501 RECIPES

FOR A LOW-C

501 RECIPES
FOR A LOW-CARB LIFE

By Gregg R. Gillespie & Mary B. Johnson

Sterling Publishing Co., Inc.
New York

10 9 8 7 6 5

Published by Sterling Publishing Co., Inc.
387 Park Avenue South, New York, NY 10016
© 2003 by Sterling Publishing Co., Inc.
Distributed in Canada by Sterling Publishing
c/o Canadian Manda Group, One Atlantic Avenue, Suite 105
Toronto, Ontario, Canada M6K 3E7
Distributed in Great Britain by Chrysalis Books Group PLC
The Chrysalis Building, Bramley Road, London W10 6SP, England
Distributed in Australia by Capricorn Link (Australia) Pty. Ltd.
P.O. Box 704, Windsor, NSW 2756, Australia

Sterling ISBN 0-7607-5416-0

TABLE OF CONTENTS

INTRODUCTION

Readers picking up this book may be doing so for any number of reasons. You might be considering a low-carb plan and want some direction. You may already be a convert and are looking to vary your meal plan with new recipes. If you are seeking a balanced approach to a low-carb diet, enjoy with flavorful and bold recipes, and you want to keep your weight in check while enjoying a healthy and happy life—this book is for you!

There are three basic elements of food—fat, protein and carbohydrate. The United States Department of Agriculture (USDA) developed a research-based guide that illustrates the relative importance of these elements. This food pyramid outlines what to eat each day and is proposed to serve as a general guideline to helping you create a healthful diet that satisfies your food preferences. The Food Pyramid focuses on controlling fat intake, because most Americans eat diets too high in fat, especially saturated fat. That means a higher intake of carbohydrates and a smaller intake of protein and fat. Not everyone, however, is aware of the good-carb-bad-carb distinction. Carbohydrates are a necessary part of a healthy diet because they provide the body with the energy it needs for physical activity and to keep organs functioning properly. Many foods rich in whole-grain carbohydrates are also good sources of essential vitamins and minerals.

The USDA food pyramid is slightly oversimplified in that it does not distinguish between different types of fats or different types of carbohydrates. It is based on the old mantra that "fat is bad," and its corollary, "carbohydrates are good." Actually, there are good fats and bad fats. The worst fats of all are the partially hydrogenated trans-fats that are ubiquitous in margarine, shortening and most store-bought baked goods. Saturated fats were not found to be as bad as once thought. But monounsaturated fats, found in nuts and olive oil, are good for you, as are the essential omega-3 fatty acids found in fish and flaxseed. There are also differences in carbohydrates. Starches, sugars and processed grains, which provide little or no nutritional value, are not nearly as good as high-fiber foods. The latter are far more nutritionally sound. Prolonging life and preventing disease are essential factors in the consideration of a diet plan. It is proven that excess pounds make people sluggish, lethargic, unmotivated, and generally thwarts one's efforts to live a long and healthy life. It is at this point that the plethora of diets out there are providing conflicting information about what is a "healthy" way to lose and maintain weight. The Atkins, Zone, and high-protein diets have proven that, if followed exactly, they can promote weight loss.

Dieting Recommendations

Ultimately, the percentage of protein you need will depend on whether you are dieting or not. If, for instance, you're a dieter on a 1,200 calorie-a-day diet and you're only eating 10 percent protein, you're not getting enough protein to support lean tissue. Even 20 percent isn't enough to support lean tissue. Studies have shown that you need to get at least 76 grams of protein, so that means you should consume the higher amounts of protein recommendations for a 1,200 calorie diet.

However, many nutritionists do stop short of recommending the very high levels of protein suggested by eating plans like the Atkins' diet because these plans so drastically cut carbohydrates - the initial phase of the Atkins' diet limits carbohydrates to 20 grams a day.

These professionals counsel moderation because carbohydrates are the major source of fiber in the diet. Just cutting carbohydrates back to 50 percent of your diet might be enough, and that would still allow for enough carbs to be within the range recommended by the USDA. The idea is to increase lean protein, decrease carbohydrates and strive for a truly healthy mix that will satisfy your hunger and not leave you feeling deprived of certain foods.

501 Recipes for a Low-Carb Life provides a plan to reduce and/or maintain a healthy weight without going to the extremes advocated by other diet plans. Treat this book as a low-carb plan that gives you sound advice on eating foods in moderation. These recipes do focus on higher protein and good fat intake while reducing carbohydrates. Combined with moderate exercise, you won't drop fifty pounds in one month, but you will learn how to cook and eat for a trim, bright lifestyle and feel on top of the world every step of the way.

Health and Carbohydrates

As mentioned above, carbohydrates fall into two groups, often referred to as "simple" or "complex." Simple carbohydrates are sugars, for example, fructose (in fruit), sucrose (table sugar), and lactose (in milk). Complex carbohydrates are starches, found in foods like potatoes and other vegetables, breads, and cereals. Whole grain foods, fruits, vegetables, and legumes (dried beans and peas) should be the source of most of the carbohydrates in the diet.

Most foods contain carbohydrates, compounds that include sugars, fiber, and starches. Carbohydrates come from a wide variety of foods—including beans, milk, popcorn, bread, potatoes, cookies, spaghetti, and cherry pie—but these foods don't all contain the same type of carbohydrate. As with dietary fat, there are no hard and fast rules about carbohydrates. Traditionally, carbohydrates that were classified as complex carbohydrates—such as bread, pasta, and other starches—were considered to be "good," and simple carbohydrates or sugars—such as table sugar, candy, and honey—were thought of as "bad." However, research now shows us that the picture is more complicated.

Much research has proven that dietary fat is not necessarily converted into body fat. Carbohydrates, on the other hand, are readily converted into fat by the action of insulin. According to many experts, most overweight people became overweight due to a condition called hyperinsulinemia — elevated insulin levels in the blood. When you eat a high-carbohydrate meal, the increased blood sugar stimulates insulin production by the pancreas. Insulin is the hormone that allows blood sugar to be used by the cells. However, a side effect of insulin is that it also causes fat to be deposited, and it stimulates your brain to produce hunger signals. So what do you do? You eat more carbohydrates, and the cycle repeats. In time, your body cells become resistant to insulin, meaning that your pancreas has to work overtime, producing up to four or five times as much insulin just to keep up with the demand. It has been shown that high levels of insulin have a deleterious effect on the body, including premature aging.

Restricting the intake of carbohydrates puts a halt to this vicious cycle. When you restrict your carbohydrate intake, your insulin levels decrease and the levels of glucagon increase. Glucagon is a hormone that causes body fat to be burned and cholesterol to be removed from deposits in the arteries.

If you severely restrict carbs, your body goes into a state of ketosis—burning fat with the subsequent production of ketone bodies in the bloodstream. The condition is called "ketonuria" if ketones are absorbed into the urine. The result of ketosis is that your blood sugar levels stabilize; your insulin level drops; and because your body is burning fat, you lose weight!

When your diet causes your body to go into a state of ketosis, you are said to be on a ketogenic diet. For most people, restricting your carbohydrate intake to fewer than 30 grams a day will induce ketonuria. Most people on ketogenic diets lose weight fairly quickly. However, although some diet experts believe that ketosis is a safe condition, it is not necessary to be in ketosis to lose weight. Keep in mind, however, that when you choose a higher level of carbohydrates than what is needed to bring on ketosis, you may have to limit your total food intake (calories) somewhat in order to lose weight.

During digestion, all carbohydrates are broken down in the intestine into their simplest form, sugar, which then enters the blood. As blood sugar levels rise, the body's normal response is to increase levels of the hormone insulin in the bloodstream. Insulin, which is released by the pancreas, helps the body's cells use this sugar for energy. This, in turn, helps bring blood sugar levels down to normal levels.

In some people, however, this response does not work properly. For example, people with type II diabetes may not have enough insulin or their insulin may not work well enough to lower the blood sugar. The result is high blood sugar levels or a condition known as insulin resistance, in which both the blood sugar and blood insulin levels remain high.

Insulin resistance may be develop because of family history, a sedentary lifestyle, ecxess weight, and/or eating a diet filled with foods that cause big spikes in blood sugar.

CARBOHYDRATES AND THE GLYCEMIC INDEX

Recently, a new system for classifying carbohydrates has received a great deal of attention, calling into question many of the old assumptions about how carbohydrates relate to health. This new system, known as the glycemic index, measures how quickly and how much blood sugar rises after a person eats a food that contains carbohydrates. Diets filled with foods that have a high-glycemic index, those which cause quick and large increases in blood sugar levels, have been linked to an increased risk for both diabetes and heart disease.

A number of factors determine a food's glycemic index. One of the most important is the level of processing. In highly processed carbohydrates, the outer bran and inner germ layer are removed from the original kernel of grain, which causes bigger spikes in blood sugar levels than would occur with less-processed grains. Whole-grain foods tend to have a lower glycemic index than their more highly processed counterparts. For example, white rice, which is highly processed, has a higher glycemic index than brown rice, which is less processed.

The number of grams of carbohydrate allowed per day varies greatly with the individual. Some people need to keep their carb count to 20 grams or less per day to lose weight. Others may successfully lose weight on 50 or 60 grams per day. Diabetics who are not obese may eat as much as 100 grams of complex carbs per day. But remember, just because you are allowed to eat 20 grams (or 50, or 60) of carbs per day doesn't mean that you can eat those in the form of sugar or starch. Make sure every gram of carbohydrate you eat is the healthier complex carbohydrates found in vegetables or whole grains. And be especially careful that your carbohydrates come from foods that have a low glycemic index.

Counting carbohydrate grams is necessary for a low-carb plan, but you mustn't lose sight of the bigger picture. Become sensitive to, and aware of, what makes up your daily food intake—type of carb, type of fat—and then shoot for a realistic standard such as 20 carbohydrate grams per serving. If your carb total per meal becomes greater than you are comfortable with, then make ingredient substitutions, always trying to create a balance.

Because you are consuming fats and oils, your appetite stays under control, because fatty foods are very satisfying. Eating a high level of fat actually causes you to lose weight faster than fasting! During a fast, your body thinks it is starving, so it kicks into a very high efficiency state of metabolism. This slows down weight loss. But with a high fat diet, combined with very low amounts of carbohydrates, your body knows it is not starving, and metabolism is maintained at a normal level. Although consuming fats is necessary for a healthy diet, try to limit consumption of trans-fats (margarine and shortening). Good fats include olive oil, flax seed oil, canola oil, oils found in nuts, and also real butter. Most fats should be the monounsaturated and saturated fats. Avoid the polyunsaturated fats when possible, except for those containing the essential omega-3 fatty acids contained in fish.

Although a low-carb, high-protein diet may result in quick weight loss, it's not a panacea for those who try to lose weight. Eating excess amounts of protein puts stress on the kidneys. Carb-restriction also affects the body's water balance in that you lose water immediately. There are two reasons that people lose weight on low carbohydrate diets. In the short term, with drastic dietary restriction of carbohydrates, the body turns to stored glycogen as a source of carbohydrate. Since glycogen is stored with water, the depletion of these stores is associated with considerable fluid loss early in the regimen. The weight lost is regained as soon as the individual resumes eating carbohydrates. The second reason is that individuals who continue to follow these diets actually consume fewer calories than they burn, either because they experience a loss of appetite, possibly related to the ketosis or because they become bored with the diet and simply begin to eat smaller quantities of food.

A "Sugar-Free" Caution...

Just because a product is labeled as "sugar-free" does not mean it is safe for diabetics or for those on a low-carb diet. Sugar-free cake mixes, snack cakes, and cookies especially should be avoided because, even though they may not technically contain sugar, the starch that's in them will quickly convert to sugar before absorption into the bloodstream. Also, the "no sugar added" items like ice cream, pies, and some candies may be loaded with sugar and other carbs. The "no sugar added" label means only that the manufacturer did not add any extra sugar beyond what is naturally present.

How the Recipes Were Selected

Choosing and developing this recipes list involved examining every ingredient, how much of it was in each recipe, and how many carbohydrates it contained. The nutritional analysis following each recipe reflects the suggested serving or portion. That way you can calculate your total carb intake per meal. (For accurate carb totals, please note that you must add the grams from a main recipe with the grams of any other recipe used that may be contained as a cross-reference.)

If a recipe greatly exceeded the standard goal of 20 grams of carbohydrates per serving, it was altered. For many recipes it was easy to simply reduce the amount of total carbs by eliminating or decreasing the carb-concentrated ingredients (such as sugar, flour, onions, potatoes and pasta). Sometimes the portion size was changed. For example, making a pasta main course into a smaller first course or side dish. Many main courses and salads were made more satisfying by increasing the protein to compensate for the carbohydrate-dense ingredients we cut back or cut out.

Whenever it was possible, homemade recipes are recommended over store-bought ingredients. The recipe for Mayonnaise (see pages 313-314) is delicious and much lower in carbs than sweetened, (whether you realized it or not!) store-bought versions. And by using the Pizza Dough recipe (see page 369), rather than prepared packaged crusts, you can enjoy the homemade pies (and calzone) without guilt and with greater satisfaction and flavor.

The Big Kahuna of carbs, pasta, presented a major problem. We all love it and eat it so often that it wasn't going away quietly just because we're on this diet. Reducing the portion size of the actual pasta, and complementing it with savory low-carb vegetables and additional protein achieved the desired goal. Note that exploring different types of noodles helped resolve the "pasta issue." Sometimes lower-carb fresh pasta is used instead of dried. Chinese and Japanese pastas to provide a new look and mouth feel—such as using flat rice-stick noodles instead of the higher-carb tagliatelle. There are also creative twists on some traditional favorites: some feature spaghetti squash, one with red clam sauce with primavera vegetables, and a Turkey Meatball Stroganoff with kale "noodles."

The satisfying, flavor-packed recipes hopefully will reduce the carb cravings, and therefore the need to eat a lot of breads. It is difficult to diminish the proportion of flour, which is the structural component of breads and its high-carb main ingredient. Instead, smaller portion sizes such as a mini muffin or a small scone or pancake are suggested.

Sugar raises another red flag in low-carb recipe development. The philosophy behind the dessert recipes is: if you have just a small taste of something sweet after a meal that may signify the end. Try some of the sweets provided to help appease a late-afternoon carb craving. Rather than raid the vending machine, choose a single Jam Bar (16 grams of carbs). This will not only satisfy you, but will also head off a feeding frenzy when you get home.

The recipe makeovers had a couple of criteria: one was nutritional and the other was the quality of the dish. The recipes collected are visually and aromatically satisfying. Some inside tips for "low-carbing" a dish are:

Use chopped raisins as a garnish and not as a handful of sugary nuggets buried within the dish.

Chop or julienne apple or tomato for garnish rather than banishing it completely.

Use fresh herbs and grated citrus rind to make up for sugars or starches—chopped fresh herbs can replace the breadcrumbs on top of gratins!

You will probably start to look at food labels more closely once you're into eating a low-carb regimen. With some quick math, you can plan your meals with savvy to get great satisfaction out of each choice, and combining the foods you buy with the dishes you make. Size is everything when it comes to diets. Portion control sounds depressing, but it is a far better alternative than depravation. Using these recipes will help you lose the weight you want but also to keep it off by changing the way you cook and eat. We'll bet that you end up liking these streamlined versions of your favorite foods even more than the old carb-heavy versions!

A Plan for Eating Out

Eating out on a low-carb diet is a trick, but it's not as hard as it may seem. The good old standby in nearly any sit-down restaurant is a grilled chicken salad, minus croutons, with blue cheese dressing. Most restaurants also offer a grilled seasoned fish, which you can have with a salad or veggies. You might also get steak, with salad or a vegetable like broccoli or green beans instead of the baked potato. Other options offered by some restaurants include grilled pork chops and grilled seafood, hamburger steak or chopped steak (no gravy). If a restaurant doesn't have any keto veggies you like, just order a side salad instead.

But there are other things you can try that are less obvious. Get a hamburger and remove the bun; eat it with a fork. This is a lot better than it sounds, if you have it with the veggies and cheese. Ask for fajitas and just eat with a fork, ignoring the tortillas. Once you're well into ketosis, you may be able to eat nachos, fried chicken or seafood, fried cheese sticks, or chicken-fried steak or chicken-fried chicken (without the gravy) without halting or reversing ketosis.

For breakfast, order a three-egg omelet filled with veggies, meats, and cheese. You'll have to eat it without toast or hash browns, but you can get an additional side of sausage or bacon. Or, if you like, get the eggs poached, scrambled, or fried with bacon, ham, steak, or sausage.

If you don't have time for a sit-down meal, you can go to a fast-food restaurant, order a breakfast sandwich or sausage and biscuit, then eat it without the bread. Skip the hash browns. For a fast lunch, you can do the same thing with hamburgers. You can also get pizza and just eat the toppings. Or get KFC Tender Roast or rotisserie chicken from Boston Market.

Remember that the restaurants are out there to make money, and there are many people on diets who require specially prepared foods. We've had waiters look at us funny, but it's very rare that we're told, "we can't do that" on a special order.

501 Recipes for a Low-Carb Life is a collection of recipes that reflects a balance of high-carb, low-carb and no-carb ingredients. The ingredient list below features foods that vary widely in carbohydrate value. Some are high in carbs and some are quite low. By providing you with these totals, you can have an at-a-glance table at your fingertips. It should be used as a helpful aid as you you make your own food choices, plan meals, cook and dine out.

1 POUND OF:	GRAMS CARBOHYDRATES
VEGGIES	
cooked beans	116.0
corn	86.3
parsnips	81.6
potatoes	81.6

1 POUND OF:	GRAMS CARBOHYDRATES
peas	65.6
carrots	46.0
beets	43.0
brussels sprouts	40.6
onions	39.2
snap beans	32.4
broccoli	23.8
mustard greens	22.2
tomatoes	21.0
asparagus	20.6
celery	16.6
spinach	15.9
cucumbers	11.0
lettuce	9.5
FRUITS	
raisins	360.7
bananas	106.3
grapes	77.8
apples	69.2
pears	68.5
pineapple	56.2
peaches	50.4
cantaloupe	37.9
grapefruit	34.8
watermelon	32.6
strawberries	31.8
BREADS	
1 English muffin	26.0
1 hamburger bun	21.6
1 small pita bread	15.6
1 slice white bread	12.4
PASTA	
fresh	248
dried	339

Gregg R. Gillespie is a prolific cookbook author with over twenty titles to his name. He lives in upstate New York.

Mary B. Johnson is a recipe developer, tester and writer. She has worked for various publications, including The New York Times. She lives in New York City.

APPETIZERS & SNACKS

GOAT-CHEESE QUESADILLAS

Yield: 24 servings

8 (6-inch) flour tortillas
4 ounces goat cheese, softened
4 small scallions, thinly sliced
freshly ground pepper to taste

2 tablespoons vegetable oil
kosher salt
TOMATO-OLIVE SALSA for
serving (see page 317)

1. Cut the tortillas into 4-inch rounds, using a small saucer as a template. Spread the tortillas with the goat cheese and sprinkle with the scallions and pepper; sandwich to make 4 quesadillas.

2. In a large skillet, heat the vegetable oil. Add the quesadillas and cook over medium-high heat until golden and crisp, about 1 minute per side. Transfer the quesadillas to a cutting board and cut each one into 6 wedges. Sprinkle with salt and top each wedge with 1 teaspoon of the salsa. Serve immediately, passing the remaining salsa separately.

Per serving: 62 calories, 6 g carbohydrates, 2 g protein, 3 g fat

MARINATED TUNA TARTARE WITH GOAT CHEESE

Yield: 4 servings

8 ounces sushi-grade tuna,
  cut into ½-inch dice
1 tablespoon olive oil
a pinch of freshly ground
  white pepper
3 ounces fresh goat cheese
½ tablespoon soy sauce
½ tablespoon mirin (sweet
  rice wine)

½ small garlic clove, minced
½ teaspoon minced fresh
  gingerroot, peeled
a pinch of cayenne pepper
salt to taste
1 tablespoon minced fresh
  chives
1 cup lightly packed small
  arugula leaves

1. In a shallow glass baking dish, drizzle the olive oil over the tuna and season with the white pepper. Cover with plastic wrap and refrigerate until chilled, or for up to 2 hours.

2. In a bowl, mash the goat cheese with the soy sauce, mirin, garlic,

ginger and cayenne and season with salt. Gently toss the marinated tuna with the goat cheese and the chives until well coated. Mound the tuna tartare on plates, garnish with the arugula and serve.

Per serving: 167 calories, 1 g carbohydrates, 21 g protein, 8 g fat

OLIVE AND TOMATO CROSTINI

Yield: 8 servings

olive oil nonstick cooking spray
8 (¼-inch-thick) baguette slices
¼ cup sun-dried tomatoes
   (not oil-packed)
½ cup pitted Calamata olives
6 leaves fresh basil, torn into
   small pieces
1 teaspoon extra-virgin olive oil
½ teaspoon finely chopped
   garlic
salt to taste
freshly ground pepper to taste

1.   Preheat the oven to 400 degrees. Lightly coat a baking sheet with cooking spray. Arrange the baguette slices on the baking sheet, lightly coat with olive oil spray and bake for about 7 minutes, or until the toasts are golden and crisp. Let cool completely on the baking sheet.

2.   In a small bowl, soak the sun-dried tomatoes in the boiling water until plump, about 10 minutes. Drain well.

3.   In a mini-processor, combine the sun-dried tomatoes, olives, basil, olive oil and garlic and pulse until finely chopped but not pureed. Transfer to a small bowl and season with salt and pepper. Spread each bread slice with 1 tablespoon of the olive mixture and serve.

Per serving: 53 calories, 8 g carbohydrates, 1 g protein, 2 g fat

HONEY-GLAZED SOYBEANS

Yield: 16 servings

Here the beans are removed from their pods and then glazed. To eat soybeans from the pods, open the pods like peanut shells and pop them into your mouth. Discard the pods.

1 pound frozen soybean pods (edamame)
salt to taste

3 tablespoons honey
2 teaspoons ground cinnamon

1. Preheat the broiler. Cook the soybeans in salted boiling water until the beans easily pop out of the pods, 6 to 8 minutes. Discard the pods and place the beans on a nonstick baking sheet.

2. Drizzle honey over the beans, sprinkle with salt and cinnamon and toss lightly. Broil until the honey caramelizes, about 10 minutes, stirring the beans a couple times to keep them from scorching. Set aside to cool and serve.

Per serving: 130 calories, 12 g carbohydrates, 10 g protein, 6 g fat

PEPPERED PEANUTS

Yield: 6 servings

Offer in bowls with drinks.

1 (7-ounce) package roasted peanuts

1 teaspoon cayenne pepper

Mix the peanuts thoroughly with the pepper.

Per serving: 192 calories, 6 g carbohydrates, 9 g protein, 16 g fat

MINI VEGGIE BITES

Yield: 16 servings

²/₃ cup grated carrot
²/₃ cup grated zucchini
²/₃ cup grated potato
1 tablespoon all-purpose flour

salt to taste
freshly ground pepper to taste
vegetable oil for frying

1. Squeeze out excess moisture from the grated vegetables: the best way is to lay them on several sheets of paper towel and cover with more paper and press down. Place the vegetables together in a bowl, add the flour and the seasoning and mix well.

2. Heat the oil in a large nonstick skillet over medium heat and add heaped tablespoons of the mixture, flattening them with a fork to make spiky round croquettes. Fry for about 5 minutes, turning halfway through. They should be golden on the outside and cooked inside.

Per serving: 34 calories, 7 g carbohydrates, 1 g protein, trace fat

BABA GANOUCHE

Yield: 16 servings

This roasted eggplant dip is a Middle Eastern specialty. Although traditionally an appetizer, it goes great as a side dish with grilled lamb but is enjoyed by vegetarians because it is rich-tasting and hearty enough to be a pita sandwich filling.

4 tablespoons olive oil
2 medium eggplants
1 large tomato, finely diced
1 handful fresh mint leaves,
   chopped
1 garlic clove, crushed
$1\frac{1}{2}$ tablespoons fresh lemon
   juice

1. Preheat the broiler. Line a baking sheet with aluminum foil and grease with half the olive oil. Slice the eggplant crosswise into $\frac{1}{4}$ -inch slices and place on the prepared baking sheet. Turn over so the oiled side is up. Sprinkle with salt and pepper and broil until charred, 2 to 3 minutes. Repeat on the other side and repeat with the remaining oil and eggplant.

2. Using a blender, puree the eggplant with the mint and garlic.

Per serving: 48 calories, 4 g carbohydrates, 1 g protein, 4 g fat

GRILLED SMOKED-MOZZARELLA WITH ZUCCHINI

Yield: 8 servings

The smoked flavors of the cheese, zucchini and sauce make this first course one to have all summer. You can roast and skin a batch of peppers at a time and have them individually packed in the freezer, waiting for use.

1 large red bell pepper, roasted, skinned, seeded and roughly chopped
1 beefsteak tomato, blanched, skinned, seeded and chopped
1/4 cup extra-virgin olive oil
1 small garlic clove, chopped
salt and pepper to taste
1 pound smoked mozzarella
1 large zucchini, sliced lengthwise into 8 slices
4 tablespoons aged balsamic vinegar
18 large basil leaves, deep-fried until crisp

1. Prepare a charcoal grill for barbecuing. Oil the grill rack.

2. Combine the bell pepper, tomato, oil and garlic in a blender and pulse until smooth. Transfer to a bowl and season with salt and pepper. Set aside.

3. Cut the mozzarella into 8 wedges and wrap each with a slice of zucchini. Cook the wrapped cheese on the grill over hot coals for 2 minutes on each side.

4. Spoon the bell-pepper sauce onto 8 plates and drizzle each portion with 1/2 tablespoon balsamic vinegar. Place 2 fried basil leaves and 1 grilled wrapped cheese on each plate and serve.

Per serving: 234 calories, 3 g carbohydrates, 12 g protein, 19 g fat

HERB FRITTELLE

Yield: 8 servings

1 pound mixed herb salad leaves such as arugula, sorrel and flat leaf parsley
1 tablespoon fresh basil
1/4 cup freshly grated Parmesan cheese
1 cup fresh breadcrumbs
3 large eggs, lightly beaten
2 tablespoons unsalted butter
sunflower oil
salt to taste
freshly ground pepper to taste

1. Place herb leaves in a medium bowl. Stir in the basil, Parmesan, breadcrumbs, eggs and seasoning.

2. Melt the butter in a large skillet. Add enough oil so that there is 1/4 inch of oil in the pan. Using 1 generous tablespoon of the mixture for each fritter, fry the frittelle a few at a time until deeply golden, about 3 minutes each side.

3. Drain on paper towels; keep warm in a low oven until the remaining frittelle are cooked.

Per serving: 105 calories, 7 g carbohydrates, 6 g protein, 6 g fat

---

CRESPELLE FRITTE (DEEP FRIED HERB PANCAKES)

Yield: 12 servings

These thin Italian pancakes are traditionally served the way the French often eat their crêpes, layered with a filling in between them or rolled around a filling. But cut like pasta and fried....That's amore!

1 cup unsifted all-purpose flour
4 eggs
3 tablespoons butter, melted
sea salt to taste
1³⁄₄ cups water

1 cup coarsely chopped mixed fresh herbs, ideally fennel feather, basil and parsley
sunflower oil for deep frying
freshly grated Parmesan cheese for serving

1. Combine the flour, eggs, 1³⁄₄ cups water and half the melted butter and a dash of salt in a blender and blend until smooth. Pour into a bowl and stir in the herbs. Using the remaining butter, make large pancakes with the batter in a large nonstick skillet. When the pancakes are cool, cut them into tagliatelle-size (about ³⁄₄-inch-wide) strips.

2. Deep fry the pancake strips, in batches, in sunflower oil for a couple of minutes, until crisp. Serve hot with grated Parmesan and sea salt.

Per serving: 110 calories, 9 g carbohydrates, 4 g protein, 6 g fat

---

GLOUCESTER CHEESE FRITTERS WITH SPICY TOMATO SAUCE

Yield: 20 servings

These are made from the same dough used to make cream puffs and éclairs. Pass them on a tray at a cocktail party or as a first course.

2 ounces unsalted butter
½ cup all-purpose flour
3 medium eggs
1 cup grated Double Gloucester
   or cheddar cheese

oil for deep frying
½ cup chopped fresh
   parsley
SPICY TOMATO SAUCE,
   warmed (see page xx)

1. Heat 5 ounces water to boiling in a saucepan with the butter. Once the mixture is at a rolling boil, add the flour all at once and beat in well with a wooden spoon until it is lump free. Allow the mixture to cool slightly and beat in the eggs one at a time. Mix in the grated cheese.

2. Fill a deep saucepan with about 2 inches of oil and heat to 350 degrees. Using a tablespoon as a measure, take equal quantities of the mixture and drop into the hot oil. Cook for 2 to 3 minutes, or until golden brown all over. Drain on paper towels and sprinkle with a little salt. Place on a serving tray and sprinkle with the parsley. Serve immediately with the sauce.

Per serving (without the sauce): 70 calories, 3 g carbohydrates, 3 g protein, 5 g fat

CERNEY CHEESE TERRINE

Yield: 12 servings

This pyramid-shaped, ash-covered goat cheese was created by Lady Angus in England's Gloucestershire region and named after the lovely village of Cerney where it is made. The cheese has a mild, citrus taste, with a delicate, goaty finish. If you can't find it, use fromage frais, which is very similar.

nonstick cooking spray
½ English cucumber, sliced
1 pound Cerney cheese, ash
   trimmed off
3 tablespoons mayonnaise
grated rind of 1 lemon
2 tablespoons mixed fresh
   herbs such as parsley, thyme,
   coriander or chives

1 tablespoon creamed
   horseradish
salt and pepper
1 envelope unflavored
   gelatin
2 tomatoes, quartered
lettuce to garnish
whole-grain bread to
   serve

1. Grease a 1 quart loaf pan with nonstick cooking spray and line with parchment paper. Grease the paper. Line the base and sides with the sliced cucumber in neat rows.

2. Place the cheese in a bowl with mayonnaise, lemon rind, herbs, horseradish and seasoning and mix well. Dissolve the gelatin in 5 tablespoons hot water and stir until clear. Leave to cool slightly, then stir into the cheese mixture. Carefully spoon into the prepared pan and level the surface with a knife. Cover with plastic wrap and chill for 1 hour until set, when the top is firm to the touch.

3. Remove the terrine from refrigerator and carefully turn out onto a platter. Remove the parchment. Garnish with the tomatoes and lettuce and serve with bread.

Per serving (without the bread): 194 calories, 3 g carbohydrates, 12 g protein, 15 g fat

MOROCCAN BEAN DIP (BYESAR)

Yield: 12 servings

This Moroccan version of the chickpea dish humus makes a wonderful appetizer or even a fast meal. Place a bowl of it in the center of a large round platter and surround it with piles of dippers such as sliced plum tomatoes, cucumbers, torn lettuce, pita bread and sesame lavash crackers.

8 ounces dried haricot or fava
  beans
3 garlic cloves, peeled and
  minced
1½ teaspoons cumin seeds
½ red onion, chopped
3 tablespoons fresh lemon juice
  or to taste
1 teaspoon chopped fresh

parsley
1 teaspoon paprika
1 teaspoon ground coriander
¼ teaspoon cayenne pepper
olive oil
salt to taste
chopped fresh or dried thyme,
  marjoram or oregano leaves,
  crushed

1. Soak the beans overnight in a large bowl with 4 cups of water. Discard any floating beans.

2. The next day drain, remove any loose skins and cover with fresh

water in a large saucepan. Add the garlic and cumin seeds and heat to boiling. Reduce the heat to low and simmer until the beans are tender, about 2 hours, depending upon the age and quality of the beans. Drain through a fine sieve so the garlic and cumin seeds stay with the beans, reserving some of the cooking liquid.

3. In batches, puree the beans with the garlic and cumin seeds in a food processor, adding the onion, lemon juice, parsley, paprika, coriander and cayenne pepper. Stir in enough olive oil and add a little of the reserved bean cooking water to give the puree a soupy consistency. Sprinkle with salt to taste and mix well.

4. Heat the puree just before serving with a little more olive oil and a sprinkling of thyme, marjoram or oregano.

Per serving: 106 calories, 12 g carbohydrates, 4 g protein, 5 g fat

TOASTED CHEESE ROUNDS

Yield: 16 servings

These open-face cheese sandwiches are rich and tasty. You can prepare the sauce ahead of time.

1 cup grated extra-sharp
  cheddar cheese
¼ cup half-and-half
1 ounce unsalted butter,
  melted

3 tablespoons beer, heated
  through
salt to taste
freshly ground pepper to taste
4 slices whole-wheat bread

1. Preheat the broiler. Place the cheese and the cream in a heatproof bowl and place the bowl over a saucepan of simmering water without the bowl touching the water. Stirring occasionally, allow the cheese and cream to form a smooth sauce, 6 to 8 minutes.

2. Meanwhile, toast the bread and cut 4 rounds from each slice of toast with a small cutter. Drizzle the butter over each piece of toast and repeat with the beer.

3. To serve: Spoon the cheese sauce over the toast rounds and season generously with salt and pepper. Broil for 2 to 3 minutes or until bubbling and golden. Serve immediately.

Per serving: 64 calories, 4 g carbohydrates, 3 g protein, 5 g fat

GUACAMOLE JAPONAISE
WITH POT-STICKER CHIPS

Yield: 6 servings

The rich avocado mixture we flavor with a Mexican accent is just as delicious seasoned with the elements that go into sushi. Hot gingerroot, spicy seasoned rice vinegar and fiery wasabi pack just as powerful a punch as a mix of chiles.

1 tablespoon black or white
  sesame seeds
1 large firm-ripe avocado
1 tablespoon shredded pickled
  ginger
3 tablespoons seasoned rice
  vinegar or 3 tablespoons

cider vinegar, mixed with
  1 teaspoon sugar
1/2 teaspoon wasabi powder or
  prepared horseradish
POT-STICKER CHIPS for dipping
  (see following recipe)

1. Place the sesame seeds in a small skillet over medium-high heat. Shake pan often until seed begins to pop, 3 to 4 minutes. Pour the seeds into a bowl and set aside to cool.

2. Cut the avocado in half and remove the pit. Scoop out the flesh from the peel and cut into small dice. Place the avocado in a bowl and add 1/2 teaspoon sesame seeds, the ginger, vinegar and wasabi. Stir gently to mix. Transfer to a serving bowl and sprinkle with the remaining sesame seeds. Serve as a dip, with the Pot-Sticker Chips.

Per serving (without the Pot-Sticker Chips): 49 calories, 2 g carbohydrates, 1 g protein, 5 g fat

POT-STICKER CHIPS

Yield: 4 servings

You can make the chips ahead and store at room temperature in an airtight container up to 2 days before serving.

nonstick cooking spray

12 round pot-sticker skins

Preheat the oven to 450 degrees. Grease a large baking sheet with nonstick cooking spray. Dip the pot-sticker skins one at a time in a bowl of water, shake off the excess and lay in a single layer on the prepared baking sheet. Bake until browned and crisp, 4 to 8 minutes, depending on the thickness of the skins. Cool on wire racks.

Per chip: 23 calories, 5 g carbohydrates, 1 g protein, trace fat

CREAMY MUSHROOMS ON TOAST

Yield: 4 servings

This is a tasty, quick appetizer or first course that is basically foolproof. The sauce is simply wine and cream mixed with the juices of the mushrooms.

1 teaspoon butter
3 ounces sliced mushrooms
1 tablespoon dry white
  wine
¼ cup half-and-half

2 scallions, trimmed and finely
  chopped
1 tablespoon chopped fresh dill
1 thin slice white bread, toasted,
  cut diagonally into quarters

1. Melt the butter in a medium nonstick skillet over medium-high heat. Add the mushrooms and cook for 2 to 3 minutes.

2. Add the white wine and reduce slightly. Add the the half-and-half, scallions and dill. Serve on the hot toast points.

Per serving: 48 calories, 4 g carbohydrates, 1 g protein, 3 g fat

ROASTED-EGGPLANT TERRINE WITH WALNUT-OIL AND FRESH-TOMATO SAUCE

Yield: 16 servings

This appetizer will elicit a chorus of "Wow!'s" and there's good reason why. The combination and contrasts of roasted and fresh vegetables, aged and fresh cheeses, and earth and ethereal seasonings will provoke requests for the recipe.

2 (1-pound) eggplants, halved lengthwise
3 eggs
1 garlic clove, crushed
½ cup fromage frais
½ cup grated pecorino cheese
½ cup provlone picante or other mature hard cheese
2 tablespoons all-purpose flour
2 teaspoons olive oil
salt to taste
freshly ground pepper to taste
nonstick cooking spray
1 red bell pepper, seeded and finely chopped
1 tablespoon finely chopped fresh basil
WALNUT-OIL AND FRESH-TOMATO SAUCE for serving (see page 337)

1. Preheat oven to 375 degrees. Place the eggplant cut side down on a baking sheet and bake until soft, about 45 minutes. Leave to cool.

2. Reduce the oven temperature to 350 degrees. Peel the eggplants, mash the flesh in a bowl and squeeze out the juice. Place the flesh in a food processor, add the eggs, garlic, fromage frais, cheeses, flour and oil and blend until smooth. Season with salt and pepper.

3. Line a 2-quart loaf pan with aluminum foil and grease with cooking spray. Pour in half of the eggplant mixture and smooth evenly. Sprinkle with the chopped pepper and basil and then pour the remaining eggplant mixture on top, smoothing evenly. Cover with foil. Place the pan in a roasting pan and add enough boiling water to come halfway up the sides of the loaf pan. Bake until the terrine is firm to touch, 55 to 60 minutes. Remove the loaf pan to a wire rack and cool the terrine completely. Refrigerate overnight or at least several hours.

4. To serve: Remove the foil from the terrine and invert the terrine onto a cutting board. Cut into ½-inch slices and place on salad plates. Drizzle with the sauce or pass the sauce separately.

Per serving (without the sauce): 81 calories, 5 g carbohydrates, 5 g protein, 5 g fat

DEEP-FRIED SAUSAGE ROLLS

Yield: 12 rolls

vegetable oil, for frying
½ cup self-rising flour
1 egg
½ cup unsweetened apple
   juice, or more if needed
6 canned Vienna sausages,
patted dry
salt to taste
freshly ground pepper to taste
flat-leaf parsley sprigs, to
   garnish
tomato ketchup, to serve

1. Heat a deep saucepan one-third full of oil to 350 degrees. Place the flour in a bowl with a pinch of salt and pepper. Make a well in the center, add the egg and slowly add the apple juice until you have achieved a smooth batter. Cut each sausage roll crosswise in half and coat each piece in the batter.

2. Deep-fry until crisp and golden brown, 3 to 4 minutes. Drain on paper towels and arrange on a serving plate and garnish with the parsley sprigs. Serve at once with the tomato ketchup.

Per roll (without ketchup): 56 calories, 5 g carbohydrates, 2 g protein, 3 g fat

THREE-PEPPER-SPICED POPCORN

Yield: 4 servings

Here's a way to flavor popcorn that goes beyond the usual butter, cheese or caramel.

1 tablespoon peanut oil
½ cup popcorn kernels
CHILI-FLAVORED SALT for
   serving (see page 312)

1. Heat a large pan with a tight-fitting lid, add the oil and the popcorn. Cover with the lid and cook for 2 to 2½ minutes, shaking the pan occasionally until the popping has almost stopped.

2. Remove the lid from the popcorn and season liberally with the flavored salt, shaking the pan until well combined. Pour the hot popcorn into a large serving bowl and serve at once.

Per serving: 60 calories, 6 g carbohydrates, 1 g protein, 4 g fat

SCALLION-SARDINE PASTRY PUFFS

Yield: 8 servings

A smear of tomato paste will combine with the sardine and pastry juices to make a succulent filling.

2 (4.23-ounce size) cans
   sardines, drained
4 scallions, chopped
1 tablespoon tomato paste
salt to taste

freshly ground pepper to taste
½ (1-pound size) package puff
   pastry (1 sheet), thawed if
   frozen
1 egg, beaten

1. Preheat the oven to 400 degrees. Combine the sardines, scallions and tomato paste in a small bowl and mix well. Season to taste and mix again.

2. Roll out the pastry into a 12-inch square. Cut into 4 squares, then cut each square in half diagonally.

3. Divide the filling between each pastry triangle, brush the edges with water and fold over. Flute or fork the edges to seal.

4. Place on a baking tray, brush with the beaten egg and bake until golden, 15 to 20 minutes. Serve warm.

Per serving: 194 calories, 11 g carbohydrates, 8 g protein, 13 g fat

---

TURKISH CHICKEN
PHYLLO TRIANGLES

Yield: 24 triangles

The small savory pastries called Tavaklu Borek are found all over the Middle East and are thought to have originated in Turkey. They can be served as appetizers or as an accompaniment to a soup or salad.

oil for greasing the pan
3 boneless, skinless chicken-
  breast halves
4 ounces butter
4 tablespoons all-purpose flour
2½ cups hot-2-percent milk
¼ cup hot chicken broth
½ cup grated Parmesan or
  Gruyère cheese
⅛ teaspoon freshly grated
  nutmeg
⅛ teaspoon salt
1 egg, lightly beaten
8 to 10 sheets phyllo pastry

1. Preheat the oven to 350 degrees. Grease a large baking sheet with oil.

2. Simmer the chicken breasts in a saucepan with just enough hot water until cooked through, 6 to 8 minutes. Remove the chicken to a plate and cool. Dice the chicken into small pieces no larger than ½ inch.

3. Melt 1 ounce of the butter in a 2-quart saucepan and whisk in the flour. Cook over low heat until bubbly and fragrant. Remove the pan from the heat and gradually whisk in the hot milk and chicken broth. Return the pan to a gentle heat and whisk the sauce until it boils and thickens, 5 to 6 minutes. Whisk in the cheese, nutmeg and salt. Remove the pan from the heat and gradually whisk in the egg and then the chicken pieces. The mixture should be fairly thick.

4. Melt 2 ounces of the butter. Stack the phyllo sheets and cut the whole stack lengthwise into 4 long strips, each about 3 inches wide. Working with 1 sheet at a time, brush with melted butter. Place a tea-spoon of filling in one corner and fold the opposite corner diagonal-ly over the filling. Fold over flag fashion to make a triangular packet. Repeat with the remaining phyllo, melted butter and filling.

5. Place these on the prepared baking sheet, with the pastry ends underneath. Melt the remaining 1 ounce of butter and use it to brush on the tops of the triangles. Bake until crisp and golden, about 20 minutes.

NOTE: *To use puff pastry, defrost a 1-pound package of puff pastry if frozen and cut it into walnut-size pieces. Roll out each into a thin 4-inch round and place a teaspoon of filling in the center of each. Fold the pastry over the filling, moisten the edges and press them together, making a half-moon shape. Brush the tops with beaten egg and bake until golden, about 20 minutes.*

Per triangle: 104 calories, 7 g carbohydrates, 6 g protein, 6 g fat

CHEESE-STUFFED APRICOTS

Yield: 12 servings

If you use dried apricots, make sure they are moist and plump.

4 ounces cream cheese
3 tablespoons crème
 fraîche
2 teaspoons grated lemon
 rind

1 pound fresh apricots, halved
 and pitted, or 8 ounces dried
 apricots
2 tablespoons chopped
 pistachio nuts

Mix the cream cheese, crème fraîche and lemon rind in a small bowl until blended and spoon into a piping bag fitted with a star or plain nozzle. Pipe the cream-cheese mixture onto the fresh apricot halves, or onto the dried apricots. Sprinkle with the pistachios to decorate.

Per serving: 65 calories, 5 g carbohydrates, 2 g protein, 5 g fat

QUESO-JALAPEÑO SQUARES

Yield: 25 servings

The sweet cheese will tone down the heat of the peppers in this easy, tasty appetizer.

2 teaspoons butter
1 cup finely chopped onion
½ (4-ounce) can jalapeño
 peppers, drained, seeded and
 chopped

2 cups grated sharp cheddar
 cheese
4 large eggs, lightly beaten
½ teaspoon salt
¼ teaspoon garlic powder

1. Preheat the oven to 350 degrees. Grease an 8-inch square baking pan and set aside.

2. Melt the butter in a nonstick skillet over medium heat. Add the onion and sauté until soft, about 5 minutes. Scatter the onion, jalapeños and cheese in the prepared pan.

3. Lightly beat the eggs in a small bowl and stir in the salt and gar-lic powder. Pour the egg mixture over the mixture in the baking dish. Bake until set, about 30 minutes.

Per serving: 54 calories, 1 g carbohydrates, 3 g protein, 4 g fat

TOMATILLO GUACAMOLE

Yield: 2 cups
(serving size: $^1/_3$ cup)

These fruits are called Mexican green tomatoes and are relatives of the red ones we can't live without. They can be cooked or eaten raw. The raw ones have a pleasant tartness that is muted when they are cooked or canned.

1 medium avocado
8 to 10 fresh tomatillos, husks removed, or 1 (11-ounce) can tomatillos, drained
1 cup chopped onion
2 tablespoons chopped fresh cilantro

2 tablespoons fresh lime juice
1½ teaspoons minced seeded serrano chile
⅛ teaspoon salt
⅛ teaspoon freshly ground pepper

1. Halve and pit the avocado and scoop out the flesh into a food processor. Quarter the tomatillos and add to the processor (if using the canned ones, drain and add without quartering). Process using the pulse motion until the desired consistency is reached. Do not over-process as a chunky texture is really nice.

2. Scrape out the mixture into a medium bowl and gently stir in the onion, cilantro, lime juice, chile, salt and pepper. Cover and refriger-ate 1 hour.

Per serving: 30 calories, 6 g carbohydrates, 1 g protein, trace fat

TOASTED SHRIMP APPETIZERS

Yield: 2 dozen appetizers
(serving size: 1 appetizer and $1/2$ teaspoon sauce)

These are a baked version of the classic Chinese deep-fried appetizer, shrimp toasts.

8 ounces medium unpeeled shrimp
1 garlic clove, peeled
2 scallions, cut into 1-inch pieces
$1\frac{1}{2}$ teaspoons cornstarch
$1\frac{1}{2}$ teaspoons dry sherry
1 egg white
$1/2$ cup sliced peeled fresh or canned water chestnuts
24 slices party-style rye bread
$1/4$ cup bottled sweet and sour sauce

1. Preheat the oven to 375 degrees. Peel and devein the shrimp and set aside.

2. Position the knife blade in the food processor bowl. With the processor running, drop the garlic through the food chute and process until minced. Add the scallions and process until chopped. Add the cornstarch, sherry and egg white and process until well blended. Add the shrimp and water chestnuts and pulse until finely chopped.

3. Spread about 1 tablespoon of the shrimp mixture over each bread slice and place spread side up on a baking sheet. Bake until shrimp mixture is cooked through, about 10 minutes.

Per serving: 33 calories, 5 g carbohydrates, 3 g protein, trace fat

SPINACH-HAM SPREAD IN BREAD BOWLS

Yield: about $3\frac{3}{4}$ cups dip

Use the toasted tops and insides of the bread bowls for making breadcrumbs or stuffing.

2 (1-pound) round loaves
   French or sourdough
   bread
1 (8-ounce) package Neufchâtel
   cheese, softened
1 (8-ounce) carton plain nonfat
   yogurt
½ cup nonfat sour cream
½ teaspoon garlic powder

1¼ cups diced leftover baked
   ham
1 (10-ounce) package frozen
   chopped spinach, thawed,
   drained and squeezed dry
1 (2-ounce) jar chopped
   pimientos, drained
2 tablespoons grated Parmesan
   cheese

1. Preheat the oven to 375 degrees. Slice off the top fourth of the loaves, using a large serrated knife. Hollow out bottom pieces, leaving a 1-inch-thick shell and reserve the tops and removed portions.

2. Place the bread bowls on a baking sheet. Cut the lids and insides of the reserved bread into bite-size pieces and place on the same baking sheet. Bake until the insides of the bowls and the removed tops and insides have dried, about 10 minutes.

3. Combine the Neufchâtel, yogurt, sour cream and garlic powder in a medium bowl and beat until smooth. Stir in the ham, spinach and pimiento. Divide the mixture between the bread bowls and sprinkle the Parmesan cheese over the spinach mixture in each bread bowl.

4. Bake until the spinach mixture is heated through, about 30 minutes.

Per tablespoon, on bread: 62 calories, 8 g carbohydrates, 3 g protein, 2 g fat

STRIPED RIBBON SANDWICHES

Yield: 32 sandwiches

If made ahead, cover sandwiches with a slightly damp paper towel and plastic wrap, and place in an airtight container. To serve, trim crusts from sandwiches. Cut each sandwich into quarters, making rectangles, squares, or triangles.

nonstick cooking spray
2½ cups chopped red bell pepper
½ cup chopped onion
1 tablespoon tomato paste
¼ teaspoon salt
⅓ teaspoon freshly ground black pepper
¾ cup coarsely shredded, seeded, peeled cucumber

4 ounces nonfat cream cheese
2 ounces blue cheese, crumbled
⅛ teaspoon cayenne pepper
16 slices very thin white bread
8 slices very thin whole-wheat bread
parsley sprigs for garnish (optional)

1. Grease a large nonstick skillet with cooking spray and heat over medium-high heat until hot. Add the bell pepper and onion and sauté until tender, about 4 minutes. Scrape the mixture into a food processor and add the tomato paste, ⅛ teaspoon salt and the black pepper. Process until smooth. Return the mixture to skillet and cook over medium-high heat until thickened, about 3 minutes. Scrape the mixture into a bowl and let it stand until cool. Cover and refrigerate until chilled.

2. Spread out the cucumber on several layers of paper towel, cover with additional paper towels and press until barely moist.

3. Combine the cream cheese, blue cheese, ⅛ teaspoon salt and the cayenne in a small bowl and stir until smooth. Stir in the cucumber, cover and chill.

4. Spread 2 tablespoons of the bell-pepper mixture over each of 8 slices of white bread and top each with a slice of wheat bread. Spread 2 tablespoons of the cucumber mixture over each slice of wheat bread and top with remaining white bread.

Per sandwich: 43 calories, 7 g carbohydrates, 2 g protein, 1 g fat

SARDINE SPREAD WITH MELBA TOAST

Yield: 30 servings

Keep cans of heart-healthy, Omega-3 rich sardines on hand for a quick appetizer. You can also use sardines that are packed in mustard or tomato sauces, and use the sauce to moisten the mixture.

2 (3¼-ounce) cans sardines in water, drained
¼ cup finely chopped scallions
1½ teaspoons prepared horse-radish
1 teaspoon dried dillweed

¼ cup plain nonfat yogurt
1 tablespoon fresh lemon juice
⅓ cup finely shredded carrot
MELBA TOAST for serving (see page 363)

Place the sardines in a small bowl and mash with a fork. Add the scallions, horseradish, dillweed, yogurt, and lemon juice and mix well. Place in a shallow serving dish and sprinkle with the carrots. Cover and refrigerate for at least 2 hours. Serve as a spread for the Melba Toast.

Per serving (without Melba Toast): 13 calories, trace carbohydrates, 1 g protein, 1 g fat

CREAMY BEAN DIP WITH GRAPEFRUIT RELISH

Yield: 30 servings

It is worth seeking out the best pita bread in town for this dip. You can also use the Indian bread called naan. Serve both at the same time for a real international exchange.

1 (about 15-ounce) can garban-zo beans (chickpeas), drained
1 (about 15-ounce) can flageolet or cannellini beans, drained and rinsed
2 garlic cloves, crushed
juice and grated rind of 1 lime
1 bunch fresh cilantro, leaves only, roughly chopped

¼ cup olive oil
1 large pink grapefruit, peeled and sectioned
1 red onion, thinly sliced
salt to taste
freshly ground black pepper to taste
warm pita bread or naan bread for dipping

1. Combine about three-fourths of the garbanzos, about three-fourths of the flageolets, the garlic, half the cilantro, all but 2 teaspoons of the oil and the lime juice and grated rind in a food processor. Process until smooth and creamy, adding a little water if necessary. Season with salt and pepper, process until mixed and taste again for seasoning.

2. Finely chop the remaining cilantro and place in a medium bowl. Add the remaining garbanzos and flageolets, the grapefruit, remaining 2 teaspoons of oil and the onion. Mix well, season to taste and mix again.

3. Pile the creamy dip into a shallow serving dish or plate and sprinkle with the grapefruit relish. Grind plenty of black pepper over all. Refrigerate until serving and serve with pita or naan for dipping.

Per serving: 53 calories, 7 g carbohydrates, 2 g protein, 2 g fat

CRUNCHY PECAN CHICKEN FINGERS

Yield: 5 servings

Dip these babies into a sweet-and-sour sauce or drizzle with honey mustard. They are even great just wrapped in a hot soft dinner roll for a soup-and-sandwich supper.

½ cup finely chopped pecans
⅓ cup cornflake crumbs
1 tablespoon chopped fresh
    parsley
1 tablespoon grated lemon rind

⅛ teaspoon salt
⅛ teaspoon garlic powder
¼ cup skim milk
12 ounces skinless, boneless
    chicken-breast halves

1. Preheat the oven to 400 degrees. Line a baking sheet with aluminum foil.

2. Combine the pecans, cornflake crumbs, parsley, lemon rind, salt, and garlic powder in a shallow bowl. Place the milk on a plate. Cut the chicken breasts into 3-inch by 1-inch strips. Dip the chicken pieces into the milk, drain off the excess and then roll in the crumb mixture. Place the chicken on the prepared baking pan and bake until tender and no longer pink, 7 to 9 minutes.

Per serving: 172 calories, 5 g carbohydrates, 18 g protein, 9 g fat

LAYERED BEAN TERRINE

Yield: 32 servings

This elegant first course is a work of art, and praiseworthy for the work involved. You're bound to be asked for the recipe! Be sure to mention that for ease and neatness, dip the spatula in a bowl of water when spreading the layers.

RED-PEPPER LAYER
1 head of garlic, top ¼ inch sliced off (for roasted garlic puree)
1 (about 15-ounce) can low-sodium garbanzo beans (chickpeas), drained and rinsed
1 (about 15-ounce) can low-sodium red kidney beans, drained and rinsed
1 medium red bell pepper, steamed for 15 minutes, cored, seeded and peeled
2 tablespoons fresh lemon juice
¼ teaspoon freshly ground black pepper
¼ teaspoon hot Hungarian paprika
freshly ground sea salt

GARBANZO-CHEESE LAYER
2 (about 15-ounce) cans low-sodium garbanzo beans
6 tablespoons freshly grated Parmesan cheese

2 tablespoons fresh lemon juice
1 tablespoon Dijon mustard
1 tablespoon plain yogurt
¼ teaspoon freshly ground white pepper

PESTO LAYER
1 (about 15-ounce) can white beans, drained and rinsed
1 cup lightly packed fresh basil leaves, rinsed and drained
2 tablespoons freshly grated Parmesan cheese
2 tablespoons fresh lemon juice
1 teaspoon mashed roasted garlic puree
¼ teaspoon freshly ground black pepper

FOR SERVING AND GARNISH
1 bunch watercress, rinsed and drained
1 pound jicama, peeled and cut into 48 wedges

1. Line an 8 by 4-inch terrine or loaf pan with a piece of plastic wrap big enough to fit over the whole terrine.

2. For the Red Pepper Layer: Preheat the oven 375 degrees. Wrap the garlic in aluminum foil and bake for 35 minutes. Immediately after it comes out of the oven, hold one end of the garlic head with a potholder. Press out the garlic with the back of a knife. (It will come out to about 1 tablespoon garlic puree, to be used for the Red-Pepper Layer and also the Pesto Layer.) Place 2 teaspoons of the roasted garlic puree and the remaining ingredients in a food processor and process for 3 minutes (you may have to do this in batches). Spread mixture evenly in the bottom of the prepared pan.

3. For the Garbanzo-Cheese Layer: Place all the ingredients for this layer in a food processor and process 4 minutes. Drop small amounts over the red pepper layer and spread gently and evenly to prevent air pockets.

4. For the Pesto Layer: Place all the ingredients for this layer into a food processor and process until smooth, about 3 minutes. Spread evenly over the Garbanzo-Cheese Layer, cover with plastic wrap and press down gently. Chill for 4 hours or overnight.

5. To serve, uncover the loaf pan. Lay a cutting board or plate over the top and invert; the loaf will fall right out. Remove the plastic wrap. Slice into 16 pieces with a thin knife, wiping off the blade between slices to make cutting easier. Cut each slice in half. Serve garnished with the watercress and jicama.

Per serving: 92 calories, 17 g carbohydrates, 5 g protein, 1 g fat

LAYERED BLACK-BEAN DIP

Yield: 12 servings

Entertaining with eats like this will guarantee you a house full of company. You can always pass crudités instead of or in addition to the jicama to use to scoop up the dip.

1 (15-ounce) can black beans, rinsed and drained
1 (4.25-ounce) can ripe olives, drained and chopped
1 small onion, finely chopped
1 garlic clove, crushed
2 tablespoons olive or corn oil
2 tablespoons fresh lime juice
¼ teaspoon salt
¼ teaspoon crushed red pepper flakes
¼ teaspoon ground cumin
⅛ teaspoon ground black pepper
1 (8-ounce) package cream cheese, softened
2 large hard-boiled eggs, peeled and chopped
1 large scallion, trimmed and sliced
1 pound jicama or assorted raw vegetables, peeled, cut into strips

1. Combine the beans, olives, onion, garlic, oil, lime juice, salt, red pepper, cumin and black pepper in a large bowl and mix well. Cover and refrigerate for 2 hours.

2. To serve, spread the cream cheese on a serving plate and cover evenly with the bean mixture. Spoon the eggs around the edge of the bean mixture and sprinkle the scallions over the center. Serve with the jicama.

Per serving: 161 calories, 11 g carbohydrates, 6 g protein, 11 g fat

MANGO AND PROSCIUTTO BITES

Yield: 50 servings

The sweet and juicy tropical fruit is the perfect mate for the salty ham.

5 firm ripe mangos
8 ounces thinly sliced prosciutto
lime wedges for garnish

Pit and cut the mango flesh to the peel into a 1-inch grid-like pattern. Turn the peel inside out and cut off the mango pieces. Quarter each prosciutto slice and wrap each quarter around a piece of mango, securing it with a wooden pick. Arrange the hors d'oeuvres on a chilled platter and serve them with the lime wedges.

Per serving: 19 calories, 4 g carbohydrates, 1 g protein, trace fat

CHINESE PORK DUMPLINGS

Yield: 20 servings

There are many bottled dipping sauces that complement these tasty appetizers, but equal portions of soy sauce, water and rice vinegar work fine. Add some chopped scallion and minced peeled fresh gingerroot and you have all you need to accent the sweet filling of pork and cabbage.

8 ounces lean ground pork
1 cup shredded Napa cabbage
1 scallion, trimmed and chopped
1 tablespoon soy sauce
salt and pepper to taste
20 wonton wrappers

1 egg, beaten
lettuce leaves for lining
  steamers
1 teaspoon dark sesame oil
bottled or homemade dipping
  sauce

1. Combine the pork, cabbage, scallion and soy sauce in a small bowl. Season with salt and pepper and marinate 30 minutes.

2. Brush the edges of each wrapper with a little beaten egg. Place a little of the pork mixture in the center of each and fold over the wrappers, pushing the filling into the center and pushing out any trapped air. Seal the edges well.

3. Place the lettuce leaves in the bottom of a steamer and place the wontons on top. Steam for 10 to 15 minutes, turning halfway through cooking and brushing with sesame oil.

Per serving: 46 calories, 5 g carbohydrates, 4 g protein, 1 g fat

---

AVOCADO COCKTAIL

Yield: 20 servings

Who needs shrimp when you can concentrate on perfectly ripe avocado? The sauce is versatile and easy to prepare.

½ cup tomato ketchup
4 ounces Neufchâtel cream
    cheese, softened
juice of 1 lemon
½ teaspoon Worcestershire
    sauce
½ teaspoon Tabasco sauce

½ teaspoon ground black pepper
½ teaspoon salt
½ head of iceberg lettuce,
    finely shredded
4 ripe avocados
4 scallions, trimmed and finely
    chopped

1. Combine the ketchup, cream cheese, lemon, Worcestershire sauce, Tabasco, black pepper and salt in a bowl and mix well. Cover and stand for about 1 hour.

2. To serve: Divide the lettuce and place it in the bottom of individual cocktail glasses. Cut the avocados in half and remove the pits. Scoop out the avocado flesh out in large pieces. Lay the avocado pieces on top of the lettuce, spoon over the sauce and garnish with the scallions.

Per serving: 177 calories, 11 g carbohydrates, 3 g protein, 15 g fat

PEANUT AND ASPARAGUS STRUDEL

Yield: 8 servings

This appetizer will probably be greeted with surprise, as peanuts play more of a starring role in it than they usually do in the cocktail-hour.

3 ounces butter
1 large onion,
    chopped
12 ounces fresh or frozen
    asparagus, thawed and
    chopped

½ cup shelled, skinned
    peanuts, chopped
salt and freshly ground black
    pepper
5 sheets phyllo pastry
¾ cup grated cheddar cheese

1. Preheat the oven to 400 degrees. In a large nonstick skillet, melt ½ ounce of the butter and sauté the onion for 3 minutes. Add the asparagus and peanuts and sauté 2 minutes longer. Remove the pan from the heat and set aside to cool. Season to taste.

2. Melt the remaining butter. Unfold the pastry sheets on a flat surface, brush each liberally with some of the melted butter, reserving a little for the top, and place the phyllo sheets on top of one another

to form layers. Scatter the asparagus mixture onto the pastry and sprinkle with ½ cup of the grated cheese.

3. Carefully roll up the strudel lengthwise and place on a baking tray. Brush with the remaining melted butter and sprinkle with the remaining cheese. Bake the strudel until crisp and golden, about 25 to 30 minutes. Serve either hot or cold in slices.

Per serving: 222 calories, 11 g carbohydrates, 7 g protein, 17 g fat

CAPPUCCINO OF ASPARAGUS AND SALMON

Yield: 6 servings

This soup gets its name from the frothy cappuccino-like "head" that comes from the hand blender used to puree it. If you don't have one, pulsing the soup in a blender with some small ice cubes will produce the airy foam.

1 pound asparagus
2 tablespoons unsalted
  butter
1 onion, sliced
1 leek, trimmed, split, rinsed
  and thinly sliced

2 garlic cloves, crushed
2 cups strong chicken broth
2 cups half-and-half
salt and pepper to taste
3½ ounces salmon, very finely
  diced

1. Snap off the tough ends from the asparagus spears and discard. Chop the remaining spears. Melt the butter in a 2-quart saucepan over medium heat and add the asparagus, onion, leek and garlic. Cook, stirring frequently, until the most of the liquid has evaporated, about 10 minutes.

2. Combine the chicken broth and cream in a separate pan and heat until gently simmering. When the vegetable mixture has finished cooking, add the hot broth mixture and cook until the vegetables are tender, about 10 minutes longer.

3. Strain the vegetables through a sieve placed over a bowl. Place the vegetables in another bowl and place in a bowl of ice water to quickly chill to prevent discoloring. Refrigerate the cooking liquid until cool.

4. To serve: Combine the cooled vegetables and cooking liquid in a clean saucepan and, using a hand blender, blend the soup, incorporating air to make it frothy. Reheat the soup until hot but not boiling and season. Place the small dices of salmon in the bottom of the serving bowls, and pour the hot soup on top—the hot soup will quickly cook the small pieces of fish on impact. Serve immediately.

Per serving: 213 calories, 11 g carbohydrates, 10 g protein, 15 g fat

BEEF CARPACCIO WITH GRILLED ASPARAGUS AND PARMESAN CRISPS

Yield: 6 servings

This is an involved creation—but great for entertaining because each part can be done ahead and then assembled for serving. The raw beef is a flavorful and textural contrast to the juicy asparagus, crisp cheese wafers and rich egg sauce. And the fresh lemon juice and shredded basil shine through as aromatic and palate-pleasing accents.

12 ounces beef tenderloin or boneless sirloin steak
1 pound medium-thick asparagus spears
olive oil for brushing

SAUCE
1 tablespoon red wine vinegar
3 eggs
4 scallions, trimmed and finely chopped

1 garlic clove, very finely chopped (optional)
2 tablespoons extra-virgin olive oil
salt and freshly ground pepper to taste

FOR SERVING
juice of ½ lemon
PARMESAN CRISPS (see following recipe)
6 fresh basil leaves, shredded

1. Cut the beef into paper-thin slices. Line 6 flat plates with plastic wrap and divide the beef among the plates, arranging the slices in one layer to cover the centers of the plates, more or less. Cover with plastic wrap. Invert each plastic-wrap encased beef packet onto the work surface and pound gently with a flat meat mallet or rolling pin until the beef is very thin. Remove the top layers of plastic wrap and cover each with one of the plates. Using the plastic wrap, lift up the beef onto the plate and quickly flip the plate to invert the beef onto it. Set aside or refrigerate until ready to serve.

2. Snap off the tough ends from the asparagus spears and discard. Peel spears if desired. Cook in boiling salted water for 3 minutes or until just tender but still quite firm. Drain and place in a bowl of ice water until completely cold. Drain the asparagus again and pat dry on a paper-towel lined baking sheet. Brush with oil and sprinkle with salt and pepper. Prepare a charcoal grill and cook the asparagus to mark them on all sides and place on a plate.

3. For the sauce: Place the vinegar in a small pan of simmering salted water, then poach the eggs until the whites are firm and the yolks are just cooked through. Drain and place in a bowl of ice-cold water to stop the cooking. Drain on paper towels. Place the poached eggs in a medium bowl and crush to a fine consistency with a fork. Add the scallions, garlic, 2 tablespoons oil, salt and pepper, and mix well. Set aside.

4. To serve: Remove the plastic wrap from the plates and brush the beef with olive oil. Sprinkle with the lemon juice and season with sea salt and pepper. Place a Parmesan Crisp on top of each carpaccio, then add the grilled asparagus and sprinkle with basil. Spoon the egg sauce around and serve.

Per serving (without the Parmesan Crisps): 301 calories, 5 g carbohydrates, 18 g protein, 23 g fat.

PARMESAN CRISPS

Yield: 16 servings

olive oil for brushing
¾ cup freshly grated Parmesan cheese

salt and freshly ground black pepper to taste

Place an 8-inch nonstick skillet over low heat, brush with a film of olive oil and then sprinkle with a thin, even layer of Parmesan. Sprinkle with salt and pepper. Cook for about 2 minutes or until the cheese melts and turns golden. Use a metal spatula to transfer the Crisps to paper towels. Repeat to make 6 Crisps in all.

Per serving: 77 calories, trace carbohydrates, 5 g protein, 6 g fat

SAVORY AVOCADO CHEESECAKE WRAPPED IN ROASTED PEPPERS

Yield: 4 servings

Eye-catching and tasty, it is even more of a delight that this appetizer is easy to make. You can use bottled roasted peppers if you do not have time to roast your own.

4 red bell peppers
2 lemons
2 large bunches fresh basil
4 garlic cloves, peeled
6 tablespoons pine nuts
6 tablespoons olive oil plus
  extra for greasing ramekins
salt to taste

freshly ground pepper to taste
2 ripe avocados, pitted and
  peeled
2 (8-ounce) packages 50-percent
  fat cream cheese, softened
1 cup fresh white breadcrumbs
toast points or raw vegetables
  for serving

1. Preheat the broiler. Quarter the peppers lengthwise and remove the seeds and membranes. Place both quartered peppers skin-side up on a baking sheet and broil until the skins are blackened, 8 to 10 minutes. Set aside to cool.

2. Grate the lemon rind and place in a food processor. Cut the lemons in half and squeeze the juice from the two halves into the processor. Reserve some basil for a garnish and add the remainder to the processor. Add the garlic, pine nuts, oil, salt and pepper and process to make a coarse dressing. Set aside.

3. Place the avocados in a medium bowl and mash with a fork until smooth. Add the cream cheese and beat together until smooth. Stir in the breadcrumbs and $1/4$ cup dressing. Squeeze the other lemon into the mixture and season to taste.

4. Remove the skins from the grilled peppers and pat the flesh dry with a paper towel. Line an 8-inch round cake pan with plastic wrap, leaving the ends of the wrap hanging over the edges of the pan. Line the pan with peppers, allowing the excess to come up and over the sides. Spread the avocado mixture over the peppers. Fold over the peppers on the sides and cover with the extending plastic wrap. Refrigerate until set, at least 2 hours.

5. To serve, remove the plastic wrap covering the cheesecake and set a serving plate on top of the mixture. Invert the cheesecake onto the plate and remove all the plastic wrap. Drizzle the remaining dressing around the plate. Garnish with the reserved basil and serve with toast points or raw vegetables.

Per serving: 190 calories, 7 g carbohydrates, 4 g protein, 17 g fat

TOMATO-GARLIC BRUSCHETTA

Yield: 16 servings

1 dash olive oil
1 tablespoon finely chopped onion
1 (8-ounce) can chopped tomatoes

1 teaspoon tomato paste
1 teaspoon finely chopped garlic
1 pinch fennel seeds (optional)
1 small (8-inch) loaf French bread

1. Heat the oil in a small nonstick skillet over medium heat and sauté the onion until tender, about 5 minutes. Stir in the tomatoes, tomato paste, garlic and fennel seeds, if using. Cook gently until thickened, about 5 minutes.

2. Slice the bread diagonally into ½-inch-thick pieces. Toast on both sides. Spread one side of each slice with the tomato mixture and serve immediately.

Per serving: 50 calories, 9 g carbohydrates, 2 g protein, trace fat

VEGETARIAN CAVIAR

Yield: 24 tablespoons
or 48 servings

These shiny "eggs" are actually mushrooms so there's nothing fishy about THIS caviar! A mixture of mushrooms will add interest to the appearance and flavor, but using one kind of mushroom will produce a more uniform spread and look like real caviar.

¼ cup minced shallots
1 tablespoon margarine
2 tablespoons vegetable
   broth
1 pound fresh mushrooms,
   cleaned and minced
1 tablespoon dry sherry
1 tablespoon minced fresh
parsley
½ teaspoon dried thyme
   leaves, crumbled
¼ teaspoon salt
⅛ teaspoon freshly ground
   black pepper
MELBA TOAST for serving
   (see page 363)

1. Melt the butter in a large nonstick skillet over medium-high heat, add the shallots and sauté until tender. Add the mushrooms and broth and cook over high heat until all liquid evaporates, about 5 minutes, stirring constantly. Stir in the sherry, parsley, thyme, salt and pepper. Remove the skillet from heat and allow mixture to cool.

2. Pack the caviar into a small crock or container and chill at least 2 hours. Serve with Melba Toast.

Per serving: 6 calories, trace carbohydrates, trace protein, trace fat

SOUPS

RIBOLLITA

Yield: 16 servings

In Italy, ribollita (literally, reboiled) usually means leftover foods. And indeed, this Tuscan soup is delicious left over or cooked in advance and reheated.

1 (19-ounce) can cannellini beans, drained and rinsed
3 slices bacon, cut crosswise into ¼-inch strips
¾ teaspoon dried rosemary, crumbled
1 onion, chopped
2 garlic cloves, minced
2 carrots, chopped
1 celery stalk, chopped
3 cups chopped cabbage (about ½ small head)

12 ounces Swiss chard, tough stems removed, leaves washed well and chopped
2 teaspoons salt
1 teaspoon freshly ground pepper
2 cups canned tomatoes with their juice
2 (1¼-inch-thick) slices country bread

1. Preheat the oven to 350 degrees. In a food processor, combine 1 cup of the beans with 1 cup water and process until smooth. Set aside.

2. In a large saucepan, cook the bacon over medium heat, stirring frequently, for 3 minutes. Add the rosemary, onion, garlic, carrots, and celery and cook, stirring frequently, until the vegetables start to soften, about 10 minutes. Add the cabbage, chard, salt, and pepper and cook, stirring, until the cabbage wilts, about 3 minutes. Stir in the tomatoes and cook, breaking them up with the back of a spoon, for 1 to 2 minutes. Add 4 cups water and bring to a simmer. Stir in the bean puree and simmer for 15 minutes.

3. Meanwhile, place the bread on a baking sheet and toast until golden, turning once, about 15 minutes. Add the remaining beans and the toasted bread to the soup. Increase the heat to medium high and bring just to a boil, stirring to break up the bread. If the soup is too thick, stir in some additional water.

Per serving: 172 calories, 20 g carbohydrates, 6 g protein, 8 g fat

FLAGEOLET BEAN SOUP

Yield: 12 servings

If you can't find the dried French beans called flageolets, which have a lovely, subtle flavor, substitute navy beans.

1½ cups dried flageolet beans
1 small onion, quartered
1 medium garlic clove
1 tablespoon fresh
  thyme
1 tablespoon coarse, (kosher)
  salt
3½ cups homemade chicken
  broth or low-sodium canned
  broth

3 fresh plum tomatoes, peeled,
  seeded, and cut into small
  cubes
½ cup half-and-half
freshly ground pepper
¼ cup flat-leaf parsley leaves,
  (optional)

1. In a medium bowl, soak the beans overnight in cold water to cover. Drain the beans and transfer them to a large saucepan. Add the onion, garlic, thyme, and 6 cups of water. Heat to boiling over high heat. Reduce the heat to low, cover tightly and simmer for 1 hour. Add 2 teaspoons of the salt and continue simmering, covered, until the beans are tender, about 20 minutes longer. Drain.

2. Transfer the beans, onion and garlic to the food processor and puree. Strain the puree into a saucepan, leaving the bean skins behind. Whisk 3 cups of the chicken broth into the puree.

3. Place the tomato cubes in a colander, sprinkle with the remaining 1 teaspoon salt and toss to coat. Let drain for 1 hour.

4. Shortly before serving, whisk the half-and-half into the soup and heat through over medium heat. If the soup is very thick, thin it with additional broth or water. Season with salt and pepper. Ladle the soup into warm soup plates and garnish each serving with a cluster of tomato cubes and a few parsley leaves.

Per serving: 113 calories, 17 g carbohydrates, 7 g protein, 2 g fat

WHITE BEAN AND SAFFRON SOUP

Yield: 12 servings

2 cups chopped onions
2 tablespoons olive oil
6 garlic cloves, chopped
1 cup dry white wine or apple juice
1½ cups dried white beans, soaked overnight, drained
8 cups vegetable broth or water

2 bay leaves
2 cups diced celery
1 cup diced carrots
1 teaspoon salt or to taste
2 teaspoons cracked black pepper
12 threads saffron
grated rind and juice of 1 lemon

In a large pot, sauté onions in olive oil on medium-high heat, stirring often until translucent and soft, about 5 minutes. Stir in garlic and sauté for 2 to 3 minutes. Add wine and stir for about 1 minute. Add beans, broth, bay leaves and heat to boiling. Reduce heat to medium and simmer for about an hour until beans are just tender. Stir in celery and carrots and simmer for 20 minutes. Add salt, pepper, saffron, lemon rind, and juice, and simmer for 10 to 20 minutes more.

Per serving: 139 calories, 20 g carbohydrates, 6 g protein, 3 g fat

COLD AVOCADO, SPINACH AND SCALLION SOUP

Yield: 6 servings

The walkways of heaven will probably be lined with avocado trees. Here's a soup to enjoy until then.

2 large ripe avocados
1 lime
4 scallions
1 (5-ounce) bag ready-to-use baby spinach
2½ cups chilled chicken or vegetable broth; more if needed

a few drops Tabasco
dash of Worcestershire sauce
salt and pepper to taste
ice cubes if desired

FOR SERVING (OPTIONAL)
lightly toasted French bread
Boursin or other cream cheese

1. Halve, pit, peel and coarsely chop the avocados. Place in a bowl and squeeze the juice from the lime over them. Toss to coat. Snip the scallions into short segments into the same bowl.

2. Reserve a few spinach leaves for garnish. Combine the remainder with the avocado mixture and, in batches, puree in a food processor. Scrape out the puree into a bowl and whisk in enough broth to get a runny but thick consistency. Season to taste with Tabasco and Worcestershire sauce, salt and pepper.

3. Pour the soup into individual bowls, add a few ice cubes if you like. Snip slivers of the reserved spinach leaves on top for garnish.

4. Serve with toasted French bread spread with Boursin or other cream cheese.

Per serving (without the bread and cheese): 106 calories, 6 g carbohydrates, 4 g protein, 8 g fat

---

CUCUMBER AND MELON GAZPACHO

Yield: 6 servings

A tomato-less gazpacho is not an oxymoron. This cold soup of vegetable and fruit juices has all the refreshing qualities of the Spanish classic.

2 large cucumbers, peeled and seeded
1 medium cantaloupe, peeled and seeded
1 bunch arugula, rinsed and patted dry
3 dill sprigs
3 mint sprigs
2 tablespoons tarragon vinegar
1 small garlic clove, peeled

1 small green chile, seeded
1½ cups carrot juice or mixed vegetable juice
³/₄ cup Greek yogurt
6 tablespoons olive oil
salt to taste
freshly ground pepper to taste

GARNISH
crushed ice
dill sprigs

1. Finely dice half of 1 cucumber and 1 slice of melon and reserve. Chop remaining cucumber and melon roughly and place in a blender with the arugula, dill, mint, vinegar, garlic, chile and half the carrot or mixed vegetable juice. (You may have to do this in batches and pour each batch into a large glass measure or bowl.) Blend to a smooth

paste and gradually blend in the remaining juice, the yogurt and oil. Season to taste with salt and pepper. Refrigerate until cold.

2. To serve, pour into 6 individual soup bowls and garnish with the reserved cucumber and melon, crushed ice cubes and sprigs of dill.

Per serving: 208 calories, 18 g carbohydrates, 4 g protein, 14 g fat

---

DEEP-FRIED TOFU IN BROTH

Yield: 4 servings

The unusual ingredients for this recipe can be found in Japanese grocery stores. You can also sprinkle bonito flakes (hana katsuo) on top of the tofu if you like.

FOR DEEP-FRIED TOFU
1 block firm tofu
3 tablespoons kuzu or potato
  spinach (katakuriko)
oil for deep frying

FOR THE BROTH
1 cup dashi (seaweed-flavored
  broth, available in granules)

3 tablespoons soy sauce
3 tablespoons mirin

FOR SERVING
5 tablespoons grated daikon
  radish with (momiji-oroshi)
  chili, or plain grated daikon
  and 1 tablespoon grated
  peeled fresh gingerroot

1. Wrap the tofu in a clean kitchen towel and place it on a slightly tilted board on the draining board. Set a small plate on top with a heavy weight or can on top. Leave for about half an hour until some of the water has drained away and the tofu is dry.

2. Cut the tofu into 8 large cubes. If using kuzu starch you will need to break up the lumps to make a fine powder. To do this put the kuzu into a strong paper bag and roll a rolling pin over it until you have a fairly fine powder. If using potato starch simply sprinkle it onto a plate and dust each piece of tofu in the starch, making sure every surface is covered.

3. Heat the oil in a saucepan to 340 degrees and drop the tofu pieces in. Fry until they are a light golden color.

4. Meanwhile, combine the ingredients for the broth in a saucepan, heat to boiling and remove from heat.

5. Place 2 pieces of tofu per person into a medium-size deep bowl.

Pour the hot broth over, until it's about one-third of the way up the tofu (it shouldn't be swimming). Shape the grated daikon into 4 little cones and place on top of the tofu in each bowl. If using ginger, also make that into little cones, and place another smaller cone of ginger on top of the daikon.

Per serving: 80 calories, 4 g carbohydrates, 6 g protein, 4 g fat

THAI CHICKEN-COCONUT SOUP

Yield: 4 servings

You don't have to go out to a restaurant to enjoy this world-famous soup. It is a fabulous first course but so delicious that you want to have lots of it as a main dish. The rice helps cool down the heat from the chiles.

FOR THE PASTE
1 tablespoon oil
2-inch piece fresh gingerroot, peeled and diced
1 tablespoon chopped fresh tender lemongrass
1 green chile, cut in half
1 red chile, cut in half
1 teaspoon coriander seeds
1 shallot
1 garlic clove

2½ cups vegetable broth
12 ounces boneless, skinless chicken breast, cut into strips
4 ounces fresh sugar snap peas or shelled fresh peas
salt to taste
freshly ground pepper to taste
juice of 1 lime
2 tablespoons shredded fresh basil

FOR THE SOUP
1 (14-ounce) can coconut milk

FOR SERVING
1 cup cooked Thai rice

1. Place all the paste ingredients in a small food processor or blender and process until smooth. Heat a wok and add the paste. Stir over medium heat for 2 minutes. Stir in the coconut milk and broth and heat to boiling. Reduce the heat to a simmer and add the chicken strips. Simmer for 5 minutes, add the peas and simmer until the chicken is cooked, 2 to 3 minutes. Season to taste. Squeeze the lime juice over the broth and sprinkle with the basil.

2. To serve, spoon some rice into each serving bowl, ladle the soup over the rice and serve at once.

Per serving: 389 calories, 18 g carbohydrates, 24 g protein, 25 g fat

QUICK BEET AND SOUR CREAM SOUP

Yield: 6 servings

This is the easiest beet soup you may ever make. It relies on the sweetness of the earthy vegetable balancing the acidity of the rich sour cream.

6 peeled beets	1 tablespoon all-purpose flour
1 tablespoon sugar	1 egg yolk
1¼ cups sour cream	1 cup croutons

1. Place 3 of the beets in a food processor and puree. Transfer to a 2-quart saucepan. Chop the remaining beets and add to the pureed beets. Add 5 cups water and the sugar. Heat to boiling and simmer until the beets are tender, about 10 minutes.

2. Meanwhile, combine ³⁄₄ cup of the sour cream and flour and whisk until blended. Whisk the mixture into the beets. Keep the soup hot over low heat.

3. Beat the egg yolk together with the remaining sour cream and divide it among 4 soup bowls. Ladle the soup into each bowl, and stir to combine it with the egg-yolk mixture. Sprinkle with the croutons.

Per serving: 164 calories, 16 g carbohydrates, 4 g protein, 10 g fat

CASHEW CURRY CHOWDER

Yield: 6 servings

This fragrant soup is full of vegetables and flavor. It is rich enough to serve as a lunch with a sandwich or will make a delicious first course with a dollop of plain yogurt added to each bowl.

2 tablespoons safflower oil	1½ cups chicken or vegetable
3 celery stalks, diced	broth
1 carrot, peeled and diced	3½ cups (2-percent) milk
1 onion, diced	salt to taste
1 russet potato, peeled and diced	ground pepper to taste
2 garlic cloves, minced	½ cup roasted cashews,
3 tablespoons curry powder	coarsely chopped

1. Heat the oil in a 3-quart saucepan over medium heat. Add the celery, carrot and onion and sauté until the onion is soft, about 5 minutes. Stir in the potato and garlic. Add the curry powder and sauté for 1 minute. Stir in the broth, milk and 3 cups water. Heat to boiling, lower heat and simmer until all vegetables are soft.

2. Puree some of the soup using a hand blender so that the broth is thickened and the soup remains chunky. Season with salt and pepper to taste. Serve, adding a generous helping of cashews to each bowl.

Per serving: 218 calories, 18 g carbohydrates, 9 g protein, 13 g fat

PEA AND CILANTRO SOUP

Yield: 6 servings

This soup can be served hot or cold.

2 ounces butter
1 large onion, finely
  chopped
2 garlic cloves, peeled and
  chopped
1 green chile, seeded and finely
  chopped
1 pound fresh or frozen peas
8 cups chicken broth

2 tablespoons chopped fresh
  cilantro
salt to taste
freshly ground pepper to taste
pinch of sugar

GARNISH
softly whipped cream
fresh cilantro leaves

1. Melt the butter in a large stockpot over medium heat and add the onion, garlic, and chile and cook, stirring, for 3 to 4 minutes. Add the peas and the broth. Heat to boiling and simmer for 7 to 8 minutes. Add the cilantro.

2. Cool the soup until it stops steaming and, in batches, puree in a blender, pouring each blended batch into a clean saucepan to re-warm if serving hot or into a bowl if serving cold.

3. Season the soup with salt, pepper and a pinch of sugar. Reheat or chill the soup as desired. Serve with a swirl of whipped cream and a few cilantro leaves.

Per serving: 258 calories, 15 g carbohydrates, 11 g protein, 17 g fat

SPINACH AND TANGERINE SOUP

Yield: 8 servings

7½ cups chicken broth
½ cup yellow split peas, soaked
1 ounce unsalted butter
¾ cup sliced scallions
1 teaspoon turmeric
8 ounces spinach, cleaned, trimmed and finely chopped
1 cup loosely packed parsley leaves, chopped
1 cup loosely packed fresh cilantro leaves, chopped plus sprigs for garnish
grated rind and juice of 2 tangerines
grated rind of 1 orange
2 tablespoons ground rice
1 cup plain yogurt, sour cream or crème fraîche

1. Heat the chicken broth to boiling in a 3-quart saucepan. Add the split peas and simmer for 10 minutes. Melt butter in a small skillet over medium heat and sauté the scallions until softened, about 5 minutes. Add the turmeric and sauté until fragrant, about 1 minute. Stir the scallion mixture into the broth and peas and rinse out the skillet with some broth.

2. Add the spinach, parsley, cilantro, grated citrus rind and tangerine juice to the soup. Cover the pan and simmer for 30 minutes.

3. Mix the ground rice with 5 ounces cold water in a cup until blended and stir into the soup. Simmer 15 minutes longer, stirring occasionally.

Serve in bowls with a little yogurt and fresh cilantro sprigs.

Per serving: 128 calories, 13 g carbohydrates, 9 g protein, 5 g fat

RICE AND PORK SOUP

Yield: 2 servings

2 tablespoons vegetable oil
2 garlic cloves, finely chopped
2¼ cups chicken broth
1 tablespoon preserved vegetable
1 tablespoon light soy sauce
¼ teaspoon ground white pepper
1 tablespoon fish sauce (either
Thai nam pla or Vietnamese nuoc mam)
2 ounces minced pork
⅔ cup boiled fragrant rice such as jasmine or more to thicken soup
fresh cilantro for garnish

1. Heat a 2-quart saucepan over medium-high heat, add the oil, and when it is hot, sauté the garlic until golden brown, about 30 seconds. Remove from the heat and set the oil and garlic aside in a small bowl.

2. In the same pan, heat the broth with the preserved vegetable. Add the soy sauce, pepper and fish sauce. Heat to simmering over medium heat. Holding the pork loosely in one hand, pull off small pieces with the other and drop into the broth. When it all has been added, cook 1 minute longer. Add the cooked rice and stir thoroughly. Cook until the rice is heated through and soft, 4 to 5 minutes. The soup should be quite thick.

3. Ladle the soup into individual bowls. Add 1 tablespoon of the garlic and oil mixture to each and garnish with cilantro leaves.

Per serving: 305 calories, 17 g carbohydrates, 13 g protein, 20 g fat

ESCAROLE SOUP WITH TURKEY MEATBALLS

Yield: 6 servings

1 pound ground turkey
2 eggs, lightly beaten
1 garlic clove, minced
1 small onion, minced
1/2 cup dried breadcrumbs
1/2 cup freshly grated Parmesan cheese
1/2 cup chopped fresh parsley
1 1/2 teaspoons salt
1/4 teaspoon fresh-ground black pepper

3 tablespoons olive oil
1/2 head escarole (about 8 ounces), leaves washed well and chopped (about 1 quart)
1 1/2 quarts canned low-sodium chicken broth or homemade broth
2 tablespoons red- or white-wine vinegar
1/4 teaspoon crushed red-pepper flakes

1. In a medium bowl, mix together the turkey, eggs, garlic, onion, breadcrumbs, Parmesan, parsley, 1/2 teaspoon of the salt, and the black pepper until thoroughly combined. Shape the mixture into twenty meatballs.

2. In a large skillet, heat 1 1/2 tablespoons of the oil over medium heat. Add half the meatballs to the pan and cook, turning, until browned on all sides, about 3 minutes. Remove the meatballs from

the pan and drain on paper towels. Repeat with the remaining 1½ tablespoons oil and the rest of the meatballs.

3. Place all the meatballs, the escarole, broth, 2 cups water, the vinegar, red-pepper flakes, and the remaining 1 teaspoon of salt in a large pot. Cover and bring to a simmer over medium heat, stirring occasionally. The meatballs should be cooked through by the time the broth comes to a simmer.

Per serving: 323 calories, 11 g carbohydrates, 26 g protein, 19 g fat

COLD BUTTERMILK BORSCHT

Yield: 7 servings

This is a beautiful soup that makes your mouth water. Serve it hot in the winter months.

nonstick cooking spray
1 teaspoon vegetable oil
²/₃ cup chopped onion
4 cups peeled diced fresh beets
2 tablespoons red-wine vinegar
1½ tablespoons brown sugar
³/₄ teaspoon dill seeds

½ teaspoon salt
¼ teaspoon coarsely ground pepper
1½ cups nonfat buttermilk
1 cup plain nonfat yogurt for serving
snipped fresh dill for garnish

1. Grease a large saucepan with cooking spray, add the oil and heat over medium-low heat until hot. Add the onion, cover and cook until tender, about 5 minutes. Add 4 cups water, the beets, vinegar, sugar, dill, salt and pepper and mix well. Heat to boiling, cover, reduce heat, and simmer until the beets are tender, about 1 hour.

2. Place one-third of the mixture in a blender, cover and process until smooth. Pour puree into a large bowl. Repeat procedure with remaining mixture. Stir in the buttermilk. Cover and refrigerate until cold.

3. To serve: Ladle soup into bowls. Add a dollop of yogurt to each and sprinkle with fresh dill.

Per serving: 79 calories, 12 g carbohydrates, 4 g protein, 2 g fat

ONION SOUP COBBLER

Yield: 8 servings

Here's a topping for French Onion Soup and that won't burn your mouth the way that traditional soaked piece of cheese-topped bread does. This tender, bumpy or "cobbled" biscuit crust is made with cornmeal and flavored with pesto.

8 cups French Onion Soup
4 cups beef broth

COBBLER TOPPING
1/2 cup all-purpose flour
1/2 teaspoon baking powder
1/4 teaspoon baking soda
1/4 teaspoon salt

1/3 cup cornmeal or fine
  semolina
1/3 cup plain yogurt
1 large egg, beaten
1 tablespoon melted butter
2 tablespoons pesto sauce
1/4 cup grated Parmesan
  cheese

1. Preheat the oven to 400 degrees. Heat the soup and broth until hot and ladle it into 8 ovenproof serving bowls or large custard cups. Place the bowls on a sturdy baking sheet.

2. Combine the flour, baking powder, baking soda, and salt in a large bowl. Stir in the cornmeal and set aside.

3. In a smaller bowl, whisk the yogurt, egg and melted butter and quickly whisk with the flour mixture. Fold in the pesto, leaving the pesto in streaks. (Do not over-mix.)

4. Drop the cobbler mixture by spoonfuls over the soup in each bowl, leaving the mounds to give a "cobbled" effect. Sprinkle with the Parmesan cheese.

5. Bake the soup on the baking sheet for easy handling until the topping has risen and is golden brown, 10 to 15 minutes.

Per serving: 176 calories, 20 g carbohydrates, 9 g protein, 7 g fat

TOFU AND FISH DUMPLING SOUP

Yield: 2 servings

The fish sauce, preserved vegetable, tofu and fish dumplings are available from Chinese grocery stores.

2 cups chicken broth
2 tablespoons Thai or
  Vietnamese fish sauce
1 tablespoon light soy sauce
1 teaspoon preserved vegetable
½ teaspoon ground white pepper

4 ounces tofu, cut into small
  cubes
8 purchased round fish
  dumplings
2 scallions, green part only, cut
  into 1-inch slivers

In a medium saucepan, combine the chicken stock, fish sauce, soy sauce, preserved vegetable and white pepper and heat until simmering. Add the tofu and dumplings and cook for 30 seconds. Add the scallions and simmer for a few seconds. Ladle into small bowls and serve.

Per serving: 228 calories, 4 g carbohydrates, 38 g protein, 6 g fat

FRUIT AND VEGETABLE SOUP

Yield: 8 servings

The vibrant colors and mix of ingredients in soup is one reason why it's one of man's oldest and most favored foods. This exotic blend of sweet and tangy flavors accents the earthy split-pea base that is at the heart of the pot. Spinach is a favorite green, but feel free to add finely shredded kale, cabbage or even the outer leaves of a head of romaine lettuce.

2 tablespoons unsalted
  butter
1 bunch scallions, trimmed
1 teaspoon turmeric
2 quarts chicken broth
¼ cup yellow split peas,
  soaked
5 cups fresh, cleaned spinach,
  finely chopped

¼ cup chopped parsley
¼ cup chopped cilantro plus
  additional whole leaves for
  garnish
grated rind of 2 tangerines
grated rind of 1 orange
juice of 3 tangerines
1 cup plain yogurt, sour cream
  or crème fraîche

1. Heat the chicken broth to boiling in a large stock pot. Add the split peas and simmer for 10 minutes.

2. Melt the butter in a 4-quart stockpot over medium heat, add the scallions and sauté for 5 minutes. Add the turmeric and cook, stirring, 1 minute. Stir in the chicken broth and heat to boiling. Add the split peas and simmer for 10 minutes. Add the spinach, parsley, cilantro, citrus rind and tangerine juice. Cover the pan and simmer

for 30 minutes. Crush some of the lentils against the pot with a large spoon or use a hand blender to thicken the broth. Ladle the soup into bowls and garnish each serving with a dollop of yogurt and some cilantro leaves.

Per serving: 154 calories, 16 g carbohydrates, 12 g protein, 6 g fat

AVOCADO AND DILL SOUP

Yield: 4 servings

This is a cold soup, perfect for dinner parties or summer picnics, and it takes only about 30 minutes to make. Serve garnished with a little extra chopped fresh dill or use chives.

2 large ripe avocados
1 cup sour cream
2 tablespoons finely chopped fresh dill
1½ cups cold vegetable stock

1 teaspoon soy sauce
salt to taste
freshly ground pepper to taste
a little chopped dill or chives for garnish

1. Cut the avocados in half and remove the pits. Scoop out the flesh and place it in a blender. Add the sour cream, dill, vegetable stock and soy sauce and blend until smooth, 1 to 2 minutes. Season with salt and pepper. Cover and refrigerate at least 20 minutes before serving.

2. To serve: Pour the soup into 4 bowls and garnish with dill or chives.

Per serving: 223 calories, 8 g carbohydrates, 3 g protein, 22 g fat

COLD SPINACH, AVOCADO AND QUARK SOUP

Yield: 8 servings

Physics majors and chefs alike brighten up when Quark is mentioned. But here you want the kind of Quark that is a thick unripened cheese. It has a rich flavor and texture—like crème fraîche—except it has little or no fat. If you can't find Quark, you can substitute tangy sour cream or yogurt.

2 ounces butter
1 (16-ounce) bag frozen
  chopped spinach
3 tablespoons flour
2¼ cups milk
2 cups chicken broth
pinch freshly grated
  nutmeg

salt and freshly ground black
  pepper to taste
2 avocados, pitted, peeled and
  chopped
2 (8-ounce) cartons Quark
  (available in specialty food
  shops or German grocery
  stores)

1. Melt the butter in a 2-quart saucepan, add the spinach and cook
for 10 minutes, stirring occasionally. Stir in the flour and cook for 1
minute. Gradually stir in the milk and chicken broth and heat to boiling. Add the nutmeg, salt and pepper and simmer for 5 to 6 minutes.

2. Stir in the avocados and Quark, reserving a little Quark for garnish. In batches, place in a food processor or blender and blend until
smooth. Transfer to a bowl and place in the refrigerator to chill.

3. To serve: Adjust the seasoning if necessary. Ladle the soup into 6 to
8 serving bowls and top each with a teaspoon of the reserved Quark.

Per serving: 210 calories, 15 g carbohydrates, 10 g protein, 14 g fat

CLASSIC HEARTY HAM
AND BEAN SOUP

Yield: 16 servings

**Soup is definitely one of the world's most happily consumed
comfort foods. Here, the smoked meat enhances the earthy
flavor of the beans. Either thyme or sage will add a soothing
fragrance and tasty seasoning. This makes a big batch, perfect for
a crowd or for stocking the freezer.**

1 pound dried navy or Great
  Northern beans
1 to 1½ pounds meaty ham
  bones or smoked pork hocks
1 large onion, chopped
1 teaspoon dried thyme or sage
  leaves, crushed (optional)

½ teaspoon seasoned salt
½ teaspoon celery salt
½ teaspoon freshly ground
  pepper
¼ teaspoon garlic powder

1. Rinse the beans and pick through them, discarding any bad ones or stray pebbles. Place the beans in a stockpot, add 6 cups water and set aside to soak overnight. (For a quicker softening method, heat the beans and water to boiling, reduce heat and simmer for 2 minutes. Remove from heat. Cover and let stand for 1 hour.)

2. Drain the beans if soaked overnight. Add 16 cups fresh water and the ham bones or pork hocks. Heat to boiling, reduce heat and simmer for 1 hour. Remove the ham bone or pork hocks and cut off the meat when cool enough to handle. Discard the bones and coarsely chop the meat.

3. Return the meat to the pan. Add the onion, thyme or sage, seasoned salt, celery salt, pepper and garlic powder. Return to boiling. Reduce the heat and simmer until the beans are tender, 45 to 60 minutes.

Per serving: 123 calories, 18 g carbohydrates, 9 g protein, 2 g fat

MUSHROOM SOUP WITH TOMATO-GARLIC BRUSCETTA

Yield: 2 servings

1 tablespoon butter
1 teaspoon vegetable oil
6 ounces mushrooms, chopped, plus a few wafer-thin slices for garnish
a pinch of freshly ground pepper
2 teaspoons all-purpose flour

1¼ cups chicken broth
½ cup half-and-half or milk
1 tablespoon heavy cream for garnish
a few leaves of fresh basil, shredded
TOMATO-GARLIC BRUSCHETTA for serving (see page 47)

1. Melt the butter in the oil in a 2-quart saucepan and sauté the chopped mushrooms with a pinch of pepper. Sauté until the mushrooms are softened, about 4 minutes. Stir in the flour until blended. Stir in the broth and heat to boiling, stirring. Simmer until the soup thickens, about 5 minutes

2. Using a hand blender, puree the mushrooms into the liquid. Stir in the half-and-half and heat through. When hot, serve quickly with

a swirl of cream over the top and a sprinkling of raw mushroom slices and basil. Serve with the Tomato-Garlic Bruschetta.

Per serving (without the Bruschetta): 182 calories, 9 g carbohydrates, 8 g protein, 13 g fat

MINESTRONE VEGETARIANO

Yield: 8 servings

¼ cup olive oil plus extra for serving
1 onion, peeled and finely chopped
2 celery stalks, washed and chopped
3 cups mixed green vegetables such as chopped spinach, cabbage, Swiss chard, lettuce leaves or spring greens
2 zucchini, cubed
1 carrot, peeled and cubed
2 ripe tomatoes, chopped
1 garlic clove, crushed
1 cup cooked cannellini or garbanzo beans
3 quarts vegetable broth or water, and more if necessary
¾ cup short stubby pasta
salt to taste
freshly ground pepper to taste
¼ cup coarsely chopped fresh flat-leaf parsley
freshly grated Parmesan cheese for serving

1. Heat the oil in a large soup pot over medium heat and add the onion. Sauté gently until soft without browning, about 7 minutes. Add the celery, green vegetables, zucchini, carrot, tomatoes and garlic. Sauté gently until the vegetables just begin to soften, about 8 minutes.

2. Add the beans and vegetable broth or water. Add more water if necessary to cover the vegetables completely. Reduce the heat to low and simmer the soup slowly until the vegetables are tender, about 30 minutes, stirring regularly. Add more liquid if necessary (use either vegetable broth or water).

3. Season the soup, heat to boiling and add the pasta. Cook gently until the pasta is al dente, tender but still firm, and transfer into soup bowls or a tureen and serve. Drizzle each serving to taste with olive oil and a sprinkle of Parmesan cheese.

Per serving: 206 calories, 18 g carbohydrates, 7 g protein, 3 g fat

SALADS

GREEK EASTER SALAD

Yield: 8 servings

1 large head romaine lettuce,
   torn into bite-size pieces
1 cucumber, peeled and thinly
   sliced
8 radishes, thinly sliced
2 scallions, thinly sliced
¼ cup plus 2 tablespoons
   extra-virgin oil

¼ cup red-wine vinegar
salt to taste
freshly ground pepper to taste
4 hard-cooked eggs, peeled
   and halved lengthwise
dill sprigs, for garnish

In a large bowl, combine the lettuce, cucumber, radishes and scallions. In a small bowl, whisk the oil with the vinegar and season with salt and pepper. Add the dressing to the salad and toss well. Top with the eggs, garnish with dill and serve immediately.

Per serving: 149 calories, 6 g carbohydrate, 5 g protein, 13 g fat

CAESAR SALAD WITH SHRIMP

Yield: 4 servings

1 loaf sourdough or country-
   style bread, cut into ¾-inch
   cubes (about 5 cups)
¾ cup plus 2 tablespoons
   olive oil
4 tablespoons lemon juice
2 garlic cloves, chopped
½ cup grated Parmesan cheese
1 teaspoon anchovy paste
2 teaspoons Dijon mustard

1 teaspoon salt
½ teaspoon fresh-ground black
   pepper
1 pound medium shrimp,
   shelled and deveined
1 head romaine lettuce,
   quartered lengthwise and cut
   crosswise into ½-inch strips
2 cups halved cherry
   tomatoes

1. Preheat the oven to 325 degrees. Toss the bread cubes with 1 tablespoon of the oil and spread on a large baking sheet. Bake until crisp on the outside and lightly browned, about 15 minutes. Let cool.

2. Meanwhile, place the lemon juice, garlic, Parmesan, anchovy paste, mustard, ½ teaspoon of the salt, and ¼ teaspoon of the pepper in a blender and blend until smooth. With the blender running, slowly add

the $^3/_4$ cup oil. As an alternative, whisk together everything but the oil and add the oil slowly, still whisking. Set the dressing aside.

3. Heat the broiler. In a broiler pan or on a baking sheet, toss the shrimp with the remaining 1 tablespoon oil, $^1/_2$ teaspoon salt, and $^1/_4$ teaspoon pepper. Broil the shrimp, turning once, until just done, about 4 minutes in all.

4. In a large bowl, combine the lettuce, tomatoes, croutons, and shrimp. Add the dressing and toss to coat.

Per serving: 395 calories, 18 g carbohydrate, 19 g protein, 28 g fat

CHERRY-TOMATO SALAD

Yield: 8 servings

2 tablespoons balsamic vinegar	salt to taste
1 tablespoon red-wine vinegar	freshly ground pepper to taste
1 large shallot, minced	3 pints cherry tomatoes,
1 teaspoon minced garlic	halved
$^1/_4$ cup plus 2 tablespoons extra-virgin oil	$^1/_3$ cup finely shredded fresh basil leaves

Whisk together the balsamic vinegar, red-wine vinegar, shallot and garlic in a large bowl. Whisk in the oil in a thin stream and season with salt and pepper. Add the tomatoes and basil and toss. Season with salt and pepper and serve.

Per serving: 121 calories, 7 g carbohydrate, 1 g protein, 11 g fat

MINTED SHRIMP SALAD

Yield: 6 servings

$^1/_2$ cup plus 1 tablespoon extra-virgin olive oil	8 ounces medium shrimp, shelled and deveined
$2^1/_2$ tablespoons sherry vinegar	$^1/_4$ cup mint leaves, torn in half
salt to taste	3 tablespoons golden raisins
freshly ground pepper to taste	(optional)
1 medium onion, finely chopped	$^1/_4$ teaspoon ground cumin
	1 pound mesclun salad greens

1. In a small bowl, whisk 7½ tablespoons of the olive oil with the sherry vinegar. Season with salt and pepper.

2. Heat the remaining 1½ tablespoons of olive oil in a large skillet. Add the onion and cook over medium heat, stirring, until softened and just beginning to brown, about 7 minutes. Add the shrimp, mint, raisins, cumin and a pinch each of salt and pepper and cook, stirring, until the shrimp are pink, about 7 minutes.

3. In a large bowl, toss the mesclun salad greens with the dressing and mound on 6 plates. Scatter the shrimp over the greens.

Per serving: 236 calories, 4 g carbohydrate, 9 g protein, 21 g fat

CANTALOUPE, MANGO AND ASIAN PEAR SLAW

Yield: 6 servings

Serve with grilled chicken, tuna, swordfis, or salmon.

1 tablespoon sugar
2 tablespoons fresh lime juice
1 tablespoon minced cilantro
1 tablespoon Asian fish sauce
½ tablespoon chile sauce,
   preferably Sriracha

1 garlic clove, minced
2 cups julienned cantaloupe
1 cup julienned carrot
½ cup julienned mango
½ cup julienned Asian pear
Boston lettuce for serving

In a bowl, dissolve the sugar in the lime juice. Stir in the cilantro, fish sauce, chile sauce and garlic. In another bowl, combine the cantaloupe, carrot, mango and Asian pear. Add the dressing, toss and refrigerate until cold.

Per serving: 56 calories, 14 g carbohydrate, 1 g protein, trace fat

WARM POACHED EGG, FRENCH BEANS AND TOMATO SALAD

Yield: 2 servings

1 small garlic clove, crushed
2 tablespoons crème fraîche
1 teaspoon Dijon mustard
1 tablespoon red-wine vinegar
salt to taste
freshly ground pepper to taste
½ (10-ounce) package frozen

French beans, cooked
according to package
directions, kept warm
2 plum tomatoes, peeled,
seeded and cut into strips
2 hot, freshly poached eggs
good olive oil for drizzling

Combine the garlic, crème fraîche, mustard and vinegar in a medium bowl, season and add a little hot water if too thick. Toss the beans and tomatoes with the dressing. Arrange the salad on two plates, place an egg on top and drizzle some oil around the edge.

Per serving: 178 calories, 10 g carbohydrate, 9 g protein, 12 g fat

TANGY BEAN SALAD

Yield: 6 servings

1¼ cups dried navy or Great
Northern beans
1 cup beef broth
3 tablespoons vinegar

1 garlic clove, minced
⅛ teaspoon salt
⅛ teaspoon pepper
4 slices bacon, chopped

1. Rinse the beans. In a large saucepan, combine beans and 4 cups cold water. Heat to boiling over high heat and then reduce heat to low. Simmer for 2 minutes. Remove the pan from the heat. Cover and let stand for 1 hour. (Or skip boiling the water and soak beans overnight in a covered pan.)

2. Drain and rinse beans. In the same pan, combine beans and 4 cups fresh water. Heat to boiling over high heat and then reduce heat to low. Cover and simmer for about 1¼ hours or until tender, stirring occasionally. Drain the beans.

3. In a small bowl, combine the beef broth, vinegar, 3 tablespoons water, garlic, salt and pepper and mix well. Pour over beans. Cover, chill 4 to 24 hours.

4. To serve, cook the bacon until crisp. Drain on paper towels. Stir into the salad.

Per serving: 149 calories, 11 g carbohydrate, 6 g protein, 9 g fat

---

APPLE SLAW

Yield: 10 servings

This is a salad and dessert in one dish, sweetened with a little honey and apples and packed with crunchy vegetables. It's perfect for a picnic or potluck supper.

½ cup pecan halves
½ cup MAYONNAISE
  (see page xx)
2 tablespoons honey
1 tablespoon fresh lime juice
1½ teaspoons yellow mustard
1½ teaspoons kosher salt
½ teaspoon freshly ground
  pepper

4 cups finely shredded green
  cabbage
3 medium Granny Smith apples,
  coarsely shredded
2 medium carrots, coarsely
  shredded
2 medium red bell peppers,
  thinly sliced
½ cup coarsely chopped chives

1. Preheat the oven to 400 degrees. Toast the pecans in a pie plate for about 5 minutes, or until fragrant. Let cool.

2. In a small bowl, combine the mayonnaise, honey, lime juice, mustard, salt and pepper. In a large bowl, combine the cabbage, apples, carrots and bell peppers. Just before serving, add the dressing, pecans and chives and toss well.

Per serving: 150 calories, 19 g carbohydrate, 2 g protein, 9 g fat

---

ALSATIAN HAM AND
GRUYÈRE SALAD

Yield: 8 servings

This is a fine place to use cold cuts or leftover meat. Thin strips of pork, lamb, beef, salami or mortadella could all be used in place of the ham. Or, for you meat lovers, try one of them in place of the cheese.

1 onion, cut into paper-thin slices

2½ teaspoons grainy Dijon mustard

2 teaspoons red- or white-wine vinegar

¼ teaspoon salt

¼ teaspoon fresh-ground black pepper

½ cup olive oil

1 pound sliced smoked ham, such as Black Forest, cut into matchstick strips

½ pound sliced Gruyère cheese, cut into matchstick strips

4 heads Belgian endive, julienned

¾ cup chopped fresh parsley

1. Place the onion in a small bowl, cover with cold water and let stand for 10 minutes. Drain the onion, rinse, and pat dry with paper towels.

2. Meanwhile, in a large glass or stainless-steel bowl, whisk together the mustard, vinegar, salt and pepper. Add the oil slowly, whisking.

3. To serve: Add the onion, ham, cheese, endives and parsley to the vinaigrette and toss.

Per serving: 352 calories, 4 g carbohydrate, 19 g protein, 29 g fat

SUGAR-SNAP NOODLE SALAD

Yield: 8 servings

This Asian-inspired salad is a spicy side dish that is nice with grilled meats and fish.

FOR THE STIR-FRY
2 tablespoons olive oil
1 red onion, sliced
1 to 2 garlic cloves, sliced
1 to 2 teaspoons ground coriander
4 dried red chiles

FOR THE SALAD
8 ounces sugar-snap peas, trimmed
8 ounces fresh Italian or Chinese vermicelli pasta

4 scallions, chopped
8 ounces button mushrooms, sliced
1 tablespoon chopped fresh cilantro
salt to taste
freshly ground pepper to taste

FOR THE DRESSING
4 tablespoons olive oil
2 teaspoons soy sauce

1. For the stir-fry: Heat the oil in a 2-quart saucepan, add the onion and cook until softened and golden, about 5 minutes. Add the garlic and ground coriander and crumble in the chiles. Fry gently over a low heat for 2 minutes.

2. Blanch the sugar-snap peas in boiling water, drain and set aside.

3. Cook the vermicelli according to the package instructions, drain in a colander and rinse until cool under running cold water. Drain well and place in a large serving bowl. Add the sugar snap peas, onion mixture, scallions, mushrooms, cilantro, almonds and seasoning to the noodles.

4. For the dressing: Whisk all the ingredients together in a small bowl until blended.

5. Pour the dressing over the noodle salad and toss to coat.

Per serving: 193 calories, 19 g carbohydrate, 5 g protein, 11 g fat

SALAD-BAR DREAM SALAD

Yield: 6 servings

This ingredient list looks like it will have you chopping all day, but fortunately you can buy most produce already trimmed, sliced and packaged in small portions. Some grocery stores even have in-house salad bars you can raid. They all add up to a tasty mix of favorite ingredients in proportions that look good and add the right amounts of juice and crunch.

½ English cucumber, seeded and cubed

6 cherry tomatoes, quartered

2 ounces button mushrooms, quartered

1 cup finely shredded red cabbage

1 cup finely shredded green cabbage

1 cup small cauliflower florets

1 cup baby carrots, peeled and thinly sliced

½ cup unsalted peanuts

½ cup chickpeas, cooked; or canned, drained and rinsed

2 tablespoons sunflower or olive oil

1 tablespoon fresh lemon juice

salt to taste

freshly ground pepper to taste

¾ cup grated cheddar cheese

1. Combine the prepared vegetables in a large bowl and toss to mix. Add the peanuts and chickpeas and toss to mix.

2. Whisk the oil and lemon juice together in a small bowl, add salt and pepper to taste, and whisk again. Drizzle the dressing over the salad and leave to stand for 30 minutes for the flavors to develop.

3. Sprinkle the cheese over the top of the salad before serving.

Per serving: 213 calories, 12 g carbohydrate, 9 g protein, 15 g fat

---

MIXED-FRUIT SALAD

Yield: 10 servings

Brightly colored, healthy and delicious, fruit salad makes a refreshing first course or dessert. The fruit salad will look most attractive if the pieces of fruit are all cut to a similar size. To give the fruit salad a special appearance, arrange on small sprigs of mint just before serving. The fruit salad is delicious served with Greek yogurt, crème fraîche or fromage frais.

2 navel oranges	1 pound strawberries
2 seedless grapefruits	1 (8-ounce) can pineapple
½ ripe cantaloupe	pieces in natural juice

1. Peel or cut the skin and pith off the orange and remove the membrane surrounding the segments. Cut each segment crosswise in half and place in a large serving bowl. Repeat with the grapefruit, cutting the segments crosswise into thirds. Cut the melon half lengthwise in half and scoop out the seeds using a spoon. Run a knife along the flesh next to the skin and discard the skin. Cut the flesh into 1-inch cubes. Add to the bowl with the oranges and grapefruits.

2. Wash the strawberries and pull out the stalk, removing the hull. Cut any large strawberries into halves or quarters and add to the fruit mixture. Add the pineapple and juice and stir gently to mix.

3. Cover and chill the fruit salad in the refrigerator for 30 to 60 minutes.

Per serving: 67 calories, 17 g carbohydrate, 1 g protein, trace fat

FETA CHEESE SALAD

Yield: 6 servings

White and rindless, feta is the cheese that makes a Greek salad so good. Traditionally, the tangy cheese is made with the milk of goats or sheep but in America you will find feta made from cows' milk.

3 cups frisée
3 cups arugula
4 ounces feta cheese
1 large red onion
2 ounces marinated sun-dried
  tomatoes

¼ cup fresh mint
  leaves
small amount of olive oil
2 tablespoons balsamic
  vinegar

1. Combine the arugula and frisée in a large bowl, breaking up the larger leaves into bite-size pieces. Crumble the feta into the salad.

2. Peel the onion and thinly slice. Cut the sun-dried tomatoes into slivers and finely shred the mint. Add the onion and sun-dried tomatoes to the salad and drizzle with a little oil. Season with salt and pepper and toss to combine. Taste and add more oil or salt and pepper if necessary.

3. Serve on a plate and drizzle with the vinegar.

Per serving: 83 calories, 6 g carbohydrate, 4 g protein, 6 g fat

GRILLED-PEPPER SALAD

Yield: 10 servings

Anchovy fillets, pitted black olives and marinated sun-dried tomatoes make this salad special. Their saltiness highlights the sweetness of the grilled peppers. Balsamic vinegar adds a mellow hint of sharpness.

6 green, red or yellow bell peppers, one kind or a mixture of any, seeded
2 tablespoons olive oil
2 tablespoons balsamic vinegar
crushed garlic to taste
mixed or one kind roughly chopped fresh herbs such as parsley, basil, thyme, marjoram and oregano
salt to taste
freshly ground pepper to taste
12 pitted black olives, slivered
4 marinated sun-dried tomatoes, roughly sliced
3 anchovy fillets, halved lengthways (optional)

1. Preheat the broiler or prepare an outdoor grill for barbecuing. Place the peppers on a roasting pan if broiling, or place them directly on the grill rack if barbecuing. Grill the peppers skin side close to the heat, turning them with tongs, until the skins are thoroughly blackened and blistered on all sides. Place the peppers into plastic bags, knot the ends and leave until the peppers are cool enough to handle. The captured steam loosens the skins so that they will strip off easily.

2. Remove the skins and seeds. Cut the peppers into strips and place in a dish with any juice they have given out. Drizzle the peppers with some olive oil. Sprinkle with the remaining ingredients and toss to mix.

Per serving: 56 calories, 6 g carbohydrate, 1 g protein, 4 g fat

GRILLED TUNA SALAD NIÇOISE

Yield: 8 servings

1 pound fresh tuna steak fillet
olive oil

VINAIGRETTE
1 to 2 garlic cloves, crushed
1 tablespoon balsamic or sherry vinegar
2 tablespoons chopped fresh chives
salt to taste
freshly ground pepper to taste
4 to 5 tablespoons olive oil

FOR THE SALAD
12 ounces small new potatoes, boiled, hot

8 ounces green beans, trimmed and cut in half
2 heads butter lettuce, separated, rinsed, dried and torn
1 (9-ounce) jar marinated artichoke hearts, drained
8 ounces cherry tomatoes, halved
8 anchovy fillets, cut in half lengthways
12 to 16 black olives
3 hard-cooked eggs, peeled and quartered into wedges

1. Preheat the broiler or prepare an outdoor grill for barbecuing. Brush the tuna steaks with a little oil.

2. While the broiler / grill preheats, make the vinaigrette: Combine the garlic, vinegar, chives, salt and pepper in a small bowl and whisk until blended. Whisk in the oil in a steady stream and whisk until smooth and thick. Adjust seasoning if necessary.

3. Broil or grill the tuna steaks for about 1 to 2 minutes each side. They should still be pink in the middle. Cut the tuna into large chunks, toss in a little dressing and leave to cool.

4. Slice the potatoes while still hot. If they are very small, leave them whole. Place in a bowl, toss with a little dressing and leave to cool.

5. Boil the green beans for about 4 minutes. Drain, run under the cold water and drain again thoroughly. Mix with the potatoes.

6. Place the remaining dressing in a large salad bowl. Just before serving, make the salad in a large bowl, starting with the lettuce and adding the tuna, vegetables, and all the remaining ingredients, mixing lightly as you go.

Per serving: 297 calories, 18 g carbohydrate, 22 g protein, 16 g fat

PINEAPPLE, POMEGRANATE AND RED-CHILE COMPÔTE

Yield: 6 servings

The torn basil leaves will give a wonderful minty freshness to the fruit salad.

1 tablespoon sugar
1 red chile, finely
   chopped
seeds from 1 pomegranate

6 slices fresh ripe pineapple,
   cut into chunks
juice of 2 limes
a few torn leaves of fresh basil

1. Combine $3^{1}/_{2}$ ounces water and the sugar in a small saucepan and stir until dissolved. Heat to boiling and simmer 2 minutes. Remove from the heat and leave to cool.

2. Pour the syrup into a large bowl and add the chopped chile and

the pomegranate seeds. Add the pineapple and the lime juice and mix well. Cover and refrigerate until chilled.

3. To serve: Sprinkle the basil over the fruit salad and spoon into compôte dishes to serve.

Per serving: 67 calories, 17 g carbohydrate, trace protein, trace fat

CRACKED-WHEAT AND CUCUMBER SALAD

Yield: 10 servings

Ground cinnamon adds its exotic aroma to this grain and vegetable salad. The fresh and juicy flavors of cucumber and fresh herbs make it refreshing on a summer day.

3 cups cracked wheat
2 English cucumbers
½ chopped fresh chives
½ cup chopped fresh parsley
¼ cup olive oil

1 tablespoon red wine vinegar
2 teaspoons ground
  cinnamon
salt to taste
freshly ground pepper to taste

1. Place the cracked wheat in a bowl and just cover with cold water. Leave to stand until the wheat has absorbed all the water, 20 to 30 minutes.

2. Meanwhile, halve the cucumbers lengthwise and scoop out the seeds. Cut each half lengthwise into thirds and then cut crosswise into ½-inch pieces. Place in a large serving bowl.

3. Drain the cracked wheat in a fine nylon sieve and press out any surplus water with the back of a large spoon. Add to the cucumbers in the serving bowl; add the chives and parsley and mix well.

4. Combine the oil, vinegar, cinnamon, salt, and pepper together in a glass measure and whisk to blend. Pour into the cucumber mixture and toss to coat. Taste and adjust the seasonings if necessary. Serve chilled. Remix before serving.

Per serving: 131 calories, 18 g carbohydrate, 3 g protein, 6 g fat

PEAR, PROVOLONE AND ARUGULA SALAD WITH CHAMPAGNE DRESSING

Yield: 4 servings

Sweet, juicy pears and salty provolone cheese are a great partnership. The combination with the unique flavor of arugula is made even more special with a special vinaigrette.

1 large bunch arugula, rinsed, dried and torn into bite-size pieces
2 tablespoons coarsely chopped fresh mint
2 tablespoons shredded

fresh basil
5 ounces CHAMPAGNE VINAIGRETTE (see page 345)
8 thin slices Comice pear
8 (2 inches by ½ inch) strips provolone cheese

Toss the arugula and herbs with half of the vinaigrette and place on salad plates. Top each with some of the pear and cheese and drizzle with the remaining vinaigrette.

Per serving: 289 calories, 10 g carbohydrate, 6 g protein, 26 g fat

RAW BEEF SALAD

Yield: 8 servings

The peppery flavor of arugula makes it the perfect salad green to accompany the fresh meat. The salty shaving of cheese and hit of fresh lemon add the high notes that make a salad exceptional.

1 (8-ounce) chunk Parmesan cheese, at room temperature
1 pound beef round steak or fillet mignon, partially frozen
fresh lemon juice

salt to taste
freshly-ground pepper to taste
2 bunches arugula, washed and trimmed
5 ounces extra-virgin olive oil

1. With a vegetable peeler, shave the Parmesan into thin slices. (You will not use all the cheese but the slices come out better if you have a large chunk to hold. Allow 4 thin slices of Parmesan per serving.)

2. Using a slicing machine, electric knife or very sharp knife, cut the beef into paper-thin slices. Arrange the slices, overlapping slightly, on four chilled plates. Sprinkle with lemon, a pinch of salt and pepper to taste.

3. Arrange the arugula over the beef. Drizzle each serving with 2 tablespoons olive oil and scatter the cheese over the top. Serve immediately.

Per serving: 310 calories, 3 g carbohydrate, 18 g protein, 25 g fat

PEAR, MANGO AND CABBAGE SALAD

Yield: 4 servings

The juicy sweet fruits and peppery cabbage make a healthy and delicious salad.

1 cup unpeeled pear cubes (cored)
1 cup fresh, ripe mango cubes, peeled
2 cups very thinly sliced green cabbage
1/4 cup unsalted pumpkin-seed-

kernels (pepitas), toasted
6 tablespoons white vinegar
2 tablespoons low-sodium soy sauce
1 teaspoon sugar
1/8 teaspoon garlic powder
1/8 teaspoon salt

1. Arrange 1/4 cup pear and 1/4 cup mango on each of 4 cabbage-lined salad plates, and sprinkle with 1 tablespoon pumpkin seeds.

2. Combine the vinegar, soy sauce, sugar, garlic powder and salt in a small bowl and stir well. Drizzle about 2 1/2 tablespoons dressing over each salad.

Per serving: 142 calories, 19 g carbohydrate, 6 g protein, 6 g fat

BABA GANOUCHE AND BULGUR WHEAT SALAD

Yield: 8 servings

This tasty combination of favorite Middle Eastern dishes can also be served as a salad with cucumbers and tomatoes or stuffed in a pita for a meal on the go. By itself, the baba ganouche is a traditional appetizer, usually served as a dip for warm pita bread.

1 cup bulgur wheat
1 tablespoon snipped fresh
  chives
1 tablespoon chopped fresh
  cilantro
salt to taste

freshly ground pepper to taste
BABA GANOUCHE (see page xx)
8 romaine lettuce leaves
fresh herb sprigs for garnish
lemon wedges for garnish and
  squeezing

1. Place the bulgur wheat in a saucepan and pour over just enough boiling water to cover. Simmer according to package directions until soft, about 12 minutes.

2. Drain the bulgur and stir in the chives, cilantro, tomato, lemon juice, salt and pepper. Mix well.

3. Serve the baba ganouche and bulgur together on a romaine lettuce leaf and garnish with fresh herbs and lemon wedges.

Per serving: 60 calories, 13 g carbohydrate, 2 g protein, trace fat

BEEF, PINK GRAPEFRUIT AND MESCLUN SALAD

Yield: 4 servings

The unusual beef and grapefruit combination is one you'll find refreshing. The horseradish is another surprise.

1 (6-ounce) beef tenderloin
  steak, cooked to desired
  doneness
6 cups mesclun (herb salad
  greens)
4 celery stalks, cut diagonally
  into thin slices

1 pink grapefruit, peeled,
  segmented and halved
½ red bell pepper, seeded and
  finely sliced
PINK-GRAPEFRUIT AND SAGE
  DRESSING for serving (see
  page 344)

1. Cut the beef into thin strips and place in a large bowl. Add the mesclun, celery, grapefruit and bell pepper, mix well and set aside.

2. Just before serving, pour the dressing into a small saucepan and heat gently until warm. Pour the dressing over the salad and toss to coat. Serve immediately.

Per serving: 233 calories, 11 g carbohydrate, 14 g protein, 16 g fat

WATERCRESS SALAD WITH BACON AND CARAMELIZED BALSAMIC BEETS

Yield: 6 servings

The peppery flavor of watercress makes a tasty mix with the smoky bacon and sweet beets. Eggs boost the protein so this could even make a nice light lunch.

6 slices of bacon
2 teaspoons olive oil
1 tablespoon balsamic vinegar
2 cups sliced cooked fresh or
   canned baby beets
salt to taste
freshly ground pepper to taste
2 tablespoons virgin olive oil

juice of 1 lemon
1 teaspoon prepared creamy
   horseradish
2 hard-cooked eggs,
   peeled
2 bunches watercress, trimmed,
   washed, drained and torn
   into bite-size pieces

1. Preheat the oven to 400 degrees. Place the slices of bacon on a rack in a broiler pan and bake for 10 to 12 minutes or until the bacon is crisp, turning the bacon halfway through cooking.

2. Meanwhile, heat the 2 teaspoons of olive oil and the vinegar in medium nonstick skillet over medium heat. Add the beets and sprinkle with salt and pepper. Sauté until the beets are glazed and the liquid has evaporated, about 5 minutes.

3. When the bacon is cooked, drain on paper towels and crumble. Combine the lemon juice, horseradish, remaining virgin olive oil, salt and pepper in a large serving bowl and whisk until blended. Grate the hard-cooked eggs into the dressing and whisk to combine. Add the watercress and toss to coat. Adjust seasoning if necessary. Sprinkle with the bacon and caramelized beets.

Per serving: 227 calories, 5 g carbohydrate, 6 g protein, 21 g fat

PEAR, MIXED GREENS AND WALNUT SALAD

Yield: 8 servings

WALNUT VINAIGRETTE
2 tablespoons sherry
   vinegar
2 small shallots, finely
   chopped
salt to taste
3 tablespoons light olive oil
2 tablespoons walnut oil

SALAD
½ cup walnut halves, chopped
2 heads romaine lettuce
2 bunches watercress
1 large bunch arugula
3 ripe comice pears, cored and
   sliced
freshly ground pepper

1. Preheat the oven to 375 degrees.

2. For the vinaigrette: Combine the sherry vinegar, shallots and a little salt in a medium bowl and whisk until the salt dissolves. Whisk in the oils to emulsify. Set aside.

3. Toast the walnuts in the oven for 10 minutes or until they begin to brown. Set aside to cool.

4. Rinse and dry the salad greens and tear them into bite-size pieces. Place in a large salad bowl and add the pears and walnuts. Toss and drizzle half the vinaigrette over the salad. Sprinkle with black pepper, gently toss to coat and taste. Add more vinaigrette and pepper if needed, and serve at once.

Per serving: 191 calories, 16 g carbohydrate, 5 g protein, 14 g fat

PINEAPPLE AND CHILI SALAD WITH QUAIL EGGS

Yield: 6 servings

2 bunches arugula, rinsed, dried and trimmed
1 large bunch watercress, rinsed, dried and trimmed
4 radishes, thinly sliced
1 mild yellow chile pepper, cut crosswise in half, seeded and thinly sliced into rings
1 small Kirby cucumber, julienned
2 thin slices fresh pineapple, cut into 1-inch pieces
4 scallions, trimmed, chopped
12 quail eggs
LIME-MINT DRESSING for the salad (see page 348)

1. Tear the arugula and watercress into bite-size pieces and place in a salad bowl. Add the radishes, chile, cucumber, pineapple and scallions and toss to mix. Poach the quail eggs and set aside.

2. To serve: Add some of the dressing to the salad and toss to coat. Add more dressing if necessary and toss.

3. Divide the salad onto 6 large plates. Serve topped with 2 quail eggs for each portion.

Per serving: 196 calories, 11 g carbohydrate, 6 g protein, 16 g fat

SCANDINAVIAN NEW-POTATO SALAD WITH SCALLIONS AND SOUR CREAM

Yield: 6 servings

1 pound small new potatoes
6 scallions, thinly sliced on the diagonal
½ cup MAYONNAISE (see page xx)
6 tablespoons sour cream or more to taste
sea salt to taste
freshly ground pepper to taste
3 tablespoons finely snipped fresh chives

1. Boil the potatoes in their skins in a saucepan of salted water until they are soft but retain a 'waxy' middle, about 20 minutes. Refresh immediately into ice water, drain well, and when cool to the touch, peel the skins and slice into thin ($^1/_8$- to $^1/_4$-inch) rounds.

2. Combine the sliced scallions, Mayonnaise and sour cream in a large bowl and season with salt and pepper. Add the sliced potatoes and mix gently but thoroughly to prevent the potatoes breaking up. Add the chives and fold in. If the mixture looks or feels too dry, add some more sour cream until moist.

Per serving: 250 calories, 15 g carbohydrate, 3 g protein, 20 g fat

---

SAUSAGE AND COUSCOUS SALAD

Yield: 8 servings

This recipe is delicious served cold, ideal for picnics and barbecues, but also hot, as a tasty supper dish served with a spicy vegetable stew.

$^3/_4$ cup dry couscous
1 pound extra-lean sausages, grilled, cooled and thinly sliced
$^1/_4$ cup finely diced dried apricots
1 medium sweet onion, finely chopped
1 tablespoon olive oil with a hint of garlic

2 tablespoons balsamic vinegar
2 tablespoons chopped fresh cilantro
1 tablespoon chopped fresh mint
salt to taste
freshly ground pepper to taste
mixed salad leaves
lemon or lime wedges for serving

1. Prepare the couscous according to package directions and set aside to cool.

2. Add the sausages, apricots, onions, oil, vinegar, cilantro, mint, salt and pepper and mix well.

3. Serve on a bed of mixed salad leaves with lemon or lime wedges.

Per serving: 222 calories, 18 g carbohydrate, 9 g protein, 13 g fat

WATERCRESS SALAD WITH TANGELOS AND POMEGRANATE SEEDS

Yield: 8 servings

Cut the pomegranate in half and remove the seeds by knocking them out. Hold the cut side of each half over a bowl and hammer the skin side with a heavy wooden spoon so the seeds fall into the bowl.

5 tangelos
2 tablespoons red-wine vinegar
2 tablespoons minced fresh basil
1/4 teaspoon freshly ground pepper

1/8 teaspoon salt
1 tablespoon walnut or vegetable oil
8 cups loosely packed trimmed watercress
1 cup pomegranate seeds

1. Grate 2 tablespoons rind from one of the tangelos into a large bowl. Squeeze 1/2 or a whole tangelo to extract 3 tablespoons juice into the bowl and add the vinegar, basil, pepper and salt. Whisk to blend. Cover and let stand 2 hours.

2. Peel and section the remaining 4 tangelos and set aside.

3. Stir the tangelo juice mixture, add the watercress and toss gently. Place 1 cup watercress mixture on each of 8 salad plates and arrange the tangelo sections and pomegranate seeds on top.

Per serving: 73 calories, 14 g carbohydrate, 2 g protein, 2 g fat

CHAING MAI SPICY CUCUMBER SALAD

Yield: 10 servings
(serving size: 1/2 cup)

This Thai-inspired salad cools the palate while firing it up at the same time.

4 medium cucumbers, peeled, halved lengthwise, seeded and thinly sliced
2 small hot red chiles, seeded, halved lengthwise and sliced
1/3 cup minced shallots
1/3 cup sliced scallions
1/2 cup rice vinegar
2 tablespoons sugar
1/2 teaspoon salt
1/4 cup chopped fresh cilantro

Combine the cucumbers, chiles, shallots and scallions in a large bowl. Combine the vinegar, sugar and salt in a glass measure, stir well and add to the cucumber mixture. Toss to coat and stir in the cilantro.

Per serving: 25 calories, 6 g carbohydrate, 1 g protein, trace fat

THAI CHILE-LIME SQUID SALAD

Yield: 5 servings
(serving size: 1/2 cup)

This spicy salad is called *laab* in Thai. Instead of squid, you can use other seafood, such as medium-size peeled shrimp, or poultry, beef or lamb. The toasted rice powder keeps the dressing from becoming watery.

3 tablespoons uncooked long-grain rice
1 pound cleaned and skinned squid
1 tablespoon grated lime rind
1/4 cup fresh lime juice
2 tablespoons sliced shallot
2 tablespoons sliced scallions
2 tablespoons Thai fish sauce (nam pla)
1 teaspoon crushed red-pepper flakes
1 tablespoon chopped fresh green chile
1 tablespoon chopped fresh mint
5 lime wedges

1. Toast the rice in a skillet over medium heat until browned, about 5 minutes, stirring occasionally. Place the rice in a blender and process until it is a powder. Set aside.

2. Cut the squid into 1/4-inch-thick rings and set aside. Heat 4 cups water to boiling in a large saucepan. Add the squid and cook just until the rings begin to curl around edges, about 30 seconds. Drain well while rinsing with cold water. Pat dry with paper towels.

3. Combine the squid, lime rind and juice, shallot, scallions, fish sauce and pepper flakes in a bowl and toss gently to mix. Spoon onto a serving platter and sprinkle with the chopped chile and mint. Serve with lime wedges for squeezing onto the salad.

Per serving: 115 calories, 10 g carbohydrate, 15 g protein, 1 g fat

SPICY BLACK-EYED PEA SLAW WITH GINGER DRESSING

Yield: 12 servings

The original recipe called for the peanuts to be added with the main ingredients. I felt this made them mushy and flavorless after the salad had been chilling a while. Adding them at serving time provided a pleasant contrast of flavor and texture.

4 cups finely shredded
   cabbage (about 1 pound)
2 cups cooked black-eyed peas
2 pickled jalapeño peppers,
   minced

GINGER DRESSING (see
   page 346)
½ cup dry-roasted peanuts,
   chopped

Combine the cabbage, black-eyed peas and jalapeños in a large bowl. Add the ginger dressing and toss well to coat. Cover and refrigerate until serving. Top with the peanuts just before serving.

Per serving: 143 calories, 10 g carbohydrate, 3 g protein, 11 g fat

BEET, GREEN BEAN AND SHALLOT SALAD

Yield: 10 servings

The earthy aroma and flavor of beets is one of the most pleasurable culinary experiences. Green beans make a happy partner to them in this tasty salad.

2 pounds small beets, tops
   trimmed
2 pounds tender green beans
3/4 cup plus 2 tablespoons
   extra-virgin olive oil
3/4 cup red wine vinegar

salt to taste
freshly ground pepper to taste
4 shallots, thinly sliced
3/4 cup chopped fresh basil
1 tablespoon chopped fresh
   mint

1. In a large saucepan, cover the beets with cold water and heat to boiling. Simmer over medium heat until tender when pierced, about 45 minutes. Drain in a colander, then rinse in cold water and slip off the skins. Thinly slice the beets crosswise and let cool.

2. Steam the green beans in a large saucepan until just tender, about 5 minutes. Rinse in cold water and drain well.

3. Whisk the oil with the vinegar in a large serving bowl and season with salt and pepper. Add the beets, beans, shallots, basil and mint to the bowl and toss to coat.

Per serving: 237 calories, 16 g carbohydrate, 3 g protein, 19 g fat

DUNGENESS CRAB COLESLAW

Yield: 8 servings

This Pacific Coast crustacean can be found from Alaska to Mexico. Their season is late fall to early winter but you can find them frozen. For convenience you can just buy a pound of lump crabmeat and proceed with step 2 of the recipe.

3 Dungeness crabs (1 1/2 to 2
   pounds each)
1 large head Napa cabbage
1 fennel bulb
1 bunch watercress

1 cup MAYONNAISE (see
   pages 313-314)
1 tablespoon tarragon
   vinegar
salt to taste

1. Place crabs in large pot and cover with cold water. Cover and place over high heat until crabs turn bright red and white foam appears at joints, about 20 minutes. Drain and rinse under cold water. Clean crab; you should have about 1 1/4 pounds of crabmeat. Reserve 1/2 cup crabmeat for garnish.

2. Using a sharp chef's knife, slice cabbage in thin strips. Quarter

fennel bulb lengthwise and remove core. Using a mandoline or Japanese vegetable cutter, shave fennel into thin strips. Pick leaves and tender stems from watercress. Combine cabbage, fennel and watercress in a large bowl. Combine Mayonnaise and vinegar in small bowl and beat until smooth. Add Mayonnaise a little at a time to cabbage, tossing gently to coat lightly but thoroughly. (You'll probably use about ⅔ cup.) Set aside 20 minutes.

3. To serve: Add crabmeat and salt to taste and toss lightly to mix, being careful not to break up chunks of crabmeat. Mound coleslaw on chilled plates and garnish with the reserved crabmeat chunks on top.

Per serving: 338 calories, 6 g carbohydrate, 17 g protein, 26 g fat

CORNBREAD, TOMATO AND CILANTRO SALAD

Yield: 4 servings
(¼ cup vinaigrette)

This is a Southwestern version of the Italian-bread salad called panzanella.

2 cups lightly crumbled
 day-old cornbread
4 plum tomatoes, chopped
4 scallions, sliced

½ cup loosely packed fresh
 cilantro leaves
LIME-CILANTRO VINAIGRETTE
 for serving (see page 347)

Combine cornbread, tomatoes, green onions and cilantro in a large bowl. Stir gently to combine so corn bread doesn't fall apart. Toss with ¼ to ⅓ cup Cilantro Vinaigrette.

Per serving: 196 calories, 20 g carbohydrate, 3 g protein, 12 g fat

A BIG GREEN SALAD

Yield: 12 servings

The tangy vinaigrette dressing can be made a few days ahead and refrigerated. Let it come to room temperature and shake well before using.

1/4 cup red-wine vinegar
2 teaspoons lemon juice
2 teaspoons Worcestershire
   sauce
1 teaspoon salt
1 teaspoon sugar or to taste
1 teaspoon freshly ground
   pepper or to taste

1/4 teaspoon minced garlic
1/4 teaspoon dry mustard
1/2 cup extra-virgin olive oil
16 cups torn mixed greens,
   such as Bibb, red lettuce
   and arugula, stems trimmed
   and leaves washed and
   crisped

1. Combine the vinegar, lemon juice, Worcestershire sauce, salt, sugar, pepper, garlic and mustard in a jar with a lid. Cover and shake until the sugar and salt are dissolved. Add the oil and shake until mixed. Adjust seasoning as needed

2. Put the crisped greens in large bowl. Add 2/3 cup of the dressing and toss gently until well mixed. Add the remaining dressing as needed.

Per serving: 91 calories, 2 g carbohydrate, 1 g protein, 9 g fat

CRUNCHY CANTALOUPE SALAD

Yield: 6 servings

Okay, it's a stretch to call a ripe melon crunchy. That's where the jicama comes in. This amazing root vegetable is a staple in Mexican cuisine and is celebrated for its juicy, crunchy qualities.

1/2 medium jicama, peeled and
   cut in julienne strips
1/2 medium cantaloupe, cut
   into 1/2-inch cubes
2 tablespoons chopped

   fresh mint
1 teaspoon grated lime rind
3 tablespoons lime juice
1 teaspoon honey
1/4 teaspoon salt

Combine the jicama, melon, mint, lime rind and juice, honey and salt in a glass or plastic bowl. Toss to coat, cover and refrigerate for about 2 hours or until well chilled.

Per serving: 43 calories, 10 g carbohydrate, 1 g protein, trace fat

ORANGE AND MINT NAPA SLAW

Yield: 6 servings

This flavor mixture works well with any type of cabbage. Napa cabbage softens quickly when dressed, so you'll want to serve it right away.

1 (1½-pound) head Napa
  cabbage
¼ cup chopped fresh mint
  plus extra sprigs for garnish
⅓ cup roasted, salted peanuts,
  chopped

5 slices bacon,
  chopped
⅓ cup orange juice
3 tablespoons white-wine
  vinegar
1½ teaspoons sugar

1. Remove 6 outer leaves from the cabbage and place one leaf on each of 6 salad plates. Set aside. Cut the head of cabbage in half lengthwise and cut each half crosswise into ¼-inch slices. Place in a large bowl, add the chopped mint and peanuts and set aside.

2. Fry the bacon over medium heat in a large skillet until crisp, about 8 minutes. Blot dry with paper towels and add to the bowl with the cabbage.

3. Remove all but 3 tablespoons of the bacon drippings from the pan and heat over high heat. Add the orange juice, vinegar and sugar, and cook, stirring, just until the drippings are melted and dressing is hot. Immediately pour the hot dressing over salad and mix quickly until well coated. Mound some salad on each leaf on the prepared plates and garnish each with a mint sprig.

Per serving: 190 calories, 10 g carbohydrate, 6 g protein, 15 g fat

EGGLESS EGG SALAD OR DIP

Yield: 4 sandwiches
or serves 6 to 8 as a dip

For a creamier type of salad, add more soy mayonnaise.

1 (10-ounce) package firm tofu,
   drained and crumbled
¼ cup finely chopped
   carrot
2 tablespoons finely chopped
   green or red bell pepper
¼ cup finely chopped celery
2 tablespoons finely chopped
   scallions

DRESSING
1 tablespoon soy mayonnaise,
   or more to taste
   2 teaspoons vinegar
1 teaspoon turmeric
½ teaspoon salt
½ teaspoon black pepper
1 teaspoon hot sauce
1 teaspoon Dijon mustard

1.   Combine the tofu and vegetables in a large bowl. In a small bowl, combine the dressing ingredients and mix well. Add the dressing to the tofu mixture and toss to coat.

Per serving: 62 calories, 4 g carbohydrate, 6 g protein, 3 g fat

CANTALOUPE, CUCUMBER AND TOMATO SALAD

Yield: 8 servings

1 small cantaloupe, casaba, or
   honeydew melon, chilled
1 English cucumber
4 large firm-ripe tomatoes, peeled
   and cubed (about 2 pounds)

DRESSING
¼ cup fresh lemon or lime
   juice

1 tablespoon finely chopped
   fresh parsley
1 tablespoon finely chopped
   fresh mint
2 teaspoons sugar
½ teaspoon salt
¼ teaspoon pepper
½ cup vegetable oil

1. Combine the lemon juice, parsley, mint, sugar, salt and pepper in a large bowl and whisk until blended. Drizzle in the oil while whisking and whisk until the dressing is smooth. If desired, cover and refrigerate until next day.

2. If made ahead, remove the bowl with the dressing from the refrigerator about 1 hour before serving. Cut the melon in half and scoop out the seeds. Cut the melon into thin wedges and remove the rind. Cut crosswise into bite-size chunks and place in a large salad bowl. Quarter the cucumber lengthwise and remove the seeds with a spoon if desired. Cut the cucumber into 1/2-inch chunks. Add the cucumber and tomatoes to the bowl with the melon.

3. Whisk the dressing again, pour over the salad and toss gently until well coated. Cover and let stand at room temperature for about 45 minutes, stirring once or twice.

Per serving: 173 calories, 13 g carbohydrate, 2 g protein, 14 g fat

TABBOULEH

Yield: 8 servings

There are so many versions of this Middle Eastern salad that you may feel overwhelmed by which one to try first. Or again. This one is a never-fail balance of the basic ingredients. Tabbouleh mavens will eventually tell you that the real secret lies in using fresh herbs, as plenty of parsley and mint are the heart of this ancient dish.

1 cup bulgur wheat
3 scallions, finely sliced
2 large ripe tomatoes, seeded, skinned and diced
2 Kirby cucumbers, diced
1/4 to 1/2 cup chopped flat leaf parsley

1/2 cup chopped fresh mint
juice of 1 lemon
1 tablespoon olive oil or more as needed
salt to taste
freshly ground black pepper

Place the bulgur in a medium bowl and cover with cold water. Let soak for 10 minutes, drain through a sieve and then squeeze out the wheat in your hand to get rid of any excess water. Place the wheat in the dried bowl and add the scallions, tomatoes, cucumber, parsley and mint. Mix, using one of your hands. Drizzle the lemon juice and 1 tablespoon oil on top and toss again. Drizzle with a little more olive oil if needed and season with salt and pepper.

Per serving: 95 calories, 18 g carbohydrate, 3 g protein, 2 g fat

SPINACH, MUSHROOM AND RADISH SALAD

Yield: 8 servings

This is a good salad to take on a picnic or to a pot luck supper. Go the extra step of garnishing it with the eggs and alfalfa sprouts before covering. To serve, just shake up the dressing and pour it on.

12 cups fresh spinach leaves, cleaned and trimmed
8 radishes, thinly sliced
4 ounces mushrooms, thinly sliced

DRESSING
2 garlic cloves, crushed
grated rind of ½ lemon
3 tablespoons fresh lemon juice

2 tablespoons walnut oil
2 tablespoons dry white wine
1 tablespoon freshly grated gingerroot
sea salt to taste
black pepper to taste

GARNISH
4 hard-cooked eggs, finely chopped
2 ounces alfalfa sprouts

1. Toss the spinach with the radishes and mushrooms in a large salad bowl. Cover with plastic wrap and refrigerate until serving.

2. Combine the garlic, lemon rind and juice, oil, wine and gingerroot in a screw-top jar and shake to combine. Season with the salt and pepper and set aside until ready to serve.

3. To serve: Shake the dressing again to combine. Drizzle over the salad and toss until evenly coated. Sprinkle the salad with the eggs and then the alfalfa sprouts. Serve.

Per serving: 88 calories, 3 g carbohydrate, 5 g protein, 6 g fat

ROASTED-VEGETABLE SALAD NIÇOISE

Yield: 12 servings

No one will notice the absence of tuna and anchovies in this classic French salad because the roasted-vegetable mix is a substantial substitute. Feel free to use heirloom potatoes and tomatoes when they are in season.

3 pounds large (about $3/4$ inch thick) asparagus spears

12 small new potatoes, cut in half

1 pound thin green beans, trimmed

1 tablespoon extra-virgin olive oil

6 black olives, pitted and sliced

3 hard-cooked eggs, peeled and halved

2 plum tomatoes, chopped

$1/2$ English cucumber, chopped

2 tablespoons fresh parsley and chives, chopped and mixed

SHALLOT-BALSAMIC VINAIGRETTE

2 shallots, finely chopped

3 tablespoons balsamic vinegar

2 teaspoons Dijon mustard

salt and freshly ground black pepper

$1/3$ cup olive oil

1. Place a heavy baking sheet in the middle of the oven and set the oven temperature to 450 degrees.

2. Wash and peel asparagus starting about $1^1/2$ to 2 inches below the tip and peeling straight down toward the cut end. Snap off the tough ends and trim straight. Place the asparagus, potatoes and green beans on a large plate and drizzle with the extra-virgin olive oil.

3. When oven reaches temperature, spread the vegetables in one layer on the baking sheet. Roast for about 5 minutes, then turn the vegetables with tongs. Continue roasting for another 2 minutes or until the asparagus are just tender. Remove from the oven. Continue roasting green beans 5 more minutes and potatoes 10 more minutes or until vegetables are tender. Cool slightly and arrange on a serving platter with the olives, eggs, tomatoes and cucumber. Sprinkle with the parsley-chive mixture.

4. Make the vinaigrette: In a small jar, combine the shallots, vinegar, mustard, and salt and pepper to taste. Shake well and add $\frac{1}{3}$ cup of oil. Shake vigorously until well combined.

5. To serve: Pour the vinaigrette over the asparagus mixture on the platter and serve immediately.

Per serving: 176 calories, 20 g carbohydrate, 6 g protein, 9 g fat

ASPARAGUS SALAD WITH ROASTED BELL PEPPERS

Yield: 8 servings

The salad can be prepared through Step 2 and refrigerated overnight. (Store the roasted peppers and the asparagus separately but bring both to room temperature before proceeding) This simple, vibrant salad depends on best-quality olive oil and balsamic vinegar because they are just about all that's combined with the sweet pepper juices to make a fruity dressing. Be sure to serve the dish warm.

2 medium red bell peppers, halved lengthwise, cored and seeded
2 medium yellow bell peppers, halved lengthwise, cored and seeded
$\frac{1}{4}$ cup extra-virgin olive oil, plus more for brushing
2 garlic cloves, minced
salt and freshly ground pepper to taste
1$\frac{1}{2}$ pounds asparagus
1 tablespoon balsamic vinegar

1. Preheat the oven to 400 degrees. Brush the skin sides of the pepper halves lightly with some of the olive oil and set them, cut side down, on a baking sheet. Bake the peppers until the skins are blistered, about 15 minutes. Remove the skins and seeds and cut the peppers into long thin strips. Place in a medium bowl and add the oil and garlic and season with salt and pepper.

2. Snap off the tough ends from the asparagus spears and discard. Cut the remaining spears into 3-inch pieces. In a large pot of boiling, salted water, cook the asparagus until just tender, about 4 minutes. Drain the asparagus and refresh under cold running water. Pat the asparagus dry with paper towels.

3. Preheat the oven to 450 degrees. Spread half of the roasted peppers in a baking dish. Arrange the asparagus on top and sprinkle with salt and pepper. Top with the remaining roasted peppers and spoon their juices on top. Bake for until bubbling, about 15 minutes. Drizzle with the balsamic vinegar and serve warm.

Per serving: 120 calories, 9 g carbohydrate, 3 g protein, 9 g fat

ASPARAGUS PASTA SALAD WITH SESAME-GINGER DRESSING

Yield: 8 servings

It may be old news that you can "stretch" your carbohydrate count from the pasta with the addition of vegetables, but the East-West combination of the flavors in this dish always manages to interest adventurous palates. The tangy dressing is also delicious on pasta-free salads made with low-carb mixtures of fruits, greens, meats, chicken and seafood.

1 package (12 ounces) fresh
  fettuccine
1 tablespoon dark sesame oil
1 pound asparagus
2 small red bell peppers, seeded,
  and cut into 1-inch-long slices

3 scallions, trimmed, chopped
3 tablespoons chopped fresh
  cilantro
SESAME-GINGER DRESSING
  (see page xx)
toasted sesame seeds for garnish

1. Cook the fettuccine according to the package directions until al dente. Drain, transfer to a medium bowl, and toss with the sesame oil.

2. Snap off the tough ends from the asparagus spears and discard. Slice the remaining spears diagonally into 1-inch pieces. Steam the asparagus just until tender, 5 to 8 minutes, and add it to the fettuccine. Add the red pepper, scallions and cilantro and toss well.

3. Add the dressing to the salad and toss to coat. Garnish with sesame seeds and serve.

Per serving: 120 calories, 20 g carbohydrate, 5 g protein, 3 g fat

ASPARAGUS, ORANGE, RED ONION AND FENNEL SALAD

Yield: 10 servings

This colorful, refreshing salad makes a dazzling appetizer or first course, too. Onions add a nice juicy crunch to the mix.

FOR THE DRESSING
2/3 cup MAYONNAISE
(see page xx)
1/2 cup buttermilk
3 tablespoons fresh basil leaves
cut in thin strips
3 tablespoons chopped fresh
parsley
2 tablespoons olive oil

2 tablespoons apple-cider
vinegar

FOR THE SALAD
24 asparagus spears
2 large fennel bulbs
4 oranges
2 red onions, thinly
sliced

1. Make the dressing: Whisk the Mayonnaise, buttermilk, basil, parsley, oil and vinegar in a medium bowl until well blended. Cover and refrigerate until cold.

2. Snap off the tough ends from the asparagus spears and discard. Cut the remaining spears into 2-inch pieces. Steam the asparagus until crisp-tender, about 2 minutes, rinse under cold running water until cool and drain. Place in a large bowl and set aside.

3. Remove the end and stalks from the fennel bulb and discard. Thinly slice the bulb and steam until just tender. Set aside until cool and add to the bowl with the asparagus.

4. Cut the peel and white pith from the oranges. Cut between the membranes to release the segments. Add to bowl with the asparagus.

5. Add the red onion to the bowl with the asparagus and mix well. Toss with about 1/2 cup dressing, or more to taste. Serve with remaining dressing on the side.

Per serving: 210 calories, 16 g carbohydrate, 13 g protein, 16 g fat

CURRIED HAM, ASPARAGUS AND TROPICAL-FRUIT SALAD

Yield: 6 servings

The spicy curry-sour cream dressing unites all the tangy, salty and sweet flavors in this luncheon main course.

1 pound asparagus, plus extra spears for garnish
1 (11-ounce) can mandarin-orange sections, drained
1 (8-ounce) can juice-pack pineapple chunks, drained
1 small stalk of celery, thinly sliced

2 cups cubed, fully cooked ham
2 tablespoons chopped onion
½ to 1 teaspoon curry powder (to taste)
1 (8-ounce) carton reduced-fat sour cream
lettuce leaves for serving

1. Snap off the tough ends from the asparagus spears and discard. Peel spears if desired. Set aside some whole spears for garnish and cut the remainder into 1-inch pieces. In a saucepan, cook all the asparagus, covered, in a small amount of boiling salted water for about 7 minutes or till crisp-tender. Drain and cool.

2. In a large bowl, combine the 1-inch pieces of asparagus, orange sections, pineapple, celery, ham and onion. Stir curry powder to taste into the sour cream and stir into the ham mixture. Chill up to 2 hours.

3. To serve: Line a salad bowl with lettuce leaves and spoon the asparagus mixture on top. Garnish with the whole asparagus spears.

Per serving: 201 calories, 20 g carbohydrate, 11 g protein, 10 g fat

SHRIMP AND ASPARAGUS SALAD WITH TRUFFLE OIL DRESSING

Yield: 6 servings

The coral color of shrimp and the spring-green asparagus make this an edible work of art. The components can be made ahead and refrigerated, making it the perfect appetizer for a sweltering summer day. Serve it on chilled plates to keep the greens crisp.

2 tablespoons butter
2 tablespoons olive oil
20 large raw shrimp, peeled
24 asparagus spears

DRESSING
juice of 2 lemons

2 tablespoons balsamic vinegar
sea salt to taste
freshly ground black pepper
½ cup white- or black-truffle
   oil or extra-virgin olive oil
8 red cherry tomatoes, halved
8 cups mixed salad greens

1. Melt the butter in the olive oil in a large skillet over medium heat and sauté the shrimp just until pink, about 4 minutes. Drain on paper towels.

2. Snap off the tough ends from the asparagus spears and discard. Peel the asparagus if skins are thick. Cook the asparagus in boiling salted water until tender. Drain, cool quickly in a bowl of ice water, drain again and cut each spear into 2 equal pieces

3. Make the dressing: Combine the lemon juice, balsamic vinegar, salt and pepper in a large bowl and whisk until smooth. Add the oil in a thin, steady stream, whisking constantly until the dressing is thick and smooth. Add the shrimp, asparagus and tomatoes, and toss to coat. Adjust seasoning if necessary.

4. Arrange the salad greens on salad plates and top with the shrimp salad.

Per serving: 286 calories, 7 g carbohydrate, 7 g protein, 27 g fat

AVOCADO CONFETTI SALAD

Yield: 4 servings

This is a guacamole-lover's delight! It's perfect as a tantalizing appetizer served in the natural bowl of the avocado peel or it can be spread out on spinach leaves for a hearty side dish.

2 small ripe avocados
2 plum tomatoes, chopped
10 Spanish olives, pitted and
  chopped
juice of 1 lime
1/4 cup diced green bell pepper
1/4 cup diced red bell pepper
1/4 cup chopped seedless
  cucumber

1/4 cup chopped red onion
1/4 cup diced peeled
  carrot
salt to taste
freshly ground pepper to
  taste
Tabasco sauce to taste
chopped fresh cilantro for
  garnish

1. Neatly cut the avocados in half lengthwise, discard the pits and carefully scoop out the shells. Reserve the shells. Finely chop the flesh and set aside in a bowl. Add the tomatoes, olives and lime juice and mix gently so the avocados do not get mushy.

2. Combine the chopped peppers, cucumber, onion and diced carrot in a medium bowl and mix well. Add to the avocados and toss gently to keep from crushing. Season with the salt, pepper and Tabasco.

3. Gently mound the salad into the avocado shells. Garnish with a light sprinkle of the cilantro.

Per serving: 155 calories, 11 g carbohydrate, 2 g protein, 13 g fat

CRISPY BACON AND AVOCADO SALAD

Yield: 6 servings

This color- and texture-rich salad makes a delicious light supper or lunchtime dish or an accompaniment for a picnic or barbecue. Use bottled balsamic dressing for convenience, or whip up a batch from your favorite recipe.

4 ounces thick-slice
  bacon
1 tablespoon olive oil
2 slices bread, cubed
1 garlic clove, crushed
12 cups mixed salad greens
4 ounces cherry tomatoes,
  halved
1 ripe avocado, pitted, peeled
  and sliced
12 black olives, halved and
  pitted
1 yellow pepper, seeded and
  diced
4 hard-cooked eggs, shelled
  and quartered lengthwise
1/3 cup bottled balsamic
  vinaigrette dressing

1. Fry the bacon in a skillet until crisp, drain on paper towels and cut into cubes. Clean the skillet, add the oil and place over medium heat. Add the bread cubes and garlic and cook until the croutons are golden, 2 to 3 minutes. Drain well on paper towels.

2. Arrange the salad greens, tomatoes, avocado slices, olives and diced pepper on a large serving platter. Sprinkle the bacon and croutons over the salad. Arrange the eggs on top. Drizzle with the vinaigrette just before serving.

Per serving: 333 calories, 13 g carbohydrate, 9 g protein, 28 g fat

CITRUS-MARINATED CHICKEN SALAD WITH AVOCADO

Yield: 4 servings

Here, the icing on the cake, or rather the salads, is a fresh (not aged or ripened) white cheese usually sold under the French name of fromage frais or fromage blanc. This is available in most cheese shops or large grocery stores. If you can't find it, you can use crème fraîche, sieved soft ricotta cheese or queso blanco, a Mexican-style fresh cheese. They all make a nice topping for the layers of juicy salad ingredients.

MARINADE
juice of 1 orange
juice of 1 lemon
juice of 1 lime
⅓ cup extra-virgin olive oil
1 teaspoon confectioners' sugar
salt and pepper to taste

SALAD
12 ounces skinless, boneless
   chicken breast, steamed or
   poached and cooled
1 ripe avocado, pitted, peeled
   and thickly sliced

juice of 1 lemon
salt and pepper to taste

FOR SERVING AND GARNISH
QUICK CUCUMBER PICKLES
   (see pages 297-298)
4 sun-dried tomatoes, sliced
2 tablespoons shredded fresh
   basil
⅓ cup fromage frais
2 fresh plum tomatoes, peeled,
   seeded and chopped
4 sprigs fresh chervil

1. For the Marinated Chicken: Combine the citrus juices, oil, sugar, salt and pepper in a medium bowl and whisk until blended. Slice the chicken and add it to the dressing. Toss to coat and marinate in the refrigerator for 1 hour in the refrigerator.

2. When ready to serve, pit, peel and thickly slice the avocado. Place in a small bowl and toss with the lemon juice. Season with salt and pepper and toss again. Set aside.

3. Arrange one-fourth of the cucumber pickles in a neat circle in the center of 4 salad plates. Place a cookie cutter or other metal ring that is About 3½ inches in diameter on top of the cucumber ring. Drain the chicken, reserving the marinade, and arrange one-fourth of the chicken in an even layer in the cookie cutter. Top with one-fourth of the avocado, then one-fourth of the sun-dried tomatoes and then one-fourth of the basil. Spread one-fourth of the fromage frais on top and remove the ring. Repeat with the remaining ingredients on 3 more salad plates to make 4 stacked salads in all.

4. To serve: Drizzle the reserved chicken marinade on each plate around each salad. Garnish each with some of the chopped fresh tomato and a sprig of chervil.

Per serving: 417 calories, 13 g carbohydrate, 25 g protein, 30 g fat

SALAD OF FRESH ASPARAGUS AND MORELS WITH BALSAMIC-PORCINI DRESSING

Yield: 4 servings

The mushroom duo here plays with the bright flavor of the asparagus. You may want to make up more creations using the trio, such as soups or pasta main courses.

32 asparagus spears, trimmed
2 tablespoons butter
8 ounces fresh morels, halved,
cleaned and trimmed
BALSAMIC-PORCINI DRESSING
(see page 344)

1. Blanch the asparagus in boiling water just until tender, about 4 minutes and immediately drain and place in a bowl of ice and water to stop the cooking and preserve the color. When cool, drain and set aside on a heat-safe plate.

2. Melt the butter in a skillet over medium heat, add the morels and sauté until they release their juices. Increase the heat to medium-high and sauté 2 to 3 minutes.

3. Pour two-thirds of the porcini dressing into a medium bowl, add the morels and toss to coat.

4. Reheat the asparagus and arrange 8 spears on each of 4 warm salad plates. Divide the morels among the spears and drizzle a little of the remaining dressing on the plate around the asparagus.

Per serving: 375 calories, 16 g carbohydrate, 7 g protein, 34 g fat

EGGS

POACHED EGGS WITH SHRIMP, SHERRY AND TOMATO-MUSTARD CHEESE SAUCE

Yield: 4 servings

This could be a show-stopping first course, lunch or supper. The elegant elements and presentation are a blast from the past. This kind of cooking is reserved for special guests.

4 large eggs
nonstick cooking spray
4 jumbo shrimp, shelled and
  deveined
1 ounce butter
2 tablespoons dry sherry
MORNAY SAUCE, warmed (see
  page 341)

½ teaspoon Dijon mustard
½ cup freshly grated Parmesan
  cheese
1 large plum tomato, seeded
  and diced
1 tablespoon chopped fresh
  cilantro
paprika for dusting

1. Poach the eggs to the desired doneness and slide into a bowl of ice-cold water to stop the cooking.

2. Arrange the oven rack so it is 6 inches from the heat source. Preheat the broiler. Grease 4 (3- to 4-inch) tall metal rings with cooking spray.

3. Cut the shrimp crosswise into ½-inch pieces. Heat a heavy skillet over medium-high heat, add the butter, and when it is melted and has just stopped bubbling, add the shrimp. Sauté quickly to sear the outside, and when they just start to turn pink, add the sherry and mustard. Quickly stir to make a glaze and stir in the tomato. Sauté just until the tomato is softened and remove from the heat.

4. Place a greased 3-inch metal ring on each of 4 heat-safe serving plates and fill each with one-fourth of the shrimp mixture. Carefully remove the eggs from the ice water and drain on paper towels. Place one of the eggs on the top of each ring of filling. Coat each with one-fourth of the Mornay Sauce, sprinkle each generously with Parmesan and with a twist, remove the rings. Broil the eggs until the eggs and sauce are heated through and the cheese is melted and bubbly, about 4 minutes.

5. Serve the eggs sprinkled with cilantro and dusted with paprika.

Per serving: 427 calories, 9 g carbohydrate, 19 g protein, 34 g fat

SPANISH-STYLE EGGS COOKED WITH PEPPERS AND TOMATOES

Yield: 4 servings

An abundance of vegetables makes a nest for these eggs as they cook. Serve at once with crusty garlic bread.

2 tablespoons olive oil
3 large red and/or green bell peppers, stemmed, seeded and sliced
1 large onion, sliced
2 large tomatoes, chopped
1 tablespoon PESTO SAUCE (see pages 320-321)

salt to taste
freshly ground pepper to taste
4 large eggs
12 black olives, pitted and chopped
1 tablespoon shredded fresh basil leaves

1. Heat the oil in a large skillet over medium heat and gently fry the peppers and onion until colored and softened, about 8 minutes. Stir in the tomatoes and Pesto and season well. Using two wooden spoons, make 4 wells in the vegetable mixture in the pan and crack an egg into each. Sprinkle the eggs with salt, black pepper, olives and basil.

2. Reduce heat and cover the pan, cook for a further 3 to 5 minutes, depending how well cooked you like your eggs.

Per serving: 301 calories, 17 g carbohydrate, 10 g protein, 23 g fat

PERSIAN OMELETTE

Yield: 3 servings

Garnish this dazzling green-flecked golden dish with watercress that has been drizzled with herb oil and tossed to coat. The juicy, peppery cress not only tastes wonderful with the eggs, but it also adds a fresh aroma to the fragrance that rises from the cooked herbs and saffron.

softened butter for greasing
the baking dish
6 eggs
2 tablespoons clarified butter
2 scallions, trimmed and chopped
1 cup loosely packed fresh
cilantro leaves, chopped
1 cup loosely packed fresh
flat-leaf parsley leaves,
chopped
1/4 cup finely snipped fresh chives
1 tablespoon finely snipped

fresh dill
1/4 teaspoon saffron threads,
crumbled
salt to taste
freshly ground pepper to taste

FOR SERVING

1 small bunch young, tender
watercress, rinsed, dried and
trimmed
BASIL OIL (see page xx)
6 tablespoons plain yogurt

1. Preheat the oven to 350 degrees. Grease a shallow 1 1/2-quart baking dish with butter.

2. Lightly whisk the eggs in a large bowl and add the clarified butter, scallions, herbs, saffron, salt and pepper. Whisk until mixed. Pour the mixture into the prepared baking dish and bake until set but still very moist, 20 to 25 minutes.

3. Meanwhile, in a medium bowl, mix the watercress with a drizzle of Basil Oil. Toss to coat.

4. To serve: Cut the omelet into wedges and place a wedge on each serving dish. Garnish with the watercress and serve with yogurt.

Per serving: 400 calories, 7 g carbohydrate, 16 g protein, 35 g fat

EGGS WITH SPICY ONION SAUCE

Yield: 4 servings

2 tablespoons ground coriander
1 teaspoon fennel seeds, ground
in a spice mill or mortar
1/2 teaspoon ground cumin
1/4 teaspoon turmeric
1/8 teaspoon cayenne pepper
1/8 teaspoon freshly ground
pepper
1/8 teaspoon cinnamon
1/8 teaspoon ground cloves
1/8 teaspoon ground cardamom

3 tablespoons vegetable oil
1/2 teaspoon mustard seeds
10 curry leaves or 2 bay leaves
1 dried red chile
2 medium onions, thinly sliced
1 teaspoon salt
1 cup chopped tomatoes
1/4 cup canned unsweetened
coconut milk
8 extra-large eggs, hard-cooked
and peeled

1. In a bowl, combine the coriander, fennel, cumin, turmeric, cayenne, black pepper, cinnamon, cloves and cardamom with ⅓ cup of water to make a paste.

2. In a large nonstick skillet, warm the oil over medium high heat and add the mustard seeds. When they begin to pop, add the curry leaves and dried red chile and cover. After most of the seeds have popped, uncover, add the onions and cook, stirring occasionally, until softened and lightly browned, about 6 minutes.

3. Add the spice paste and salt and cook over medium heat for 5 minutes, adding a few tablespoons of water if the pan is dry. Add the tomatoes and ¾ cup of water and simmer over low heat, stirring occasionally, until the tomatoes are soft and the sauce is thick. Add the coconut milk and eggs, spooning the sauce over the eggs. Heat to simmering, cover and cook over low heat until the eggs are heated through. Serve at once.

Per serving: 298 calories, 9 g carbohydrate, 14 g protein, 24 g fat

EGG AND ASPARAGUS CASSEROLE

Yield: 6 servings

Creamy fresh-mushroom sauce and a crunchy cracker topping make this mix a favorite side dish or light main course for lunch.

2 ounces butter plus extra for greasing baking dish
½ cup chopped celery
¼ cup all-purpose flour
½ teaspoon salt
½ teaspoon dry mustard
dash of pepper
1¾ cups milk

1 teaspoon chicken bouillon granules
4 ounces mushrooms, chopped
1 (16-ounce) package frozen cut asparagus
3 eggs, hard-cooked, shelled and sliced
½ cup crushed saltine crackers

1. Preheat the oven to 375 degrees. Butter a 10-inch by 6-inch by 2-inch baking dish and set aside.

2. Melt the butter in a 2-quart saucepan over medium heat and cook the celery 2 minutes. Blend in the flour, salt, mustard and pep-

per. Add the milk and bouillon granules, heat to boiling and cook, stirring, until thickened and bubbly. Stir in mushrooms and set aside.

3. Cook the asparagus according to package directions, drain thoroughly and set aside. Reserve 1/2 cup asparagus and 1 egg for garnish. In the prepared baking dish, arrange the remaining asparagus and egg slices and pour the mushroom sauce over all. Cover and bake for 15 minutes. Arrange the reserved asparagus and sliced egg on top, sprinkle with the crushed crackers and bake, uncovered, 10 minutes longer.

Per serving: 228 calories, 17 g carbohydrate, 9 g protein, 15 g fat

PUFFY BAKED OMELET WITH ZUCCHINI-TOMATO SAUCE

Yield: 4 servings

You don't need an ovenproof skillet to bake this omelet—it's cooked in a baking pan. Be sure your guests are gathered at the table and waiting when the cooking time is up.

nonstick cooking spray
6 egg yolks
1/2 teaspoon onion powder
1/4 teaspoon salt
1/4 teaspoon freshly ground black pepper

6 egg whites
1 (14 1/2-ounce) can stewed tomatoes, undrained and cut up
1/2 medium zucchini, quartered lengthwise and cut crosswise into 1/4-inch slices

1. Preheat the oven to 350 degrees. Grease an 8-inch square baking dish with nonstick cooking spray and set aside.

2. Beat the egg yolks, onion powder, salt and 1/8 teaspoon of the black pepper until thick and yellow, about 4 minutes. Set aside. Beat the egg whites until soft peaks form when the beaters are raised. Fold the egg whites into egg-yolk mixture using a rubber spatula and spread the mixture evenly into the prepared dish. Bake until a knife inserted near the center comes out clean, 22 to 25 minutes.

3. Meanwhile, combine the tomatoes and their juices, zucchini and the remaining black pepper in a small saucepan and heat to boiling. Reduce the heat to low, cover and simmer until the zucchini is tender,

about 5 minutes. Uncover and simmer until the juices have reduced to a nice coating consistency, 10 to 12 minutes. To serve, cut the omelet into quarters and serve with the sauce.

Per serving: 143 calories, 8 g carbohydrate, 11 g protein, 8 g fat

TOMATO-SEAFOOD FRITTATA

Yield: 8 servings

One man's omelet is another man's scrambled eggs. But both the Italians and Spanish make a sturdy, portable egg cake that can sit around awhile in a picnic basket, while a bottle of white wine chills in a cold stream. But fresh out of the oven, this rich tomato-red mixture of vegetables, shrimp, squid and crabmeat will not get as far as the dining-room table. A salad with a tangy lemon vinaigrette is all that is needed.

1 small white onion, unpeeled, left whole, plus 1 medium white onion, finely chopped
2 garlic cloves, unpeeled
5 bay leaves
1½ to 2 teaspoons salt
1 pound unshelled shrimp
½ pound cleaned squid, diced
1 pound lump crabmeat, picked over
1 pound tomatoes, peeled, seeded, and chopped
¼ cup chopped flat-leaf parsley
2 jalapeño peppers, seeded and finely chopped
2 tablespoons flour
4 eggs, separated
1 tablespoon olive oil

1. Combine the whole onion, garlic, bay leaves, 1 teaspoon salt and 2 quarts water in a stockpot or large saucepan. Heat to boiling over high heat, then reduce the heat and simmer 5 minutes. Add the shrimp and cook 3 minutes, skimming off any froth.

2. Remove the shrimp with a slotted spoon, drain well, transfer to bowl and set aside to cool. Remove and discard the onion and garlic from the stockpot, add the squid and cook 3 minutes. Remove squid from the pot, drain and set aside. Reserve the seafood broth for another purpose (it makes delicious fish soup).

3. When the shrimp are cool enough to handle, peel, devein and finely chop. Combine the shrimp, squid, crabmeat, chopped onion, tomatoes, parsley and peppers in a large bowl and mix well. Sprinkle

with the flour and $\frac{1}{2}$ to 1 teaspoon more salt and toss again until no flour can be seen.

4. Beat the egg whites in bowl until slightly stiff peaks form. Beat the egg yolks, 1 at a time, into the seafood mixture until thoroughly incorporated. With a rubber spatula, carefully fold in the egg whites.

5. Heat the oil in a skillet over medium-high heat until hot and fragrant. Reduce the heat to low. Pour or spoon seafood mixture into pan, smoothing it with spatula to spread it evenly down to the bottom of pan. Cook uncovered 8 minutes. Flip the cake by sliding onto pan lid or plate and slipping it back into pan. Cook until golden on underside, about 3 minutes. Serve hot, cut into wedges.

Per serving: 216 calories, 8 g carbohydrate, 31 g protein, 6 g fat

ROQUEFORT SOUFFLÉ

Yield: 6 to 8 servings

Testing a soufflé may make you nervous for it's more than meets the eye. A soufflé should be hot, soft, and creamy in the center, so it will have a crusty wall and a totally different, almost saucy, middle. Testing should not deflate it. Use a thin metal skewer so you cannot only see that it is clean when inserted after the baking time; it should also feel hot to the touch so you'll know the heat of the oven has penetrated the dish and egg mixture.

7 tablespoons butter	6 egg yolks
2 tablespoons fine dried breadcrumbs	$\frac{3}{4}$ cup crumbled Roquefort cheese
6 tablespoons all-purpose flour	$\frac{1}{3}$ cup cream cheese
$1\frac{1}{2}$ cups milk	7 egg whites
salt to taste	$1\frac{1}{2}$ tablespoons cornstarch

1. Preheat the oven to 375 degrees. Grease a soufflé dish with 1 tablespoon of the butter and sprinkle with the breadcrumbs as if dusting with flour. Invert the dish and shake out excess crumbs.

2. Melt the remaining 6 tablespoons butter in saucepan over low heat. Add the flour and stir frequently over low heat 5 minutes but do not let brown. Heat the milk and a pinch of salt to boiling and

add to the flour-butter mixture. When the sauce is smooth and very thick, beat in the egg yolks 1 at a time. Add the Roquefort and cream cheese, stirring over low heat until melted and smooth. Set aside.

3. Beat the egg whites and cornstarch until stiff peaks form. Fold one-fourth of the whites into the cheese mixture. Fold in remaining whites and spoon into the prepared soufflé dish. Bake 45 minutes to 1 hour.

Each of 8 servings: 287 calories, 10 g carbohydrates, 11 g protein, 23 g fat

MUSHROOM-PARMESAN SOUFFLÉ

Yield: 6 to 8 servings

Cheese and mushrooms make a heady marriage of flavors and aromas in the airy medium supplied by egg whites. If you can find or want to spring for the white truffle oil, it will add an even deeper earthy tone to the one set by the mushrooms.

1½ ounces dried porcini or shiitake mushrooms
2 teaspoons plus 1 tablespoon olive oil
2 tablespoons grated Parmesan cheese
3 garlic cloves, minced
1 shallot, minced

¼ cup cornstarch
1 teaspoon salt
6 egg whites
¼ teaspoon cream of tartar
2 tablespoons white truffle oil (optional)
PARMESAN CHEESE SAUCE for serving (see page 324)

1. Place the dried mushrooms in small bowl and add 2 cups boiling water. Let soak 20 minutes. Drain mushrooms, reserving soaking liquid and strain liquid through cheesecloth. Process mushrooms in food processor or blender until pieces are size of red pepper flakes.

2. Preheat the oven to 325 degrees. Grease a soufflé dish with 2 teaspoons olive oil. Sprinkle the dish with Parmesan as if dusting with flour and set aside.

3. Heat the remaining 1 tablespoon olive oil over medium-low heat in a small skillet. Add the garlic and shallot and cook, stirring often, until softened and aromatic, 3 to 5 minutes. Add the cornstarch and gradually whisk in 1½ cups reserved porcini liquid, making up difference with water if necessary. Raise heat to medium-high and heat the liquid to boiling, stirring constantly. Boil until thickened, about 3 minutes. Place the mixture in large bowl and add mushrooms and salt to taste. Let mixture cool to room temperature.

4. Beat the egg whites and cream of tartar until stiff peaks form. Fold $1/4$ of the beaten egg whites into the mushroom mixture. Fold in remainder of beaten egg whites and the truffle oil. Spoon the mixture into the prepared soufflé dish and bake until a thin metal tester or toothpick comes out clean, about 1 hour.

5. Serve the soufflé immediately, topping each serving with Parmesan Cheese Sauce and 1 teaspoon white truffle oil.

Each of 8 servings, without Parmesan Cheese Sauce: 75 calories, 8 g carbohydrate, 4 g protein, 3 g fat

MEATS

MEXICAN STYLE LOIN OF PORK

Yield: 12 servings

4 cups fresh orange juice
6½-pound boneless loin of
  pork
16 pasilla chiles
12 guajillo chiles
½ onion
6 ounces cider vinegar
20 garlic cloves

2 teaspoons dried thyme
6 whole cloves
2 teaspoons ground cumin
2 teaspoons dried oregano
2 (2-inch) sticks cinnamon
6 whole allspice
4 tablespoons coarse salt
4 tablespoons lard

1. Preheat the oven to 350 degrees.

2. In a small saucepan, heat half of the orange juice until warm.
Toast the chiles on an iron skillet and let them soak in the warm
orange juice for 20 minutes. Transfer the chiles and the orange juice
they soaked in to a blender, add the onion and vinegar and puree.
Set aside.

3. In a mortar, grind the garlic, thyme, cloves, cumin, oregano, cinnamon, allspice and salt. Add the pureed chiles and stir well. Place in
a large nonreactive baking dish and stir in the remaining orange juice.

4. Use a fork to pierce the loin of pork all over. Transfer to the baking pan or dish, turn to coat with the chili and orange sauce and
refrigerate, covered, for at least 6 hours, preferably overnight. Turn
frequently.

5. Remove the loin of pork from the refrigerator 2 hours before
roasting, drain it and pat dry with paper towels. Smear lightly with
the lard. Return it to the marinade and let stand in the marinade at
room temperature.

6. Remove the loin of pork from the refrigerator 2 hours before
roasting, drain it and pat dry with paper towels. Pour the marinade in
a 3-quart saucepan and set aside. Place the roast in a roasting pan,
cover with aluminum foil and roast for 1 hour, basting every 20 minutes with the pan juices. Turn the meat over, cover and roast until
done (the internal temperature reaches 170 degrees), about 1 more
hour, basting every 20 minutes with the pan juices. Turn the oven
temperature up to 450 degrees, uncover the meat and roast for 5 to

10 minutes or until browned, being careful not to let it burn. Let it stand for 15 minutes before slicing.

7. While the roast sits, boil the marinade about 5 minutes. Strain and boil until reduced to a thickened sauce consistency and serve extra to accompany the sliced pork.

Per serving: 398 calories, 12 g carbohydrates, 40 g protein, 20 g fat

HERB AND HONEY ROAST PORK

Yield: 6 to 8 servings

1 (3-½-pound) boneless loin of pork, with the rib rack bones if possible
3 garlic cloves, cut into slivers
12 fresh sage leaves
3 tablespoons peanut oil
salt to taste
freshly ground pepper to taste
2 thyme sprigs, leaves removed
2 large onions, each cut into 8 wedges
1 carrot, peeled, halved lengthwise and cut crosswise into 1-inch pieces
1 bouquet garni
2 tablespoons honey
2 tablespoons red-wine vinegar

1. Prepare the pork the day before you are going to roast it. Make a small incision with the tip of a small knife in the roast and insert a sliver of garlic in it. Repeat with the remaining garlic evenly all over the roast.

2. Place the sage leaves in a bowl and sprinkle them with salt and pepper. Roll up the sage leaves and their seasoning into little cylinders and insert them into the pork with the aid of a small sharp knife. Rub the roast all over with 1 tablespoon of the olive oil, the salt, pepper and thyme. Wrap the roast in plastic wrap and place into the refrigerator.

3. After a day of marinating, remove the roast, wipe it and let it come up to room temperature. Preheat the oven to 475 degrees.

4. Heat the remaining 2 tablespoons of oil in a roasting pan in the oven. When hot, add the onions, carrot and bouquet garni, sprinkle with salt and pepper and toss to coat. Push the vegetables to the side and place the pork loin on the rack made with the rib bones if you have them.

5. Place the roast in the oven for 10 minutes, turning down the temperature to 400 degrees. Leave to roast for $1^1/_2$ hours. Remove the roast from the oven, immediately brush with the honey and loosely cover with foil. Leave to rest 15 minutes before carving. Place the vegetables in a bowl and keep warm.

6. Place the roasting pan on the stovetop on medium heat. Add the vinegar and $1^1/_4$ cups water and heat to boiling, stirring with a wooden spoon to loosen the browned bits in the pan. Boil to reduce the liquid to a thin gravy consistency and serve with the carved pork.

Each of 8 servings: 368 calories, 11 g carbohydrates, 44 g protein, 16 g fat

GARLIC AND LIME PORK CHOPS

Yield: 8 servings

Marinating pork is like gilding the lily, but why not? The combined influence of Asian, Mexican and European flavors in these chops' bath shows just how international our palates have become. Turning the marinade into a sauce is an inspired move. Serve the chops with rice and red onion marmalade.

GARLIC AND LIME MARINADE
6 garlic cloves, crushed
2 tablespoons soy sauce
2 tablespoons grated peeled
    fresh gingerroot
2 tablespoons Dijon mustard
$1/_2$ cup lime juice
2 ounces sunflower oil
2 ounces olive oil

$1/_2$ hot red chile, finely
    diced
8 ($3/_4$-inch thick) pork chops,
    trimmed

GARNISH
crisp-fried sugar-snap peas
lime wedges
fresh cilantro leaves

1.   Combine the marinade ingredients in a heavy-duty zip-top plastic food-storage bag. Add the pork chops, remove any excess air, and seal. Lay the bag in a baking dish and refrigerate for 1 day or overnight, turning the bag occasionally.

2.   Preheat the broiler. Remove the pork from the marinade and place on a rack in a broiler pan. Pour the marinade in a small saucepan and heat to boiling. Let the marinade simmer while broiling the chops for 5 minutes on each side.

3. Serve the chops with a drizzle of the boiled marinade. Garnish with crisp-fried sugar-snap peas, lime wedges and fresh cilantro leaves.

Per serving: 368 calories, 11 g carbohydrates, 44 g protein, 16 g fat

PORK CHOPS WITH CIDER, APPLE JUICE AND BLACK PEPPER

Yield: 4 servings

The mix of slightly alcoholic cider with natural apple juice makes a juicy quick sauce for the rich, sweet meat. Cracked pepper adds visual interest and flavor.

4 (6-ounce) boneless pork chops
½ tablespoon butter
½ tablespoon extra-virgin olive oil
salt to taste

freshly ground pepper to taste
4 to 6 tablespoons dry fermented cider
2 tablespoons unsweetened apple juice

1. Trim any fat from the meat. Melt the butter in the olive oil or butter in a heavy skillet over medium-high heat and cook the meat on both sides until it is done to your liking. (Do not overcook.)

2. Season, particularly with coarsely ground black pepper, and place on serving plates. Pour the cider and apple juice in the pan, boil and scrape up any browned bits and spoon on to the steaks. Serve immediately.

Per serving: 357 calories, 4 g carbohydrates, 35 g protein, 22 g fat

THAI PORK CHOPS

Yield: 4 servings

These juicy, spicy pork chops are easy to coat and quick to cook. There will be seasoning mix left over for your next batch or for cooking chicken or fish.

THAI SEASONING

18 low-sodium sesame-flavored Melba toasts

1 tablespoon garlic powder

1 tablespoon ground ginger

1 teaspoon sugar

½ teaspoon cayenne pepper

4 lean center-cut loin pork chops, ½-inch thick

1 tablespoon low-sodium soy sauce

nonstick cooking spray

1. Place the Melba toasts in a food processor, and process until finely crushed. Combine the crushed Melba toasts and remaining ingredients in a zip-top heavy-duty plastic bag, seal bag, and shake well. Store tightly sealed, shake well before each use. Use as a coating mix for pork or poultry.

2. Preheat the oven to 450 degrees. Grease a baking sheet with cooking spray.

3. Trim the fat from the pork chops, and brush pork with soy sauce. Place ⅓ cup Thai Seasoning in a large zip-top heavy-duty plastic bag. Add chops, seal bag, and shake to coat. Place chops on the prepared baking sheet and bake until the chops are cooked through, about 15 minutes.

Per serving: 283 calories, 12 g carbohydrates, 24 g protein, 15 g fat

PLUM PORK WITH WATER CHESTNUTS

Yield: 4 servings

Serve hot with rice or noodles.

1¼ pounds pork tenderloin

12 peeled fresh or canned water chestnuts

¼ cup vegetable oil

3 tablespoons cornstarch

3 tablespoons plum sauce

1 tablespoon vinegar

1. Cut the pork into ½-inch cubes. Cut the water chestnuts in half and pat dry with paper towels.

2. Heat the oil in a wok until hot over medium-high heat.

3. Dust the pork with cornstarch, stir-fry in hot oil until brown and set aside. Add the water chestnuts and stir-fry until golden brown.

Add to the pork. Carefully drain off the oil and wipe out the wok with paper towels. Add the plum sauce, 5 tablespoons water and the vinegar to the wok and mix well. Heat until boiling over medium heat, add the pork and water chestnuts, and cook, stirring, until heated through and coated with sauce, about 1 minute.

Per serving: 265 calories, 18 g carbohydrates, 30 g protein, 7 g fat

CLASSIC HONEY-GLAZED BAKED HAM

Yield: 23 servings
(serving size: 3 ounces)

Your house will become a fragrant temple as this ham cooks, and your table will become filled with worshipers once it's sliced. Serve side dishes aplenty to show off how well the sweet flavor goes with just about everything.

6½-pound reduced-sodium smoked fully cooked ham
40 whole cloves
nonstick cooking spray
¼ cup firmly packed

brown sugar
¼ cup honey
3 tablespoons unsweetened pineapple juice
½ teaspoon dry mustard

1.   Preheat the oven to 425 degrees. Grease a wire roasting rack with cooking spray and place in a roasting pan.

2.   Score the "top" of the ham in a diamond pattern and push a clove into each of the diamonds. Place the ham on the rack in the pan.

3.   Combine the sugar, honey, pineapple juice and mustard in a small saucepan and mix well. Heat to boiling and cook 1 minute. Remove the pan from the heat and when the glaze has cooled, brush it over the ham.

4.   Bake the ham for 5 minutes. Reduce the heat to 325 degrees and bake 1 hour, basting the ham with sugar mixture every 15 minutes.

Per serving: 154 calories, 5 g carbohydrates, 24 g protein, 5 g fat

CRUSTED HAM WITH ORANGE-MADEIRA SAUCE

Yield: 32 servings
(serving size: 4 ounces)

1 (12- to 13-pound) bone-in smoked ham
1½ cups medium-dry Madeira
2 cups coarse fresh bread-crumbs
½ cup finely chopped fresh flat-leaf parsley
3 large garlic cloves, minced

3 tablespoons unsalted butter, melted
2 tablespoons Dijon mustard
½ teaspoon kosher salt
2 large navel oranges
½ teaspoon finely grated orange rind

1. Preheat the oven to 325 degrees. Set the ham in a large roasting pan, fat side up. Using a sharp knife, score the fat all over in a cross-hatch pattern. Pour 1 cup of the Madeira over the ham and cover tightly with foil. Bake the ham for about 3½ hours, or until heated through.

2. In a medium bowl, toss the breadcrumbs with the parsley. In a small bowl, combine the garlic, melted butter and mustard and work into the breadcrumbs with your fingers. Season with the salt.

3. Uncover the ham and baste with the pan juices and transfer to a large platter. Pour the pan juices into a medium saucepan. Return the ham to the roasting pan and raise the oven temperature to 375 degrees. Pat the breadcrumb mixture all over the top of the ham, pressing it firmly into the fat. Return the ham to the oven and bake for about 30 minutes longer, or until the breadcrumb coating is crisp and golden brown. Transfer the ham to a cutting board and let rest for 15 minutes.

4. Meanwhile, using a sharp knife, peel the oranges, removing all the bitter white pith. Working over a bowl to catch the juices, cut the oranges between the membranes to release the sections; you should have ½ cup of juice. Add the orange sections, orange juice and the remaining ½ cup of Madeira to the juices in the saucepan. Cover and simmer over low heat for 10 minutes. Remove from the heat, add the rind and keep warm.

5. Using a long, thin knife, carefully slice the ham, holding the crumbs in place with one hand while you cut. Arrange the ham slices on a platter. Sprinkle any fallen crumbs over the ham and serve with the orange sauce.

Per serving: 265 calories, 11 g carbohydrates, 21 g protein, 14 g fat

PAN-FRIED TENDERLOIN STEAKS PUTTANESCA

Yield: 4 servings

Hickory-smoked salt adds a sultry depth to the double-tomato sauce.

2 tablespoons sun-dried
  tomato tidbits
1³⁄₄ cups chopped unpeeled
  tomato
¹⁄₃ cup dry red wine
¹⁄₄ cup chopped fresh
  basil
¹⁄₄ cup chopped pitted ripe
  olives
1 garlic clove, crushed

4 (4-ounce) beef tenderloin
  steaks, well trimmed
1 tablespoon Worcestershire
  sauce
¹⁄₄ teaspoon hickory-smoked
  salt
¹⁄₄ teaspoon freshly ground
  pepper
nonstick cooking spray
fresh basil sprigs for garnish

1. Combine the sun-dried tomato and ¹⁄₂ cup boiling water in a bowl and let stand 10 minutes.

2. Drain the sun-dried tomato and add the tomato, wine, basil, olives and garlic; mix well and set aside.

3. Brush the Worcestershire sauce over the steaks and sprinkle with the smoked salt and the pepper.

4. Grease a large nonstick skillet with cooking spray and heat over medium-high heat until hot. Add the steaks and cook until browned, about 1 minute on each side. Reduce the heat to medium-low and cook until they are the desired degree of doneness, about 4 minutes longer on each side. Place the steaks on a hot serving platter, set aside and keep warm.

5. Add the tomato mixture to the drippings in the skillet and cook over medium-high heat until heated through, about 3 minutes, stirring occasionally. Serve the sauce over the steaks. Garnish with the basil sprigs.

Per serving: 369 calories, 9 g carbohydrates, 22 g protein, 26 g fat

CURRIED HAM-RAISIN ROLL-UPS

Yield: 12 roll-ups

You can use 24 to 36 very thin slices of sandwich-type packaged or deli-sliced ham instead of the thick slices. Use 2 to 3 slices to obtain desired $\frac{1}{8}$-inch thickness.

2 cups cooked rice	1 teaspoon dried parsley flakes
CURRY SAUCE	12 slices ham, $\frac{1}{8}$-inch
2 tablespoons minced onion	thick

1. Preheat the oven to 325 degrees. Grease a shallow large baking dish.

2. Combine the rice, $\frac{1}{2}$ cup of the Curry Sauce, the onion and parsley in a bowl. Divide the rice mixture into 12 portions and spread one portion over each ham slice. Roll up and place seam side down in the prepared dish. Stir the remaining Curry Sauce and check its consistency for pouring, adding a bit more hot milk if necessary. Pour it over the Ham Roll-Ups and spread evenly. Bake, uncovered, until heated through and bubbly, 25 to 30 minutes.

Per roll-up: 188 calories, 14 g carbohydrates, 8 g protein, 11 g fat

NEW-YORK-MINUTE STEAKS

Yield: 4 servings

When you're hungry, time is everything. So what better way to get on with the nighttime than this quick skillet steak dinner?

1 large egg
1 teaspoon salt
¼ teaspoon freshly ground
  pepper

¾ cup fine dried breadcrumbs
1½ tablespoons butter
1½ pounds minute
  steaks

1. Beat the egg with 2 teaspoons water, the salt and pepper in a shallow bowl until blended. Spread out the breadcrumbs on a plate.

2. Working with one steak at a time, dip the steaks into the egg mixture and then into the crumbs to coat on both sides. Place the prepared steaks between 2 sheets of waxed paper and press lightly with your hand to make sure the crumbs stay on.

3. Melt the butter in a very large nonstick skillet over medium-high heat. Add the steaks and brown on both sides, cooking to degree of desired doneness.

Per serving: 358 calories, 15 g carbohydrates, 40 g protein, 14 g fat

GRILLED STEAK WITH BLACK BEANS

Yield: 4 servings

In South America, piquant chimichurri sauce is a favorite accompaniment to grilled meats. Serve bread alongside to soak up the sauce—you won't want to miss a drop.

2 tablespoons vegetable
  oil
1 onion, chopped
3 garlic cloves, minced
1 cup cooked black beans,
  homemade or drained and
  rinsed canned black beans
1 cup canned low-sodium
  chicken broth or homemade
  broth

⅔ cup canned crushed
  tomatoes in thick puree
1 (7-ounce) jar sliced pimentos,
  drained
1 bay leaf
1 teaspoon salt
1½ pounds sirloin steak, about
  1 inch thick
¼ teaspoon freshly ground
  pepper

1. In a medium saucepan, heat 1 tablespoon of the oil over medium low heat. Add the onion and garlic and cook, stirring occasionally, until translucent, about 5 minutes. Add the beans, broth, tomatoes, pimentos, bay leaf, and 1/2 teaspoon of the salt. Simmer until thickened, about 20 minutes. Remove the bay leaf.

2. Light the grill or heat the broiler. Rub the steak with the remaining oil, sprinkle with the remaining salt and the pepper. Grill or broil for 4 minutes. Turn, cook to your taste, about 4 minutes longer for medium-rare. Cut into thin diagonal slices. Top the beans with the steak and sauce.

Per serving: 546 calories, 18 g carbohydrates, 39 g protein, 35 g fat

LAMB IN AN HERB CRUST

Yield: 2 servings

Baked garlic cloves make a good side dish, with a little fried parsley.

1 cup fine fresh breadcrumbs
1 cup chopped fresh flat-leaf
  parsley
grated rind of 1/2 lemon

Dijon mustard
1 rack uncut lamb chops, end
  bones trimmed and fat
  removed

1. Preheat the oven to 400 degrees. Mix together the breadcrumbs, parsley and lemon in a small bowl. Smother the lamb in mustard. Take handfuls of crumb mix and shape it on to the lamb.

2. Place the lamb on a rack in a broiler pan. Roast for 15 minutes.

Per serving: 269 calories, 14 g carbohydrates, 26 g protein, 12 g fat

GRILLED SPICY SOUTHWESTERN FLANK STEAK WITH CORN SALSA

Yield: 4 servings
(includes ¼ cup corn salsa per serving)

The earthy flavors of the spice rub mix with the meat juices and sizzle to a heady fragrance. Sweet corn and tomatoes make a juicy salsa the perfect sidekick.

1 teaspoon ground cumin
1 teaspoon ground coriander
½ teaspoon chili powder
1 pound lean flank steak
½ cup medium-hot

picante sauce
2 garlic cloves, crushed
nonstick cooking spray
EASY CORN SALSA for serving
(see page 316)

1. Combine the cumin, coriander and chili powder in a cup, mix well and rub into the steak. Place the steak in a zip-top plastic food-storage bag and add ½ cup of the picante sauce and the garlic. Turn the bag to distribute the ingredients over the steak. Marinate in refrigerator at least 8 hours, turning bag occasionally.

2. Remove steak from bag, discarding marinade.

3. Prepare an outdoor grill for barbecuing. Coat a grill rack with cooking spray.

4. Set the grill rack over medium-hot coals and heat until hot. Place the steak on the rack and cook 8 minutes on each side or until desired degree of doneness. Using tongs, transfer the steak to a cutting board, cover loosely with aluminum foil and let stand 10 minutes to allow the juices to settle.

5. Cut the steak diagonally across the grain into thin slices. Serve the corn salsa over the steak.

Per serving: 206 calories, 7 g carbohydrates, 24 g protein, 9 g fat

STIR-FRIED GINGER AND BRANDY BEEF

Yield: 2 servings

10 ounces beef, slightly frozen for easier slicing

2-inch piece peeled fresh gingerroot, finely chopped

2 tablespoons brandy

1½ tablespoons soy sauce

1½ tablespoons oyster sauce

1 teaspoon cornstarch

½ teaspoon freshly ground pepper

2 tablespoons vegetable oil

2 tablespoons white wine

2 tablespoons beef broth

2 scallions, trimmed and shredded

2 tablespoons chopped fresh cilantro

1. Preheat the oven to 200 degrees. Heat an oven-safe serving plate or baking dish.

2. Thinly slice the beef and place in a shallow bowl. Add the ginger, brandy, soy sauce, oyster sauce, cornstarch and pepper and toss to coat.

3. Heat the oil in a wok until smoking. Add the beef and stir-fry 1 minute. Add the wine and broth and stir-fry until the beef is the desired doneness, 1 to 2 minutes longer. Transfer to the hot plate and garnish with scallions and cilantro.

Per serving: 428 calories, 11 g carbohydrates, 30 g protein, 24 g fat

---

SLOW-COOKER CORNED-BEEF DINNER

Yield: 12 servings

This is a modernized version of the old-fashioned slow-cooked stovetop recipe, which can cook for about 4 hours less time on the stove, but you should be home when it is cooking.

2 whole cloves
1 bay leaf
1 tablespoon packed brown
  sugar
¼ teaspoon freshly ground
  pepper
3½-pound corned beef
1 small head cabbage

(about 2 pounds), cut into
  8 wedges
6 medium carrots, peeled and
  cut into chunks
4 medium potatoes, peeled
  and cut into chunks
2 medium onions, peeled and
  quartered through the root

1. Combine 2 cups boiling water, the cloves, bay leaf, sugar and pepper in a 6-quart slow-cooker. Add the corned beef and the cabbage wedges, carrots, potatoes and onions. Cover and cook on LOW for 10 to 12 hours or on HIGH for 5 to 6 hours. Discard the bay leaf before serving.

Per serving: 413 calories, 19 g carbohydrates, 27 g protein, 26 g fat

RUMP STEAK WITH RED WINE AND SHALLOTS

Yield: 1 serving

1 (8-ounce) rump steak
salt to taste
freshly ground pepper to taste
2 teaspoons oil

2 tablespoons butter
4 shallots, thinly sliced
⅓ cup red wine
⅓ cup veal broth

1. Sprinkle the steak on both sides with salt and pepper. Melt 1 tablespoon of the butter in the oil over medium-high heat and brown the steak on both sides, about 3 minutes per side, or to desired doneness inside. Remove to a plate and keep warm.

2. Add the shallots to the drippings in the skillet and sauté until softened, about 3 minutes. Add the wine and boil until reduced to 2 tablespoons. Add the broth and boil until the sauce measures about ¼ cup. Whisk in the remaining butter until melted, adjust the seasoning, and pour over steak.

Per serving: 657 calories, 11 g carbohydrates, 54 g protein, 38 g fat

LAMB AND CARROT MEATLOAF

Yield: 6 servings

1 pound lean ground lamb
2 garlic cloves, crushed
3 large carrots, peeled and grated finely
1 to 2 teaspoons ground cumin
1 teaspoon ground cinnamon
1 large onion, grated
2 tablespoons tomato paste
1¼ cups fresh breadcrumbs
2 eggs, beaten
salt to taste
freshly ground pepper to taste

1. Preheat the oven to 375 degrees. Line a 2-quart loaf pan with aluminum foil.

2. In a large bowl, mix all the loaf ingredients together thoroughly and season well. Press the mixture into the prepared pan and cover with aluminum foil.

3. Cook the loaf about 1 hour, or until firm and a skewer or knife when inserted comes out clean. Allow the loaf to sit in its pan for 10 minutes before turning out and slicing.

Per serving: 406 calories, 14 g carbohydrates, 23 g protein, 29 g fat

GORGONZOLA CHEESEBURGERS ON CROSTINI

Yield: 4 servings

8 ounces ground sirloin or chuck

salt to taste
freshly ground pepper to taste
8 thin slices pancetta
4 ounces Gorgonzola cheese cut into 4 (³/₄-inch-thick) slices
4 slices Italian bread
1 large garlic clove, sliced in half
8 basil leaves, shredded
½ cup chopped tomato
¼ cup chopped red onion
extra-virgin olive oil for drizzling

1. Preheat the broiler or prepare an outdoor grill for barbecuing. Shape the meat into 4 patties and season on both sides with salt and pepper. Wrap each hamburger with 2 slices of pancetta.

2. Broil the burgers about 5 inches from the heat source or grill the burgers over a medium-hot fire for about 4 minutes, or until the pancetta is nicely browned. Flip the burgers and top them with the Gorgonzola. Grill for about 4 minutes longer, or until nicely browned on the second side and cooked through.

3. Meanwhile, rub the cut sides of the garlic over the bread and grill the bread on both sides until lightly toasted. Combine the basil, tomato and onion in a small bowl and sprinkle with salt and pepper. Toss to mix.

4. To serve: Place one crostini on a serving plate. Top with the basil mixture and drizzle with oil. Set the burgers on top and serve at once.

Per serving: 485 calories, 13 g carbohydrates, 24 g protein, 31 g fat

STEAKS WITH STILTON RAREBIT

Yield: 2 servings

2 (8-ounce) beef tenderloin steaks
salt to taste
freshly ground pepper to taste
1 tablespoon olive oil
1 cup red wine
1¼ cups homemade beef broth
2 ounces Stilton cheese
¼ cup milk

¼ cup beer
1 egg yolk
1 tablespoon breadcrumbs
½ teaspoon dry mustard
Worchestershire sauce to taste
Tabasco sauce to taste
1 ounce butter, softened
1 tablespoon PESTO SAUCE (see page xx)

1. Season the steaks well with salt and pepper. Heat the olive oil in a large skillet over medium-high heat and cook the steaks until well browned on both sides and to almost the desired degree of doneness on the inside, 5 to 6 minutes in all. Remove the steaks from the pan to a small roasting pan.

2. Add the wine to the pan and heat to boiling over high heat. Boil

until it is reduced by half and add the beef broth. Boil until the liquid is reduced to 1 cup. Set aside.

3. Combine the egg yolk, breadcrumbs, mustard, Worcestershire sauce and a dash of Tabasco in a small saucepan. Whisk in the milk and beer and season well. Crumble in the Stilton cheese and heat, whisking, until the cheese is melted.

4. Preheat the broiler. Pour the Stilton rarebit over the steaks and broil until golden brown on the top. Remove from the grill and place in the 2 bowls. Season the hot, reduced sauce and whisk in the butter to give the sauce a nice glaze. Whisk the pesto into the sauce, pour it round the steaks and serve.

Per serving: 868 calories, 9 g carbohydrates, 60 g protein, 56 g fat

BEEF TENDERLOIN STEAK 'EN PERSILLADE' WITH RED-WINE SAUCE

Yield: 3 servings

The buttery persillade or parsley topping to the steaks provides an appetizing aroma as it broils in a final act of cooking the steaks. The red-wine sauce is easy to assemble.

1 bunch flat leaf parsley
2 garlic cloves
8 ounces butter, melted, plus 1 ounce, softened
salt to taste
freshly ground pepper to taste

1½ cups red wine
1½ cups triple-strength chicken broth
3 (8-ounce) beef tenderloin steaks
¾ cup fresh breadcrumbs

1. For the topping: Pick off the leaves from the parsley sprigs and plunge into a small saucepan of boiling water. Drain through a sieve and immediately cool down under running cold water. Place in a blender with the melted butter, garlic, salt and pepper. Blend until completely smooth. Set aside.

2. For the wine sauce: Pour the wine into a wide saucepan and boil until reduced to about 3 ounces. Add the broth and boil until the

total liquid measures about 6 ounces and is almost syrupy. Season to taste. Whisk in the softened butter until melted. Keep warm but do not boil or the sauce will separate.

3. Preheat the broiler. Place the steaks on a rack in a broiler pan and broil as you like them cooked. Smear a good layer of parsley mixture on top of each and sprinkle with the breadcrumbs. Return to the grill until the crust is golden brown and sizzling, watching the whole time to prevent the mixture from burning. Transfer the steaks to individual plates and pour the wine sauce around each.

Per serving: 1102 calories, 10 g carbohydrates, 52 g protein, 86 g fat

PAN-FRIED BLACK-PEPPER STEAKS WITH PINK-PEPPERCORN SAUCE

Yield: 4 servings

There are a few hard and fast rules to follow when cooking steaks. First, you know the pan is hot enough when the butter is nut-brown. Anything less means that the meat will stew! As far as testing a steak for doneness, start checking the steaks after they have been cooking for about 4 minutes in total. Undercook them slightly anyway, to allow for the time they will keep warm while you make the sauce and dish up.

BLACK-PEPPER STEAK
1 tablespoon crushed black peppercorns
4 (6-ounce) beef tenderloin steaks
1 ounce butter

Pink-Peppercorn Sauce
1 small onion, finely chopped
1 garlic clove, finely chopped
2 tablespoons brandy

½ cup red wine
½ cup beef broth
2 tablespoons heavy cream
1 tablespoon fresh snipped fresh chives
1½ teaspoons pink peppercorns
salt to taste
freshly ground pepper to taste
POTATO-MUSHROOM MASH for serving (see page 281)

1. Press the crushed peppercorns onto the steaks. Melt the butter in a large skillet over medium-high heat until it is nut brown. Fry the steaks 2 minutes on each side, until they are well browned on the

outside and done to your liking, rare or medium. Remove them from the pan, cover and keep warm.

2. Add the onion and garlic to the fat remaining in the pan and cook for about 3 minutes, until they have softened. Pour in the brandy and wine and boil until the liquid has reduced by half. Add the beef broth and boil again until it has reduced by half. Stir in the cream, chives and pink peppercorns and season to taste.

3. Arrange the steaks and Potato-Mushroom Mash on the plates and spoon the sauce over the meat.

Per serving (with the Potato Mash): 554 calories, 17 g carbohydrates, 39 g protein, 33 g fat

BROILED STEAK
AU POIVE TO ORDER

Yield: 4 to 6 servings

Extra-thick steaks are so dramatically received, and you only have to watch them carefully to make them perfect. It's a risk to cook them too long on one side so plan to spend the last 5 minutes in front of the broiler to control the surface browning and interior goings on.

1/4 cup red-wine vinegar
1 tablespoon vegetable oil
3 pounds T-bone or porterhouse steak (or steaks), as thick as 2 inches

1 teaspoon salt
1 teaspoon freshly ground pepper
1 teaspoon dried basil leaves, crushed

1. Preheat the broiler and arrange the oven racks so the surface of the steaks will be 4 inches from the flame or heat element.

2. Combine the vinegar and oil in a deep shallow bowl and whisk until blended. Dip the steak or steaks on both sides in the vinegar mixture, drain off the excess and place on the broiler rack over a broiler pan.

3. Combine the salt, pepper and basil in small cup. Press half of the mixture onto both sides of the steak or steaks and place on the

broiler rack. Broil until the surface is seared and sizzling, about 5 minutes. Turn the steaks over and press the remaining seasoning onto the uncooked side or sides. Cook to the desired degree of doneness, which may mean turning thick steaks over again, cooking 2 or so minutes per side.

Each of 6 servings: 319 calories, 0 g carbohydrates, 48 g protein, 13 g fat

HEARTY MEAT LOAF
WITH FRESH CORN

Yield: 6 servings
(serving size: 1 slice) plus 3 slices for sandwiches

Take a survey and you'll be surprised how well meat loaf scores on the list of comfort foods. Maybe it's because the leftovers make such enviable brown-bag lunches.

nonstick cooking spray
2 teaspoons vegetable oil
1½ cups chopped onions
1 cup diced celery
1 large garlic clove, crushed
1¼ teaspoons dried basil
3/4 teaspoon dried oregano
  leaves
½ teaspoon salt
½ teaspoon celery salt
⅛ teaspoon freshly ground
  pepper
2 tablespoons cider vinegar
1½ pounds ground beef round
½ cup dried breadcrumbs
1½ cups fresh corn kernels,
  divided
¼ cup chopped fresh parsley
1 large egg
¼ cup tomato sauce

1. Preheat the oven to 350 degrees. Grease a broiler pan with the cooking spray.

2. Heat the oil in a large skillet over medium-high heat. Add the onions, celery and garlic and sauté until tender and lightly browned, about 5 minutes. Add the basil, oregano, salt, celery salt and pepper and cook 2 minutes. Remove from the heat and stir in vinegar. Set aside to cool.

3. Crumble the beef into a large bowl. Add the cooled onion mixture, the breadcrumbs, ½ cup of the corn and the parsley and set aside.

4. Place the remaining corn and the egg in a food processor and process until almost smooth. Add to meat mixture and stir well. Although the mixture will be wet, shape it into a 9-inch-by-4-inch loaf and place it on the prepared broiler pan.

5. Bake the meat loaf for 30 minutes. Brush the loaf all over with the tomato sauce and bake 35 minutes longer. Let stand 5 minutes before slicing.

Per serving: 266 calories, 19 g carbohydrates, 30 g protein, 8 g fat

BANKRUPTCY STEW

Yield: 8 servings

If you're going into or coming from the condition stated in this recipe title, you may find stomach-filling solace in this tasty dish. But even if you just want to keep the wolves from the door, this is certainly an economical main course for a crowd. The fresh parsley will add a wealth of flavor.

nonstick cooking spray
2 pounds lean boneless beef round steak, cut into 1-inch cubes
4 large potatoes, peeled and cubed
3 large carrots, peeled and thinly sliced
1 large green bell pepper, thinly sliced
1 large celery stalk, chopped
1 large yellow onion, thinly sliced
½ cup tomato sauce
¼ cup finely chopped fresh parsley
1 bay leaf

Grease a large Dutch oven with the cooking spray and heat over medium-high heat until hot. Add the beef cubes and brown on all sides, gradually adding up to ½ cup water until all the meat is browned. Add the vegetables and the tomato sauce, cover and simmer until the meat is tender, about 1½ hours.

Per serving: 368 calories, 11 g carbohydrates, 44 g protein, 16 g fat

BURGUNDIAN-STYLE SAUSAGE STEW WITH GARLIC BREAD TRIANGLES

Yield: 4 servings

This is as hearty and satisfying as its classic, chunks-of-beef counterpart. The wine you choose can influence the flavor more than any other ingredient. Try it with red wines from California, Italy, New Zealand or South Africa. You can vicariously travel around the globe in one dish!

1 tablespoon vegetable oil
12 shallots, peeled and halved
   lengthwise
1 pound beef sausages
4 thick slices of bacon, diced
1 to 2 garlic cloves, crushed
6 ounces button mushrooms,
   sliced
1¼ cups beef broth
1¼ cups red wine

½ teaspoon prepared mustard
2 tablespoons chopped fresh
   thyme leaves
1 tablespoon cornstarch
   blended in a little cold
   water
salt to taste
freshly ground pepper to taste
GARLIC BREAD TRIANGLES
   (optional, see page 357)

1. Heat the oil in an ovenproof casserole and add the shallots and sausages and cook until lightly golden, 8 to 10 minutes, stirring occasionally.

2. Add the bacon, garlic and mushrooms and cook 3 to 4 minutes.

3. Add the broth, wine, mustard, most of the thyme, the cornstarch mixture, salt and pepper. Heat to boiling and simmer gently 20 to 25 minutes, stirring occasionally.

4. Serve the stew sprinkled with the remaining chopped thyme and the bread triangles arranged around the edge.

Per serving (without the bread triangles): 627 calories, 17 g carbohydrates, 22 g protein, 47 g fat

STOVETOP STEAK AND MUSHROOMS IN STOUT GRAVY

Yield: 4 servings

The aroma of this stew cooking will bring everyone into the kitchen. It's even great cooked a day ahead to allow the flavors time to mingle.

2 pounds chuck steak
seasoned flour
2 tablespoons vegetable oil
1½ pounds onions, roughly
  chopped
8 ounces mushrooms, cleaned
and quartered lengthwise
1¼ cups Guinness or other
  stout
1¼ cups beef broth or water
pinch of grated nutmeg
salt and pepper to taste

1. Cut the meat into fairly large chunks and roll in seasoned flour.

2. Heat the oil over medium-high heat in a heavy Dutch oven and brown the meat chunks in batches, removing the meat from the pan to a bowl as it browns. Add the onions to the fat in the pan and sauté for 2 to 3 minutes. Add the mushrooms and sauté 1 minute.

3. Return the meat to the pan and add the Guinness, broth, nutmeg, salt and pepper. Heat until the liquid is boiling, reduce the heat to low, cover and simmer gently until the meat is tender, about 2 hours.

Per serving: 336 calories, 15 g carbohydrates, 33 g protein, 15 g fat

SAUERBRATEN

Yield: 6 servings
(serving size: 3 ounces roast and ½ cup sauce)

This is one of the world's most tender, delicious and beloved beef dishes. German for "sour roast" because of the vinegary marinade and cooking liquid, the dish is actually sweetened by all the flavorful goodies it is cooked with by the time it's ready to eat.

1 (2-pound) lean boneless
   rump roast

MARINADE
1 cup cider vinegar
1 medium onion, thinly
   sliced
6 black peppercorns
4 whole cloves
4 allspice berries

1 bay leaf
$\frac{1}{2}$ teaspoon salt
$\frac{1}{4}$ teaspoon pepper
nonstick cooking spray
1 cup chopped onion
$\frac{1}{2}$ cup diced carrot
$\frac{1}{2}$ teaspoon sugar
$\frac{1}{4}$ cup all-purpose flour
finely shredded carrot
   (optional)

1. Trim the fat from roast. Place the roast in a large heatproof bowl and set aside.

2. Combine 5 cups water, the vinegar, onion, peppercorns, cloves, allspice berries and bay leaf in a saucepan and heat to boiling. Pour the hot mixture over the roast, cover and marinate in the refrigerator for 2 days, turning the roast twice each day.

3. Remove the roast from the marinade. Reserve the marinade. Pat the roast dry with paper towel and sprinkle with salt and pepper.

4. Grease a large Dutch oven with cooking spray and place over medium heat until hot. Add the roast and brown on all sides. Remove the roast from the pan and set aside.

5. Re-coat the pan with cooking spray. Add the chopped onion and diced carrot and sauté until crisp-tender, about 3 minutes. Stir in the sugar. Add the roast and reserved marinade. Heat to boiling, cover, reduce heat, and simmer 1 hour. Turn roast over and cook until tender, about 1 hour longer.

6. Remove the roast from pan, set aside and keep warm. Strain the cooking liquid through a sieve into a bowl and discard the solids. Return the cooking liquid to the pan. Place the flour in a bowl, gradually whisk in 3 tablespoons water until smooth. Whisk the flour into the cooking liquid. Heat to boiling, whisking constantly, over medium-high heat. Reduce the heat to medium and cook until slightly thickened, about 10 minutes.

7. Cut the roast into $\frac{1}{4}$-inch-thick slices and arrange on a serving platter. Pour a small amount of cooking liquid over roast. Garnish with shredded carrot, if desired. Pass the remaining cooking liquid separately.

Per serving: 216 calories, 8 g carbohydrates, 35 g protein, 4 g fat

BEER-BRAISED BEEF BRISKET

Yield: 12 servings

A big chunk of meat, a bottle of beer, and Thou. This is a recipe for the tender-meat lovers who don't want to fuss with a lot of ingredients unless they are necessary. Here, the delicious flavor is the sum of every element but without the burp.

4-pound beef brisket, trimmed
1/2 teaspoon freshly ground pepper
1 cup sliced onion, separated into rings
1/2 cup chili sauce
3 tablespoons brown sugar
2 garlic cloves, crushed
1 (12-ounce) bottle of beer
2 1/2 tablespoons all-purpose flour
parsley sprigs for garnish
tomato slices for serving

1. Preheat the oven to 350 degrees. Place the brisket in a 13 by 9 by 2-inch baking dish. Sprinkle the brisket with the pepper and arrange the onion rings on top.

2. Combine the chili sauce and the next 3 ingredients, stir well, and pour over brisket. Cover and bake for 3 hours. Uncover and bake until the brisket is tender, about 20 minutes.

3. Place the brisket on a serving platter, reserving the cooking liquid. Set the brisket aside and keep warm.

4. Pour 1 1/2 cups of the cooking liquid into a small saucepan. Place flour in a small bowl. Gradually add 1 1/4 cups water, blending with a wire whisk. Whisk into the cooking liquid. Heat to boiling, whisking, until the gravy is thickened, about 2 minutes, whisking constantly.

5. To serve, slice the brisket and place on a platter. Garnish with parsley sprigs and serve with the gravy and sliced tomatoes.

Per serving: 266 calories, 8 g carbohydrates, 33 g protein, 10 g fat

CURRIED BEEF AND POTATOES

Yield: 4 servings

Feel free to add leftover cooked vegetables such as carrots, green beans and squash to the mixture.

12 ounces top round beef steak
8 ounces potatoes, peeled, halved and thinly sliced
$1/2$ cup beef broth
2 teaspoons cornstarch
$1/4$ teaspoon salt
nonstick cooking spray

$3/4$ cup chopped onion
$3/4$ cup chopped green or red bell pepper
1 tablespoon vegetable oil
1 teaspoon curry powder
1 medium tomato, coarsely chopped

1. Partially freeze the meat. Thinly slice across the grain into bite-sized strips and set aside.

2. Cook the potatoes in boiling water until tender. Drain and set aside.

3. Combine the beef broth, cornstarch, and salt. Set aside.

4. Grease a wok or large skillet with cooking spray. Heat over medium-high heat. Add the onion and stir-fry 2 minutes. Add the bell pepper and stir-fry until the vegetables are crisp-tender, about 2 minutes. Remove to a bowl.

5. Add the oil to hot wok. Add the beef and curry powder. Stir fry until cooked to the desired doneness, 2 to 3 minutes. Push beef from center of the wok. Stir broth mixture to recombine and add to center of wok. Heat to boiling, stirring until thickened. Stir in onion mixture, potatoes and tomato. Cook, stirring, until heated through.

Per serving: 209 calories, 17 g carbohydrates, 22 g protein, 6 g fat

GRILLED CALF'S LIVER WITH MADEIRA SAUCE

Yield: 4 to 6 servings

Serve the liver on a bed of braised red cabbage.

2 pounds (4 to 6 slices) thinly
 sliced calf's liver
1 to 2 tablespoons unsalted
 butter

salt to taste
freshly ground pepper to taste
5 ounces malmsey Madeira
¼ cup snipped fresh chives

1. Rinse, dry and skin liver. Cut out any veins and sinew using a sharp pair of scissors.

2. Heat a heavy nonstick skillet until over medium-high heat. Add 1 tablespoon butter and swirl the pan to melt the butter. Return the pan to the heat and when the butter stops bubbling, add 3 to 4 slices of liver. Cook briefly until browned, 1 to 2 minutes, and turn and cook on the other side. The liver should be just pink in the middle. Remove the liver from the pan and keep warm while using the remaining butter to cook the remaining liver.

3. Add the Madeira to the pan, scraping up all the meaty bits into it. Check and adjust the seasoning. Add a handful of chopped chives and serve with liver.

Each of 6 servings: 258 calories, 10 g carbohydrates, 27 g protein, 9 g fat

CHEESE-STUFFED BURGERS

Yield: 4 servings

Here's a special formula for those who take a tasty burger seriously. There are many variations of it you can try that are as simple as using different chutneys instead of mustard and ketchup or red onion marmalade instead of raw sliced onions.

1½ pounds lean ground beef

½ onion, grated or very finely chopped

½ tablespoon Worcestershire sauce

1 tablespoon minced fresh parsley

leaves from 2 sprigs of thyme, finely chopped

1 egg, lightly beaten

oil, or a combination of oil and butter for grilling or frying

salt to taste

freshly ground pepper to taste

4 1-ounce chunks of cold cheddar or blue cheese

TO SERVE

1 cup shredded lettuce

4 tomato slices

4 thin slices onion

4 sliced dill pickles

sauces and relishes as desired

1. Mix the beef with the onion, Worcestershire sauce, parsley, thyme, salt and pepper in a large bowl. Use your fingers to squish it together thoroughly. Add a little beaten egg to hold it together and divide into 4 equal portions. Shape each into a nice round burger about ¾-inch thick. Push a fairly deep thumbprint into the middle of the patties and place a large lump of cold cheese in the indentation.

2. To grill, brush each burger with a little oil and cook under a thoroughly preheated grill until browned and crusty on the outside, but until moist and tender on the inside and the cheese is melting. To fry, heat a little oil or oil and butter in a skillet and fry the burgers over a high heat until nicely browned outside and done to your taste on the inside.

3. Serve the burger on a plate with lettuce, tomato, onion and pickles, salt, pepper and whatever sauces or relishes you happen to like best.

Per serving: 578 calories, 4 g carbohydrates, 41 g protein, 43 g fat

VENETIAN-STYLE CALF'S LIVER WITH BALSAMIC VINEGAR

Yield: 2 servings

When the craving for liver and onions hits, here's a quick way to satisfy it. The juices from the onion and liver will marry well with the sweet and tangy flavor of the balsamic vinegar.

1 to 2 tablespoons olive oil
1 large onion, thinly sliced
1 fresh thyme sprig
2 (6-ounce) slices calf's liver,
cut into thick strips
splash of balsamic vinegar
2 tablespoons chopped
flat-leaf parsley

Heat 1 tablespoon oil in a nonstick skillet over medium heat, add the onion and cook until tender, about 5 minutes. Add the thyme and liver and fry to the desired doneness, adding more oil if necessary. Add the balsamic vinegar and stir to scrape up any browned bits.

Per serving: 319 calories, 15 g carbohydrates, 31 g protein, 14 g fat

VEAL MEATBALLS WITH TOMATO AND ONION SAUCE

Yield: 4 servings

1 pound lean minced veal
1 egg
1 tablespoon fresh bread-
crumbs
2 garlic cloves, minced
1 tablespoon chopped fresh
parsley
1½ cups chopped Spanish
onions
sea salt to taste
fresh ground black pepper to
taste
1 teaspoon all-purpose flour
2 tablespoons olive oil
2 small tomatoes, seeded and
chopped
⅓ cup white wine
¼ cup chicken broth

1. Mix the meat, egg, breadcrumbs, garlic, parsley and half the onions in a bowl until blended and season with salt and pepper. Shape into small meatballs and dust with the flour.

2. Heat the oil in a large nonstick skillet over medium heat and brown the meatballs on all sides. Remove to a plate. Add the remainder of the onions to the pan and cook until soft and golden, about 15 minutes. Add the wine, broth and chopped tomato and season to taste. Return the meatballs to the pan, cover and simmer until the meatballs are cooked through, about 40 minutes.

Per serving: 401 calories, 10 g carbohydrates, 38 g protein, 21 g fat

GRILLED VEAL CHOPS WITH ROQUEFORT BUTTER

Yield: 4 servings

Braise some shredded Savoy cabbage and mushrooms to soak up the blue-cheese butter. Follow with a green salad.

8 ounces unsalted butter, softened
8 ounces Roquefort cheese
1 garlic clove, crushed
Tabasco sauce, to taste
½ bunch parsley, leaves only

4 (8-ounce) veal chops, trimmed
salt to taste
freshly ground pepper to taste
olive oil
1 lemon, quartered

1. Place the butter, half the Roquefort, the garlic and a few drops of Tabasco in a food processor. Blend until completely smooth.

2. Blanch the parsley leaves for 5 seconds in a small saucepan of boiling water. Refresh in cold water, dry and chop coarsely. Beat the parsley into the butter mixture. Crumble the remaining Roquefort and fold into the butter mixture. Shape the butter into a roll, wrap up in plastic wrap and chill.

3. Preheat the oven to 350 degrees. Preheat a cast iron ridged grill pan on the stovetop.

4. Season the chops, brush with a little oil and roast in the oven, turning every 3 to 4 minutes on both sides on the grill pan to give an attractive cross-hatched pattern. (If the grill pan isn't large enough to hold all the chops, mark them in the grill pan on the stovetop and place in a large roasting pan.) Roast the chops for 15 minutes. This will give you a good pink chop. If you prefer it well cooked, leave for 5 minutes longer. Remove from the oven and allow to rest for 15 minutes in a warm place.

5. Place a chop on each plate and garnish with a couple of slices of the Roquefort butter and a lemon wedge.

Per serving: 825 calories, 2 g carbohydrates, 47 g protein, 70 g fat

LAMB IN DEVILLED SAUCE

Yield: 6 servings

1 (2-pound) breast of lamb
salt to taste
freshly ground pepper to taste
2 teaspoons oil
1 carrot, peeled and chopped
1 onion, chopped
1 clove garlic, crushed

1¼ cups chicken broth
4 tablespoons English mustard
1 teaspoon cayenne pepper
2 ounces butter, melted
½ cup fine dried breadcrumbs
1½ recipes DEVILLED SAUCE
    for serving (see page 326)

1. Sprinkle the lamb with salt and pepper. Heat the oil over medium-high heat in a Dutch oven and brown the meat well on both sides. Add the vegetables and brown well on all sides. Add the stock, cover and simmer over low heat until tender, 1½ to 2 hours.

2. Remove the lamb from the pan when it has cooled. Remove the bones and weight down the lamb to flatten it. Refrigerate until chilled.

3. Preheat the broiler. Cut the breast meat into 3-inch pieces and spread with the mustard. Dust with cayenne pepper, dip into the melted butter and roll in the breadcrumbs. Place on a baking sheet.

4. Broil until crisp, turning once, 5 to 6 minutes. Serve with Devilled Sauce.

Per serving: 511 calories, 13 g carbohydrates, 17 g protein, 43 g fat

VEAL SCALLOPS WITH MARSALA SAUCE

Yield: 2 servings

Veal is a tender, delicate meat and its texture complements the creamy wine sauce. Complete the meal with a crisp green salad and steamed baby vegetables.

2 veal scallops
1 egg
¼ cup fresh white
   breadcrumbs
2 tablespoons olive oil
¼ cup Marsala or sweet
   sherry

4 heaped tablespoons crème
   fraîche
salt to taste
freshly ground pepper to taste
⅓ cup toasted pinenuts
flat-leaf parsley sprigs for
   garnish

1. Gently pound the scallops with the flat side of a meat mallet or rolling pin to a ¼-inch thickness. Place the egg in a shallow bowl and beat until thin. Place the breadcrumbs in another shallow bowl. Dip each scallop into the egg and then the breadcrumbs.

2. Heat the oil in a large skillet over medium-high heat. Fry the scallops until browned, about 2 minutes on each side. Remove to a serving platter and keep warm.

3. Add the Marsala or sherry to the skillet and simmer for 1 minute. Stir in the crème fraîche and warm through. Season with salt and pepper.

4. Spoon the sauce onto two warmed serving plates. Place the schnitzel on top, sprinkle with the pinenuts and garnish with sprigs of parsley.

Per serving: 617 calories, 18 g carbohydrates, 47 g protein, 36 g fat

LAMB CHOPS WITH VEGETABLES

Yield: 3 servings

2 tablespoons olive oil
1 small onion, finely chopped
1 ripe tomato, ends trimmed,
   cut into 3 thick slices
salt to taste
freshly ground pepper to taste
8 ounces kale, washed, stalks
   and thick veins trimmed off,

   leaves shredded
3 (1-inch-thick) lamb chops
1 small eggplant, ends trimmed
   and cut crosswise into
   ¼-inch thick slices
1 cup red wine
1 ounce butter
1 tablespoon tapenade

1. Heat 2 teaspoons of the olive oil in a large nonstick skillet over medium heat. Add the onion and sauté until tender, about 5 minutes. Sprinkle the tomato slices on one side with salt and pepper and place in the skillet. Sprinkle the kale around the tomatoes and add drizzle with 2 tablespoons water. Cover the pan and let steam until the kale is wilted, stirring occasionally, and the tomatoes have heated through, about 5 minutes.

2. Meanwhile, season the chops with salt and pepper and rub on all sides with 2 teaspoons of the olive oil. Place on a rack in a broiler pan. Repeat with the eggplant slices and broil the lamb and eggplant until browned and sizzling, about 3 minutes on each side.

3. Remove the vegetables and place on a paper-towel-lined plate. Place a 3- or 4-inch metal ring on each of 3 plates and add to each one-third of the eggplant slices, then tomatoes and kale in layers. Cover and keep warm. Leave the pan on the heat and add the red wine, butter, salt and tapenade, whisking to form a sauce.

4. To serve: Remove the rings and place a lamb chop on top of each stack. Pour the sauce over the top.

Per serving: 462 calories, 16 g carbohydrates, 34 g protein, 24 g fat

APPLE-GLAZED RIB LAMB CHOPS

Yield: 8 servings

Tired of always serving mint jelly with lamb? The sweet flavor of apple juice will have everyone chewing on the bones.

½ cup unsweetened apple juice
⅓ cup firmly packed brown sugar
¼ teaspoon dry mustard

1/8 teaspoon ground cloves
8 (6-ounce) lean lamb rib chops, trimmed
nonstick cooking spray

1. Combine the apple juice, brown sugar, mustard and cloves in a large zip-top heavy-duty plastic bag. Add the chops, seal the bag, and marinate in the refrigerator 2 hours, turning bag occasionally.

2. Remove the chops from the bag, reserving marinade. Preheat the broiler.

3. Coat a broiler rack with cooking spray and place the rack in a broiler pan. Place the chops on the broiler rack and broil 5¹/₂ inches from the heat 9 minutes on each side or to desired degree of doneness, basting frequently with the reserved marinade.

Per serving: 212 calories, 5 g carbohydrates, 23 g protein, 11 g fat

QUICK LAMB CASSOULET

Yield: 8 servings

A classic cassoulet takes days to assemble and hours to make. This streamlined version is a way to have the essence of the labor-intensive dish without feeling guilty about taking a few shortcuts.

1 tablespoon olive oil
6 slices bacon, coarsely chopped
2 pounds boneless lamb leg steaks, cut into cubes
1 onion, finely chopped
1 garlic clove, crushed
1 carrot, peeled and diced
1 (14-ounce) can chopped tomatoes
³/₄ cup red wine

³/₄ cup hot lamb or beef broth
¹/₄ teaspoon dried rosemary, crumbled
¹/₄ teaspoon thyme leaves, crumbled
1 (14-ounce) can haricot beans, undrained
salt to taste
freshly ground pepper to taste
1 cup chopped fresh parsley

1. Heat the oil in a large skillet over medium heat and add the bacon and lamb. Cook until browned. Add the onion and garlic and cook until soft, about 5 minutes. Add the carrots and cook, stirring, 2 minutes. Add the tomatoes, wine, broth and herbs. Cover and cook for 20 minutes until the meat is tender.

2. Stir the beans into the cassoulet, heat until bubbly and season with salt and pepper. Spoon the cassoulet into a heatproof serving dish and sprinkle the parsley on top.

Per serving: 374 calories, 19 g carbohydrates, 30 g protein, 18 g fat

LAMB MEAT LOAF

Yield: 8 servings

This curry-flavored meat-loaf recipe made the rounds years ago, when kaffir lime leaves were unknown here. Most people used bay leaves instead, or even lemon or orange leaves from a back-yard tree. However, it takes the kaffir leaves to add the proper touch of delicate, lemony perfume. You can find them in East Indian grocery stores.

2 slices white bread
1 cup milk plus extra for
  soaking bread
2 tablespoons butter
2 onions, thinly sliced
1 apple, peeled and diced
1½ pounds ground lamb
¼ cup raisins
12 blanched almonds, coarsely
  chopped

2 tablespoons sugar
2 tablespoons cider vinegar
¼ teaspoon salt
¼ teaspoon freshly ground
  pepper
2 eggs
6 single kaffir lime leaves
1 teaspoon turmeric
cooked white rice (optional)
chutney (optional)

1. Preheat the oven to 350 degrees. Soak the bread in a bowl with enough milk to cover until soft, then squeeze dry.

2. Melt the butter in a large nonstick skillet over medium heat and sauté the onions and apple until tender and not browned, about 7 minutes. Add the soaked bread, lamb, curry powder, raisins, almonds, sugar, vinegar, salt and pepper. Beat one egg and add and mix thoroughly.

3. Pack the mixture lightly into 9 by 5-inch loaf pan or baking dish. Arrange the lime leaves on top. Bake for 1 hour. Beat the remaining egg in a glass measuring cup with the milk. Stir in the turmeric. Pour mixture over meat loaf and bake 15 minutes longer. Serve with rice and chutney, if desired.

Per serving: 396 calories, 18 g carbohydrates, 19 g protein, 28 g fat

GRILLED INDIAN GROUND LAMB KABOBS (KOFTE)

Yield: 4 servings

A salad of tomato, lettuce and cucumber with a dill-yogurt dressing is a good accompaniment.

2 thick slices day-old white
bread, crusts removed
1 pound best-quality lean
ground lamb or beef
1 onion, grated or very finely
chopped
1 teaspoon ground cumin,
(optional)

salt to taste
freshly ground pepper to
taste
olive oil for broiling

TO SERVE
crushed red-pepper flakes
dried oregano

1.   Preheat the broiler. Soak the bread in water in a bowl for 10 minutes. Drain, squeeze dry and crumble into a food processor. Add the meat, onion, cumin (if used), salt and pepper and process until well mixed. Scrape the mixture into a bowl and knead it with your hands for a few minutes until smooth and cohesive.

2.   Divide the mixture into 12 portions and roll each one into either a tubby sausage shape or portions the size of a baby rugby ball. Thread three kabobs onto each of 4 skewers, place on a rack in a broiler pan and brush with oil. Broil for 5 to 6 minutes until just cooked through but still slightly pink at heart, turning once.

3.   For those who want to spice them up, serve with chili and oregano

Per serving: 364 calories, 9 g carbohydrates, 20 g protein, 27 g fat

SPANISH LAMB STEW

Yield: 4 servings

Fried bread, onion and garlic form to become el machado, the pounded mixture that will thicken the sauce at the end of the cooking time.

1 (2-pound) boneless leg of
   lamb, trimmed
4 tablespoons Spanish olive oil
   or more if needed
1 onion, chopped
4 to 5 garlic cloves, sliced
1 bay leaf
1 slice stale bread,

crusts removed
1 teaspoon Spanish paprika
1 pinch chili powder
4 1/2 ounces red wine
salt to taste
freshly ground pepper to
   taste
1 sprig fresh thyme (optional)

1. Cut the lamb into 3 by 2-inch pieces. Heat the oil in a wide saucepan or deep skillet. Add the onion, garlic and bay leaf and fry gently until the onion is tender and golden, about 7 minutes. Discard the bay leaf. Scoop the onion and garlic out into a mortar (or small grinder) and pound to a paste.

2. In the same oil (add a little more if you need to), fry the bread over a medium heat until nicely browned and crisp. Break the bread into the onion/garlic mixture and pound it in. If you have a processor that can handle small quantities, onion, garlic and bread can all be pureed together.

3. Take the pan off the heat while you are busy pounding and stir the paprika and chili powder into the oil, followed by the meat. Return to a gentle heat and pour in the wine. Season with salt and pepper, and add the thyme (if used). Cover tightly and cook over a very low heat, stirring occasionally, until the meat is tender, 10 to 15 minutes. Stir in the machado and simmer until the sauce is thick and moist, but not runny, about 5 minutes. Adjust the seasoning and serve.

Per serving: 473 calories, 6 g carbohydrates, 48 g protein, 25 g fat

GARLIC-HONEY BUTTERFLIED LEG OF LAMB

Yield: 6 servings

You only need a little know-how and a sharp boning knife to butterfly a leg of lamb, which basically means to bone it without cutting all the way through the leg and spreading it out or "butterflying" it to form a sheet, like wings. But you can ask your butcher to do this for you.

MARINADE

1 garlic clove, peeled and crushed

½ cup vegetable oil

2 tablespoons honey

2 tablespoons bottled Asian plum or duck sauce

2 tablespoons soy sauce

1 teaspoon ground coriander

1 teaspoon ground cumin

1 (3½-pound) leg of lamb, skinned, trimmed, boned and butterflied

1. Line a large roasting pan with heavy-duty aluminum foil. Combine the garlic, oil, honey, sauces and spices in a blender and blend until smooth. Place the lamb in the prepared roasting pan, coat on all sides with the marinade and let stand for several hours at room temperature.

2. Preheat the oven to the hottest temperature, at least 450 degrees. Place the pan with the lamb on the middle oven rack and cook until crisp all over and pink inside, about 30 minutes. Yes, 30 minutes.

3. Allow the lamb to rest for 10 minutes in a warm place before carving. Carve into thick slices. Reheat the juices left from carving and pour them over the lamb.

Per serving: 539 calories, 9 g carbohydrates, 43 g protein, 36 g fat

LAMB NIÇOISE

Yield: 6 servings

LAMB AND MARINADE

¼ cup olive oil plus 2
   tablespoons for cooking
   the lamb
12 leaves fresh basil, chopped
juice of 1 lemon
1 garlic clove, crushed
salt to taste
freshly ground pepper to
   taste
2 loins of lamb
3 long sprigs fresh rosemary

VEGETABLES

8 ounces small new potatoes
1 red bell pepper, seeded
1 eggplant
2 red onions
2 tablespoons olive oil
salt to taste
freshly ground pepper to taste
2 cups cherry tomatoes
12 pitted black olives
BASIL OIL for drizzling
   (see page xx)

1. For the lamb and marinade: Mix ¼ cup olive oil, the basil, garlic, lemon juice, salt and pepper in a shallow baking dish. Add the lamb and roll in the marinade to coat. Cover and let stand, turning the lamb occasionally, for as long as possible, preferably overnight in the refrigerator.

2. The next day or when ready to cook, prepare the vegetables: Preheat the oven to 400 degrees. Slice the new potatoes in half lengthwise. Dice the eggplant and red bell pepper in similar-size pieces and cut the red onion into quarters. Place the vegetables in a shallow roasting pan, drizzle with oil, season and roast at the top of the oven in a single layer until almost tender, about 30 minutes. Remove the vegetables from the oven, add the cherry tomatoes and olives, toss and return to bottom of oven for a further 15 minutes.

3. Meanwhile, heat 2 tablespoons olive oil in an oven-safe skillet or Dutch oven over high heat. Drain the lamb and pat it dry with paper towels. Sear it on all sides in the skillet. If the rosemary is long enough, bind it to the sides of the lamb with string. If not, just poke it underneath as it goes into the oven. Finish the lamb in the top of the oven for 10 to 15 minutes, depending on how you like it cooked.

4. To serve: remove the lamb from the oven and rest in a warm place. Stack the roasted vegetables in the center of warmed plates. Slice the lamb and sit it on top of the vegetables. Drizzle with Basil Oil and serve.

Per serving: 453 calories, 17 g carbohydrates, 16 g protein, 37 g fat

MOUSSAKA

Yield: 8 servings

6 tablespoons vegetable oil
1 onion, chopped
2 garlic cloves, minced
1 pound ground lamb
½ cup red wine
1 tablespoon tomato paste
1 (15-ounce) can crushed tomatoes in thick puree
1 bay leaf
1 (3-inch) cinnamon stick

⅛ teaspoon ground allspice
salt
freshly-ground pepper
1 eggplant (about 1 pound), peeled and cut crosswise into ¼-inch slices
4 ounces Neufchâtel or cream cheese
¼ cup soy milk or 2-percent milk
¼ cup grated Parmesan cheese

1. Preheat the broiler. In a large nonstick skillet, heat 1 tablespoon of the oil over medium heat. Add the onion and garlic, cook until starting to soften, about 3 minutes. Add the lamb and cook until the meat loses its pink color, about 2 minutes. Stir in the wine, tomato paste, tomatoes, bay leaf, cinnamon, allspice, ½ teaspoon salt, and ¼ teaspoon pepper. Heat to boiling. Reduce the heat. Simmer, covered, for 10 minutes.

2. Brush both sides of the eggplant slices with the remaining 5 tablespoons oil and sprinkle lightly with salt and pepper. Place the eggplant slices on a large baking sheet and broil, 6 inches from the heat, until browned, about 5 minutes. Turn and broil until browned on the other side, about 5 minutes longer.

3. In a small saucepan, combine the cream cheese, milk, ⅛ teaspoon salt, and a pinch of pepper. Warm over low heat until just melted.

4. Oil a 2-quart baking dish. Layer half the eggplant in the dish, half the meat sauce. Sprinkle with half the Parmesan. Repeat with the remaining eggplant, meat sauce, and Parmesan. Spoon the cream-cheese sauce on top, broil until just starting to brown, 1 to 2 minutes.

Per serving: 350 calories, 10 g carbohydrates, 14 g protein, 28 g fat

MEDALLIONS OF LAMB WITH CREAMY CABBAGE

Yield: 4 servings

4 (6-ounce) lamb tenderloin
  steaks, trimmed
a splash of olive oil
1 tablespoon olive oil
4 slices bacon, chopped
1 large onion, peeled and finely
  chopped
1 garlic clove, peeled and finely chopped

1 carrot, peeled and finely
  chopped
½ head Savoy cabbage, finely
  shredded
1 cup chicken broth
1 cup heavy cream
salt to taste
freshly ground pepper to
  taste

1. Brown the steaks on each side in a splash of hot olive oil in a skillet over medium-high heat. Reduce the heat and cook 3 minutes on each side for medium-rare or until the meat is done to your liking. Remove to a plate, cover and keep warm.

2. Add the tablespoon of olive oil to the same skillet and cook the chopped bacon over medium heat until golden brown. Remove with a slotted spoon and drain on paper towels.

3. Drain off all but 1 tablespoon bacon drippings. Add the onion, garlic and carrot to the pan and cook until softened, about 5 minutes. Add the cabbage and cook, stirring, until just tender, about 3 minutes. Add the broth and heat to boiling, stirring with a wooden spoon to dislodge the sediment from the bottom of the pan. Add the cream, heat to boiling and season to taste. Carve the lamb in thick oblique slices and serve it with the cream cabbage.

Per serving: 667 calories, 14 g carbohydrates, 42 g protein, 49 g fat

POULTRY

CRUNCHY CHILI CHICKEN

Yield: 4 servings

Slice some juicy, fresh tomatoes while you steam green beans and new potatoes to serve with this dish.

3 tablespoons cornmeal
1 tablespoon all-purpose flour
1 tablespoon chili powder
1 teaspoon ground cumin
1 teaspoon dried oregano
  leaves

½ teaspoon salt or to
  taste
cayenne pepper to taste
4 boneless, skinless chicken
  breast halves
1 tablespoon vegetable oil

1. Combine the cornmeal, flour, chili powder, cumin, oregano, salt and cayenne in a shallow dish.

2. Press chicken into mixture to coat all over. Heat the oil in a non-stick skillet over medium heat until hot and cook the chicken, turning once, until it is no longer pink inside, 10 to 15 minutes.

Per serving: 176 calories, 8 g carbohydrates, 28 g protein, 3 g fat

TANGY GARLIC-LIME CHICKEN

Yield: 4 servings

Asian fish sauce is as versatile a seasoning as soy sauce. A little goes a long way because both the taste and smell are notoriously strong.

4 boneless, skinless
  chicken-breast halves
2½ cups vegetable oil
5 garlic cloves, chopped
juice of 2 limes
1 tablespoon soy sauce

1 tablespoon Thai or
  Vietnamese fish sauce
  (optional) or salt to
  taste
1 teaspoon sugar
2 red chiles, sliced finely

1. Cut each chicken breast into 8 pieces. Heat the oil in a deep skillet over medium-high heat until it sizzles when a little piece of bread is added and fry the chicken pieces, in batches, until golden brown, draining chicken on paper towels after cooking.

2. Pour out the oil and clean the pan. Add ¼ cup water, the lime

juice, soy sauce, fish sauce, sugar and chiles. Add the chicken and simmer until tender, about 10 minutes. Pick out some of the garlic and discard before serving.

Per serving: 173 calories, 3 g carbohydrates, 28 g protein, 5 g fat

---

GRAPEVINE- AND ROSEMARY-SMOKED CORNISH GAME HENS

Yield: 8 servings

Grapevine cuttings are available at some specialty shops and home center stores. Soak the dried vine cuttings and the rosemary sprigs in water before adding to the grill fire. Cuttings that are green inside when snapped in two do not need to be soaked.

4 Cornish game hens
6 large garlic cloves
⅓ cup fresh rosemary leaves, lightly crushed, plus handfuls of fresh rosemary sprigs for grilling
1 tablespoon fresh

marjoram leaves
freshly ground black pepper
1 small bunch fresh thyme
½ cup extra-virgin olive oil
kosher or coarse sea salt
1 dozen grapevine cuttings

1. Rinse hens and pat dry. Split along backbone with shears, and cut away and discard backbone. Open out hens on work surface, skin-side up. With the palm of hand, push sharply and hard on breast-bones to crack and flatten breasts. Make a slit in skin at base of each thigh and tuck end of each drumstick in slit to anchor it.

2. Place hens in a large shallow non reactive bowl or pan. Put garlic through a garlic press and spread onto birds. Sprinkle rosemary, marjoram and generous grindings of pepper on birds and rub seasonings into surface. Layer whole thyme sprigs on and between birds. Pour olive oil over birds and turn to coat. Marinate in refrigerator at least 2 hours, turning occasionally, or overnight.

3. Remove the hens from the refrigerator 20 minutes before cooking. Heat a gas grill to medium or place coals at sides of grill, leaving center as indirect cooking area. When coals are ashen and glowing,

add rosemary stalks and cuttings to coals. Place game hens over indirect heat, skin-side up, and salt to taste. Grill hens 15 minutes, then turn skin-side down and sprinkle with salt to taste. Add more vine cuttings if needed. Grill hens until cooked through, about 15 more minutes. Move to hottest part of fire during last 5 minutes of cooking to crisp skin. Cut in half to serve.

Per serving: 335 calories, 0 carbohydrates, 29 g protein, 24 g fat

CHICKEN FRICASSEE

Yield: 4 servings

This hearty, brothy stew is even better made a day ahead of time so the flavorful juices of the chicken and all the vegetables can marry.

3 celery stalks
1 carrot, peeled
2 tomatoes
2 leeks
2 cups coarsely shredded
    green cabbage
nonstick cooking spray
4 skinless, boneless chicken-
    breast halves

1/2 cup dry white wine
2 garlic cloves, crushed
2 teaspoons chopped fresh or
    1 teaspoon dried tarragon
1 teaspoon caraway seeds
1 bay leaf
3 (14 1/2-ounce) cans reduced-
    sodium chicken broth
chopped parsley for garnish

1. Cut the celery and carrots into 1-inch slices. Quarter, skin and seed the tomatoes. Trim the leeks, cut off the tough green, and split them. Rinse well and cut crosswise into 1/2-inch pieces. Core the cabbage and cut into 8 wedges.

2. Grease a 4- to 5- quart saucepan with cooking spray and place over medium heat. Add the chicken breasts and cook on each side until lightly browned. Add the leeks, celery, garlic and wine and cook 5 minutes. Add the carrots, tomatoes, cabbage, tarragon, caraway seeds, bay leaf and chicken broth. Heat to boiling over high heat, reduce heat to low and cook, covered, until the vegetables are tender, about 30 minutes. Remove the bay leaf.

3. Spoon the chicken and vegetables into heated soup plates with some of the broth. Sprinkle each with parsley.

Per serving: 285 calories, 18 g carbohydrates, 36 g protein, 5 g fat

TARRAGON CHICKEN PATTIES

Yield: 4 servings
(serving size: 1 patty and 1 tablespoon sauce)

If you can't find ground chicken, you can buy boneless, skinless thighs and grind them in a food processor.

1 pound ground raw chicken
 thighs
½ cup chopped onion
¼ cup fine dried breadcrumbs
2½ tablespoons dried parsley
 flakes
½ teaspoon dried thyme
 leaves
½ teaspoon freshly ground

 pepper
¼ teaspoon salt
1 egg white
¼ cup all-purpose flour
nonstick cooking spray
1 teaspoon olive oil
½ cup dry white wine
½ teaspoon dried tarragon
 leaves

1. Combine the chicken, onion, breadcrumbs, parsley, thyme, pepper, salt and egg white in a bowl and mix gently but thoroughly.

2. Divide the chicken mixture into 4 equal portions and shape each into a ³⁄₄-inch-thick patty. Place the flour in a shallow dish, dredge the patties in flour and set aside.

3. Grease a nonstick skillet with cooking spray, add the oil and heat over medium heat until hot. Add the patties and cook 3 minutes on each side. Cover and cook until no longer pink in the center, about 3 minutes longer.

4. Remove the patties from the skillet, set aside and keep warm. Add the wine and tarragon to the skillet and heat to boiling, scraping the bottom of the pan with a wooden spoon to loosen any browned bits. Cook until the wine is reduced by half, about 1 minute.

Per serving: 232 calories, 13 g carbohydrates, 25 g protein, 6 g fat

CHICKEN BREASTS
IN RED-WINE SAUCE

Yield: 8 servings

You can omit the confit portion of this for a quicker preparation of the long-cooking classic.

1 tablespoon plus 2 ounces butter
8 ounces shallots, peeled and parboiled until tender
2 tablespoons sugar
1¼ cups chicken broth
¼ bottle fruity red wine
1 teaspoon vegetable oil
8 ounces smoked ham or bacon, cut into 1-inch-by-½-inch lardons
1 pound button mushrooms
2 whole boneless chicken breasts, split (4 halves)
CHICKEN CONFIT (optional)
chopped tomatoes for garnish
fresh basil sprigs for garnish

1. Melt 1 tablespoon of the butter in a medium nonstick skillet over medium heat and add the shallots. Sprinkle with the sugar and turn to coat. Cook, shaking the pan frequently until the sugar has melted and glazed the shallots. Set aside and keep warm.

2. Place the chicken broth in a 2-quart saucepan and boil until it has reduced by half. Add the wine and set aside.

3. For the chicken: Preheat the oven to 350 degrees. Heat 1 teaspoon vegetable oil in a clean Dutch oven on the stovetop over medium-high heat and fry the lardons until they render their fat and are crisp. Remove to a plate. Add the mushrooms and cook until browned. Remove to a bowl. Pan-sear the chicken breasts skin-side down. Turn and sear the other side. Roast the breasts in the oven until they are cooked through, turning over once, for 7 to 10 minutes in all.

4. To serve: Reheat the shallots, lardons and mushrooms. Slice the chicken breasts diagonally into ¼-inch pieces and, keeping the breasts assembled, transfer each to a warm dinner plate. Reheat the sauce to boiling and remove from the heat. Whisk in the remaining 2 ounces butter until it melts and thickens the sauce. Serve the sauce around the chicken. Place a leg of Chicken Confit, if used, on top of the chicken. Garnish with piles of the chopped tomatoes, ham or bacon lardons, shallots and mushrooms and a basil sprig on each dish.

Per serving (without the Chicken Confit): 681 calories, 19 g carbohydrates, 47 g protein, 43 g fat

CHICKEN CONFIT

Yield: 4 servings of chicken

This special dish applies an ancient method of preserving meat, usually goose, duck or pork, whereby the cooked-in-its-own-fat meat becomes as soft as butter but not as greasy. A seal of fat prevents the meat from spoiling. Here, chicken legs take a turn at short-term immortality. Turn them into something even more amazing by crisping up the skin so the tender flesh has something to contrast with. The confit fat can be used for cooking instead of butter or oil and it can also add an amazing richness to steamed vegetables.

1 quart rendered chicken,
   duck or goose fat
4 whole chicken legs
1 small red onion, sliced
12 garlic cloves, peeled
1 (3-inch) stick cinnamon

2 whole star anise
rind of 1 orange or
   lemon
1 teaspoon salt
½ teaspoon freshly ground
   pepper

1. For the confit: Preheat the oven to 300 degrees. Place the chicken fat in a heavy deep casserole or Dutch oven and bake until melted. Add the chicken legs and add all the confit ingredients, season with salt and pepper and mix well, pressing the chicken legs down into the fat. Cover with foil or the pan lid and bake until the chicken has almost fallen off the bone, about 2 hours. Remove the confit from oven and set aside until the mixture has totally cooled. Remove the legs from the confit juices and place on a baking sheet. Bake until the skin is crisp, about 25 minutes.

2. Preheat the oven to 350 degrees. Cut the crisped chicken legs in half at the joint and serve.

Per chicken leg: 70 calories, 0 carbohydrates, 8 g protein, 4 g fat

GRILLED LEMON CHICKEN WITH ONION SAUCE

Yield: 6 servings

Dark-meat chicken reaches its potential in the barbecue pit. It stays moist, even without the skin, and adapts to any seasoning. The onion sauce conveniently cooks alongside the chicken.

½ cup fresh lemon juice
1 tablespoon vegetable oil
1 vegetable-flavored bouillon
  cube
2 teaspoons minced fresh
  thyme
¼ teaspoon freshly ground
  pepper

6 skinless chicken
  drumsticks
6 skinless chicken thighs
4 large onions, thinly sliced
  and separated into rings
2 bay leaves
1 garlic clove, crushed
nonstick cooking spray

1. Combine the lemon juice, oil and bouillon cube in a large bowl, and stir until the bouillon cube dissolves. Add the thyme, pepper, chicken, onions, bay leaf and garlic and toss well to coat. Cover and marinate in the refrigerator at least 2 hours.

2. Remove the chicken to a bowl. Place the marinade in the center of a sheet of heavy-duty aluminum foil and gather the edges of the foil together to form a pouch. Tightly seal the edges and set aside.

3. Prepare an outdoor grill for barbecuing. Grease the grill rack with cooking spray and place over the coals. Arrange the chicken on the grill rack and grill 20 minutes. Turn the chicken over and place the foil pouch on the grill rack. Grill until chicken is done and onions are tender, about 20 minutes, turning the foil pouch occasionally. Discard the bay leaves.

Per serving: 223 calories, 11 g carbohydrates, 28 g protein, 7 g fat

DAY-AFTER-THANKSGIVING HASH

Yield: 2 to 3 servings

4 tablespoons butter
½ onion, finely diced
1 small garlic clove, crushed
½ teaspoon chopped fresh
   rosemary
1 cup cooked brussels sprouts,

   coarsely chopped
salt and pepper to taste
2 cups shredded cooked turkey
1 cup cooked mashed potatoes
½ cup leftover gravy
1 bunch chives, chopped

1. Melt the butter in a large nonstick skillet over medium heat and sauté the onion, garlic and rosemary until fragrant, about 3 minutes. Add the brussels sprouts and season with salt and pepper. Cook, stirring, until hot. Fold in the turkey and mashed potatoes and stir to combine. Stir in the gravy.

2. Leave the hash mixture to cook and form a crust underneath, then break it up and cook until the pieces are crispy but still moist. Sprinkle with the chives before serving.

Each of 3 servings: 403 calories, 20 g carbohydrates, 32 g protein, 22 g fat

CHICKEN STROGANOFF WITH TARRAGON

Yield: 4 servings

You can cook some sliced mushrooms in with the chicken to stretch the portions and add an extra "stroganoff" touch.

2 ounces butter
4 large boneless, skinless
   chicken breasts sliced into
   ½-inch strips
leaves from 8 sprigs tarragon
a dash of brandy

a dash of sherry
½ cup heavy cream
½ cup low-fat plain
   yogurt
salt and pepper
fresh lemon juice to taste

1. Melt the butter in a large skillet and add the chicken and tarragon. Cook over high heat, stirring frequently, until the chicken is slightly colored on all sides for about 3 minutes.

2. Add the brandy or sherry, cream and yogurt. Let it simmer for a few minutes to thicken and finish cooking the chicken. Season to taste and add a good squeeze of lemon juice. Taste again, to make sure you have the right balance of flavors.

Per serving: 410 calories, 3 g carbohydrates, 42 g protein, 25 g fat

CHICKEN BURGERS IN PARMA HAM

Yield: 2 servings

The sweet and salty ham wrap makes a tasty crust when fried. The burger stays tender and moist inside.

12 ounces ground chicken
1 large onion, diced and cooked
1 red chile, seeded and chopped
½ cup grated Parmesan cheese
½ cup fresh white breadcrumbs

1 tablespoon chopped sage
salt to taste
freshly ground pepper to taste
4 slices Parma ham

1. In a mixing bowl, combine the chicken, cooked onion, chile, cheese, breadcrumbs and sage and mix well. Season with salt and pepper.

2. Take 2 pieces of ham and lay over each other in a cross. Take half of the chicken mix and pat into a burger shape, placing in the middle of the cross, then fold the pieces of ham over into a parcel shape. Repeat with the remaining chicken mixture and ham. Cook the burgers on a hot oiled griddle pan over medium heat for 10 to 12 minutes or until cooked through.

Per serving: 433 calories, 15 g carbohydrates, 54 g protein, 16 g fat

CHICKEN WITH PINENUTS AND RED PEPPER

Yield: 2 servings

The flavor of a pepper when it is roasted is so intense that a little goes a long way. The crème fraîche is a rich medium and makes a decadent sauce.

1 red bell pepper
salt to taste
freshly ground pepper to taste
1 pinch chili powder or
  cayenne pepper
1 tablespoon all-purpose flour
2 boneless, skinless chicken-
  breast halves
1½ tablespoons sunflower oil

2 tablespoons sliced scallions
1 teaspoon chopped fresh
  tarragon plus extra for garnish
1 teaspoon Dijon mustard
2 tablespoons pinenuts plus
  1 tablespoon chopped for
  garnish
1 (8-ounce) container crème
  fraîche

1. Preheat the broiler. Halve and seed the pepper and broil on a baking sheet until the skins turn black. Place the pepper in a plastic bag until cool. Peel away the skin and cut the flesh into narrow strips.

2. Blend the seasonings with the flour and coat the chicken breast halves with the mixture. Heat the oil in the skillet and cook the chicken until golden brown and almost tender. Add the scallions and stir over the heat for several minutes or until golden. Add nearly all the roasted-pepper strips, the tarragon, mustard, pinenuts and crème fraîche. Stir until blended and heat through.

3. Serve topped with the remaining strips of red pepper and the extra tarragon and pinenuts.

Per serving: 586 calories, 15 g carbohydrates, 34 g protein, 44 g fat

CHICKEN STIR-BOIL

Yield: 4 servings

Stir-fry has a buddy that needs a PR campaign. Here chicken is cooked twice, with the skin on. Then the cut, skinned pieces are finished cooking with a trio of vegetables that was "sautéed" in broth. The result is a bowl of tender, plump vegetables and meat in a bath of flavorful juices.

2 cups chicken broth
1/4 teaspoon olive oil
4 (6-ounce) boneless chicken breasts with skin on
8 ounces fresh mushrooms, quartered
8 ounces frozen lima beans
1 (8-ounce) can whole water chestnuts, drained

1 tablespoon chopped fresh dill
1 tablespoon fresh lemon juice
1/4 teaspoon freshly ground salt
1/4 teaspoon freshly ground pepper
1/4 teaspoon cayenne pepper
2 teaspoons arrowroot mixed with 1 teaspoon of water

1. Pour the chicken broth into a large skillet and boil until reduced to 1/2 cup, about 15 minutes.

2. While the broth is reducing, brush a large skillet over medium high heat with the oil and place the chicken breasts skin-side down in the skillet to brown, turning them every 2 minutes for a total of 10 minutes.

3. Remove the skillet from the heat, transfer the chicken to a plate and pull off and discard the skin. Slice the chicken into 2 by 1/2-inch strips. If you see a little pink color, don't worry, the chicken will cook a bit more in the next step. Blot the skillet with a paper towel to absorb the excess fat.

4. Pour 1/4 cup water into the skillet and deglaze over a high heat, scraping all the residues up into the liquid. Add the chicken broth. The moment it comes to a boil, add the mushrooms, lima beans and water chestnuts and "stir-boil" until just tender, about 5 minutes.

5. Stir in the cooked chicken and heat through. Stir in the dill, lemon juice, salt, black pepper and cayenne.

6. Remove from the heat and tip the pan so that the juices collect

in a clear space. Stir in the arrowroot mixture, return to heat and stir until thickened. Serve in bowls and don't miss a single drop.

Per serving: 421 calories, 22 g carbohydrates, 44 g protein, 17 g fat

CHICKEN AND SPINACH WITH WHITE-WINE AND MUSHROOM SAUCE

Yield: 8 servings

World-wide, the ingredients in this dish seem to go 'round and round' in all manner of combinations, always pleasing with the finale. This incarnation is vibrant with quick-cooked flavors and aromas.

3 ounces butter
1 teaspoon vegetable oil
4 boneless chicken-breast halves
½ cup dry white wine
2 tablespoons finely chopped shallots
5 ounces wild or button mushrooms, sliced
¼ cup heavy cream or crème fraîche
3 cups fresh rinsed baby spinach leaves
salt to taste
freshly ground pepper to taste
1 tablespoon minced fresh parsley

1. In a large nonstick skillet, melt 1 ounce of the butter in the oil over medium heat. Place the chicken skin-side down and cook slowly, 10 to 12 minutes, allowing the skin to turn a nice golden brown color. Turn over and cook until juices run clear, a further 7 to 10 minutes.

2. Remove the chicken from the pan and keep warm. Pour off any fat and put the pan over high heat.

3. Pour half of the wine into the hot pan and scrape with a wooden spoon to release any caramelized bits of chicken from the pan. Pour the deglazed liquid into a pitcher and set aside.

4. Clean the pan and return to medium heat. Add 1 ounce of the remaining butter and cook the shallots for 1 minute without coloring them. Add the mushrooms and sauté quickly, again without col-

oring. Add the remaining wine and deglazed liquid to the pan, turn up the heat and reduce the liquid by one-third. Add the cream. Heat to boiling, season with salt and pepper to taste and remove from the heat, keeping it warm.

5. In a very hot wok, add the remaining butter and at the same time throw in the spinach. Stir continuously and in seconds the spinach will wilt and be cooked. Season with salt and pepper and serve under the chicken breast.

6. Reheat the sauce, stir in the chopped parsley and pour the sauce around the chicken and spinach.

Per serving: 440 calories, 4 g carbohydrates, 33 g protein, 31 g fat

CHICKEN STUFFED WITH FRESH GINGER AND SCALLIONS

Yield: 4 servings

White wine and heavy cream combine to flavor and enrich the sauce. It lightly coats the chicken and a bed of stir-fried potatoes and sugar snap peas.

3 tablespoons olive oil
4 (6-ounce) boneless chicken breasts with the skin on
1 bunch scallions, trimmed and finely chopped
1-inch piece fresh gingerroot, peeled and finely chopped
salt to taste
freshly ground pepper to taste

FOR THE SAUCE
½ cup dry white wine
½ cup chicken broth
½ cup heavy cream
1-inch piece fresh gingerroot, peeled and thinly sliced
1 bunch scallions, trimmed and finely chopped
POTATO AND SUGAR-SNAP SAUTÉ for serving (see page 276)

1. Preheat the oven to 325 degrees. Line a baking pan with aluminum foil.

2. Heat 2 tablespoons of the oil in a skillet over a medium-high heat and cook the chicken until just golden brown on the outside but still raw in the center. Remove it to a plate and let cool a little.

3. Add another tablespoon of oil to the pan and stir in the scallions and ginger. Gently fry for 5 minutes, until softened but not colored. Remove the pan from the heat and season lightly.

4. Using a sharp knife, make 4 oblique cuts, evenly spaced, to the center of each chicken breast. Push a little of the scallion and ginger mixture into each cut so that the flavors penetrate well into the meat. Transfer the chicken to the prepared baking pan and bake 10 to 12 minutes, or until the chicken is cooked through.

5. For the sauce: Pour the wine into a small pan and reduce it by half. Add the chicken broth and reduce by half. Stir in the cream, ginger and scallions. Heat to simmering and season to taste.

6. Serve each chicken breast on a bed of the Potato and Sugar-Snap Sauté with the sauce spooned over the chicken.

Per serving: 638 calories, 16 g carbohydrates, 40 g protein, 44 g fat

CHICKEN TIKKA

Yield: 4 servings

These East Indian kabobs are family-friendly and party-perfect because the chicken can marinate in the refrigerator up to 2 days in advance of serving. You can find the spices and other special ingredients at East Indian grocery stores.

1½ pounds boneless, skinless chicken breasts or thighs
1½ tablespoons fresh lemon juice
1 teaspoon salt
1 teaspoon sugar
⅓ cup plain yogurt
⅓ cup half-and-half
1 tablespoon finely grated peeled fresh gingerroot
2 teaspoons pureed garlic
2 teaspoons ground cumin
1 teaspoon ground coriander
1 teaspoon balti garam masala
1 teaspoon turmeric
½ teaspoon chili powder
1 tablespoon besan (garbanzo bean or chickpea flour)
oil for greasing the foil
2 ounces melted butter for basting

TO GARNISH
raw onion rings
lemon wedges
tomato wedges
chopped fresh green chile

1. Cut the chicken into 1-inch chunks and place in a mixing bowl and add the lemon juice, salt and sugar. Mix thoroughly and set aside for 30 minutes.

2. Beat the yogurt and cream together in a bowl until smooth and add the remaining ingredients except for the oil, butter and the garnish. Pour the marinade over the chicken and stir to distribute and mix well. Cover and leave to marinate for 3 to 4 hours or overnight in the refrigerator. Once marinated it can be left in the refrigerator up to 48 hours.

3. Preheat the broiler to high. Line a grill pan with aluminum foil and brush with a little oil. Thread the chicken pieces onto skewers, leaving a slight gap between each piece. Place the skewers in the prepared grill pan and cook 4 inches from the element for 5 minutes. Baste generously with melted butter, reduce heat slightly and cook for a further 5 minutes. Turn the skewers over and brush with more butter. Cook for 4 to 5 minutes, remove the chicken from the skewers and place in a serving dish. Garnish with the onion, lemon, tomatoes and chili.

Per serving: 256 calories, 9 g carbohydrates, 42 g protein, 5 g fat

CHICKEN STEWED IN STOUT

Yield: 6 servings

The deep, roasted-barley flavor of stout makes this a decidedly unique and delicious approach to chicken and the traditional vegetables in a stew.

2 tablespoons oil
1 ounce butter
20 baby onions
1 chicken, cut into 8 pieces
1/4 cup gin
1 tablespoon all-purpose flour
1 1/4 cups Guinness or other dark stout

8 ounces button mushrooms, small
1 celery stalk, sliced
1 carrot, peeled and sliced
3 slices white bread
1/4 cup crème fraîche
1 tablespoon chopped fresh parsley

1. Preheat the oven to 350 degrees. Heat the oil and butter in a Dutch oven. Add the onions and sauté until browned. Add the chicken pieces and brown on both sides. Add the gin and carefully ignite. When the flames subside, sprinkle with the flour and cook, stirring, for 1 to 2 minutes. Add the Guinness, heat to boiling, and cook, stirring with a wood-

en spoon to loosen any browned bits, until the bubbles have subsided.

2. Add the mushrooms, carrot and celery. Heat to boiling, cover and bake for 40 to 45 minutes.

3. Meanwhile, toast the bread. Cut out 4 heart shapes from each slice with a cookie cutter and keep warm.

4. Skim off any fat from the stew. Reheat the stew and whisk in the crème fraîche. Adjust the seasoning and serve with the heart-shaped croutons.

Per serving: 384 calories, 19 g carbohydrates, 31 g protein, 16 g fat

RED MOLE WITH TURKEY

Yield: 16 servings

This is a classic combination. The earthy flavor of the sauce meets and matches the rich meaty taste of the bird. You may start a new Thanksgiving tradition!

1 whole (about 4 pounds)
   boneless turkey breast with
   skin on or 2 (2-pound) turkey
   breast halves
salt and pepper

2 tablespoons olive oil

RED MOLE
sesame seeds for garnish
watercress sprigs for garnish

1. Cut the whole turkey breast into 2 halves. Sprinkle the turkey breast halves with salt and pepper. Heat 1 tablespoon of the oil in an 8- or 9-quart Dutch oven over medium-high heat. Brown one turkey-breast half, skin-side down first, on all sides, about 10 minutes total, and remove to a platter. Repeat with the remaining oil and turkey-breast half.

2. Preheat the oven to 325 degrees. Remove the fat from the pan and add the Red Mole. Heat slowly over medium heat until boiling. Add the turkey-breast halves and cover. Bake until an instant-read thermometer placed in the center of the turkey-breast halves registers 150 degrees, about 40 minutes, or until the meat is only a faint pink if you cut into it.

3. Remove the turkey to a cutting board, cover with foil and let stand for 10 minutes.

4. To serve, slice the turkey into ½-inch thick slices and arrange them overlapping on a deep platter. Thin the mole sauce if necessary with hot water to a coating consistency. Taste and adjust the sugar and/or salt if necessary. Ladle a generous amount of sauce over the turkey and pass more at the table. Sprinkle the turkey with sesame seeds and garnish with watercress.

Per serving: 386 calories, 16 g carbohydrates, 37 g protein, 20 g fat

CHICKEN LEGS WITH JERUSALEM ARTICHOKES

Yield: 6 servings

A hands-on approach to meat separates the real cooks from the wanna-be's. Here, to get most chicken off the bones and have them in the perfect pieces, you have to be committed and dig in.

8 (8-ounce) whole chicken legs
1 teaspoon olive oil
1 yellow onion, peeled and thinly sliced
2 garlic cloves, peeled, crushed and chopped
½ (6-ounce) can low-sodium tomato paste
2 cups chicken broth
12 ounces Jerusalem artichokes, peeled and coarsely chopped
1¼ cups de-alcoholized white wine
1 tablespoon plus 1 teaspoon minced fresh oregano leaves
½ teaspoon freshly ground pepper
¼ teaspoon freshly ground salt
1 cup black olives
1 tablespoon chopped fresh parsley

1. Preheat the oven to 425 degrees. Place the chicken pieces on a rack in a roasting pan and bake for 50 minutes.

2. Meanwhile, heat the oil into a large saucepan over medium-high heat and fry the onion and garlic until translucent, about 4 minutes. Stir in the tomato paste until completely incorporated, turn up the heat a notch, allowing the natural sugars in the tomato paste to go light brown and caramelize, about 10 minutes.

3. Pour in the broth, artichokes, 1 cup of the wine, 1 tablespoon of the oregano, half of the black pepper and the salt, cover and simmer for 8 minutes. Add the olives to the sauce and heat through.

4. Remove the chicken from the oven and transfer the chicken to a bowl. Pour the chicken drippings from the pan into a fat strainer pitcher and allow the fat to rise to the top. Place the pan on the stovetop, add the remaining wine and scrape up the residues. Add the chicken cooking liquid to the sauce until the fat comes to the level of the spout. Whisk the sauce to combine, boil until it has reduced to a nice coating consistency and keep warm.

5. Remove the skin from the cooked chicken, using a bowl of ice water to cool down your fingers. It's about 3 seconds between dips for normal, 4 seconds for macho and 5 seconds for super macho. I must say that tongs don't do a good job, so get in and let your fingers do the working. Separate into major meat pieces according to muscle lines and add to the sauce. Stir in the remaining oregano and pepper.

6. To serve, spoon into individual bowls and garnish with parsley.

Per serving: 345 calories, 17 g carbohydrates, 39 g protein, 10 g fat

CURRIED APRICOT CHICKEN

Yield: 6 servings

Steaming hot lemon rice or rice pilaf makes a traditional side dish for curried dishes.

6 boneless, skinless chicken-breast halves
¼ cup whole-milk plain yogurt
2 teaspoons grated fresh peeled gingerroot
2 teaspoons garlic puree
10 dried apricots
1 green chile, seeded and chopped
3 tablespoons sunflower or vegetable oil
1 medium onion, finely sliced

2 teaspoons ground coriander
1 teaspoon ground cumin
½ teaspoon garam masala
½ to 1 teaspoon chili powder
½ teaspoon freshly grated nutmeg
1 teaspoon salt or to taste
½ teaspoon sugar
⅓ cup half-and-half
2 tablespoons chopped fresh cilantro

1. Cut each chicken breast diagonally into 2 to 3 chunky pieces. In a large mixing bowl, blend the yogurt, ginger and garlic together.

Add the chicken, mix well, cover and leave to marinate for 1 hour.

2. Roughly chop the apricots and soak them in 1 cup hot water in a bowl for 15 minutes. Pour the apricots and their soaking liquid into a blender, add the green chile and puree. Set aside.

3. In a heavy saucepan heat the oil over a medium heat and fry the onions until they are soft and lightly browned, 8 to 9 minutes.

4. Add all the spices (coriander through nutmeg) and cook for 1 minute. Add the marinated chicken and increase the heat slightly. Fry the chicken for 4 to 5 minutes until the pieces turn opaque. Add ¼ cup lukewarm water, cover the pan and reduce the heat to low. Simmer for 15 minutes.

5. Add the salt, sugar and pureed apricot/chile mixture. Cover the pan and simmer 15 minutes.

6. Add the half-and-half and cook, uncovered, for 5 minutes or until the sauce has reduced to the desired thickness. Taste and adjust the seasoning if necessary.

7. Stir in the cilantro, remove from heat and serve.

Per serving: calories, g carbohydrates, g protein, g fat 13 Calories, trace Total Fat, (13% calories from fat),trace Protein, 3g Carbohydrate, 0mg Cholesterol, 3mg Sodium

HOT-HOT CHICKEN

Yield: 4 servings

Serve with basmati rice and naan bread, raita or fruit chutney. Please note, this is a hot spicy dish. If you want it milder, use a tried-and-tested palate-safe sauce.

1 tablespoon vegetable oil
1 medium onion, roughly
  chopped
1 garlic clove, finely chopped
salt to taste
freshly ground pepper to taste
4 boneless, skinless chicken
  breast halves, chopped
into chunks
CURRY SAUCE made with hot
  curry powder (see page 324,
  omit the raisins)
4 medium tomatoes, skinned,
  seeded and roughly chopped
2 tablespoons chopped fresh
  cilantro

1. Preheat the oven to 350 degrees. Place the oil in a skillet over a medium heat and add the onion and garlic.

2. Season the chicken pieces with salt and freshly ground pepper and add them to the skillet. Brown the chicken pieces and then pour the contents of the skillet into a 2-quart baking dish. Pour the curry sauce over the chicken and mix the sauce through the chicken and onion. Cover the dish and bake the chicken for 45 minutes, adding the tomatoes, 10 minutes before the end of the cooking time.

3. Sprinkle with the cilantro just before serving.

Per serving: 501 calories, 19 g carbohydrates, 34 g protein, 33 g fat

GREEK CHICKEN

Yield: 4 servings

Packed with interesting flavors, these pita-bread sandwiches are a satisfying meal.

¼ cup plain Greek yogurt
2 tablespoons humuus
1 teaspoon ground cumin
1 teaspoon ground coriander
½ teaspoon turmeric
3 tablespoons fresh lime juice
1 tablespoon chopped fresh mint
pinch of salt

4 boneless, skinless chicken-breast halves, cut into thin strips
2 tablespoons BASIL OIL FOR SERVING (see page 313)
4 white pita bread loaves
mixed salad greens
sliced tomatoes
sliced yellow bell pepper

1. Mix together the yogurt and humuus in a bowl, cover and refrigerate.

2. In a shallow bowl blend together the cumin, coriander, turmeric, lime juice, mint and salt. Add the chicken to the spice mixture, mix well to coat chicken, cover and leave to marinate in a cool place for at least 30 minutes, stirring occasionally.

3. Heat the basil oil in a large skillet over medium heat and fry the chicken until cooked through, 8 to 10 minutes, stirring occasionally until golden.

4. Toast the pita loaves on each side until golden brown. Cut in half crossways, open up and fill with the chicken mixture. Add salad leaves, tomato slices and yellow bell pepper slices. Top with a generous spoonful of the humuus-yogurt mixture and serve immediately.

Per serving: 297 calories, 20 g carbohydrates, 31 g protein, 10 g

KIWI, LIME AND COCONUT CHICKEN

Yield: 4 servings

4 boneless, skinless chicken
  breast halves

MARINADE
2 to 3 kiwifruit, peeled and
  diced
1 tablespoon sherry vinegar
1 tablespoon lime juice
salt to taste
freshly ground pepper to taste

TO COOK
1 ounce butter
1 tablespoon olive oil
1 tablespoon honey

SAUCE
5 ounces canned coconut milk
3 tablespoons heavy cream
  (optional)
2 kiwifruits, peeled and diced
2 scallions, trimmed and
  minced
finely grated peel of 1 lime
salt to taste
freshly ground pepper to
  taste

TO GARNISH
1 tablespoon finely chopped
  parsley

1. Cut the chicken breasts into good-sized strips about ½ inch thick and 3 inches long.

2. Prepare the marinade by mixing together the diced kiwifruit, sherry vinegar, lime juice and seasoning in a shallow baking dish. Add the chicken strips, toss to coat and leave to marinate for 30 minutes.

3. To cook the chicken, melt the butter in the oil in a large nonstick skillet, add the honey and, when bubbling, add the chicken. The honey will sweeten the chicken during cooking, but be careful not to overcook. Cook, stirring for about 5 minutes, until the chicken is almost cooked and the liquid in the pan has reduced.

4. Add the coconut milk and, if liked, the cream. Add the diced kiwifruit, scallions, lime peel, salt and pepper. Simmer gently for 5 to 6 minutes over a low heat until the chicken is cooked through. Cooking time will vary with the thickness of the cooked chicken fillets, but test just before serving. Garnish with finely chopped parsley.

Per serving (with heavy cream): 360 calories, 12 g carbohydrates, 29 g protein, 23 g fat

TEX-MEX TURKEY STIR-FRY

Yield: 4 servings

You can cut up and measure all your ingredients up to a day ahead of cooking. That way when you come home after work and hit the door starving, you can have dinner on the table in less than 15 minutes.

1 pound turkey-breast cutlets	1/4 teaspoon ground cumin
1 large green bell pepper	1 teaspoon vegetable oil
1 large onion	1 cup corn kernels
nonstick cooking spray	3/4 cup bottled thick and
1 1/4 teaspoons chili powder	chunky salsa

1. Cut the turkey cutlets into 2 1/2 by 1/2-inch thick strips. Cut the onion crosswise into thin slices and separate into rings. Seed the pepper and cut into thin slices.

2. Coat a large nonstick skillet with cooking spray, and heat over high heat until hot. Add the turkey and stir-fry 3 minutes. Stir in the chili powder and cumin and stir-fry 1 minute. Remove the turkey to a bowl and set aside.

3. Add the oil to the skillet and heat over medium-high heat. Add the onion and pepper and stir-fry 3 minutes. Return turkey to skillet, and stir in the corn and salsa. Stir-fry until heated through, about 2 minutes.

Per serving: 257 calories, 15 g carbohydrates, 27 g protein, 10 g fat

WHISKY CHICKEN CURRY WITH ROASTED ALMONDS AND CREAM

Yield: 2 servings

2 boneless, skinless chicken breast halves
2 tablespoons oil
1 tablespoon butter
1 heaping tablespoon finely chopped onion or shallot
1 teaspoon curry powder
1 teaspoon grated rind of orange
salt to taste

freshly ground pepper to taste
2 tablespoons whisky
½ cup heavy cream

GARNISH
¼ cup roasted slivered almonds
sliced orange segments
1 teaspoon finely chopped fresh parsley

1. Cut the chicken into bite-size pieces. Heat 1 tablespoon of oil in a large nonstick skillet or wok over medium-high heat and briskly stir-fry the chicken pieces until almost fully cooked, about 5 minutes. Remove from pan and keep warm.

2. Add the remaining oil and butter to the pan and when the butter melts, add the onion and curry powder. Reduce the heat to low and cook gently for 2 to 3 minutes.

3. Return the chicken pieces to the pan and add the orange rind and seasoning.

4. Warm the whisky in a metal ladle, set alight and pour over the chicken, shaking the pan as you do so. Stir in cream and heat through until bubbling and slightly thickened.

5. Serve chicken on plates topped with almonds and garnished with orange segments plus some finely chopped parsley.

Per serving: 692 calories, 16 g carbohydrates, 34 g protein, 53 g fat

BACON-WRAPPED CHICKEN LOAF

Yield: 8 servings

This cold meat loaf can be an appetizer when spread on crackers, an elegant first course with pickles, or a tasty sandwich filling. Use the flavorful cooking fat and juices instead of butter on vegetables.

1 large chicken (about 4 pounds) or two 2-pound chickens, poached until tender and cooled
3/4 cup chicken broth
1 shallot or small onion, finely chopped
a pinch of ground cloves
a pinch of ground allspice
2 tablespoons butter
12 slices bacon
salt and pepper to taste
1 cup clarified butter

1. Remove the skin and bones from the chicken and finely chop the meat. Place the meat in a medium bowl and add the stock, shallot, cloves and allspice. Mix well and season with salt and pepper. In batches, pulse in a food processor or blender until smooth.

2. Preheat the oven to 350 degrees. Grease a 9 by 5 by 3-inch loaf pan with 1 tablespoon of the butter. Stretch each slice of bacon until it is as thin as possible without breaking it, holding one end while lightly pressing toward the other end with the flat side of a knife. Line the pan with the bacon, reserving some for the top. Add the chicken mixture and spread it to flatten the top. Dot the top with pieces of the remaining tablespoon butter and then cover with the reserved bacon and wrap the whole pan tightly in heavy-duty aluminum foil.

3. Place the loaf pan in a roasting pan on the middle oven rack and add enough boiling water to reach halfway up the side of the casserole. Place an ovenproof weight or another loaf pan partially filled with water on top of the filled loaf pan to weight it down while cooking. Bake until an instant-read thermometer inserted through the foil into the center of the loaf reads 165 degrees, about 1 hour. Let cool, covered, and then run a knife around the edges and leave to get cold.

4. When cold, press down with a spoon, pour the clarified butter over the top, and keep in a cold place until ready to serve.

Per serving: 589 calories, 1 g carbohydrates, 33 g protein, 50 g fat

TURKEY AND PESTO PATTIES WITH GRILLED RED ONIONS

Yield: 2 servings

You can turn these into appetizers for 4 by making the patties smaller or shaping them into little meatballs.

8 ounces ground
  turkey
⅓ cup dried breadcrumbs
2 tablespoons PESTO SAUCE
  (see pages 320-321)

salt and freshly ground black
  pepper
Char-GRILLED RED-ONION
  WEDGES for serving (see
  page 286)

1. Combine the turkey with the breadcrumbs and pesto and season with salt and pepper.

2. Form the turkey mixture into small patties and fry for 6 to 7 minutes on each side or until cooked. Serve with the Char-Grilled Red-Onion Wedges.

Per serving: 391 calories, 19 g carbohydrates, 24 g protein, 15 g fat

TURKEY-VEGETABLE STIR-FRY

Yield: 2 servings

Fresh bean sprouts are so earthy, crisp and juicy that you'll want to make a special trip to Chinatown or a special produce department just to get them.

nonstick cooking spray
8 ounces turkey-breast cutlets,
  cut into 2-inch-by-½-inch
  strips
1 garlic clove, minced
1 teaspoon Dijon mustard
½ teaspoon grated peeled
  fresh gingerroot

⅛ teaspoon dried thyme
  leaves
⅛ teaspoon salt
pinch of ground white pepper
1½ cups fresh bean sprouts
½ cup coarsely shredded
  carrot
¼ cup sliced scallions

Grease a wok or large nonstick skillet with cooking spray and heat over amedium-high heat until hot. Add the turkey and stir-fry 5 minutes. Add the garlic, mustard, gingerroot, thyme, salt and pepper and stir-fry 30 seconds. Add the bean sprouts, carrot and scallions and stir-fry 1 minute longer.

Per serving: 217 calories, 8 g carbohydrates, 28 g protein, 8 g fat

---

TURKEY MEATBALL STROGANOFF WITH MUSTARD-GREEN "FETTUCCINE"

Yield: 6 servings

Horseradish and grape jelly are the surprise ingredients in these tender, sweet and sour meatballs.

MEATBALLS
½ teaspoon light olive oil
¼ teaspoon dark sesame oil
1 small onion, finely diced
2 large garlic cloves, peeled and chopped
1 pound ground turkey
¼ cup matzo meal
2 tablespoons liquid egg substitute
1 tablespoon prepared horseradish
2 teaspoons dried thyme leaves
½ teaspoon fresh lemon juice
¼ teaspoon freshly ground

black pepper
⅛ teaspoon freshly ground sea salt
2 cups low-sodium V-8 juice
1 tablespoon all-fruit grape jelly
15 medium mushrooms, stems trimmed
1 tablespoon cornstarch
2 teaspoons dried sage leaves, crumbled
1 teaspoon ground cumin

FOR SERVING
8 cups cleaned, trimmed, fettuccine-width shreds of raw mustard greens

1. Heat the oils in a small skillet over medium heat and fry the onion and garlic for 2 minutes. Place the turkey in a large bowl, add the cooked onions and garlic, the matzo meal, egg substitute, horseradish, thyme, lemon juice, pepper and salt and mix well. Shape the mixture into balls, using ¼ cup of the mixture to make each meatball. Set aside.

2. Combine the V-8 juice, 1 cup water and the jelly in a small Dutch oven over medium-high heat and heat to boiling, stirring to dissolve the jelly. Add the meatballs and the mushrooms and simmer for 20 minutes. Remove from the heat. Mix the cornstarch with 2 tablespoons water until dissolved and stir into the sauce. Heat to boiling and cook until thickened and clear, about 30 seconds. Season with sage and cumin and keep warm.

3. Steam the mustard greens until just tender and keep warm.

4. To serve: Make a fettuccine-greens nest on each individual plate, nestle in 3 each of the turkey meatballs and 3 or 4 mushrooms, and ladle $1/2$ cup of the sauce over the top.

Per serving: 212 calories, 19 g carbohydrates, 19 g protein, 8 g fat

NUTTY TURKEY BURGERS

Yield: 4 servings

The texture of these tender burgers is made more interesting with an assortment of toasted nuts.

1 pound ground raw turkey
1 medium onion, chopped
$1/2$ cup chopped toasted mixed
   nuts
$3/4$ cup fresh breadcrumbs
1 teaspoon dried mixed
   herbs
salt to taste
freshly ground pepper to taste
2 eggs, beaten
oil for shallow-frying

TO COAT
2 tablespoons all-purpose
   flour
1 egg, beaten
$3/4$ cup fresh breadcrumbs
oil for shallow frying

FOR SERVING
4 cups mesclun greens tossed
   with a little olive oil, red-wine
   vinegar, salt and pepper

1. Place the burger ingredients in a bowl and mix gently but thoroughly. Shape into eight $1/2$-inch thick, 3-inch rounds.

2. To coat, place the flour on a plate, the egg in a shallow bowl and the breadcrumbs on another plate. Coat the burgers with the flour. Dip into the beaten egg and then coat with the breadcrumbs. Refrigerate for 10 minutes to firm up the patties.

3. Shallow fry the burgers in hot oil in a skillet over medium heat until golden brown on both sides, 10 to 15 minutes in all. Serve immediately on a bed of mesclun salad.

Per serving: 431 calories, 19 g carbohydrates, 30 g protein, 26 g fat

HONEY-TURKEY FAJITAS

Yield: 8 servings

You can substitute chicken breast or pork tenderloin for the turkey. These margarita-inspired seasonings go well with many meats.

1 pound (uncooked) turkey
  breast
juice and grated rind of 1 lime
juice of 1 orange
1 red chili pepper, finely diced
2 tablespoons tequila
2 tablespoons olive oil
1 tablespoon strong-flavored
  honey

1 teaspoon chopped fresh
  cilantro plus additional
  for serving
salt and pepper to
  taste
8 warm flour tortillas
1 (8-ounce) container crème
  fraîche or sour cream for
  serving

1. Cut the turkey into strips no longer than your little finger. Place in a large bowl and add the lime juice and grated rind, orange juice, chili, tequila, oil, honey and 1 teaspoon cilantro. Mix well. Cover and marinate in the refrigerator for 4 to 6 hours.

2. When ready to serve, heat a heavy, nonstick skillet. Drain the turkey, reserving the marinade. Add the turkey to the skillet and cook rapidly to brown quickly. Add the marinade and heat to boiling over medium high heat while stirring the turkey. Cook until the turkey is glazed and the marinade has sizzled away. Season with salt and pepper.

3. Sprinkle the tortillas with a little water and heat for 30 seconds in another skillet. Place a little turkey on each tortilla, fold and serve with a little crème fraîche and chopped cilantro.

Per serving: 292 calories, 20 g carbohydrates, 16 g protein, 15 g fat

ROAST QUAIL WITH JUNIPER BUTTER

Yield: 2 servings

Allow one, two or three birds per person. A first-course is probably a single-bird portion but as a main dish, the amount depends on the appetite. Use your hands so you can get to all the flavorful meat.

6 tablespoons butter, softened
3 tablespoons chopped fresh
  parsley
1 tablespoon juniper berries,
  crushed
1 tablespoon fresh lemon juice
salt to taste
freshly ground pepper to taste

6 quail (preferably trussed)
6 slices of bacon
6 slices white bread, toasted,
  crusts removed

GARNISH
celery leaves
parsley sprigs

1. Blend the butter with the juniper berries, chopped parsley, salt and pepper. Shape into a log on a sheet of waxed paper and roll up. Place in the freezer to harden.

2. Place the rack in the center of the oven. Preheat the oven to 500 degrees. Season the quail with salt and pepper. Wrap 2 strips of bacon around each quail and secure underneath with toothpicks. Place the birds in a roasting pan and roast for 5 minutes. Turn the birds over using tongs and roast until cooked to desired doneness, about 10 minutes

3. To serve: Place a slice of the toast on each dinner plate and top with the quail to absorb the juices. Slice the juniper butter and arrange the slices over the quail. Garnish with celery leaves and parsley sprigs and serve immediately.

Per serving: 419 calories, 13 g carbohydrates, 24 g protein, 30 g fat

PHEASANT BRAISED WITH RED CABBAGE AND APPLES

Yield: 4 servings

1 pheasant
2 ounces butter
1 slice bacon, diced
1 onion
1 garlic clove
4 cups shredded red cabbage
1 large apple, peeled, cored

and diced
¼ cup red wine
2 tablespoons wine vinegar
1 tablespoon soft brown sugar
salt to taste
freshly ground pepper to
    taste

1. To cut up the pheasant: Cut the pheasant in half and remove the breasts (on the bone) with the wings attached. Cut off the pinion and second joint on each wing and discard. Cut off the legs and separate at the joints. Discard the backbone.

2. Heat a Dutch oven over medium-high heat. Melt the butter and brown the pheasant joints all over. Remove and place to one side. Reduce the heat, add the diced bacon and fry until crisp. Add the onion and garlic and cook until colored lightly. Add the shredded cabbage, diced apple, red wine, vinegar and sugar. Season well.

3. Place the pheasant breasts on the vegetables and place the leg joints on top. Cover and simmer for 20 minutes. Remove the breasts and simmer the legs for a further 20 minutes. Serve the pheasant on the cabbage mixture with the juices spooned over.

Per serving: 451 calories, 18 g carbohydrates, 44 g protein, 22 g fat

ANCHO-CASHEW MOLE
WITH GRILLED QUAIL

Yield: 4 servings

The smoky grilled flavor of the quail goes nicely with this mole sauce. Try it with grilled pork, chicken or fish.

8 quail, dressed
oil for grilling
salt and pepper
1 cup ANCHO-CASHEW

MOLE SAUCE (see page 333)
½ chopped toasted cashews
  for garnish

1. Prepare an outdoor grill for barbecuing or preheat the broiler. Oil the grill rack and arrange it about 8 inches from the hot coals

2. Tie each quail's legs together with kitchen string and place on a baking sheet. Brush with oil and sprinkle with salt and pepper. Place breast side down on the grill rack and cover the grill. Cook about 8 minutes, checking a few times to make sure they are not burning. Move the coals to one side and place the quail on the other side. Cover and grill until the leg bones move easily, about 4 to 6 minutes longer.

3. Heat the mole sauce in a small saucepan until hot. Spoon ¼ cup onto each of 4 plates and top each portion with 2 quail. Sprinkle with cashews and serve.

Per serving: 422 calories, 16 g carbohydrates, 46 g protein, 19 g fat

FISH

ROMAINE-WRAPPED SEA SCALLOPS WITH YOGURT-WINE SAUCE

Yield: 4 servings

Try this with thick pieces of salmon. The sauce and vegetables will go nicely together and the colors will dazzle.

⅓ cup sliced scallions
1 tablespoon low-sodium soy sauce
1 teaspoon vegetable oil
¼ teaspoon crushed red-pepper flakes
1 pound sea scallops
½ cup Gewurztraminer or

other semi-sweet white
4 large romaine lettuce leaves
½ cup clam juice
1 tablespoon white vinegar
1 bay leaf
½ cup plain nonfat yogurt
¼ cup diced red bell pepper

1. Combine the scallions, soy sauce, oil and pepper flakes in a heavy-duty food storage bag and squeeze to mix well. Add the scallops to the bag and seal top. Marinate in the refrigerator 30 minutes.

2. Heat the wine to simmering in a large nonstick skillet over medium heat. Add the lettuce leaves, cover, reduce heat to low and cook for 3 minutes or until the lettuce wilts. Remove the pan from the heat.

3. Remove the lettuce from the skillet with a slotted spoon, reserving the wine, and set on a plate. Spoon ½ cup of the scallop mixture onto the center of each lettuce leaf. Fold in 4 sides of the lettuce leaf to cover the scallop mixture and form a packet.

4. Add the clam juice, vinegar, and bay leaf to the reserved wine in skillet and heat to boiling. Carefully place each lettuce packet, seam side down, into the skillet. Cover, reduce heat and simmer 5 minutes. Remove the pan from the heat and let stand, covered, 5 minutes.

5. Remove the packets with a slotted spoon onto individual serving plates and keep warm.

6. Discard the bay leaf. Heat the cooking liquid to boiling over medium-high heat and cook until reduced to 2 tablespoons, about 7 minutes. Remove the pan from the heat and scrape the bottom with a

wooden spoon to loosen any browned bits. Gradually add the yogurt to skillet, whisking until smooth. Spoon 2 tablespoons of the sauce around each packet and sprinkle each with 1 tablespoon bell pepper.

Per serving: 156 calories, 7 g carbohydrates, 21 g protein, 2 g fat

TROUT FILLETS
WITH CAPERS AND OLIVES

Yield: 4 servings

Crispy fish takes to piquant, salty seasoning. The vermouth and lemon juice sauce becomes the trout's best friend when the capers and olives are added.

¼ cup yellow cornmeal
½ teaspoon paprika
¼ teaspoon freshly ground pepper
4 (6-ounce) skinless rainbow- or brook-trout fillets
1 tablespoon olive oil
1 garlic clove, minced
½ cup dry vermouth

2 tablespoons chopped pitted Niçoise olives
2 tablespoons drained capers
2 tablespoons minced fresh parsley
1½ tablespoons fresh lemon juice
½ teaspoon cornstarch
¼ teaspoon salt

1. Combine the cornmeal, paprika and pepper on a plate and dredge the fillets in the mixture. Heat the oil in a large nonstick skillet over medium-high heat. Add the fillets and cook 2 minutes on each side or until browned, about 2 minutes on each side. Remove the fillets from the skillet, set aside and keep warm. Wipe out the skillet with paper towels.

2. Combine the garlic, vermouth, olives, capers, parsley, lemon juice, cornstarch and salt in the skillet and stir until well blended. Heat to boiling over medium-high heat and cook until slightly thickened, about 1 minute, stirring constantly. Spoon 2 tablespoons sauce over each fish fillet.

Per serving: 388 calories, 8 g carbohydrates, 36 g protein, 15 g fat

SCALLOPS WITH BLACK-BEAN NOODLES

Yield: 2 servings

SCALLOPS
2 tablespoons red-wine vinegar
1 tablespoon salt
1 red bell pepper, roasted, skinned and sliced
2 tablespoons olive oil
3 to 4 dashes Tabasco sauce
6 scallops, cut in half horizontally

SAUCE
2 tablespoons white wine
2 tablespoons fish broth
2 tablespoons heavy cream
2 ounces butter

BLACK-BEAN NOODLES
2 tablespoons bottled Chinese black bean sauce
pinch of sugar
1/2 ounce Chinese cellophane noodles, soaked and drained

1. Heat the red-wine vinegar and salt together in a pan. Add the bell pepper slices and simmer for 1 minute. Drain the pepper slices and return them to the pan. Add 1 tablespoon of the olive oil and the Tabasco and reheat for 1 to 2 minutes.

2. Heat the remaining olive oil in a wok. Add the scallops and stir-fry for 1 to 2 minutes. Stir in the peppers and fry for a further minute or until the scallops are just cooked. Season.

3. Meanwhile, reduce the wine, fish broth, and cream for 2 to 3 minutes or until thickened. Add the cooking juices from the scallops and peppers and reduce for a further minute. Beat in the butter and season with salt and pepper.

4. In a wok, heat the black-bean sauce with the sugar. Add the noodles and stir-fry for 1 to 2 minutes or until heated through.

5. To serve: Pile half the noodles on the center of each of 2 plates. Place a cooking ring on each pile and in each layer the scallops and peppers finishing with a layer of scallops. Spoon the cream sauce around.

Per serving: 536 calories, 20 g carbohydrates, 16 g protein, 43 g fat

CRAB AND ASPARAGUS STEW IN FENNEL BOWLS

Yield: 2 appetizer
or lunch servings

Here's a quick-to-assemble light course that's perfect for pre-the-atre dining or a cozy luncheon with a friend.

1 fennel bulb
1 teaspoon olive oil
1 tablespoon chopped shallots
½ cup diced peeled and
  seeded tomato
1 teaspoon chopped garlic
8 ounces cooked asparagus, cut
  into 1-inch pieces on the
  diagonal

½ cup light fish or chicken
  broth
1 cup lump crabmeat, cleaned
2 tablespoons butter
salt to taste
freshly ground black pepper to
  taste
2 tablespoons chopped parsley
  for garnish

1. Trim the ends off the fennel and slice the bulb lengthwise across the widest part. Remove the outer shell. Repeat on the other side of the bulb. Steam or blanch the shells until they are just tender. Keep warm.

2. Heat the oil in a small skillet, add the shallots and cook 30 seconds, stirring. Add the tomatoes and garlic and cook, stirring, 2 minutes. Add asparagus and stock. Heat to boiling, add the crabmeat and stir in the butter. Season to taste with salt and pepper.

3. To serve: Place a fennel bowl on each of 2 plates and spoon the stew into the bowls. Sprinkle with the parsley.

Per serving: 246 calories, 12 g carbohydrates, 7 g protein, 16 g fat

FRUITS OF THE GARDEN AND SEA EN PAPILLOTE

Yield: 4 servings

You'll enjoy serving and devouring these surprise packages. All the aromas, flavors and juices stay sealed inside the parchment paper.

3/4 cup fresh corn kernels

1/2 cup coarsely shredded
carrot

1/4 cup frozen green peas,
thawed

1/4 cup sliced scallions

8 ounces cod or other lean
white fish fillet, cut into
1-inch pieces

12 large shrimp (3/4 pound),
peeled and deveined

4 large sea scallops
(1/2 pound)

1/4 teaspoon salt

1/8 teaspoon freshly ground
pepper

2 tablespoons freshly grated
Parmesan cheese

2 tablespoons fresh lemon
juice

1. Preheat the oven to 425 degrees. Combine the corn, carrot, peas and scallions in a bowl and mix well.

2. Cut 4 (15-inch) squares of parchment paper. Fold each square in half, open each and place 1/4 cup of the corn mixture near the fold. Arrange one-fourth of the cod, 3 shrimp, and 1 scallop in a single layer over the corn mixture and sprinkle the salt and pepper evenly over the seafood. Spoon an additional 1/4 cup corn mixture over each serving, top each with 1 1/2 teaspoons cheese and drizzle with the lemon juice.

3. Fold the paper and seal the edges with narrow folds. Place the packets on a baking sheet.

4. Bake the packets until puffed and lightly browned, about 11 minutes. Place the packets on individual serving plates, cut open and serve immediately.

Per serving: 229 calories, 11 g carbohydrates, 39 g protein, 2 g fat

TRIPLE-ORANGE SCALLOP AND SHRIMP KABOBS

Yield: 4 servings

Fresh citrus goes well with seafood and here sweet oranges give more than a little squeeze of juice from a wedge.

8 ounces fresh or frozen scallops, thoroughly rinsed
1 garlic clove, minced
½ cup fresh orange juice
1 teaspoon finely grated orange peel
2 tablespoons soy sauce
1 teaspoon grated peeled fresh gingerroot
¼ teaspoon cayenne pepper
12 large fresh or frozen large shrimp, peeled and deveined
12 fresh or frozen pea pods
1 orange, cut into 8 wedges

1. For the marinade, combine the garlic, orange juice, orange peel, soy sauce, gingerroot and cayenne in a plastic food-storage bag set in a deep bowl. Halve any large scallops. Add the scallops and shrimp to the marinade and seal the bag. Turn and squeeze the bag to coat the seafood. Marinate in the refrigerator 30 minutes.

2. Meanwhile, prepare an outdoor grill for barbecuing or preheat the broiler. Drain the seafood, reserving the marinade. If using fresh pea pods, cook in boiling water about 2 minutes, drain. Or, thaw and drain frozen pea pods. Wrap 1 pea pod around each shrimp. Thread pea pods and shrimp onto four 10- or 12-inch skewers alternately with scallops and orange wedges.

For grilling outdoors: Grill kabobs on an uncovered grill directly over medium-hot coals for 5 minutes. Turn and brush with marinade. Grill 5 to 7 minutes more or until the shrimp turn pink and the scallops are opaque. Brush occasionally with marinade.

For broiling: Place kabobs on the unheated rack of a broiler pan. Broil 4 inches from the heat for 4 minutes. Turn and broil 4 to 6 minutes more or until the shrimp turn pink and the scallops are opaque. Brush occasionally with marinade.

Per serving: 110 calories, 11 g carbohydrates, 14 g protein, 1 g fat

STOUT-HEARTED HERRINGS

Yield: 6 servings

The bittersweet flavor of the dark beer called stout enhances the natural saltiness of these delicious, fine-textured fatty fish.

12 filleted fresh herrings
1½ cups Guinness or other
  stout
5 ounces vinegar
1 teaspoon brown
  sugar

¼ teaspoon salt
1 onion, cut into rings
10 whole cloves
4 white peppercorns
4 black peppercorns
2 bay leaves

1. Preheat the oven to 350 degrees. Wash the herring fillets and roll up, starting from the tail and place in a baking dish.

2. Combine the stout, vinegar, brown sugar and salt, mix well and pour over the herrings. Sprinkle the fish with the onion, cloves, peppercorns and bay leaves, pushing the solid seasonings into the liquid as much as possible. Cover with parchment or aluminum foil and bake until the herrings are tender, about 20 minutes. Remove the herrings from the oven and cool before serving.

Per serving: 618 calories, 6 g carbohydrates, 67 g protein, 33 g fat

CHEESY COD PIE

Yield: 8 servings

You can substitute flounder for the cod or even use a mix of your favorite shellfish. Add some cooked leftover vegetables with the fish for an even tastier and colorful dish.

nonstick cooking spray
3 pounds skinless cod filets
3 cups heavy cream
1¼ cups chopped
  mushrooms
¼ cup finely chopped shallots
2 tablespoons chopped fresh
  parsley
1 teaspoon chopped fresh

  thyme
salt to taste
freshly ground pepper to taste
milk for glazing the scones
1 cup grated cheese, preferably
  mature cheddar or a mixture
  of cheddar and Parmesan
8 CHEDDAR CHEESE SCONES,
  unbaked (see page 361)

1. Preheat the oven to 450 degrees. Grease a 3-quart round baking dish with cooking spray and arrange the cod on the bottom.

2. Heat the cream in a 2-quart saucepan until hot. Add the mushrooms, shallots, parsley and thyme. Mix well. Pour the sauce over the fish and sprinkle with two-thirds of the cheese.

3. Arrange the scones on top of the sauce so that they just about cover the surface. Glaze them with a little milk, and sprinkle with the remaining grated cheese. Bake until the fish is cooked through and the scones are golden brown, 25 to 30 minutes.

Per serving: 646 calories, 20 g carbohydrates, 37 g protein, 46 g fat

PEPPERED TARRAGON HALIBUT

Yield: 4 servings

Halibut tastes superb on its own, so you do not need to mess with a good thing. A few seasonings and a homey, spiced side dish are all you need.

¼ cup olive oil
4 (6-ounce) halibut fillets
a large pinch of black
  pepper

a large pinch of chopped fresh
  tarragon leaves
ANISE CARROT PUREE for
  serving (see page 285)

1. Heat the olive oil in a skillet. Season the halibut with fresh cracked black pepper. Pan-fry the fillets on both sides in the oil until cooked, 5 to 10 minutes according to the thickness. Sprinkle the halibut with the chopped fresh tarragon and serve.

Per serving (with the carrot puree): 459 calories, 8 g carbohydrates, 36 g protein, 31 g fat

FRIED FISH STICKS

Yield: 8 servings

½ cup all-purpose flour
salt to taste
freshly ground pepper to taste
3 large eggs
1 cup fine cracker crumbs

1¼ pounds skinless striped
  bass fillets, cut into
  3 by ½-inch strips
vegetable oil for frying
lemon wedges for serving

1. Place the flour in a shallow bowl and season generously with salt and pepper. Crack the eggs into another shallow bowl and beat well. Place the cracker crumbs in a third bowl and season with salt and pepper.

2. Dredge the fish strips in the flour. Dip the strips in the beaten eggs and coat completely with the seasoned crumbs. Arrange the fish fingers on a large baking sheet, cover with plastic wrap and refrigerate for at least 1 hour or overnight.

3. In a medium saucepan, heat 2 inches of oil to 375 degrees. Fry the fish sticks 4 or 5 at a time until golden brown and just cooked through, about 3 minutes. Using a slotted spoon, transfer the fried fish to paper towels to drain. Serve at once with lemon wedges.

Per serving: 178 calories, 12 g carbohydrates, 17 g protein, 6 g fat

SPAGHETTI SQUASH WITH RED CLAM SAUCE

Yield: 4 servings

The brilliant yellow of the squash makes it a more attractive partner than pasta for this red sauce. If you like things spicy-hot, add a pinch of crushed red-pepper flakes.

1 tablespoon olive oil
4 garlic cloves, minced
½ cup chopped green bell pepper
¼ cup minced scallions
1 (6½-ounce) can minced clams, undrained
2 tablespoons tomato paste
2 teaspoons dried oregano leaves
1 teaspoon sugar
1 (14½-ounce) can no-salt-added whole tomatoes, undrained and chopped
4 cups cooked spaghetti squash
fresh oregano sprigs for garnish

1. Heat oil in a large nonstick skillet over medium-high heat. Add the garlic, bell pepper and scallions and sauté until softened, about 5 minutes. Drain the liquid from the clams into the skillet and add the tomato paste, oregano and sugar. Whisk to blend the tomato paste into the clam juice. Add the tomatoes and their liquid and heat to boiling. Simmer, uncovered, until reduced to 2 cups, about 15 minutes, stirring frequently. Remove from the heat and stir in clams.

2. Reheat the spaghetti squash and place on a hot platter. Spoon the sauce on top and garnish with the oregano sprigs.

Per serving: 146 calories, 20 g carbohydrates, 8 g protein, 5 g fat

CLASSIC SEAFOOD GUMBO

Yield: 8 servings

This fish- and vegetable-packed stew/soup is a crowd-pleaser. Add more fresh jalapeño to taste if you like it spicy. Adding cooked long-grain rice to the bowl while you eat is traditional to cool the palate down as you continually fire it up.

FOR THE BROTH
1 pound unpeeled large raw shrimp
4 large chicken wings
1 carrot, sliced
1 large onion, sliced
1 celery stalk, sliced
1 handful mixed fresh herbs such as parsley, thyme and oregano

FOR THE GUMBO
4 tablespoons bacon fat, lard or vegetable oil
5 tablespoons all-purpose flour
3 strips of bacon, cut into ¼-inch-wide strips
1 pound plum tomatoes, roughly chopped

8 ounces okra, thickly sliced
2 onions, chopped
1 large celery stalk, sliced
1 green bell pepper, seeded and chopped
1 green jalapeño chile, thinly sliced
1 large thyme sprig
2 bay leaves
8 ounces skinned boneless chicken, cut into 2-inch pieces
20 small clams or mussels, cleaned
4 ounces crabmeat
2 scallions, cut into 1-inch lengths
1 tablespoon chopped fresh parsley
salt to taste
freshly ground pepper to taste

1. For the Broth: Peel the shrimp and set the meats aside. Place the shells, 8 cups water and the rest of the broth ingredients in a large pan and heat to boiling. Reduce the heat to low and simmer until the broth is aromatic and well flavored, about 1 hour. Strain through a colander into another pan.

2. For the Gumbo: Heat the oil in a large pan, add the flour and cook on a gentle heat, stirring continuously, until golden biscuit brown. Add the bacon and cook for another 2 minutes. Gradually add the broth, stirring constantly until blended. Heat to boiling and add the tomatoes, okra, onions, celery, bell pepper, jalapeño, thyme and bay leaves. Reduce the heat to low and simmer 5 minutes. Add the chicken and simmer until the chicken is tender and the vegetables are soft, about 20 minutes longer. Add the shrimp and clams or

mussels and simmer, stirring several times, until the shrimp are cooked through and the shellfish have opened (discard any unopened shellfish). Stir in the crabmeat, scallions, parsley, 1 1/2 teaspoons each salt and black pepper.

Per serving: 376 calories, 14 g carbohydrates, 28 g protein, 23 g fat

NORWEGIAN LOBSTER WITH CHILE-GARLIC MAYONNAISE

Yield: 1 serving

6 ounces sea salt
1 (1 1/2- to 2 1/2-pounds) lobster
2 tablespoons MAYONNAISE (see pages 313-314)
1 red chile, seeded and finely chopped

1 to 2 garlic cloves, crushed
SCANDINAVIAN NEW-POTATO SALAD WITH SCALLIONS AND SOUR CREAM (see page 203)
butter-lettuce leaf

1. Heat 1 gallon of water to boiling and add the sea salt. (This is about the same strength as seawater.) When the water comes to a rolling boil, drop in the lobster and cover with the lid. Reduce the heat when the water returns to a boil. Cook the lobster for 10 to 15 minutes for a 1 1/2-pound lobster and 15 to 20 minutes for a lobster up to 2 1/2 pounds. These times start when the water returns to the boil. Do not boil hard, just a gentle simmer.

2. Place the lobster on a chopping board and push the pointed end of a knife right through the carapace on the line that runs down the middle of the back of the body section; bring the knife down on to the chopping board cutting right through the tail, severing the body into two sections. Remove the stomach from the body (just behind the mouth) and also remove the intestine, which runs down to the tail. Clean out the rest of the inside and reserve the coral meat and enjoy.

3. Cut the meat into good-size pieces and replace in the lobster shells.

4. To serve, mix the chile and garlic with the Mayonnaise. Place a dollop in the space left by the removal of the stomach. Serve the potato salad on the side in a lettuce-leaf bowl.

Per serving (with the potato salad): 567 calories, 15 g carbohydrates, 20 g protein, 46 g fat

INDIVIDUAL CRAB IMPERIAL SOUFFLÉS

Yield: 4 servings

This is an individual presentation of the classic American dish. You can serve it as an appetizer in smaller portions, in buttered scallop shells of any size. Scale down the cooking time according to the amount of mixture used per shell. Pass little demitasse spoons or cocktail forks for easy eating at a stand-up soirée.

3 tablespoons butter

1 green bell pepper, seeded and finely diced

2 tablespoons chopped canned or bottled pimiento

2 tablespoons all-purpose flour

1 teaspoon salt

1/4 teaspoon freshly ground pepper

3/4 cup milk

1/4 cup plus 2 tablespoons MAYONNAISE (see page 313)

3 large egg yolks

1 teaspoon fresh lemon juice

1/2 teaspoon dry mustard

1/4 teaspoon Worcestershire sauce

1 pound lump crabmeat, picked over

3 large egg whites at room temperature

1. Preheat the oven to 350 degrees. Grease four 8-ounce ramekins.

2. Melt the butter in a large skillet over medium-high heat and sauté the green pepper until softened, about 3 minutes. Add the pimiento, flour, salt and pepper and stir until blended. Stir in the milk and 1/4 cup of the Mayonnaise and cook until the mixture boils and thickens.

3. Remove the pan from the heat. Whisk in the egg yolks, lemon juice, mustard and Worcestershire sauce until blended. Fold in the crabmeat until coated and spoon into the prepared ramekins.

4. Beat the egg whites in a deep bowl until stiff peaks form when the beaters are raised. Add the remaining 2 tablespoons Mayonnaise and fold in just until blended. Spoon the egg-white mixture over the crab mixture in the ramekins. Bake until golden and hot, 15 to 20 minutes. Serve immediately.

Per serving: 456 calories, 8 g carbohydrates, 29 g protein, 34 g fat

GRILLED TERIYAKI TUNA WITH FRESH PINEAPPLE

Yield: 6 servings

Fruit is wonderful grilled alongside fish, poultry or meat. Choose firm types and brush with oil before placing on the grill to keep its sugars from caramelizing and sticking to the rack.

¼ cup low-sodium teriyaki or soy sauce
3 tablespoons honey
3 tablespoons mirin (sweet rice wine)
2 teaspoons minced peeled fresh gingerroot
½ teaspoon hot sauce

1 garlic clove, minced
6 spears peeled and cored ripe pineapple
6 (4-ounce) tuna steaks, ³/₄ inch thick
nonstick cooking spray
scallion brushes for garnish (optional)

1. Combine the soy sauce, honey, mirin, gingerroot, hot sauce and garlic in a large baking dish. Cut the pineapple lengthwise into 6 spears. Add the pineapple and tuna to the mixture in the baking dish, turning to coat. Cover and marinate in refrigerator 30 minutes, turning every 10 minutes.

2. Prepare an outdoor grill for barbecuing or preheat the broiler. Remove the tuna and pineapple from marinade, reserving marinade.

3. Grease a grill rack or broiler pan with cooking spray. Place the grill rack on the grill over medium-hot coals. Place the tuna and pineapple on the grill rack or broiler pan and cook 4 minutes on each side until the tuna is medium-rare or desired degree of doneness, basting tuna and pineapple occasionally with the reserved marinade. Garnish with the scallion brushes.

Per serving: 219 calories, 20 g carbohydrates, 30 g protein, 1 g fat

CRAB AND TOFU DUMPLINGS

Yield: 6 to 8 servings

Guests will be surprised when you tell them that there is tofu at the heart of these tasty appetizers.

4 ounces firm tofu, drained
4 ounces crabmeat
1 egg yolk
1-inch piece peeled fresh gingerroot, grated
2 tablespoons finely chopped
scallion

2 tablespoons all-purpose
flour
2 teaspoons soy sauce, plus
extra for serving
¼ teaspoon salt
oil for deep frying
lime wedges for serving

1. Press the tofu through a coarse sieve into a bowl and add the crab, egg yolk, ginger, scallion, flour, soy sauce and salt. Deep-fry bite-size portions until golden and drain on paper towels.

2. Serve with fresh lime and a little soy sauce.

Each of 8 servings: 43 calories, 2 g carbohydrates, 4 g protein, 2 g fat

MUSSELS MARINIÈRE

Yield: 4 servings

Make sure all your mussels are alive before cooking. Any mussels that do not close when slightly tapped on a work surface should be discarded.

1 tablespoon olive oil
⅔ cup chopped shallots
1¼ cups fish stock, homemade
or from bouillon cubes
5 ounces dry white wine
2 garlic cloves, crushed
1 pound mussels, scrubbed and

beards removed
2 tablespoons coarsely
chopped flat-leaf parsley
salt to taste
freshly ground pepper to taste
2 tablespoons half-and-half or
heavy cream (optional)

1. Heat the oil over low heat in a 3-quart saucepan and add the shallots. Cover until softened, 3 to 4 minutes. Add the stock, wine and garlic, and heat to boiling.

2. Stir in the mussels. Heat to boiling, cover and simmer over medium heat until the mussels open, about 3 minutes.

3. Gently stir in the parsley and season to taste, adding the half-and-half or cream just before serving. Serve in shallow bowls.

Per serving: 183 calories, 10 g carbohydrates, 15 g protein, 7 g fat

SEAFOOD BURGERS

Yield: 4 servings

Orange roughy is a thick, dense white fillet of deep-water fish from the northeast coast of New Zealand that is readily available at larger fish departments and specialty fish stores.

8 ounces medium shrimp, boiled for 30 seconds, peeled and deveined
8 ounces orange roughy fillets, skinned, cut into small pieces
¼ teaspoon salt

¼ teaspoon cayenne pepper
3 scallions, trimmed and coarsely chopped
4 medium white mushrooms
1 tablespoon snipped fresh dill
2 egg whites
¼ cup fine dried breadcrumbs

1. Preheat the oven to 400 degrees. Place half of the shrimp and half of the roughy in a food processor and process 10 pulses, then transfer to a large bowl. Repeat with the remaining shrimp and fish. Sprinkle with the salt and cayenne pepper.

2. Place the scallions, mushrooms and dill in the processor and pulse 5 times. Add to the seafood, pour in the egg whites and mix well. Form into 4 patties and set aside.

3. Spread the breadcrumbs out on a plate. Place the patties on top and press firmly, coating both sides with the crumbs, and transfer to a baking sheet. Bake until cooked through, about 10 minutes.

Per serving: 145 calories, 8 g carbohydrates, 23 g protein, 2 g fat

ALASKAN SALMON-SALAD SANDWICHES

Yield: 6 sandwiches

These are lunchtime fare but fancy enough for little tea sandwiches. The tangy yogurt and lemon juice in the dressing brightens the mixture more than mayonnaise could.

1 (15½-ounce) can Alaskan
  salmon
⅓ cup plain nonfat yogurt
⅓ cup chopped scallions

⅓ cup chopped celery
1 tablespoon lemon juice
freshly ground pepper to taste
6 pita breads

1. Drain the salmon and place in a large bowl. Separate into flakes using a fork. Stir in the yogurt, scallions, celery, lemon juice and pepper and mix well.

2. Cut a slice off of a pita edge so you can open it. Place the slice at the bottom of the pocket to help absorb the juices from the filling. Repeat with the remaining pitas.

3. To serve, spoon the salad into the pitas.

Per serving: 189 calories, 17 g carbohydrates, 18 g protein, 5 g fat

PARSLEY-AND-CHIVE-PACKED SALMON-COD CAKES

Yield: 8 servings

You say potato and I say fish cake. It's an association thing. This mix of fresh herbs, fish and, yes, potatoes, makes even meat-lovers agree that there are burgers and then there are fish cakes. Let's call the whole thing delicious. The directions call for using a metal spatula to shape the fish cakes. It's really the key to shaping them because using your hands actually warms the fish mixture and makes it sticky and more difficult to shape. Use two spatulas for speed and efficiency. Soon you will become the neighborhood fish-cake meister, and, you've been warned, there's no turning back!

12 ounces potatoes, peeled
  and freshly boiled
1 ounce butter, melted
salt to taste
freshly ground pepper to taste
6 ounces salmon fillet, skinned
6 ounces cod fillet, skinned
6 scallions, peeled and finely
  sliced
4 tablespoons chopped fresh
  parsley

2 tablespoons chopped fresh
  chives
grated rind and juice of
  1 lemon

FOR FRYING
1 beaten egg
6 tablespoons fine fresh white
  breadcrumbs
1 ounce unsalted butter
4 tablespoons sunflower oil

1. Mash the potatoes with the melted butter, salt and freshly ground pepper in a medium bowl. Set aside.

2. Season the salmon and cod with salt and pepper. Heat a little water and a splash of lemon juice in a shallow pan and lightly poach the seasoned salmon and cod until just cooked. Remove the fish from cooking liquid and flake.

3. Place the mashed potato and flaked fish into a large mixing bowl. Add the scallions, herbs, lemon rind and scallion and mix well. Taste and adjust the seasoning if necessary. Roll teaspoonfuls of the mixture into balls and flatten the top and sides with a small spatula to form small fish cakes. Pour the beaten egg onto a plate and the bread-crumbs onto a second plate. Dip the fishcakes first in the beaten egg and the breadcrumbs to coat. Pat smooth with a small spatula.

4. Heat a cast iron or heavy base skillet. Melt the butter in the oil over medium heat and fry the fish cakes on all sides until crisp, golden and hot. Cook in two batches, keeping the first batch hot while cooking the second. Drain on paper towels. Serve with lemon wedges or perhaps a parsley sauce.

Per serving: 224 calories, 11 g carbohydrates, 11 g protein, 15 g fat

CRISPY SALMON ON STIR-FRIED VEGETABLES

Yield: 4 servings

Here, grilled salmon kabobs and an array of crisp-tender vegetables get coated in a soy, honey and herb sauce. Leave the skin on the salmon so you can enjoy the contrasting texture with the tender flesh.

4 salmon fillets with the skin on
salt and pepper
2 teaspoons dark sesame oil
2 teaspoons vegetable oil
2 garlic cloves, finely chopped
1 chile, finely chopped
1 teaspoon grated peeled fresh
   gingerroot
6 stalks asparagus, cut in pieces

2 heads bok choy, chopped
3 scallions, sliced into 1-inch
   pieces
2 ounces broccoli florets
2 handfuls baby spinach leaves
2 ounces sugar snap peas
½ cup vegetable broth
½ recipe SOY-HONEY FRESH-
   HERB SAUCE (see page339)

1. Soak bamboo or wooden skewers in water for 30 minutes before cooking.

2. Cut each salmon steak into 6 even slices and thread onto the bamboo skewers. If the skewers are too long, cut off the ends. Heat a nonstick griddle or seasoned grill pan and cook the salmon skin side down until crisp and golden and season to taste. Repeat on the other side, but don't overcook or the flavor will be spoiled.

3. While the salmon is cooking, heat a wok and add the sesame and vegetable oils. Raise the temperature and add the garlic, chile and ginger. Cook for 1 minute and then add the remaining vegetables in this order: asparagus, bok choy, scallions, broccoli, baby spinach and sugar snap peas, stir-frying briefly after each addition. The broth needs to be added continuously from this point, and the whole dish needs to cook for 2 minutes.

4. Re-stir the sauce mixture and stir into the wok. Cook until the liquid boils.

5. Serve some of the stir-fried vegetables on a plate topped with the salmon. Serve immediately while everything is still hot.

Per serving: 121 calories, 17 g carbohydrates, 5 g protein, 5 g fat

GRILLED BUTTERFLIED SHRIMP WITH LEMON AND CHILE

Yield: 6 servings

30 large fresh shrimp, unshelled
grated rind and juice of 1 lemon
2 garlic cloves, finely diced
1 chile, finely diced

2 tablespoons olive oil
salt to taste
freshly ground pepper to taste
chopped fresh cilantro to garnish

1. Cut the shrimp along the inner side and fold the sides back flat, pulling out the intestinal tract if there is one. Place the shrimp in a large bowl and sprinkle with the lemon rind and lemon juice, garlic, diced chile, which will begin to marinate them. Drizzle with the olive oil. Set aside for only 30 minutes.

2. Preheat a grill pan or prepare an outdoor grill for barbecuing.

3. Cook the shrimp shell side only for 2 to 3 minutes or just until the shrimp turn pink. Place on a platter or in a bowl and sprinkle with a little salt, pepper and cilantro.

Per serving: 91 calories, 1 g carbohydrates, 9 g protein, 5 g fat

CRAB AND SALMON CAKES WITH LEMON-CILANTRO SAUCE

Yield: 8 to 10 servings

Serve these hot with salad and garlic and lemon dressing.

1¼ pounds salmon fillets

1 pound crabmeat, picked over for shells and flaked

3 scallions, finely chopped

⅔ cup dried breadcrumbs

½ cup MAYONNAISE (see pages 313-314)

juice of ½ lemon, or more to taste

1 teaspoon Tabasco sauce, or more to taste

1 egg, beaten

oil for shallow frying

LEMON-CILANTRO SAUCE (see page 323)

1. Poach and drain the salmon and pat dry with paper towels. Place in a large bowl and separate into flakes with a fork. Gently press any excess moisture from the crabmeat and add to the salmon. Add the remaining ingredients except the egg and mix gently but thoroughly, Adjust the seasoning and add the beaten egg, stirring gently just until the mixture holds together.

2. Press the mixture into a 3-inch round cutter to form small cakes. Refrigerate the cakes on a baking sheet for at least 30 minutes before frying.

3. Heat a thin layer of oil in a large nonstick skillet over medium heat. Pan-fry the cakes on both sides until golden and heated through, watching them carefully to avoid scorching. Serve immediately with the sauce.

Each of 10 servings: 299 calories, 12 g carbohydrates, 24 g protein, 26 g fat

LOBSTER THERMIDOR

Yield: 2 servings

Food legend has it that this dish was named by Napoleon after the eleventh month (July 19–August 17) of the French Revolutionary Calendar, the official calendar of the first French republic from 1793 to 1805.

1 whole lobster
salt and pepper
1 ounce butter, melted
BECHAMEL SAUCE (see
   page 342)
1 raw egg yolk

2 tablespoons heavy cream
1 tablespoon brandy or to taste
1/2 teaspoon Dijon mustard or
   to taste
4 tablespoons freshly grated
   Parmesan cheese

1. Preheat the oven to 425 degrees. Split the lobster in half lengthwise, remove the gritty sac and discard. Crack the claws. Place the lobster on a baking sheet. Season the lobster with salt and pepper and roast in for 10 minutes, basting with the melted butter.

2. Meanwhile, heat the Bechamel Sauce in a small saucepan until hot. Whisk the egg yolk, cream and brandy in a small bowl and add some of the hot sauce. Whisk this mixture back into the sauce. Whisk in the mustard and 2 tablespoons of the cheese.

3. Remove the lobster meat from the shells and slice it. Place the meat in a bowl and mix it with enough of the Bechamel Sauce to coat. Replace the meat in the shells, top with the remaining sauce and sprinkle with the remaining cheese. Bake until browned and bubbly.

Per serving: 549 calories, 14 g carbohydrates, 28 g protein, 41 g fat

COD BAKED IN A HERB-CRUMB CRUST WITH TOMATO SALSA AND ARUGULA

Yield: 3 servings

You can use most any other thick fish fillets in this recipe. Thinner pieces are fine but you have to cut down on the baking time.

FOR THE COD

1 pound 1-inch-thick cod fillets
salt and pepper to taste
1/2 cup fine dried breadcrumbs
1 small bunch parsley, rinsed,
   dried and finely chopped
1 small bunch basil, rinsed,
   dried and sliced

1/4 cup olive oil
1/2 recipe BEEFSTEAK-TOMATO
   AND BASIL SALSA (see
   page 319)

FOR SERVING

2 small bunches arugula, rinsed
   and dried

1. Preheat the oven to 375 degrees. Grease a 1 1/2-quart baking dish.

2. Place the cod fillets in the prepared baking dish and season well. Mix the breadcrumbs with the chopped parsley, sliced basil and olive oil. Cover the cod with the mixture, pressing down lightly. Bake for 10 minutes.

3. When the cod is about 2 minutes away from being cooked, sauté the arugula in a nonstick skillet until wilted, about 3 seconds. Arrange the arugula on 4 plates, top with the cod and spoon the salsa over all.

Per serving: 453 calories, 17 g carbohydrates, 32 g protein, 29 g fat

CURRIED FISH WITH COCONUT

Yield: 4 servings

This spicy mixture is also suitable for cooking shrimp and chunks of boneless, skinless chicken. Serve with cooked white rice.

1/2 tablespoon sunflower oil
1 large onion, chopped
1 bay leaf
1 tablespoon mild curry
   powder
1 tablespoon flaked
   unsweetened coconut
2 teaspoons turmeric
2 cups vegetable broth

1 (10-ounce) package frozen cut
   green beans, thawed
1 pound thick cod or salmon
   fillets, skinned and cut into
   1 1/2-inch cubes
4 ounces Greek yogurt
salt and freshly ground pepper
fresh cilantro for garnish,
   roughly chopped

1. In a large skillet or wok, heat the oil over medium heat and fry the onion until softened. Add the bay leaf, curry powder, coconut and turmeric. Cook over medium-low heat for 2 minutes. Stir in the broth and simmer for 3 to 4 minutes.

2. Add the green beans and simmer 2 minutes. Add the fish pieces, pushing them into the liquid, and season. Cover and cook gently for 2 minutes or until the fish is just cooked.

3. Meanwhile, mix the yogurt with a little water to reach the consistency of heavy cream. Pour the mixture into the pan and gently mix through until piping hot. Sprinkle with the cilantro and serve at once.

Per serving: 170 calories, 10 g carbohydrates, 23 g protein, 4 g fat

BAKED TILAPIA WITH WHITE WINE AND HERBS

Yield: 2 servings

2 (8- to 10-ounce) fresh whole tilapia, cleaned and scaled
5 ounces fruity white wine
1 to 2 garlic cloves, finely chopped
¼ cup chopped fresh mixed herbs
2 large scallions, trimmed, sliced diagonally
salt to taste
freshly ground pepper to taste
1 tablespoon butter, softened
1 teaspoon cornstarch, blended with a little cold water
2 tablespoons crème fraîche

1. Preheat the oven to 350 degrees. Grease a shallow baking dish large enough to hold the fish. Lightly oil a piece of aluminum foil large enough to cover the baking dish.

2. Arrange the tilapia side by side in the prepared pan and pour the wine over the fish. Sprinkle with the garlic, most of the herbs, the scallions, salt and pepper. Dot half the butter over each fish.

3. Cover the fish with the prepared piece of foil and crunch the foil around the dish to seal tightly. Bake until the fish are cooked through (the eyes will be white), 30 to 35 minutes.

4. Transfer the tilapia to a serving dish and keep warm. Pour the cooking juices into a small saucepan, stir in the blended cornstarch and simmer until thickened and clear, about 2 minutes. Stir in the crème fraîche, pour over the fish and sprinkle with the remaining herbs. Serve immediately.

Per serving: 370 calories, 5 g carbohydrates, 28 g protein, 21 g fat

GRILLED TROUT WITH A HORSERADISH CRUST

Yield: 1 serving

2 skinless trout fillets
1 tablespoon olive oil plus
    extra for greasing the pan
1 slice whole-wheat bread,
    ground into small, coarse
    crumbs
2 teaspoons creamed
    horseradish
1 tablespoon chopped
    fresh parsley

grated rind of ½ lemon

FOR THE DRESSING
1 teaspoon Dijon mustard
juice of ½ lemon
salt to taste
freshly ground pepper to
    taste
2 tablespoons virgin olive oil
1 cup mixed crisp salad leaves

1. Preheat the broiler. Brush a broiler pan with oil. Sprinkle the trout fillets with salt and pepper.

2. In a bowl, mix together the bread, horseradish, parsley, 1 tablespoon olive oil and the lemon juice together. Spread this mixture over the trout fillets and place under the grill for 5 minutes to cook.

3. For the dressing: Mix the mustard and lemon juice together in a bowl. Add a little salt and pepper and whisk the oil in very slowly. Mix the salad leaves with a little of the dressing and place on a large dinner plate. Drizzle the remaining dressing around the outside of the plate. Place the crusted trout on top of the salad leaves and serve warm.

Per serving: 715 calories, 19 g carbohydrates, 41 g protein, 57 g fat

ONE-DISH
MEALS

CURLY-ENDIVE SALAD WITH BACON AND POACHED EGGS

Yield: 4 servings

4 cups ½-inch cubes good-quality white bread
6 tablespoons olive oil
salt to taste
freshly ground pepper to taste
8 ounces sliced bacon, cut crosswise into ½-inch strips
2 small heads curly endive, (about 18 ounces in all), torn into bite-size pieces
3 tablespoons plus 1 teaspoon red- or white-wine vinegar
4 eggs
1 garlic clove, minced
½ teaspoon dried thyme leaves

1. Place a large skillet over medium heat. Toss the bread cubes with 2 tablespoons of the oil and ¼ teaspoon each of salt and pepper. Place them in the pan and cook, stirring frequently, until crisp and brown, about 5 minutes. Remove the croutons from the pan.

2. Add the bacon to the pan and cook until crisp. Remove and drain. Place in a large glass or stainless-steel bowl with the endive. Pour off all but ¼ cup of the fat from the pan.

3. Fill a saucepan two-thirds full with water. Add the 1 teaspoon vinegar and heat to boiling. Break each egg into a cup or small bowl and slide one at a time into the water. Reduce the heat to a bare simmer. Poach the eggs until the whites are set but the yolks are still soft, about 3 minutes. Remove with a slotted spoon and drain on paper towels. Sprinkle with salt and pepper.

4. To the fat in the pan, add the remaining 4 tablespoons oil, the garlic, thyme, and ¼ teaspoon each of salt and pepper. Warm the dressing over medium-low heat, stirring occasionally, until the garlic barely starts to brown, about 2 minutes. Add the remaining 3 tablespoons vinegar and remove from the heat. Toss the dressing with the endive and bacon until the endive wilts slightly. Add the croutons and toss again. Place on plates. Top each salad with a warm egg.

Per serving: 436 calories, 18 g carbohydrates, 15 g protein, 34 g fat

FRIED TORTILLAS WITH CHORIZO

Yield: 6 servings

½ cup vegetable oil
6 flour tortillas
¼ cup warm refried beans
4 ounces white cheese
1 onion, finely chopped

8 ounces chorizo, crumbled,
 fried and drained
½ cup chopped tomatoes
2 green chiles, chopped
 finely

1. Heat the oil in a skillet and toss each tortilla in it for 1 minute, turning once and removing from the oil when just light brown. Drain the tortillas on paper towels and keep them warm.

2. Spread each tortilla with a thin layer of the hot refried beans. Sprinkle each with some of the cheese, onion, chorizo, tomatoes and chiles. Serve immediately.

Per serving: 365 calories, 20 g carbohydrates, 17 g protein, 24 g fat

LENTIL-TURKEY CHILI CASSEROLE

Yield: 12 servings

Use any lentils that catch your fancy: green, yellow, red or a mix. They are like chameleons in adapting their beany flavor to any seasoning, and they cook so quickly that you'll find it possible to make this dish from scratch at short notice.

1 pound ground turkey
1 medium onion, chopped
1 stalk celery, chopped
½ small green bell pepper,
 seeded and chopped
1 cup dried lentils
nonstick cooking spray

1¼ cups cooked brown
 rice
1 (6-ounce) can tomato paste
1 (1.25-ounce) package taco-
 seasoning mix
½ teaspoon chili powder or
 more to taste

1. Combine the turkey, onion, celery, green pepper and 1 cup water in a medium saucepan. Heat to boiling over medium heat, and cook until the turkey is cooked through, stirring with a wooden spoon to break up the turkey into little pieces. Stir in the lentils and 3 cups water, cover and simmer over low heat until the lentils are tender, about 40 minutes.

2. Preheat oven to 375 degrees. Lightly grease a 2-quart casserole with cooking spray.

3. Add the rice, tomato paste, taco seasoning and ½ teaspoon chili powder to the lentil mixture and mix well. Heat to boiling and cook 5 minutes. Adjust seasoning and add more water if necessary to make the mixture juicy but not soupy. Spoon the chili into the prepared casserole and bake, uncovered, 25 minutes. Let stand 5 minutes before serving.

Per serving: 160 calories, 20 g carbohydrates, 12 g protein, 4 g fat

BRIE RACLETTE

Yield: 4 servings

8 ounces Brie, rind removed
6 cups broccoli flowerets
1 pound mushrooms, halved or quartered if large
2 tablespoons vegetable oil
½ teaspoon salt
1 small apple, cored, cut into 16 chunks
1 cup walnut halves
½ cup cocktail onions

1. Preheat the oven to 400 degrees. Cut the Brie into thin slices and divide the cheese among four small ovenproof dishes or ramekins.

2. Heat a saucepan of water to boiling and cook the broccoli until tender, about 5 minutes. Remove the broccoli with a slotted spoon and drain on paper towels.

3. Place the mushrooms on an aluminum-foil lined baking sheet. Drizzle with the oil, sprinkle with the salt, and toss to coat. Roast the mushrooms until browned and tender, turning once, 10 to 15 minutes. Remove the pan from the oven and turn the oven off.

4. Place the dishes of cheese in the oven and leave until the cheese just melts, 5 to 10 minutes.

5. Meanwhile, pile the broccoli, mushrooms, apple pieces, walnuts and cocktail onions on individual plates. Serve each portion of melted Brie immediately, along with the vegetables, apple and nuts for dipping.

Per serving: 495 calories, 20 g carbohydrates, 23 g protein, 40 g fat

HOT MUFFULETTA

Yield: 6 servings

This sandwich, a New Orleans specialty, is usually served unheated, probably because the weather in The Big Easy is usually so hot and steamy. In addition to its unconventional melted cheese, this version is made with a crusty baguette. (Try keeping things crisp, even with air conditioning, when the humidity outside is 100 percent!) For more variety, use a combination of chopped, pitted black olives, such as Calamata, and green olives with pimientos in the salad for both color and flavor.

1 (10-ounce) jar green olives with pimientos, drained and chopped
¼ cup chopped fresh parsley
1½ teaspoons dried oregano leaves
1 garlic clove, minced

3 tablespoons olive oil
1 14-inch, thin baguette, split, most of the inside removed
8 ounces sliced hard salami
8 ounces sliced ham
8 ounces sliced provolone

1. Preheat the oven to 350 degrees. In a small bowl, combine the chopped olives with the parsley, oregano, garlic and oil. Spread some of the olive mixture on the bottom half of the bread.

2. Top the olive salad with the salami, ham, and provolone. Cover with the tops of the bread and cut into 6 sandwiches. Wrap each sandwich in aluminum foil. Bake until the cheese melts, about 15 minutes.

Per serving: 513 calories, 20 g carbohydrates, 24 g protein, 37 g fat

CARROT, ONION AND OAT BRAN CASSEROLE

Yield: 4 servings

1 cup chopped onion
1 cup shredded carrots
1 garlic clove, minced
1½ cups skim milk
½ cup oat bran
2 tablespoons chopped fresh parsley

½ teaspoon salt
1/8 teaspoon ground nutmeg
1/8 teaspoon pepper
1 cup shredded cheddar or Monterey Jack cheese
4 egg whites

1. Preheat the oven to 325 degrees. In a large saucepan combine the onion, carrots, garlic, and 2 tablespoons water. Heat to boiling, reduce the heat to low and simmer, covered, until the vegetables are tender, about 10 minutes, stirring occasionally. Do not drain.

2. Stir in the milk, oat bran, parsley, salt, nutmeg, and pepper. Heat to boiling over medium-high heat, stirring constantly. Cook and stir for 2 minutes. Remove from heat, add the cheese and stir until melted. Cool slightly.

3. In a large mixing bowl beat the egg whites until stiff peaks form when the beaters are raised. Fold in the onion mixture and pour into an ungreased 1½-quart soufflé dish. Bake until the top is brown and a knife inserted near the center comes out clean, about 50 minutes. Serve immediately.

Per serving: 234 calories, 20 g carbohydrates, 17 g protein, 12 g fat

DRIED-FRUIT AND BULGUR-STUFFED CABBAGE LEAVES

Yield: 12 servings

This Old-World staple of home cooking has evolved with every generation stirring the melting pot. Here, it keeps to its tomato-sauce roots but emerges as a meatless, sweet-and-spicy, high-fiber and cheesy model of its former self. An abundance of hazelnuts adorns its new incarnation.

12 large outer leaves from a large Savoy cabbage
2 tablespoons vegetable oil
1 medium carrot, peeled and finely grated
1 onion, finely chopped
½ cup bulgur wheat or long-grain rice
¼ cup dried apricots, finely chopped
3 tablespoons raisins
½ teaspoon ground allspice
salt and freshly ground black pepper to taste
½ cup hazelnuts, toasted and chopped
1 cup ricotta curd cheese or skimmed milk soft cheese
1 (14-ounce) can chunky chopped tomatoes

1. Preheat the oven to 350 degrees. Heat a large pot of water to boiling, add the cabbage leaves, and boil until softened, 1 to 2 minutes. Drain, reserving ½ pint of the cooking water, and refresh in

cold water. Drain thoroughly, then pat each leaf dry with a clean kitchen towel. Cut out the tough stalk from each leaf.

2. In a small saucepan, heat the oil and sauté the carrot and onion until softened, about 3 minutes. Stir in the bulgur, apricots, raisins, allspice, salt and pepper and mix well. Add the reserved cooking water and heat to boiling. Reduce the heat and simmer until all the liquid has been absorbed, about 10 minutes. Set aside to cool.

3. Add the hazelnuts and ricotta to the bulgur mixture and taste for seasoning. Divide the mixture among the cabbage leaves and fold the leaves over as if making an eggroll to enclose the filling.

4. Arrange the cabbage parcels in a shallow casserole dish and spread the tomatoes on top. Cover with the lid or foil and bake until bubbly, about 30 minutes

Per serving: 150 calories, 15 g carbohydrates, 5 g protein, 9 g fat

CRISPY TOFU CUBES WITH PEANUT DIPPING SAUCE

Yield: 4 servings

SAUCE

¼ cup chopped roasted peanuts
1 tablespoon sugar
2 tablespoons water
2 teaspoons Chinese white rice vinegar or cider vinegar
1 tablespoon finely chopped

fresh cilantro
½ teaspoon salt
½ teaspoon chili oil
12 ounces tofu cut into 1-inch cubes
1¼ cups peanut oil for deep-frying

1. Combine the sauce ingredients together in a small bowl, mix well and set aside.

2. Pat the tofu dry with paper towels. Heat the 1¼ cups oil in a deep-fat fryer or a large wok until it almost smokes. Deep-fry the tofu cubes in two batches. When each batch of tofu cubes is lightly browned, remove and drain well on paper towel.

3. Arrange the tofu cubes on a platter and serve the peanut sauce separately as a dipping sauce.

Per serving: 217 calories, 9 g carbohydrates, 12 g protein, 17 g fat

PAN-FRIED TOFU "STEAKS" WITH HOT CHILE

Yield: 1 serving

2 (½-inch-thick) slices tofu
1 tablespoon oil
2 tablespoons sweet soy sauce
1 teaspoon garlic chili paste

1 tablespoon chopped fresh
  cilantro
2 tablespoons chopped
  scallion

Heat the oil in a skillet over medium heat and fry the tofu slices until light brown on both sides, about 2 minutes. Combine the soy sauce and chili paste in a small bowl and add the cilantro and scallions. Mix well and pour on top of the tofu.

Per serving: 216 calories, 9 g carbohydrates, 8 g protein, 18 g fat

PINTO BEAN AND MUSHROOM IN PITA BREAD

Yield: 2 servings

1 teaspoon lard or oil
1 garlic clove, chopped
½ cup cooked pinto beans
2 mushrooms, thinly sliced
2 tablespoons roughly
  chopped fresh cilantro

1 pita loaf, warmed, cut crosswise in half
2 tablespoons salsa
2 tablespoons sour cream
2 tablespoons grated cheddar
  or Monterey jack cheese

1. Heat the oil in a nonstick or cast-iron skillet over medium heat. Add the garlic and beans and fry until just the garlic has softened, about 3 minutes. Add the mushrooms and cilantro and heat through, about 2 minutes.

2. Spoon the bean mixture into the pita halves. Spoon the salsa and sour cream on top and sprinkle with the cheese.

Per serving: 163 calories, 18 g carbohydrates, 7 g protein, 8 g fat

STOVETOP EGGPLANT PARMESAN

Yield: about 4 servings

4 ½ ounces olive oil
8 cups diced eggplant
1 large onion, chopped
2 garlic cloves, peeled and
  roughly chopped
2 large beefsteak tomatoes,
  skinned and chopped

1 bay leaf
salt to taste
freshly ground pepper to
  taste
8 ounces whole-milk
  mozzarella cheese, shredded
½ cup grated Parmesan cheese

1. Heat 4 ounces of the oil in a large, deep skillet over medium heat and sauté the eggplant until tender and browned. Remove to a bowl.

2. Fry the onion and garlic gently in the same skillet in the remaining 2 tablespoons of the oil until softened and lightly browned, about 7 minutes. Add the tomatoes, bay leaf and salt and pepper. Simmer gently for 15 minutes. Stir in the eggplant, cover loosely and simmer gently until the mixture has thickened, 20 to 30 minutes, stirring occasionally. Try to find the bay leaf and discard. Sprinkle with the mozzarella and then the Parmesan. Cover and heat until the cheeses melt.

Per serving: 538 calories, 20 g carbohydrates, 19 g protein, 49 g fat

CROISSANT WITH PESTO, PARMA HAM, PLUM TOMATOES AND TALLEGIO

Yield: 1 serving

This is a dream of a sandwich. The tender, buttery croissant will have you licking your fingers.

1 croissant
2 teaspoons PESTO SAUCE (see
  pages 320-321)
3 slices taleggio cheese

1 thin slice of Parma ham
1 plum tomato, chopped
freshly ground pepper to taste
olive oil for drizzling

1. Cut the croissant in half and spread the pesto on the base. Next add the tallegio, Parma ham, plum tomatoes and ground pepper.

2. Place on a baking sheet and heat about 5 inches away from the broiler for 4 minutes or until the cheese melts. Drizzle with olive oil and serve immediately.

Per serving: 328 calories, 16 g carbohydrates, 4 g protein, 23 g fat

CHEESY EGG AND VEGETABLE CASSEROLE

Yield: 4 servings

This is a vegetable version of macaroni and cheese without the macaroni. It will win the hearts of kids whose idea of vegetables is French fries and tomato ketchup.

nonstick cooking spray
1/2 cup chopped onion
1 cup frozen mixed vegetables
1 1/4 cups skim milk
1 tablespoon cornstarch
2 teaspoons instant chicken bouillon
1/8 teaspoon freshly ground
pepper
1/2 cup shredded cheddar cheese
1 teaspoon Dijon-style mustard
4 hard-cooked eggs, peeled and sliced
1 large tomato, cut lengthwise and thinly sliced crosswise

1. Preheat the oven to 350 degrees. Grease an 8 by 1 1/2-inch round baking dish with cooking spray.

2. Combine the onion and 1 cup lightly salted water in a small saucepan and boil for 5 minutes. Add the mixed vegetables and cook 5 minutes more or until tender; drain well.

3. Meanwhile, for the sauce, in a medium saucepan mix the milk with the cornstarch, bouillon granules, and pepper. Cook and stir over medium heat until thickened and bubbly. Stir in the cheese and mustard and cook, stirring, until the cheese is melted. Spread the vegetables in the bottom of the prepared dish. Top with the egg slices. Pour and spread the sauce over the vegetable mixture.

4. Bake, uncovered, for 20 minutes. Arrange tomato slices on top. Bake, uncovered, 5 minutes more or until heated through.

Per serving: 200 calories, 14 g carbohydrates, 14 g protein, 10 g fat

BEAN AND BACON CROISSANT SANDWICH

Yield: 1 serving

Here's a midnight snack or a quick meal you can pull together with what's on hand in the refrigerator.

1 croissant
2 tablespoons warm baked
  beans

2 slices crispy bacon
¼ cup grated Gruyère
  cheese

Cut the croissant in half. Spread the beans over the cut side of the bottom half and top with the bacon. Sprinkle with the cheese and broil until the cheese melts. Cover with the croissant top and serve immediately.

Per serving: 744 calories, 20 g carbohydrates, 24 g protein, 63 g fat

CARAMELIZED TOMATO OPEN-FACE SANDWICHES

Yield: 4 servings

If you like, you can put a slice of goat's cheese or soft blue cheese on top of the roll before returning it to the broiler.

1 to 2 garlic cloves, finely
  chopped
1 tablespoon olive oil
1 tablespoon finely chopped
  fresh basil
salt to taste

freshly ground pepper to
  taste
2 plum tomatoes, halved
  lengthwise
1 tablespoon tomato puree
4 whole-grain rolls, halved

1. Preheat the broiler. Mix the garlic with the oil and brush over a nonstick baking sheet.

2. Spread the tomato halves with the tomato puree and sprinkle with the basil. Place on the baking sheet. Broil until they begin to brown, about 2 minutes.

3. Place 1 or 2 artichoke halves and a tomato half on each roll, and place on the baking sheet. Broil until they caramelize nicely, about 2 minutes. Cool a few minutes before serving.

Per serving: 142 calories, 20 g carbohydrates, 5 g protein, 6 g fat

LIME-MARINATED TURKEY TACOS

Yield: 4 servings

A flavorful marinade makes the strips of turkey breast tender and extra flavorful.

FOR THE MARINADE
1 garlic clove, crushed
grated rind and juice of ½ lime
2 tablespoons taco relish
1 teaspoon chopped fresh
  cilantro

FOR THE FILLING
1 pound turkey breast, cut into
½-inch strips
1 tablespoon vegetable oil

TO SERVE
8 taco shells
2 cups shredded lettuce
2 plum tomatoes,
  chopped
2 tablespoons taco relish

1. Combine garlic, lime rind and juice, relish and cilantro in a shallow glass baking dish. Add the turkey and turn to coat. Cover and refrigerate for 2 to 3 hours, turning once or twice.

2. Heat the oil in a large skillet or wok over medium-high heat. Drain the turkey and stir-fry until crisp and golden, about 10 minutes.

3. Heat the taco shells according to package directions. Divide the turkey among the shells and top with the lettuce, tomatoes and relish.

Per serving: 289 calories, 12 g carbohydrates, 27 g protein, 15 g fat

TURKEY, CHEDDAR AND CRANBERRY FLAN

Yield: 8 servings

Alternative fillings can be used including other left over meats or fish. For a vegetarian flan, chopped mixed vegetables and grated cheese is ideal.

1½ cups sifted all-purpose flour

¾ cup grated cheddar cheese

pinch of dry mustard

8 tablespoons butter, melted, plus 1 tablespoon unmelted butter

1 small onion, chopped

2 cups diced cooked turkey

¼ cup fresh cranberries

1 tablespoon chopped fresh parsley

salt to taste

freshly ground pepper to taste

¾ cup plus 1 tablespoon crème fraîche

2 eggs

1. Preheat the oven to 375 degrees.

2. Sift the flour into a bowl, add the cheese and mustard and mix well. Add 8 tablespoons melted butter and 1 to 2 tablespoons of water, enough to mix together to form a soft dough.

3. Mold the pastry into an 8-inch tart pan with a removable bottom, and prick the pastry with a fork. Line with parchment paper, fill with dried peas or beans or aluminum pie weights and bake for 15 minutes.

4. Meanwhile, prepare the filling: Melt the remaining 1 tablespoon butter in a saucepan, add the onion and cook gently until soft, 2 to 3 minutes. Add the turkey, cranberries, parsley, salt and pepper and mix well.

5. Combine the crème frâiche and eggs in a bowl, mix well and pour over the turkey mixture. Mix well.

6. Spoon out the peas, beans or pie weights from the pastry shell and remove the parchment. Pour the turkey mixture into the pastry case and bake until firm to the touch and lightly golden brown, 35 to 40 minutes.

Per serving: 355 calories, 20 g carbohydrates, 18 g protein, 22 g fat

CREAMED, MASHED ROOT VEGETABLES WITH SAUSAGES AND CRANBERRY CHUTNEY

Yield: 4 servings

The elements of this substantial dish remind one of winter. But the sausages could always be grilled over an outdoor fire in the summer.

CHUTNEY

1 tablespoon sugar
4 tablespoons fresh cranberries
2 tablespoons fresh orange
   juice
2 small potatoes, peeled and
   diced
4 ounces baby parsnips, peeled
and diced
1 ounce butter
2 tablespoons heavy cream
salt to taste
freshly ground pepper to
   taste
4 pork sausage links, cooked
   and hot

1. For the chutney: Combine 5 ounces water and the sugar in a small saucepan and stir until dissolved. Add the cranberries and simmer until the cranberries begin to break down, 5 to 6 minutes. Remove 1 tablespoon cranberries, reserve, and add the orange juice to the pan. Set aside the chutney.

2. Cook the potatoes and parsnips covered with salted boiling water in a 2-quart saucepan until tender, about 15 minutes. Drain the potatoes and parsnips and mash with the butter and the cream. Season with salt and pepper and keep warm. Serve with the sausages and chutney. Garnish with the reserved cranberries.

Per serving: 215 calories, 19 g carbohydrates, 5 g protein, 14 g fat

CHALLAH LATKES

Yield: 8 servings

This recipe was adapted from an L. A. Times article, "Eight Days of Latkes" by Judy Zeidler. Judy wrote, "Jewish delis choose challah as their No. 1 choice for making French toast. I discovered challah also makes a delicious dessert latke, especially when topped with orange marmalade or ice cream."

8 (about ³⁄₄-inch thick) slices
   challah (egg bread)
3 eggs, lightly beaten
1 tablespoon confectioners'
   sugar plus extra for serving
³⁄₄ cup milk
1 tablespoon grated orange
   rind
oil for frying
orange marmalade for serving

1. Using a 2¹⁄₂ to 3-inch round cookie cutter, cut each slice of bread into a round. In a large bowl combine eggs, 1 tablespoon powdered sugar, milk and orange rind. Place each slice of bread in egg mixture and let soak on both sides.

2. Heat the oil in a large nonstick skillet over medium-high heat. Using a metal spatula, carefully transfer bread rounds into skillet and fry bread until golden brown on both sides and egg mixture is cooked, about 5 minutes. Arrange on heated serving plates, sprinkle with powdered sugar and top with a spoonful of orange marmalade.

Per serving: 148 calories, 19 g carbohydrates, 6 g protein, 5 g fat

GREEN RICOTTA GNOCCHI

Yield: 4 servings

These are also called malfatti and, more affectionally, "nude ravioli" because they are dumplings of filling without any pasta around them. Be sure to thoroughly wring out the spinach or Swiss chard because too much moisture will cause the dumplings to break up while cooking.

1 pound spinach or Swiss chard
1½ cups ricotta cheese
3 large eggs and 1 more if needed
1 cup freshly grated Parmesan cheese
1/8 teaspoon ground white pepper
½ teaspoon grated nutmeg
2 to 3 tablespoons all-purpose flour
6 tablespoons butter, melted

1. Remove the stems and thick veins from the spinach or chard and steam or boil until tender, 5 to 10 minutes. Drain and cool, then squeeze tightly in your hands to remove as much water as possible. Place the spinach or chard on a board and finely chop or process very briefly in a food processor. (You do not want to puree the greens.)

2. Place the spinach or chard in a bowl, add the ricotta and mix thoroughly but gently, using your hands. Add 1 egg and mix it in, then add ½ cup Parmesan cheese and mix again. Add 2 more eggs, mix again and season with the nutmeg and pepper. If the texture is moist enough to shape, don't add any more eggs. If you need to, lightly beat one more egg and mix in just enough of it to moisten the mixture. Add just enough flour to hold the mixture together.

3. Using two tablespoons, scoop up some of the mixture and, transferring it back and forth between the spoons, roll it into an elongated egg shape, dipping the spoons lightly in flour if necessary to prevent sticking. Repeat with the remaining mixture.

4. Lay the gnocchi gently on a floured surface or tray, making sure they do not touch or overlap, and leave them to rest for about an hour.

5. Heat a large saucepan of salted water to boiling, very carefully add the dumplings and gently boil until they bob up to the surface, about 2 minutes.

6. Gently scoop the dumplings out of the boiling water using a slotted spoon, arrange them carefully on a warmed serving platter or in a warmed bowl. Pour the butter over the gnocchi and dust with the remaining cheese. Serve at once.

Per serving: 415 calories, 9 g carbohydrates, 22 g protein, 33 g fat

TURKEY SKILLET STIR-FRY WITH SPINACH AND RED PEPPER

Yield: 4 servings

Cook the vegetables until just tender-crisp. They will be juicier and more interesting with a little crunch.

12 ounces of turkey breasts
2 tablespoons sunflower oil
2 onions, sliced
2 garlic cloves, finely chopped
1 red bell pepper, seeded and
  finely sliced
1½ ounces shiitaki mush-
  rooms, rehydrated according

to package directions
2 tablespoons sherry
1 (8-ounce) package baby
  spinach leaves
2 tablespoons soy sauce
1 teaspoon dark sesame oil
salt to taste
freshly ground pepper to taste

1. Pound the turkey gently between two pieces of plastic wrap. Remove the plastic and cut the turkey into thin strips. Heat the oil in a large skillet and cook the turkey breasts for 3 minutes. Remove from the pan and keep warm.

2. Add 1 tablespoon of oil to the pan and stir-fry the onions, garlic, red pepper and mushrooms for 2 to 3 minutes.

3. Blend the sherry with the cornstarch in a cup and gradually stir it into the onion mixture. Add the turkey and spinach and cook gently until the spinach wilts, 7 to 8 minutes. Stir in the soy sauce and sesame oil. Season with salt and pepper.

Per serving: 294 calories, 19 g carbohydrates, 23 g protein, 14 g fat

SICILIAN EGGPLANT AND OLIVE STEW

Yield: 6 servings

3 to 4 celery stalks, including
　leaves, chopped
1 large onion, chopped
1 tablespoon salted capers
3 tablespoons olive oil
1 large (2¼-pound) eggplant,
　cut into 1-inch chunks

20 green olives
3 tablespoons tomato paste
1 tablespoon sugar
1 tablespoon white wine vine-
　gar
salt to taste
freshly ground pepper to taste

1. Blanch the celery and onion in lightly salted boiling water for a few minutes and drain. Set aside.

2. Meanwhile, soak the capers in a small bowl of water for 10 minutes and drain. Set aside.

3. Heat half the oil in a large nonstick skillet over medium heat, add half the eggplant chunks and fry until brown and tender. Remove to a bowl and repeat with the remaining eggplant, adding the first batch to the second when it is finished. Add the onion, celery and all the remaining ingredients.

4. Stir well, and cover and cook for about 15 minutes, adding 1 to 2 tablespoons of water if the sauce gets too thick during cooking. Remove the lid towards the end of cooking to evaporate some of the liquid if necessary. Season to taste with salt and pepper.

Per serving: 108 calories, 150 g carbohydrates, 3 g protein, 4 g fat

PAN-FRIED PARMESAN POLENTA WITH GRILLED PORTOBELLO MUSHROOMS AND 30-MINUTE TOMATO SAUCE

Yield: 24 triangles
with topping and sauce

olive oil for greasing the pan

1 tablespoon olive oil

POLENTA

3⅓ cups milk
2 ounces butter
salt to taste
freshly grated nutmeg to taste
1½ cups fine semolina or cornmeal
¼ cup freshly grated Parmesan
  cheese plus extra for serving
2 eggs
1 tablespoon butter

MUSHROOMS

14 ounces portobello mushrooms, carefully wiped off
  and stalks removed (do not
  wash)
oil for broiling
salt to taste
freshly ground pepper to taste
30-MINUTE TOMATO SAUCE,
  warmed (see page 335)
BASIL OIL (see page 313)

1. Grease a 12 by 6-inch baking sheet with olive oil and set aside.

2. For the polenta: Combine the milk, butter and a pinch each of salt and nutmeg in a 2-quart saucepan and heat to boiling over medium heat. Gradually add the semolina in a steady stream while stirring continuously with a wooden spoon. Cook, stirring, until the mixture comes loose off the sides and bottom of the saucepan. Remove the pan from the heat and add ¼ cup of the grated Parmesan cheese and the eggs and mix well. Taste and adjust the seasoning. Immediately turn the polenta onto the prepared baking sheet and spread with a spatula until completely even and flat. This has to be done at great speed as the semolina mixture sets very quickly. Set aside and cool.

3. Turn out the pan of cooled polenta onto a work surface or cutting board. Cut into 3 by 2½-inch triangles.

4. For the mushrooms: Preheat the broiler. Place the mushrooms on

a baking sheet and brush with oil. Season with salt and pepper. Broil the mushrooms until they are tender, turning to cook on all sides, about 5 minutes in all.

5. Preheat a seasoned nonstick griddle over medium heat. Melt the butter in the oil on the griddle and fry the polenta triangles on both sides until golden brown. Transfer to a serving platter and sprinkle with additional Parmesan cheese.

6. To dress the dish, place a small ladle of hot tomato sauce into a large soup plate, place six pieces of polenta in a circle, top with a ring of four or five pieces of grilled mushrooms in the center and drizzle some basil oil over the top. Serve immediately. Additional Parmesan cheese can be served on the side.

Per triangle: 150 calories, 13 g carbohydrates, 6 g protein, 9 g fat

---

SMOKY GREEN-BEAN STEW

Yield: 6 servings

Vegetables take center stage in this dish but the smoky flavor of a turkey wing adds depth and meaty richness.

1 smoked turkey wing
1 medium yellow onion, diced
2 garlic cloves, minced
2 pounds green beans,

trimmed, halved
8 ounces red-skinned new potatoes (6 small potatoes)
salt to taste
pepper to taste

1. Place a large heavy saucepan over medium heat and let preheat for about 3 minutes, Add the turkey wing, and cook, turning the wing several times until it is browned and begins to release some of its oil. Add the onion and cook, stirring, until browned, about 3 minutes. Add the garlic and fry 1 minute.

2. Add the green beans, potatoes and enough water to just cover the vegetables. Heat to boiling and simmer over medium heat until the potatoes are tender, 35 to 45 minutes, depending on size of potatoes. Pull the turkey meat off the bones and shred. Stir into the stew. Season with salt and pepper.

Per serving: 169 calories, 20 g carbohydrates, 12 g protein, 6 g fat

SKILLET CASSEROLE WITH SAUSAGE AND FLAGEOLETS

Yield: 6 servings

Flagelolets are immature kidney beans that have been removed from their pods while they are young and tender. They are especially prized for their delicate flavor and beautiful pale-green color. If you can't find them, substitute navy beans.

1 tablespoon vegetable oil
12 ounces sausage, chopped into bite-size pieces
1 large onion, thinly sliced
6 ounces button mushrooms, quartered
1 large green bell pepper, seeded and diced
4 tablespoons all-purpose flour
1 cup dry red wine, more if needed
1 tablespoon Worcestershire sauce
1 (14-ounce) can chopped tomatoes
1 (14-ounce) can flageolets, drained
salt to taste
freshly ground pepper to taste
2 tablespoons crème fraîche

1. Heat the oil in a large skillet over medium heat and sauté the sausage, onion, mushrooms and bell pepper until the onion is soft, about 8 minutes.

2. Sprinkle the flour over the sausage and vegetables and cook for 2 minutes, stirring constantly.

3. Gradually add the wine and Worcestershire sauce, stirring constantly.

4. Add the tomatoes and flageolets and heat to boiling, stirring gently to keep the beans intact. Season with salt and pepper, stir in the crème fraîche and heat until warmed through.

Per serving: 330 calories, 19 g carbohydrates, 13 g protein, 20 g fat

CORN AND TOFU PIE

Yield: 4 servings

This imaginative combination of East meets West ingredients shows why quiches have never gone out of style. The tender custard makes it work.

1 teaspoon margarine
2 tablespoons fine dry breadcrumbs
1 (12-ounce) package tofu,
  drained and cut into 1-inch
  chunks
2 egg whites
1 large egg
³⁄₄ cup shredded regular or
  low-fat cheddar cheese
¹⁄₃ cup low-fat or skim milk
¹⁄₂ teaspoon dried oregano

leaves, crushed
¹⁄₄ teaspoon ground black pepper
¹⁄₈ teaspoon salt
¹⁄₈ teaspoon garlic powder
1 tablespoon chopped fresh
  parsley (optional)
1 tablespoon dried minced
  onion
1 (7-ounce) can whole-kernel
  corn, drained
1 medium tomato

1. Preheat the oven to 350 degrees. Grease a 9-inch pie dish with the margarine over the bottom and sprinkle with the breadcrumbs to coat the dish. Set the dish aside.

2. Combine the tofu, egg whites, whole egg, ¹⁄₂ cup of the cheese, the milk, oregano, pepper, salt and garlic powder in a blender or food processor bowl. Cover and blend or process until smooth.

3. Pour into a bowl and stir in the corn, parsley and dried onion. Pour into the prepared pie plate. Bake, uncovered, until a knife inserted near the center comes out clean, 30 to 35 minutes.

4. Cut the tomato into thin wedges and arrange wedges over the pie in a starburst pattern. Sprinkle with the remaining cheese. Bake until the cheese melts, about 3 minutes.

Per serving: 261 calories, 18 g carbohydrates, 19 g protein, 14 g fat

SAFFRON BROWN RICE
AND MUSHROOMS
UNDER PRESSURE

Yield: 12 servings

You can cook this in a saucepan but it will take about 20 minutes longer once the ingredients are combined.

1 clove garlic, minced
1½ cups long-grain brown rice, rinsed and drained
1 pound button mushrooms, cut into ½-inch slices
1 medium carrot, peeled and diced

1 teaspoon fennel seeds
½ teaspoon salt or to taste
ground black pepper to taste
¼ teaspoon saffron threads
chopped fresh parsley for garnish

Combine the leeks, garlic and 1 tablespoon water in a pressure cooker over medium heat and cook, stirring, for 2 to 3 minutes. Add 2 cups boiling water, the rice, mushrooms, carrot, fennel seeds, ½ teaspoon salt, ¼ teaspoon pepper and the saffron. Mix well, cover, lock, and immediately bring to high pressure. Keep there for 25 minutes. Remove from heat and cool for 10 minutes, after which release/open cooker. Stir, transfer to a serving bowl and sprinkle with parsley.

Per serving: 98 calories, 20 g carbohydrates, 3 g protein, trace fat

TVP AND SALSA WRAPS

Yield: 10 servings

Pinto beans get an extra boost of nutrition from the soybeans in TVP (texturized vegetable protein). Juicy homemade salsa and a generous amount of shredded cheddar add fresh flavors. The burritos may be made ahead, kept wrapped, and baked before serving. Unwrap, place on cookie sheet, brush tops lightly with oil if desired and bake at 350 degrees about 20 minutes.

½ cup dried pinto beans
3 garlic cloves, minced
1 bay leaf
½ cup textured vegetable protein (TVP) granules or flakes
2 teaspoons chili powder
1 teaspoon ground cumin
1 teaspoon salt
½ teaspoon dried oregano

leaves
1 tablespoon olive oil
1 small onion, chopped
hot sauce to taste
5 (8-inch) tortillas or chapattis (available in East Indian grocery stores)
½ recipe TWO-TOMATO-AVOCADO SALSA (see page 319)

1. The day before serving: Combine the beans and 3 cups water in a large bowl and set aside to soak overnight.

2. The next day: Drain and rinse the beans and combine with 3 cups fresh water, the garlic and bay leaf in a 2-quart saucepan. Heat to boiling and simmer until the beans are tender, 1 to 1½ hours. Drain the beans in a sieve placed over a bowl. Return the bean liquid to the saucepan. Add the TVP, ½ cup hot water, the chili powder, cumin, salt and oregano, mix well and set aside.

3. Heat the oil in a large skillet, add the onion and sauté until softened, about 7 minutes. With a slotted spoon, drain and add the TVP mixture to the onion and cook a few minutes more. Stir in the cooked beans, then transfer mixture to a food processor and process until smooth, adding the bean liquid as necessary to make the mixture a chili-like thickness. Taste and add a little hot sauce.

4. To assemble: Heat a griddle or skillet over medium heat until a few drops of water dance on the surface. Dry fry each tortilla on both sides until the surface of the tortilla begins to bubble and brown slightly. Keep them warm in a thick towel. When all are heated, place one-fifth of the filling down one side of a tortilla and roll up. Repeat with the remaining tortillas and filling. Cut each tortilla in half. Serve with the salsa.

Per serving: 173 calories, 20 g carbohydrates, 11 g protein, 6 g fat

TWO-BEAN BAKED CALZONE

Yield: 6 servings

Of the two beans in this vegetarian dish, the borlotti may be the mystery guest. Popular in Italian and Portuguese cooking, these reddish-streaked, medium-size tan nuggets are known in America as cranberry beans. If you can't find them, pinto beans are an acceptable substitute, with red kidney beans next in line. Serve the calzone with a crisp green salad.

1 (12-inch) round PIZZA
  DOUGH (see page 368)
1 garlic clove, crushed
2 tablespoons roughly
  chopped fresh parsley

FILLING
1/3 cup cooked canellini beans
1/3 cup cooked borlotti beans
1 cup canned plum tomatoes,

drained and chopped
4 ounces extra-sharp cheddar
  cheese, grated
2 tablespoons chopped fresh
  basil leaves
2 tablespoons sun-dried
  tomato paste
1 teaspoon brown sugar
freshly ground black
  pepper

1. Preheat the oven to 400 degrees. Lightly grease a nonstick baking sheet or round pizza pan. Place the pizza-dough round on the pan and press the garlic and parsley into the dough.

2. Combine the beans, chopped tomatoes, cheese, basil, tomato paste, sugar and pepper in a large bowl, mix well and spoon over half of the dough. Wet the edges of the dough with water and fold over to form a large turnover. Flute the edges to seal.

3. Dust the calzone lightly with flour and bake until golden, cooked through and crisp, 25 to 30 minutes.

Per serving: 171 calories, 19 g carbohydrates, 8 g protein, 7 g fat

SWEET ONION 'N' SWISS QUICHE

Yield: 6 servings

This easy recipe uses the microwave for cooking the onions and "baking" the pie.

3/4 cup thinly sliced sweet
onion
2 tablespoons butter
1 baked pie shell made from
LOWFAT PASTRY (see pages
390-391)
2 1/2 cups shredded Swiss

cheese
2 firm tomatoes, sliced
1 (5-ounce) can evaporated
milk
2 large eggs
1 teaspoon dried Italian
seasoning

1. Combine the onion and butter in a 2-quart glass measure or casserole. Cover with plastic wrap or a lid, loosely venting the container. Microwave on HIGH power 5 1/2 to 6 1/2 minutes. Remove the onion with a slotted spoon and place in the pie shell. Sprinkle the cheese over the onions and arrange the tomato slices on top.

2. To the onion cooking liquid remaining in the measure, add the milk, eggs and Italian seasoning and beat well. Pour the milk mixture over the ingredients in the pie shell.

3. Microwave on MEDIUM-HIGH power (70 percent) until center is almost set, 10 to 12 minutes, rotating the dish midway through cooking. Let stand 10 minutes before cutting.

Per serving: 394 calories, 20 g carbohydrates, 19 g protein, 26 g fat

GRILLED GARDEN BURGERS

Yield: 4 servings

Fire up the barbecue and get ready for these vegetable-packed, tasty turkey or beef burgers. You can shape them ahead of time and keep them refrigerated until you are ready to cook.

1 egg white
1/4 cup fine dry bread crumbs
1/4 cup finely shredded carrot
1/4 cup finely chopped onion
1/4 cup finely chopped green
pepper
1/2 teaspoon salt

1/8 teaspoon pepper
1 pound ground turkey or lean
beef
2 tablespoons grated Parmesan
cheese
nonstick cooking spray
1 medium tomato, sliced

1. In a large bowl combine the egg white, breadcrumbs and, if using beef, 2 tablespoons water. Stir in the carrot, onion, green pepper, salt, and pepper. Add the ground meat and Parmesan cheese and mix well. Shape meat mixture into four $3/4$-thick patties.

2. Prepare an outdoor grill for barbecue. When the coals are ready, grease a cold grill rack with nonstick cooking spray and place the rack on a grill. Grill the burgers over medium coals for 7 minutes. Turn and grill 8 to 11 minutes or until no pink remains. Place 1 tomato slice on each burger and grill 1 minute longer.

Per serving: 227 calories, 9 g carbohydrates, 23 g protein, 11 g fat

HAM AND POTATO HASH

Yield: 3 servings

A skillet supper is so nice because all the flavors are concentrated in one pan—and there's not a lot of cleanup! This combination of foods also makes a nice brunch dish.

nonstick cooking spray
8 ounces ground fully
   cooked ham
1 cup sliced celery
$1/2$ cup chopped
   onion
1 small potato, peeled and
   chopped

1 cup fresh or frozen cut green
   beans
$1/4$ teaspoon dried thyme,
   crushed
$1/8$ teaspoon ground black
   pepper
1 tablespoon grated Parmesan
   cheese

1. Grease a large skillet with nonstick cooking spray. Heat the skillet over medium heat and add the ham, celery, and onion. Cook, stirring and breaking up the ham with a wooden spoon, until the vegetables are tender, about 10 minutes. Stir in the potatoes, fresh green beans, if used, $1/2$ cup water, thyme, and pepper. Heat to boiling and reduce the heat to low. Cover and simmer for 20 minutes or until the potatoes are tender and most of the liquid is absorbed. If using frozen green beans, add to ham and potato mixture the last 7 minutes of cooking.

2. To serve, sprinkle with Parmesan cheese.

Per serving: 209 calories, 17 g carbohydrates, 16 g protein, 9 g fat

TURKEY-BROCCOLI MELT

Yield: 4 servings

Here's a complete meal so satisfying that you can't dismiss it as "just" an open-face sandwich.

1 (16-ounce) package frozen
  broccoli spears
4 teaspoons prepared
  mustard
4 slices whole wheat bread,
  toasted
4 slices deli turkey breast
¼ cup shredded sharp cheddar
  cheese
1 cup fresh alfalfa sprouts

1. Preheat the broiler. Cook the broccoli according to package directions. Drain and set aside.

2. Spread 1 teaspoon mustard over each bread slice and place on a baking sheet. Top each with 1 turkey slice, 3 broccoli spears and 1 tablespoon cheese.

3. Broil 3 inches from heat 1½ minutes. Top with ¼ cup sprouts.

Per serving: 183 calories, 20 g carbohydrates, 17 g protein, 6 g fat

SPANISH RICE AND BEANS

Yield: 6 servings

This paella-like mix is a vegetarian's delight. The fiery color comes from the saffron, tomato and pimiento. The rich sherry flavor mixes well with the salty olives and earthy garbanzo beans.

2 tablespoons olive oil
¼ cup cooked garbanzo beans
  (chickpeas)
½ teaspoon cayenne pepper
1 medium yellow onion, diced
  (2 cups)
10 medium garlic cloves,
  crushed
1 cup uncooked long-grain
  white rice
1½ teaspoons saffron strands
2 cups vegetable broth
1 cup dry sherry
1 ripe medium tomato, diced (1
  cup)
1 (14-ounce) can sliced pimientos, drained and diced
¼ cup frozen petite peas
20 pitted black olives, cut in
  half
salt and freshly ground black
  pepper to taste

1. Preheat the oven to 350 degrees. Heat the oil over high heat in a large nonstick skillet. Add the garbanzo beans and cayenne and sauté 1 minute. Remove to a plate, lower the heat to medium high, add onion and garlic, and sauté 5 minutes. Add the rice and sauté a few seconds. Sprinkle the saffron over the mixture and add the broth. Heat to simmering and add the sherry, tomato and pimientos. Return the garbanzos to the skillet. Cover and simmer 15 minutes.

2. Stir in the peas and olives, cook 1 minute and season with salt and pepper.

Per serving: 190 calories, 20 g carbohydrates, 3 g protein, 7 g fat

PAELLA WITH CHICKEN, SHRIMP AND SQUID

Yield: 6 servings

For a different flavor, mussels can be added at the beginning with the squids.

1³/₄ cups chicken broth
1 teaspoon saffron threads
¹/₂ cup olive oil
4 chicken thighs, bone in, with skins
1 small Spanish onion, chopped
3 ounces cleaned fresh squid rings
1 plum tomato, skinned, seeded and diced
²/₃ cup paella rice or risotto rice
1 teaspoon paprika
a pinch of chili powder
sea salt to taste
freshly ground pepper to taste
20 small shrimp, with shells
2 garlic cloves, crushed
chopped fresh parsley for garnish
lemon wedges for garnish

1. Combine the broth and saffron in a small saucepan and heat almost to boiling. Keep hot.

2. Preheat the oven to 325 degrees. Heat a 9-inch cast-iron skillet or paella pan over medium-high heat until hot. Add the oil and heat until hot. Brown the chicken pieces and onions until the chicken is golden brown on both sides and the onions are wilted, about 6 minutes. Add the squid and sauté 30 seconds. Add the tomatoes and

sauté until the liquid evaporates, 1 to 2 minutes. Add the rice and stir until coated with oil. Add the hot saffron broth, paprika, chili powder, salt and pepper. Stir briefly to mix together and when the broth is boiling, reduce the heat. Simmer over low heat until the chicken has almost cooked through, the rice is tender and the mixture is no longer soupy and some liquid remains, about 10 minutes.

3. Stir in the shrimp and garlic. Bake until the liquid has evaporated, about 15 minutes. Remove from the oven and cover with foil. Let stand 10 minutes. To serve, sprinkle with the parsley and garnish with the lemon.

Per serving: 424 calories, 20 g carbohydrates, 20 g protein, 29 g fat

BEAN AND FRESH VEGETABLE TART

Yield: 8 servings

Mexicans have many types of beans and make many different types of savory pies with them. This one has a flour crust.

Nonstick cooking spray
3/4 cup all-purpose flour
1 cup shredded cheddar cheese
1 1/2 teaspoons baking powder
1/2 teaspoon salt
1/3 cup milk
1 egg, slightly beaten
2/3 cup cooked garbanzo beans
2/3 cup cooked kidney beans

1 (8-ounce) can tomato sauce
1 small green bell pepper, seeded and chopped
1 small onion, finely chopped
2 teaspoons chili powder
2 teaspoons fresh or 1/2 teaspoon dried oregano leaves (preferably Mexican)
1/4 teaspoon garlic powder

1. Preheat the oven to 375 degrees. Grease a 10-inch pie plate with nonstick cooking spray.

2. Mix the flour, 1/2 cup cheese, the baking powder and salt in a medium bowl. Stir in the milk and egg until blended and spread over the bottom and up the sides of the prepared pie plate.

3. Combine the beans, tomato sauce, bell pepper, onion, chili pepper, oregano and garlic powder in a medium bowl and mix well. Spread the mixture into the pie plate and sprinkle with the remaining 1/2 cup cheese.

4. Bake the pie until the edges are puffy and light brown, about 25 minutes. Let stand 10 minutes before cutting.

Per serving: 171 calories, 20 g carbohydrates, 9 g protein, 6 g fat

SPAGHETTI-SQUASH PRIMAVERA

Yield: 5 servings

This vegetable alternative to pasta doesn't need to offer any apologies for being less than strands of al dente wheat. It is deliciously juicy and crunchy and beautifully golden. Serve chilled or at room temperature.

2 cups broccoli florets
2 cups cooked spaghetti
  squash
1 cup sliced fresh mushrooms
1 cup julienned yellow squash
9 ounces frozen sugar snap
  peas, thawed
1/4 cup sliced scallions
2 tablespoons balsamic
  vinegar

2 teaspoons olive oil
2 garlic cloves, crushed
1 tablespoon chopped fresh
  parsley
3/4 teaspoon dried basil
1/8 teaspoon salt
1/8 teaspoon freshly ground
  pepper
1/4 cup freshly grated fresh
  Parmesan cheese

1. Cook the broccoli in a saucepan of boiling water for 1 minute. Drain, place in a large bowl and add the spaghetti squash, mushrooms, yellow squash and sugar-snap peas in a bowl, toss gently and set aside.

2. Whisk the vinegar and oil in a small bowl until blended. Whisk in the garlic, parsley, basil, salt and pepper until blended, add to the vegetable mixture and toss well. Sprinkle with the Parmesan cheese.

Per serving: 92 calories, 11 g carbohydrates, 5 g protein, 4 g fat

TURKEY-VEGETABLE CHILI

Yield: 4 servings

You can use the spicy vegetable-juice cocktail if you want a little more kick. Bloody Mary mix also adds a lot of sizzle.

nonstick cooking spray
1 cup chopped green bell
  pepper
3/4 cup chopped celery
1/2 cup chopped carrot
1/2 cup chopped onion
1 pound ground turkey

2 teaspoons chili powder
1 teaspoon dried Italian seasoning
1 1/4 cups vegetable-juice cocktail
1 (8-ounce) can no-salt-added
  tomato sauce

1. Grease a large nonstick skillet with cooking spray and heat over medium-high heat until hot.

2. Add the bell pepper, celery, carrot and onion and sauté until tender, about 8 minutes. Add the turkey, chili powder and Italian seasoning and cook until the turkey is browned, about 2 minutes, stirring and breaking it up with a wooden spoon. Add the cocktail juice and tomato sauce, mix well and heat to boiling. Reduce the heat and simmer, uncovered, until thickened, about 30 minutes, stirring occasionally.

Per serving: 234 calories, 15 g carbohydrates, 22 g protein, 10 g fat

BEEF AND BLACK-BEAN CHILI

Yield: 12 servings

Although black beans are especially alluring visually, other sweet, mouth-pleasing beans can be used with great success here. If you can't find epazote, a pungent herb that adds flavor and also helps to reduce the gas in beans, add a splash of vinegar.

2 cups black beans or Jacob's Cattle, red kidney or pinto beans
2 teaspoons dried epazote (optional), available at Mexican grocery stores
4 teaspoons cumin seeds
2 teaspoons dried oregano leaves, preferably Mexican
3 onions, finely diced
3 tablespoons vegetable oil
4 garlic cloves, coarsely chopped
1 pound lean ground beef
2 to 3 tablespoons ground red chili
salt to taste

4 teaspoons sweet paprika
2 cups peeled, seeded and chopped tomato, juice reserved
1 to 2 teaspoons pureed chipotle chili
1/4 cup chopped fresh cilantro
dash of red wine vinegar or sherry vinegar (optional)

GARNISH
sour cream
1 poblano or long green chili, roasted and peeled and sliced
cilantro sprigs

1. Sort and rinse the beans and place in a large pot. Add 6 cups water and set aside to soak overnight. (Or heat the beans and water to boiling, reduce heat and simmer for 2 minutes. Remove from heat. Cover and let stand for 1 hour.)

2. Drain the beans if soaked overnight and place in a large pot. Add the epazote and enough water to cover by 4 inches. Heat to boiling and cook for 5 to 10 minutes, removing any surface scum. Lower the heat and simmer, partially covered.

3. While the beans cook, toast the cumin seeds in a large dry skillet over medium heat until fragrant, add the oregano and cook for 5 seconds, shaking the pan so the seasonings don't burn. Cool on a plate and grind to a powder.

4. Sauté the onions in the oil in the same skillet over medium heat for 7 to 8 minutes. Add the garlic and sauté until tender. Add the ground beef and brown well, breaking the meat into little pieces with a wooden spoon. Add the cumin mixture, 2 tablespoons ground red chili, 1 1/2 teaspoons salt and the paprika and mix well. Lower the heat and cook until the onions are soft, another 5 minutes. Add the tomatoes and juice, 1 teaspoon chipotle puree and the cilantro. Simmer the mixture for 15 minutes and add it to the beans.

5. Continue cooking until the beans are completely soft, about 30 minutes, adding boiling water if necessary to keep the water level at least an inch above the beans. Taste and season with more ground red chili, chipotle and salt, and add a dash of vinegar if needed. Ladle the beans into bowls and garnish with a spoonful of sour cream, the chili strips and a sprig of cilantro.

Per serving: 231 calories, 14 g carbohydrates, 11 g protein, 15 g fat

SOFT CHICKEN-CABBAGE TACOS

Yield: 8 servings

Red cabbage adds a lot of crunch inside the tender tortillas. Splurge by adding a spoonful of sweet and tart Mango-Lime Salsa.

8 7-inch flour tortillas	½ teaspoon salt
3 cups shredded cooked chicken breast	½ cup sour cream
	2 cups thinly sliced red cabbage

1. Preheat the oven to 350 degrees. Wrap tortillas tightly in foil. Place the chicken on a sheet of foil and sprinkle with the salt. Toss to coat and wrap up tightly. Bake the packets of tortillas and chicken for 10 minutes.

2. To serve: Spread 1 tablespoon sour cream over each tortilla. Divide the chicken evenly among tortillas, top each with ¼ cup cabbage and fold in half.

Per serving: 215 calories, 19 g carbohydrates, 18 g protein, 7 g fat

SMOKED TURKEY-AND-WATERCRESS PITAS WITH SPICY MUSTARD SAUCE

Yield: 4 servings
(serving size: 1 pita half)

Everyone likes a good sandwich and this has all the elements for a house favorite. Watercress adds a peppery juiciness to complement the smoked turkey.

¼ cup plain yogurt
2 tablespoons spicy hot mustard
2 large pita breads, cut crosswise in half

4 slices smoked turkey breast
8 (¼-inch thick) slices tomato
1 cup loosely packed trimmed watercress
½ cup shredded Swiss cheese

Mix the yogurt with the mustard in a small bowl and spread evenly on the inside of each pita half. Place 1 turkey slice, 2 tomato slices and ¼ cup watercress on each half and sprinkle with 2 tablespoons of the cheese.

Per serving: 237 calories, 20 g carbohydrates, 18 g protein, 10 g fat

PASTA

CAMPANELLE WITH ROAST VEGETABLES, FETA CHEESE AND BASIL

Yield: 4 servings

This ruffled, bell-flower shaped pasta is readily available, but if you can't find it, use another pasta with an energetic squiggly or spiral shape.

2 tablespoons BASIL OIL
(see page 313)
1 small red onion, cut into 8 wedges
1 to 2 garlic cloves, crushed
1 small red bell pepper, seeded and cut into 8 pieces
1 small green bell pepper, seed-ed and cut into 8 pieces
1 small zucchini, cut into 2-inch chunks
1 small yellow squash, cut into 2-inch chunks
1 cup campanelle or other twisted-shape pasta, cooked and drained
¼ cup crumbled feta cheese
1 small bunch fresh basil, leaves removed, rinsed, drained and shredded
salt to taste
freshly ground pepper to taste

1. Preheat the oven to 400 degrees

2. Place the oil in a large roasting pan or baking dish and tilt the pan to spread it out. Place the pan on the top oven shelf of the hot oven for 2 to 3 minutes. Carefully remove the pan from the oven and add the onion, garlic, peppers, zucchini and squash. Mix the vegetables with the oil and roast them until tender, 35 to 40 minutes.

3. Add the freshly cooked and drained campanelle, feta cheese, basil and seasoning to taste and mix well.

Per serving: 182 calories, 20 g carbohydrates, 5 g protein, 9 g fat

LINGUINE WITH TUNA, LEMON AND ARUGULA

Yield: 4 first-course servings

3 tablespoons extra-virgin olive
   oil
2 garlic cloves, finely chopped
1 small dried red chile,
   crushed
1 (7-ounce) can tuna in olive
oil, drained and flaked
4 ounces linguine
1 bunch arugula, washed and
   dried, leaves coarsely chopped
juice of 1 lemon, or to taste
salt to taste

1. In a 3-quart saucepan, heat the oil over medium-low heat and gently cook the garlic and chile. As the garlic begins to change color, add the tuna and stir. Keep warm.

2. Cook the pasta in a large pot of salted boiling water. When the pasta is al dente, add the arugula and immediately drain the pasta and arugula in a colander. Add the pasta mixture to the tuna mixture. Drizzle with half the lemon juice. Using two wooden spoons, lift up and stir pasta and arugula until the tuna is evenly distributed. Taste and add more lemon juice and salt if needed. Serve at once.

Per serving: 257 calories, 20 g carbohydrates, 18 g protein, 12 g fat

SOBA NOODLES WITH SHRIMP, VEGETABLES AND SAFFRON SAUCE

Yield: 8 servings

Japanese soba (buckwheat) noodles can be found at Asian grocery stores. If you can't find them, use angel-hair pasta (cappellini).

4 ounces fresh snow peas
4 ounces soba noodles
2 teaspoons vegetable oil
2 large scallions, trimmed and
   julienned
2 garlic cloves, finely chopped
1 medium carrots, peeled and
julienned
2 ounces shiitake mushroom
   caps, thinly sliced
8 ounces medium shrimp,
   shelled and deveined
SAFFRON SAUCE, warm (see
   pages 329-330)

1. Trim ends off peas and remove the strings. Thinly slice each pea lengthwise. Set aside.

2. Cook the soba noodles in 3 quarts boiling water in a dutch oven for 2 minutes. Drain and rinse with cold, running water. Drain well and set aside.

3. Heat the vegetable oil in a large nonstick skillet over medium heat. Add the scallions and garlic and sauté 2 minutes. Add the sliced snow peas and carrots and sauté 1 minute. Add the mushroom caps and sauté 2 minutes. Add the shrimp and cook until pink, about 1 minute, stirring constantly. Add the soba and cook until heated through, about 1 minute, stirring constantly.

4. Place the noodle mixture in a large shallow serving bowl. Pour the sauce on top and toss to coat.

Per serving: 141 calories, 20 g carbohydrates, 5 g protein, 7 g fat

CELLOPHANE NOODLES WITH VODKA-FLAVORED PESTO SAUCE

Yield: 6 servings

8 ounces Chinese rice
  vermicelli noodles
6 tablespoons PESTO SAUCE

(see pages 320-321)
2 tablespoons vodka, or to taste
salt

1. Soak the noodles in a bowl of hot water until soft, about 10 minutes, and drain. Place the pasta in a large heated serving bowl.

2. Place the Pesto Sauce in a small bowl and stir in the vodka to form a paste. Add a little of the mixture to the pasta and toss to coat. Taste and add more of the pesto, thinned a little bit for easier distribution with hot water, and toss again. Taste for salt and adjust if necessary. Serve immediately.

Per serving: 142 calories, 10 g carbohydrates, 2 g protein, 9 g fat

RICE-STICK "LINGUINE" WITH GREEN-BEANS, MUSHROOMS AND GORGONZOLA SAUCE

Yield: 6 first-course
or light lunch servings

This is a delicious accompaniment for most pasta shapes but the flat strands of this Chinese pasta are really special. Serve with a crisp mixed green salad for a special lunch. East meets West and chopsticks for all!

4 ounces Chinese rice-stick
  noodles
4 ounces haricots verts or tender trimmed green beans
1 ounce butter
6 ounces mushrooms,
  sliced

4 ounces Gorgonzola cheese,
  crumbled
$2/3$ cup heavy cream
2 tablespoons shredded fresh
  basil
salt to taste
freshly ground pepper to taste

1. Soak the noodles in a baking dish of hot water until soft, about 15 to 20 minutes, and drain

2. Cut the beans into 1-inch pieces on the diagonal and steam, covered, in a 3-quart saucepan in $1/4$ cup boiling, salted water for 3 minutes. Add the mushrooms and steam until softened, about 2 minutes. Add the Gorgonzola and cream and stir over medium heat until the cheese melts, 3 to 4 minutes. Stir in almost all of the basil and season to taste.

3. Reheat the noodles and place in a large shallow serving bowl. Pour the sauce over the pasta and toss to coat. Sprinkle with the reserved basil.

Per serving: 271 calories, 20 g carbohydrates, 6 g protein, 19 g fat

HOISIN-FLAVORED VEGETARIAN NOODLES

Yield: 4 servings

The Chinese exploit the intense, sweet fruit flavor of hoisin sauce to enrich a dish and make it seem even more satisfying than it is. This is efficient when it comes to meatless meals, where dishes such as these noodles depend on seasoning to enhance the other few but thoughtfully chosen ingredients.

1 (2-ounce) bundle Chinese rice vermicelli noodles
2 tablespoons vegetable oil
1 tablespoon garlic puree
4 ounces fresh bean sprouts
8 ounces bok choy
2 eggs, lightly beaten
2 tablespoons hoisin sauce
2 tablespoons Chinese chili sauce
1 tablespoon low-sodium soy sauce
1/2 teaspoon black pepper
chopped scallions for garnish

1. Soak the noodles in a bowl of hot water until soft, about 10 minutes, and drain. Chop the bok choy into thin strips.

2. Heat the oil and fry the garlic until light brown. Add the bean sprouts, noodles and bok choy and stir-fry over high heat for 2 minutes. Add the eggs and toss well with the noodles. Add the remaining seasonings and stir-fry rapidly for 1 minute.

3. Serve with chopped scallions.

Per serving: 189 calories, 20 g carbohydrates, 6 g protein, 10 g fat

CHICKEN LIVERS AND LEMON WITH FRESH TAGLIATELLE

Yield: 6 to 8 servings

A little brandy or Marsala rises to the robust flavor of chicken liver. Freshly grated lemon rind adds a lively aroma.

8 ounces chicken livers
1 ounce butter
8 scallions, sliced
1 thyme sprig
1 garlic clove, crushed
salt to taste
freshly ground pepper to taste
1 tablespoon brandy or
    Marsala
finely grated rind of 1 lemon
8 ounces fresh tagliatelle
1 tablespoon oil
$^1/_4$ cup freshly grated Parmesan
    cheese

1. Trim the chicken livers, removing any greenish parts. Rinse and pat dry with paper towels.

2. Melt half the butter in a large skillet, add the scallions and thyme and cook until the scallions are soft but not colored. Add the garlic and cook for 1 minute longer.

3. Add half the chicken livers and cook, turning frequently, until brown on the outside but still pink in the center. Remove and discard the sprig of thyme. Place the chicken liver mixture into a food processor and process until smooth. Season to taste with salt and pepper.

4. Heat the remaining butter in the skillet until foaming and cook the remaining chicken livers as before. Add the brandy or Marsala and lemon rind to the pan and cook for 1 minute. Season lightly with salt and pepper and return the processed chicken-liver mixture to the pan. Mix thoroughly.

5. Cook the tagliatelle in a large saucepan of boiling salted water to which the oil has been added, until al dente. Drain and return to the pan. Add the chicken-liver mixture and mix thoroughly. Transfer to a large serving dish, sprinkle with the Parmesan cheese and serve immediately.

Each of 8 servings: 160 calories, 18 g carbohydrates, 9 g protein, 5 g fat

SALMON AND CAVIAR PASTA

Yield: 8 first-course servings

This appetizer or main course is as delicious and easy as it is elegant and beautiful. Champagne would be perfect with it.

2 shallots
2 garlic cloves
1 tablespoon butter
3$\frac{1}{2}$ ounces dry white wine
1 cup fresh fish broth
2 cups penne or rigatoni
1 ounce salmon roe caviar
6 large fresh scallops

1 (4-ounce) salmon fillet, diced
$\frac{1}{4}$ cup mixed chopped fresh
   flat leaf parsley, fresh basil
   and fresh chervil
salt to taste
freshly ground pepper to taste

1. Peel and dice the shallots and garlic. Melt the butter in a medium nonstick skillet over medium heat and sauté the shallots and garlic until softened, about 3 minutes. Add the white wine and broth, heat to boiling over medium-high heat and boil until reduced by half. Add the cream and boil until the liquid has thickened.

2. Meanwhile, cook the pasta in boiling salted water according to package directions. Drain the pasta and place in a large serving bowl.

3. Add the salmon to the wine sauce and remove the pan from the heat. Let stand 1 minute or until the salmon barely cooks through. Stir in the chopped herbs, season to taste and pour over the pasta. Toss to coat and sprinkle caviar on top. Toss again before serving.

Per serving: 294 calories, 19 g carbohydrates, 18 g protein, 15 g fat

FRESH SALMON LASAGNE WITH TOMATO DRESSING

Yield: 4 servings

This is an easy-to-make and glamorous-to-serve entrée. If beef-steak tomatoes are out of season, use eight of the ripest plum tomatoes you can find.

DRESSING
3 beefsteak tomatoes, chopped
$\frac{1}{2}$ cup olive oil
$\frac{1}{3}$ cup balsamic vinegar
$\frac{1}{4}$ cup snipped fresh chives
   plus 8 whole chives for
   garnish

salt to taste
freshly ground pepper to taste
nonstick cooking spray
8 (3-ounce) thin slices fresh
   salmon fillets
8 cooked short lasagne
   noodles, warm

1. For the dressing, combine the tomatoes, oil, vinegar and snipped chives in a small saucepan. Season with salt and pepper and heat through. Keep warm.

2. Grease a nonstick skillet with cooking spray. Pan-fry the salmon fillets. On each of 4 dinner plates, place a piece of salmon, then top with a noodle, then a piece of salmon, and then another noodle on top. Spoon some warm dressing over each portion and cross 2 whole chives over each.

Per serving: 623 calories, 20 g carbohydrates, 40 g protein, 42 g fat

FRIED EGG NOODLES

Yield: 8 side-dish servings

8 ounces dried Chinese egg
  noodles
1 tablespoon oil
1 tablespoon soy sauce

1 tablespoon oyster sauce
6 ounces broth or water
1/4 teaspoon freshly ground
  pepper

1. Soak the noodles in boiling water until softened, about 1 minute. Drain in a colander and rinse well with cold water. Squeeze off excess water.

2. Preheat the wok or skillet over medium-high heat. Add the oil and swirl it around the wok and add the noodles and toss until hot.

3. Add all the sauces and continue to stir. Add the broth or water around the edges of the wok and continue to stir for 1 minute more.

4. Turn onto a plate and serve.

Per serving: 124 calories, 20 g carbohydrates, 4 g protein, 3 g fat

PASTA AND VEGETABLES IN BROTH

Yield: 2 servings

1 tablespoon butter
1 carrot, peeled and thinly
  sliced
1/4 cup chopped broccoli
3 cups fish stock; or beef,

  chicken or vegetable broth
1/2 cup cooked pasta
1/2 cup fresh bean sprouts
1/4 cup fresh peas
toasted sesame seeds for garnish

1. Melt the butter in a 2-quart saucepan over medium heat. Add the carrot and broccoli, cover and cook until softened, 2 minutes. Add the stock or broth, pasta, bean sprouts and peas. Simmer until the carrots are cooked through, 3 to 4 minutes. Pour into soup bowls and sprinkle with the toasted sesame seeds.

Per serving: 209 calories, 18 g carbohydrates, 14 g protein, 9 g fat

EGG NOODLES WITH CHICKEN AND VEGETABLES

Yield: 8 first-course servings

6 ounces dried Chinese egg
  noodles
8 ounces chicken breast
1 medium carrot, peeled and
  julienned
4 ounces green beans, trimmed
  and cut in half lengthwise
1 cup julienned daikon radish

2 tablespoons soy sauce
1 tablespoon oyster sauce
1 tablespoon oil
1 red chile, sliced (optional)
2 sprigs fresh cilantro, leaves
  only

1. Soak the noodles in boiling water until softened, about 1 minute. Drain in a colander and rinse well with cold water. Squeeze off excess water. Slice the chicken breast into thin pieces.

2. Heat the oil in a wok over medium-high heat and add the chicken pieces and vegetables. Stir-fry until the chicken is almost cooked through. Add the noodles and heat through. Add the soy sauce and the oyster sauce and stir-fry until the chicken and noodles are coated. Let cook 2 minutes, until heated through and the chicken is cooked.

3. Turn out the noodle mixture onto a serving plate and garnish with the slices of chile and cilantro leaves. Serve hot.

Per serving: 145 calories, 18 g carbohydrates, 11 g protein, 3 g fat

CELLOPHANE NOODLES WITH GARLIC-PEANUT SAUCE

Yield: 8 first-course servings

These noodles are also called bean thread noodles because they are made from mung beans. They are found in Chinese grocery stores and are packaged in bundles of varying weights.

2 (2-ounce) bundles Chinese rice vermicelli noodles
1 cup creamy peanut butter
1 cup chicken or vegetable broth or more if necessary
3 tablespoons rice vinegar
2 tablespoons dark sesame oil
2 tablespoons minced fresh cilantro
2 tablespoons soy sauce
1 teaspoon minced garlic
1/2 teaspoon sugar
1/2 teaspoon dry mustard
4 scallions (white and green parts), cut into 1/2-inch pieces
2 tablespoons toasted sesame seeds

1. Cut the noodles with scissors into 5-inch or 6-inch lengths. Place them in a metal or other heatproof bowl and cover with boiling water. Allow them to soften, stirring occasionally, for 5 minutes. Drain in a colander and refresh under cold running water. Dry by patting with paper towels and place in a shallow serving bowl.

2. Combine the peanut butter and 1/2 cup of the broth, the vinegar, oil, cilantro, soy sauce, garlic, sugar and mustard in a blender. Blend until smooth, starting out using a pulse motion. With the machine running, pour in 1/2 cup more broth through the opening in the lid. Process until blended and smooth, adding a little more broth if necessary to make the sauce a pourable consistency.

3. Pour the peanut sauce over the noodles and toss to coat well. Sprinkle with scallions and the sesame seeds and toss again. Serve at room temperature.

Per serving: 295 calories, 20 g carbohydrates, 9 g protein, 21 g fat

STIR-FRIED CHINESE NOODLES WITH SHRIMP

Yield: 6 first-course servings

The noodles for this classic dish are made from mung bean paste and are as clear as glass. They are softened and cooked in the tasty broth mixture and soak up all the flavors of the other ingredients.

1 (2-ounce) bundle Chinese rice vermicelli noodles
3 tablespoons vegetable oil
4 shallots, thinly sliced
2 garlic cloves, thinly sliced
8 ounces green shrimp, shelled and deveined
1 cup chicken broth
1 tablespoon fish sauce
2 scallions, finely sliced
fresh cilantro leaves for garnish
1 jalapeño pepper, seeded and slivered

1. Cut the noodles into 3-inch pieces with a pair of scissors. Heat the oil in a wok and stir-fry the shallots and garlic until golden. Add the shrimp and stir-fry for 1 minute, then add noodles, chicken broth and fish sauce. Cook until the noodles are soft and have absorbed the liquid. Add the scallions. Turn out the mixture onto a deep platter. Sprinkle with the cilantro and jalapeño.

Per serving: 183 calories, 19 g carbohydrates, 9 g protein, 8 g fat

WARM BOW TIES AND DUCK WITH PINK-GRAPEFRUIT AND SAGE DRESSING

Yield: 4 first-course servings

The contrasting shapes, textures and flavors of this festive pasta dish make it a great conversation piece at the beginning of dinner.

1 cup uncooked bow ties, spirals, elbows or other medium pasta shape
2 cups cooked shredded duck meat and crisp skin, warm or
at room temperature
PINK-GRAPEFRUIT AND SAGE DRESSING (see page 344)
2 tablespoons chopped fresh cilantro

Cook and drain the pasta according to the package directions. Place in a serving bowl and add the duck and dressing. Toss to mix and coat. Sprinkle with the cilantro and serve.

Per serving: 348 calories, 18 g carbohydrates, 9 g protein, 22 g fat

VEGETABLES
& SIDE DISHES

GOLDEN FRIED CARDOONS

Yield: 8 servings

If you want a European vacation in a single bite, then try one of these tasty morsels! Popular in France, Italy and Spain, cardoons get shelf space in America only in ethnic markets and only during the Christmas holidays. So seek out these celerylike vegetables with a flavor that is a combination of artichoke, salsify and celery. Intrigued? Fried, they are a user-friendly introduction to the many ways they are delicious. They're also a good source of potassium, calcium and iron.

2 tablespoons white vinegar
4 large cardoon ribs (1 pound), ends and leaves trimmed
2 large egg yolks
1 large egg
1 cup homemade dry breadcrumbs
$\frac{1}{4}$ cup freshly grated Parmesan cheese
salt to taste
freshly ground pepper to taste
vegetable oil for frying
lemon wedges for serving

1. Combine 2 quarts water and the vinegar in a large bowl. Using a vegetable peeler, remove the tough outer strings of the cardoon ribs. Cut the ribs into 2-inch lengths, adding them to the vinegar water as you work. Drain the cardoon ribs, transfer them to a large saucepan of lightly salted water and boil until very tender, about 30 minutes. Drain and pat dry, let cool.

2. In a shallow bowl, combine the egg yolks, 1 tablespoon water and the egg. In another bowl, toss the crumbs with the Parmesan, salt and pepper. Dip the cardoon in the eggs and dredge in the crumbs, pressing to help them adhere. Shake off any excess and set the cardoon on a waxed-paper-lined baking sheet.

3. In a medium skillet, heat $\frac{1}{2}$ inch of vegetable oil over medium-high heat. When the oil is very hot, add the cardoon, 5 or 6 pieces at a time, and fry until golden and crisp, about $1\frac{1}{2}$ minutes per side. Transfer the cardoon to a wire rack set over a baking sheet. Sprinkle lightly with salt and serve hot or at room temperature with lemon wedges.

Per serving: 118 calories, 13 g carbohydrates, 5 g protein, 5 g fat

KIWI RAITA

Yield: 4 servings

This cold sauce goes especially well with grilled lamb in any form. Try it with kebabs, burgers or in pita sandwiches made with grilled lamb.

½ teaspoon black mustard
   seeds
½ teaspoon cumin seeds
¼ teaspoon coriander seeds
2 kiwifruit, peeled and
   coarsely chopped
½ cup plain low-fat yogurt
¼ cup low-fat sour cream

¼ cup finely chopped
   onion
½ tablespoon coarsely
   chopped fresh cilantro
⅛ teaspoon pure red chili
   powder or crushed
   red-pepper flakes
salt to taste

1. In a dry skillet, combine the mustard, cumin and coriander seeds and toast over medium heat, stirring, until fragrant, about 3 minutes. Coarsely grind the seeds in a spice grinder or mortar.

2. In a bowl, combine all but 1 tablespoon of the kiwi with the yogurt, sour cream and onion. Stir in the ground seeds, cilantro and chile powder and season with salt. Cover and refrigerate until cold. Garnish with the reserved kiwi and serve.

Per serving: 80 calories, 10 g carbohydrates, 3 g protein, 4 g fat

BROCCOLI WITH ASPARAGUS, PROSCIUTTO AND TOASTED PECANS

Yield: 4 servings

3½ tablespoons unsalted butter
⅓ cup chopped pecans
2½ cups peeled and
   shredded broccoli stalks

(from 3 pounds broccoli)
½ cup asparagus tips
½ teaspoon salt
4 thin slices prosciutto

1. In a small skillet, melt ½ tablespoon of the butter over low heat. Add the pecans and sauté until lightly browned, 2 to 3 minutes. Transfer to a plate to cool.

2. Steam the broccoli and asparagus together until just tender, about 3 minutes. Drain well and toss with the remaining 3 table-spoons of butter and the salt. Mound the vegetables on plates or in bowls and sprinkle the pecans on top. Arrange a slice of prosciutto alongside and serve.

Per serving: 200 calories, 5 g carbohydrates, 5 g protein, 19 g fat

CHICKPEA FRENCH-FRIES

Yield: 6 servings

2 cups chickpea flour
2 tablespoons minced fresh
  parsley
1 garlic clove, minced

1/2 teaspoon freshly ground
  pepper
salt
vegetable oil for deep frying

1. In a heavy medium saucepan, combine the chickpea flour with the parsley, garlic, pepper and 1 teaspoon salt. Whisk in 2$\frac{1}{3}$ cups water in a thin stream until a smooth paste forms. Boil the mixture over medium high heat, whisking constantly until very thick, about 5 minutes. Beat with a wooden spoon until smooth.

2. Scrape the dough into a 12 by-7$\frac{1}{2}$-inch baking pan and smooth the surface. Let cool to room temperature. Press a piece of plastic wrap directly on the dough and refrigerate for at least 6 hours or overnight.

3. In a 3-quart saucepan, heat 2 inches of oil to 350 degrees. Unmold the chickpea dough onto a cutting board. Cut it in half lengthwise and slice crosswise into $\frac{1}{2}$-inch-wide sticks. Fry the chickpea sticks in 2 batches until golden brown, 2 to 3 minutes. Using a slotted spoon, transfer the fries to paper towels to drain. Sprinkle with salt and serve at once.

Per serving: 134 calories, 18 g carbohydrates, 7 g protein, 4 g fat

HARICOTS VERTS WITH VIDALIA ONIONS AND SESAME SEEDS

Yield: 8 servings

8 medium Vidalia or other
  sweet onions
salt to taste
freshly ground pepper to taste
1 cup homemade chicken or
  canned low-sodium broth
1½ teaspoons white sesame
  seeds
¼ cup extra-virgin olive oil
2 tablespoons Champagne
  vinegar
1½ teaspoons Asian sesame oil
½ teaspoon black sesame
  seeds
8 ounces haricots verts or thin
  green beans
6 scallions, white and tender
  green parts, thinly sliced
  diagonally
½ small red onion, finely diced

1. Preheat the oven to 400 degrees. Peel the onions, leaving the root ends intact. Cut off the onion tops and scoop out the centers with a spoon or melon-ball scoop, leaving the outer 2 layers intact. Arrange the hollowed-out onions in a large baking dish and season them well inside and out with salt and pepper. Pour the chicken broth into the baking dish, cover with foil and bake for about 35 minutes, or until the onions are tender. Using a slotted spoon, transfer the onions to a large platter and let cool.

2. Meanwhile, in a small dry skillet, toast the white sesame seeds over medium high heat, stirring, until lightly browned, about 2 minutes, let cool. In a small bowl, whisk together the olive oil, vinegar, sesame oil, white and black sesame seeds and a pinch of salt.

3. In a large saucepan of lightly salted boiling water, cook the green beans until just tender, about 6 minutes. Drain the beans, cool under running water and drain again. Pat dry with paper towels. Cut the beans into 1-inch lengths and transfer them to a large bowl. Add the scallions, red onion and sesame dressing, season with salt and toss. Fill the onions with the bean salad and serve.

Per serving: 135 calories, 14 g carbohydrates, 3 g protein, 8 g fat

BRAISED RED RADISHES

Yield: 6 servings

30 red radishes with leaves
1 teaspoon kosher salt

³/₄ teaspoon sugar
¹/₄ cup extra-virgin olive oil

1. Trim the radish leaves to ¹/₄ inch and halve the radishes length-wise. Place the radishes in a medium saucepan and the kosher salt, sugar, oil and 1¹/₂ cups water. Heat to boiling over high heat and lower the heat to medium. Cover and simmer until the radishes are tender, about 12 minutes.

2. Using a slotted spoon, transfer the radishes to a serving bowl. Boil the cooking liquid over high heat until reduced to ¹/₄ cup, about 15 minutes. Season with salt and pour the liquid over the radishes.

Per serving: 86 calories, 1 g carbohydrates, trace protein, 9 g fat

BRAISED RED ONIONS, PEAS AND LETTUCE WITH DILL

Yield: 8 servings

²/₃ cup olive oil
3 medium red onions, finely
  chopped
3 (10-ounce) packages

frozen peas
salt and freshly ground pepper
4 cups shredded lettuce
¹/₄ cup chopped dill

Heat the oil in a large saucepan. Add the onions and cook over medium heat, stirring occasionally until softened but not browned, about 5 minutes. Add the peas and 3 cups water and season with a large pinch each of salt and pepper. Heat to boiling and simmer over medium heat until the water has evaporated and the peas are very tender, about 20 minutes. Add the lettuce and dill and cook until tender, about 5 minutes. Serve hot.

Per serving: 261 calories, 19 g carbohydrates, 6 g protein, 19 g fat

ROASTED CHIOGGIA BEETS WITH FETA AND RASPBERRY VINEGAR

Yield: 8 servings

Chioggia beets are a sweet accent to tangy feta cheese. Use imported sheep's milk cheese to get the best flavor.

½ cup raspberry vinegar
3 tablespoons honey
1 medium shallot, minced
kosher salt
coarsely cracked black pepper
¼ cup grapeseed oil
8 small beets, washed

and trimmed
1 tablespoon unsalted butter,
 cut into small bits
4 ounces feta cheese, thinly
 sliced
1 handful spicy baby greens,
 such as mizuna, for garnish

1. Preheat the oven to 350 degrees. In a medium bowl, whisk together ¼ cup of the raspberry vinegar, 1½ tablespoons of the honey, the shallot, ½ teaspoon of salt and ½ teaspoon of pepper. Whisk in the grapeseed oil until emulsified.

2. Arrange the beets so they fit snugly in a single layer in a deep baking dish. Add enough water to barely cover the beets and add the remaining ¼ cup of vinegar and 1½ tablespoons of honey and the butter. Season with salt and pepper. Cover with foil and bake for 50 to 60 minutes, or until the beets are tender when pierced with a knife. Let cool slightly.

3. Drain and peel the beets and slice them ¼ inch thick. Add them to the honey dressing and let cool for up to 4 hours.

4. To serve, arrange half the beet slices on 8 small plates and cover with the feta. Top with the remaining beet slices and drizzle each serving with about 1 tablespoon of the dressing. Garnish with the greens and serve.

Per serving: 172 calories, 16 g carbohydrates, 4 g protein, 11 g fat

BUTTERNUT SQUASH WITH CARDAMOM AND CINNAMON

Yield: 8 servings

1 (2½-pound) butternut
 squash, peeled, seeded and
 cut into 1-inch cubes
6 cardamom pods, crushed
 with the back of a knife
6 whole cloves
3 (3-inch) cinnamon sticks,
 broken in half
3 bay leaves
1½ tablespoons unsalted
 butter, melted
3 tablespoons plum sauce
 warmed, plus extra for serving
salt to taste

In a medium bowl, toss the butternut squash with the cardamom, whole cloves, cinnamon sticks and bay leaves. Bring water to a boil in a large steamer and add the spiced squash, cover and steam until tender, about 15 minutes. Discard the spices. Transfer the squash to a bowl and add the butter and 3 tablespoons of plum sauce. Season with salt and toss gently. Serve extra plum sauce on the side.

Per serving (without extra plum sauce): 96 calories, 20 g carbohydrates, 2 g protein, 2 g fat

CANADIAN BACON, POTATO AND SWISS-CHARD GRATIN

Yield: 4 servings

Grated Gruyère cheese melts among ribbons of leafy Swiss chard and slices of Canadian bacon and potato. The dish bakes until the cheese on top is a crusty golden brown.

2 tablespoons butter
8 ounces Swiss chard, large stems
 removed, leaves cut crosswise
 into about 1-inch ribbons
1 garlic clove, minced
½ teaspoon salt
½ teaspoon fresh-ground black
 pepper
8 ounces baking potatoes
 (about 2), peeled and cut
 into about ⅛-inch slices
1½ cups grated Gruyère cheese
8 ounces sliced Canadian bacon
⅔ cup canned low-sodium
 chicken broth or homemade
 broth

1. Preheat the oven to 425 degrees. In a medium skillet, melt 1 tablespoon of the butter over medium low heat. Add the Swiss chard and cook until it starts to wilt, about 1 minute. Stir in the garlic and $1/8$ teaspoon each salt and pepper. Cook until no liquid remains in the pan, about 2 minutes.

2. Butter an 8-by-8-inch baking pan or similarly sized gratin dish. Layer one-third of the potatoes in the dish and top with $1/8$ teaspoon each salt and pepper, one-third of the cheese, and half the Canadian bacon. Spread the Swiss chard in a single layer. Top with half the remaining potatoes and sprinkle with $1/8$ teaspoon each salt and pepper. Spread half the remaining cheese and the remaining Canadian bacon over the potatoes. Add the remaining potatoes to the dish, sprinkle with the remaining $1/8$ teaspoon each of salt and pepper, and top with the remaining cheese and 1 tablespoon butter. Pour the chicken broth over all.

3. Cover the gratin with aluminum foil and bake for 15 minutes. Remove the foil and continue baking until the potatoes are tender and the top is golden brown, about 30 minutes longer. Let stand 2 to 3 minutes before cutting.

Per serving: 349 calories, 14 g carbohydrates, 25 g protein, 22 g fat

CREAMY SALSIFY WITH HORSERADISH

Yield: 6 servings

2 tablespoons white vinegar
1 pound black salsify
salt
3 tablespoons heavy cream
2 tablespoons unsalted butter

$3/4$ teaspoon finely grated fresh horseradish root
freshly ground white pepper
parsley leaves for garnish

1. In a large bowl, combine 2 quarts water with the vinegar. Peel the salsify under cool running water. Cut the roots into 4-inch lengths, adding them to the vinegar water as you work. Drain the salsify, transfer to a medium saucepan and add 2 quarts of fresh water and a generous pinch of salt. Heat to boiling and cook over medium high heat until tender, 8 to 10 minutes.

2. Drain the salsify, reserving 3 tablespoons of the cooking water. In a food processor, combine the salsify and the reserved cooking water with the cream, butter and horseradish and puree until smooth. Season with salt and white pepper. Work the puree through a fine sieve and serve hot, sprinkled with parsley.

Per serving: 122 calories, 14 g carbohydrates, 3 g protein, 7 g fat

SPICY RED LENTILS

Yield: 8 servings

Lentils do not need to be soaked the way dried beans do, so you can make this dish when you are seized with inspiration and the desire for an exotic, spicy side dish.

3 ounces vegetable oil
1 medium onion, thinly sliced
2 cinnamon sticks
8 ounces red lentils
½ teaspoon chopped fresh ginger
2½ cups vegetable broth
½ teaspoons chili powder

salt to taste
½ lemon
1 garlic clove, chopped
2 red bell peppers, chopped
½ fresh green chile, chopped
2 bay leaves crumbled
⅓ cup roughly chopped fresh cilantro leaves

1. Heat 2 ounces of the oil in a large, deep saucepan over a medium-low heat and cook three-fourths of the sliced onion until soft, about 5 minutes. Add the cinnamon sticks, lentils and ginger, and cook for about 10 minutes, stirring frequently. Add the broth, 2½ cups hot water and the chili powder. Season with salt, heat to the boiling and boil rapidly for 10 minutes.

2. Squeeze the juice from the lemon half and add to the pan with the squeezed lemon shell. Cook 50 minutes, stirring frequently.

3. Meanwhile, chop the remaining sliced onion. Heat the remaining oil in a small skillet and cook the chopped onion, garlic, red bell peppers, chile and bay leaves about 10 minutes, or until the onion is browned.

4. When the lentils are tender, remove the lemon shell. Add the chopped-onion mixture, including the oil, to the lentils. Sprinkle with chopped cilantro and serve hot.

Per serving: 204 calories, 19 g carbohydrates, 8 g protein, 11 g fat

OKRA WITH SPICED YOGURT

Yield: 4 servings

This chilled vegetable salad makes a satisfying lunch-in-a-bowl or serve it as an accompaniment to a main meal.

1 pound okra, trimmed, cut into 1-inch chunks
2/3 cup plain Greek yogurt
1 bunch scallions, trimmed and finely sliced
2 tablespoons coarsely chopped fresh cilantro
1/4 teaspoon ground cumin
1/4 teaspoon ground coriander
1/4 English cucumber, finely diced
salt to taste
freshly ground pepper to taste
2 plum tomatoes, diced

1. Cook the okra in boiling salted water until tender, about 10 minutes. Drain in a colander and cool.

2. Meanwhile, mix together the yogurt, scallions, cilantro, spices, cucumber, salt and pepper in a serving bowl. Add the cooled okra and stir until coated. Refrigerate until chilled. Stir in the tomatoes just before serving.

Per serving: 80 calories, 15 g carbohydrates, 5 g protein, 1 g fat

FRESH SOYBEANS WITH POTATO CUBES

Yield: 4 servings

1 to 2 small dried red chiles
1 tablespoon vegetable oil
1 teaspoon minced garlic
8 ounces potatoes, peeled and cubed
1 cup shelled green soybeans,
fresh or frozen
1 teaspoon soy sauce
salt to taste
freshly ground pepper to taste
1 teaspoon sugar (optional)

1. Heat a nonstick wok or a large skillet over medium-high heat. Crush the chile peppers and stir-fry in oil for 30 seconds, until some smoke rises. Add the garlic and stir-fry another 10 seconds. Add the potato cubes and stir-fry for 5 minutes. (The potato cubes should he half cooked, with color changed, but not soft enough to break up.)

2. Add the soybeans and keep stir-frying for another 5 to 7 minutes, until both potatoes and beans are tender. (Make sure that you don't overcook the young soybeans. They should be greener when they are raw.)

3. Add the soy sauce and season to taste with salt and pepper. Add the sugar, if using. Stir everything quickly, to coat. Turn out onto a warmed platter before sugar has a chance to burn.

Per serving: 174 calories, 19 g carbohydrates, 10 g protein, 8 g fat

HONEY-GLAZED ENDIVE

Yield: 6 servings

6 medium heads Belgian
   endive, root ends trimmed
3 tablespoons honey
juice of 1 lemon

salt to taste
1 ounce butter
freshly ground pepper to
   taste

1. Pack the endives into a deep large skillet in a single layer. Drizzle with the honey and lemon juice, add a little salt and dot with the butter. Pour over enough water to almost cover. Cover and heat to boiling over medium-high heat.

2. Uncover, reduce the heat to medium-low and simmer gently until the water has virtually all evaporated, leaving just a thick syrup, turning once or twice. Start turning the endive in the syrup as they begin to brown, so that they are nicely coated in the caramelized syrup. Remove the pan from the heat before they burn and serve.

Per serving: 106 calories, 17 g carbohydrates, 3 g protein, 4 g fat

STIR-FRIED GREEN VEGETABLES WITH HONEY-MINT SAUCE

Yield: 6 servings

HONEY-MINT SAUCE

2 tablespoons chopped fresh cilantro
1 tablespoon chopped fresh mint
2 tablespoons vegetable broth
2 tablespoons soy sauce
1 teaspoon cornstarch
1 teaspoon honey

FOR THE VEGETABLES

2 teaspoons dark sesame oil
2 teaspoons vegetable oil
2 garlic cloves, finely chopped
1 chile, finely chopped
1 teaspoon grated peeled fresh gingerroot
6 stalks asparagus
2 heads bok choy, chopped
3 scallions, sliced into 1-inch pieces
2 ounces broccoli florets
2 handfuls baby spinach leaves
2 ounces sugar snap peas
1/2 cup vegetable broth

1. For the sauce, combine the cilantro, mint, 2 tablespoons of the vegetable broth, the soy sauce, cornstarch and honey in a small bowl and mix well. Set aside.

2. For the vegetables, heat a wok over medium heat and add the sesame and vegetable oils. Raise the temperature to medium-high and add the garlic, chile and ginger. Cook for 1 minute and then add the remaining vegetables in this order: asparagus, bok choy, scallions, broccoli, baby spinach and sugar snap peas, stir-frying briefly after each addition. The remaining 1/2 cup broth needs to be added continuously from this point, and the whole dish needs to cook for 2 minutes.

3. Re-stir the sauce mixture and stir into the wok. Cook until the liquid boils and is thickened and clear. Serve immediately.

Per serving: 77 calories, 10 g carbohydrates, 4 g protein, 4 g fat

GRILLED MEDITERRANEAN VEGETABLES AND MOZZARELLA

Yield: 4 servings

2 small zucchini, each sliced diagonally into 6 pieces
1 small eggplant, cut in half lengthwise then each half cut crosswise
1 large red bell pepper, peeled, seeded and cut in 4 length-wise
1 large mozzarella, quartered into wedges
½ cup olive oil
juice of 1 lemon

salt to taste
freshly ground pepper to taste

GARNISH
20 leaves opal basil
1 bunch arugula, washed and shredded
10 green olives, pitted
10 black olives, pitted
10 sun dried tomatoes, shredded
rind and juice of 1 lemon

1. Preheat the broiler. Combine the zucchini, eggplant and peppers in a medium bowl. Place the mozzarella in a small bowl. Drizzle the vegetables with 3 tablespoons of the oil and toss to coat. Drizzle the mozzarella with 1 tablespoon of the oil and toss to coat.

2. Heat a broiler pan until it reaches smoking point. Add the egg-plant mixture and broil 3 minutes, stirring to brown on all sides. Remove the vegetables to a baking sheet. Wipe the pan out and grill the mozzarella for 30 seconds. Add to the grilled vegetables. Drizzle with the remaining olive oil and all but 2 tablespoons of the shredded opal basil and toss to coat with the salt and pepper.

3. In a medium bowl, combine the arugula, olives, dried tomatoes and the lemon rind and juice. Toss to coat.

4. To serve: Arrange the vegetables and mozzarella on 4 dinner plates. Sprinkle the arugula mixture over the vegetable mixture and then sprinkle with the reserved shredded basil leaves.

Per serving: 545 calories, 14 g carbohydrates, 25 g protein, 45 g fat

EAST INDIAN CABBAGE

Yield: 4 servings

This is a traditional side-dish with an Indian meal.

1 tablespoon butter
1 tablespoon vegetable oil
1 medium onion, sliced
1 (1-inch) piece peeled and
  grated fresh gingerroot
8 ounces green cabbage,
  shredded
1 teaspoon ground turmeric

1 teaspoon salt
1/2 teaspoon paprika
1 tablespoon fresh lemon
  juice
1 teaspoon curry powder
  (garam masala)
plain yogurt for serving
  (optional)

1. Heat a wok or large skillet until hot, add the butter, oil and the onion and stir-fry for 1 minute over high heat, stirring all the time. Add the ginger and cook for 1 minute. Add the cabbage, turmeric, salt and paprika and stir-fry for 2 minutes.

2. Stir in the lemon juice and the curry powder and serve with yogurt, if desired.

Per serving: 73 calories, 4 g carbohydrates, 1 g protein, 7 g fat

POTATO AND SUGAR-SNAP SAUTÉ

Yield: 4 servings

2 large baking potatoes, peeled
2 tablespoons olive oil
1 garlic clove, peeled and finely
  chopped

8 ounces sugar snap peas
salt to taste
freshly ground pepper to
  taste

Dice the potatoes into 1/2-inch pieces and dry on paper towels. Heat the oil in a skillet and sauté the potatoes until golden brown and tender. Add the garlic and sugar snap peas and sauté 1 to 2 minutes. Season with salt and pepper and toss to coat. Cover and keep warm until ready to serve.

Per serving: 121 calories, 13 g carbohydrates, 3 g protein, 7 g fat

CORN FRITTERS

Yield: 6 servings

You can use 1 cup of fresh corn kernels or thawed, frozen corn. The colorful Mexican-style canned corn is another alternative.

2 large eggs
2 tablespoons self-rising
  flour
2 tablespoons milk

1 (8-ounce) can whole kernel
  corn, drained
salt and pepper to taste
6 tablespoons corn oil

1. Break the eggs into a bowl, sift in the flour and add the milk. Mix together until smooth with a fork. Add the corn and a little salt and pepper, and mix again.

2. Heat the oil in a skillet. Add a tiny drop of the corn batter and when it sizzles, the oil is hot enough. Place 3 separate tablespoons of the batter in the skillet to make 3 pancakes. Cook them for about 3 minutes or until they start to look firm and brown on the bottom. (If the oil is spattering, turn down the heat a little.)

3. With a spatula, turn the fritters over and cook on the other side for a couple of minutes. Drain the fritters on paper towels and keep in a warm place, such as a warm oven, while you cook all the remaining batter the same way.

Per serving: 190 calories, 10 g carbohydrates, 4 g protein, 16 g fat

PAN-GRILLED BABY LEEKS WITH MUSTARD-HONEY DRESSING

Yield: 6 to 8 servings

This grilling technique works well for other members of the onion family. Try grilling fat scallions, thick rounds of sweet onions and dramatic wedges of red onion.

2 pounds baby leeks, trimmed,
  split and rinsed well
1 tablespoon olive oil

1 teaspoon chopped fresh sage
MUSTARD-HONEY DRESSING
  (see page 345)

1. Lightly brush a cast-iron grill pan or griddle with the ridged side up with oil and heat. Add the leeks and cook until tender, 4 to 5 minutes, turning occasionally and brushing with the remaining oil. Turn the heat off and immediately sprinkle with the sage. Transfer to a serving platter.

2. Drizzle the dressing over the leeks while they are warm and serve.

Each of 8 servings: 210 calories, 18 g carbohydrates, 2 g protein, 16 g fat

SPICY CAULIFLOWER-CASHEW STEW

Yield: 6 servings

This is a perfect side dish to serve with beef curry or mutton curry and plain boiled rice.

2 teaspoons sunflower oil
½ teaspoon fenugreek seeds
1 to 2 long, slim, dried red chiles, chopped
¾ cup roasted shelled cashews, split
3 ounces green beans, cut into 1-inch pieces
1 medium cauliflower, cut into ½-inch florets

1 teaspoon salt
1½ ounces ghee or unsalted butter
1 medium onion, finely chopped
1 teaspoon turmeric
⅔ cup coconut milk
½ teaspoon tamarind concentrate or 1 tablespoon fresh lime juice

1. Heat the oil in a small saucepan over a low heat and fry the fenugreek and chiles until they are just a shade darker. Remove from the heat and cool. Crush with a pestle and mortar to make a paste using the oil in which they were fried.

2. Combine the cashews and green beans in a large saucepan with 2 cups water and heat to boiling. Reduce the heat, cover and cook for 5 minutes. Add the cauliflower and salt. Cover and cook for a further 5 minutes. Add the crushed spice paste and stir well. Remove from the heat.

3. In a separate pan, heat the ghee or butter over a medium heat and fry the onions until they are a pale golden color, about 6 minutes. Stir in the turmeric and fry for 1 minute. Stir this into the vegetables along with all the ghee or butter.

4. Add the coconut milk to the vegetables. Return to the heat and heat to a gentle simmer.

5. Add the tamarind (but not the lime juice) and stir gently until dissolved. Cook gently without a lid for 5 to 6 minutes. If using the lime juice, add it now and remove from the heat.

Per serving: 250 calories, 14 g carbohydrates, 6 g protein, 21 g fat

ZUCCHINI-PITA SANDWICHES WITH GOLDEN SHALLOT-GARLIC SAUCE

Yield: 10 servings

The fragrant garlic sauce turns these baby-squash sandwiches into a feast.

1 pound baby or small
  zucchini
5 pita breads, warmed and split
  in half

2 tablespoons butter, softened
GOLDEN SHALLOT-GARLIC
  SAUCE (see page 323)
olive oil for drizzling

1. Fifteen minutes before serving, heat a saucepan of water to boiling. Preheat the oven to 350 degrees to warm the pita bread.

2. If the zucchini are very small and tender cook them whole, otherwise, quarter lengthways and cut in half crosswise so they will fit into the pita halves. Drop the zucchini into boiling water and cook until just tender, 2 to 3 minutes. Drain thoroughly.

3. Smear the insides of the pita-bread halves generously with softened butter and spread generously with sauce. Arrange the zucchini in the pita halves. Drizzle a little olive oil over each. Serve immediately.

Per serving: 122 calories, 15 g carbohydrates, 4 g protein, 5 g fat

CREOLE VEGETABLES

Yield: 6 servings

The stars of Cajun cuisine are the "holy trinity" of celery, green bell peppers and onions. They are joined here with several other vegetables to do battle with some fiery seasoning.

2 tablespoons vegetable oil
2 garlic cloves, finely chopped
1 (14-ounce) can chopped
  tomatoes
½ teaspoon Cajun seasoning
½ teaspoon cayenne pepper

2 celery stalks, chopped
1 green bell pepper, diced
1 onion, chopped
1 yellow zucchini,
  chopped
1 green zucchini, chopped

1. Heat 1 tablespoon of the oil in a large skillet and add the garlic. Cook for several minutes, then add the tomatoes and continue to cook for several minutes. Stir in the Cajun seasoning.

2. In another skillet, heat the remaining 1 tablespoon oil and add the celery, bell pepper, onion and zucchini. Stir-fry over high heat for several minutes, until the vegetables start to soften but are still crisp. Pour the sauce over the vegetables, cover and simmer over low heat for 15 minutes. Serve hot.

Per serving: 87 calories, 11 g carbohydrates, 12 g protein, 5 g fat

BOK CHOY WITH OYSTER SAUCE

Yield: 6 servings

The small heads of this juicy cabbage resemble a bunch of wide celery with dark green leaves. It can be used raw in salads, as a recipe ingredient, or it can be the star, as in this recipe.

1½ pounds of small heads of
  bok choy
1 tablespoon oil

2 tablespoons oyster sauce
a dash of salt, or more
  to taste

1. Remove the outer leaves of each bok choy and cut crosswise into 3-inch sections (hearts) from the root end up. Wash well and drain. Separate the leaves from the stalks.

2. Heat the oil in a wok over medium heat and add the stalks and a dash of salt. Stir-fry until they are softened but still crisp, about 3 minutes. Add the leaves and stir-fry until wilted.

3. Add the oyster sauce and salt to taste. Stir well and serve hot.

Per serving: 39 calories, 4 g carbohydrates, 1 g protein, 3 g fat

CREAMED LEEKS WITH ORANGE

Yield: 4 to 6 servings

In this skillet side dish, the sweet and citrus glaze is infused with the mild onion juices of the noble leek. Serve it with roast pork, chicken or fish.

5 large leeks, trimmed
3 tablespoons butter, and more
  if necessary
finely grated rind and juice of
  1 orange
1 cup sour cream or

crème fraîche
salt to taste
freshly ground pepper to
  taste
1 squeeze of lemon juice, or
  more to taste

1. Cut the leeks into 2-inch lengths and shred finely. Melt 3 tablespoons butter in a large skillet over medium heat and add the leeks. Stir to mix and add the orange juice and a little salt and pepper. Cover and simmer gently together for 10 minutes or so, stirring occasionally, until the leeks are just tender.

2. Uncover and boil off most of the watery juices until all that remains is a few tablespoons of buttery liquid. Stir in the orange rind. Heat to simmering and cook for 3 to 5 minutes, until very thick and creamy.

3. Stir in the sour cream until blended and season with salt, pepper and lemon juice. Taste and adjust seasoning. If not using immediately, spear a small piece of butter on the tip of a knife and rub it over the surface to prevent a skin forming.

Each of 6 servings: 170 calories, 13 g carbohydrates, 2 g protein, 13 g fat

POTATO-MUSHROOM MASH

Yield: 4 servings

1 ounce butter
1 small onion, finely chopped
1 garlic clove, finely chopped
4 ounces mushrooms, wiped
and chopped
2 small potatoes, peeled and
freshly boiled

2 teaspoons fresh parsley,
chopped
1 teaspoon whole-grain
mustard
1/4 cup heavy cream
salt to taste
freshly ground pepper to taste

Melt the butter in a medium skillet and sauté the onion and garlic over medium heat for about 5 minutes, or until they have softened and are golden. Add the mushrooms and sauté for 1 minute. Add the potatoes and crush them with a fork until they are broken up. Stir in the parsley, mustard and cream. Season to taste, cover and keep warm until you are ready to serve.

Per serving: 157 calories, 12 g carbohydrates, 3 g protein, 12 g fat

CAULIFLOWER STIR-FRIED WITH GINGER AND CILANTRO

Yield: 4 servings

It is important to cook the cauliflower just until crisp-tender or it will develop a strong cabbage flavor.

1/4 cup olive oil
4 thin slices peeled fresh
gingerroot
1 large cauliflower, cut into
delicate florets

3/4 teaspoon salt or to taste
freshly ground pepper to taste
1/4 cup minced fresh cilantro
generous squeezes of lemon
juice

1. Pour the oil into a large wok or skillet and set over a medium-high heat. When hot, add the ginger. Stir-fry 10 seconds, pressing on the ginger to flavor the oil.

2. Add the cauliflower and salt and stir-fry 2 to 3 minutes, until the

cauliflower starts to soften. Add ¼ cup water. Cover and cook on medium-high heat 2 to 3 minutes longer, or until the cauliflower is tender but crisp. Uncover and boil away extra liquid, if there is any. Remove the ginger slices if desired.

3. Stir in the pepper, cilantro and lemon juice and serve.

Per serving: 178 calories, 12 g carbohydrates, 5 g protein, 14 g fat

CARAMELIZED BABY ONIONS

Yield: 4 servings

The sugar glaze and roasting will sweeten the onions inside and out.

1 ounce butter
3 tablespoons sugar
1 pound baby onions, peeled

2 to 3 tablespoons balsamic vinegar

1. Preheat the oven to 400 degrees. Melt the butter and sugar in a small saucepan over medium heat and add the onions. Stir until well coated and add the balsamic vinegar. Cook, stirring occasionally, for 10 minutes.

2. Transfer the onions to a 1-quart baking dish. Bake the onions until tender when pierced with a skewer, 15 to 20 minutes. Serve hot.

Per serving: 130 calories, 19 g carbohydrates, 1 g protein, 6 g fat

COCONUT-FLAVORED GREEN BEANS

Yield: 4 servings

The mix of East Indian spices and coconut will make you see a different side of green beans. The onions add a meaty supporting role.

2 onions
1-inch piece gingerroot
8 ounces green beans
½ cup shredded coconut
1 tablespoon vegetable oil

1 teaspoon ground coriander
1 teaspoon ground turmeric
salt to taste
freshly ground pepper to taste

1. Peel and finely chop onions and ginger. Trim the green beans. Dry-fry the coconut in a large nonstick skillet over medium heat, stirring, until golden-brown. Transfer the coconut to a small cup and set aside.

2. Heat the oil in the same skillet over medium heat and add the onions and ginger. Sauté for 5 minutes. Add the green beans and sauté for 2 minutes.

3. Add the 2 tablespoons water, the coconut, coriander, turmeric, salt and pepper. Cover and cook over low heat until beans are cooked, 5 to 10 minutes, stirring often,.

Per serving: 190 calories, 17 g carbohydrates, 3 g protein, 13 g fat

CAULIFLOWER AND TOMATO GRATIN

Yield: 6 servings

The crunchy buttery topping is like a savory streusel.

1 head cauliflower, broken into florets
4 tomatoes, sliced
1 teaspoon fresh thyme leaves or ½ teaspoon dried leaves, crushed
salt to taste
freshly ground pepper to taste

1 ounce butter

FOR THE TOPPING
⅔ cup rolled oats
1 cup grated cheddar cheese
salt to taste
freshly ground pepper to taste
4 ounces butter

1. Preheat the oven to 400 degrees. Lightly butter a 2-quart baking dish.

2. Cook the cauliflower in salted, boiling water, or steam it until almost tender. Drain and pack it tightly in the prepared dish. Cover with the tomato slices, sprinkle with the thyme leaves, salt and pepper and dot with the butter.

3. For the topping: Mix the oats, grated cheese, salt and pepper together in a bowl. Melt the butter and stir enough of it into the mixture with a palette knife to make a crumbly mixture. Cool slightly then scatter over the vegetables in a thick layer. Bake for about 30 minutes until the topping is golden brown and crisp. Serve immediately.

Per serving: 334 calories, 19 g carbohydrates, 10 g protein, 26 g fat

CELERIAC BAKED IN CREAMY GRUYÈRE SAUCE

Yield: 6 servings

This simple combination of ingredients is just as delicious with celeriac as it is with potatoes. You can try it with most other vegetables or a mix of just your favorite ones.

3 tablespoons butter
1 garlic clove, crushed
1 pound celeriac, peeled with a
  paring knife

salt to taste
freshly ground pepper to taste
1 cup grated Gruyère cheese
2 cups heavy cream

1. Preheat the oven 375 degrees. Generously grease a shallow baking dish with half the butter. Rub the crushed garlic over the inside of the dish.

2. Cut the celeriac into thin wedges and place in the prepared dish. Sprinkle with salt and pepper and top with the grated Gruyère. Dot the remaining butter over the wedges and carefully pour over the cream.

3. Bake until golden brown and the celeriac is tender, 40 to 50 minutes. Cover with foil during cooking if over-browning.

Per serving: 389 calories, 16 g carbohydrates, 4 g protein, 36 g fat

ASIAGO GRITS

Yield: 4 servings

The sharp, salty flavor of the Asiago cheese makes a delicious addition to the creamy corn grits.

2¼ cups low-sodium chicken
  broth
¼ teaspoon salt
⅛ teaspoon freshly ground
  pepper

3 garlic cloves, chopped
1 cup uncooked regular grits
½ cup 2-percent milk
1½ cups grated Asiago
  cheese

Combine 1¾ cups water and the broth, salt, pepper and garlic in a large saucepan and heat to boiling. Gradually stir in the grits. Cover, reduce heat, and simmer until thickened, about 15 minutes, stirring occasionally. Remove from heat and stir in the milk and cheese.

Per serving: 165 calories, 8 g carbohydrates, 14 g protein, 9 g fat

ANISE-CARROT PUREE

Yield: 4 servings

Be careful not to over-flavor the carrots with the star-anise powder. Adding it gradually and tasting as you go is the safest way to try the recipe for the first time.

¼ cup olive oil
8 ounces carrots, peeled
2 shallots, thinly sliced
2 garlic cloves, crushed

1 teaspoon star anise powder
salt to taste
freshly ground pepper to
  taste

1.   Dice the carrots into small pieces. Heat the oil in a large nonstick skillet over medium heat and add the shallots and garlic. Cover and cook until soft and light brown, about 7 minutes. Add the carrots and enough water to barely cover, season lightly and bring to the boil. Cover and cook the carrots until soft and most of the liquid has evaporated, about 20 minutes.

2.   Puree the carrot mixture with a blender or use a potato masher, leave it as chunky as you like. Add the star-anise powder, a little at a time and keep tasting carrots until the correct flavor is obtained.

Per serving: 153 calories, 8 g carbohydrates, 1 g protein, 14 g fat

SWISS CHARD WITH SPICY CHILE-PEPPER VINEGAR

Yield: 6 servings

2 pounds Swiss chard or
  collard greens

SPICY CHILE-PEPPER VINEGAR
(see page 313)

Remove stems and center ribs from the Swiss chard, and wash the leaves thoroughly. Combine Swiss chard and ¼ cup water in a large Dutch oven, cover and cook over medium heat for 5 minutes or until tender. Serve with the seasoned vinegar.

Per serving: 32 calories, 7 g carbohydrates, 3 g protein, trace fat

CHAR-GRILLED RED-ONION WEDGES

Yield: 2 servings

1 red onion, cut into wedges
olive oil for brushing

salt to taste
freshly ground pepper to taste

1. Preheat the broiler or prepare an outdoor grill for barbecuing over indirect heat.

2. Brush the red-onion wedges with a little olive oil and place on a broiler pan or grill rack. Broil or grill until softened and lightly charred on both sides, 15 to 20 minutes.

Per serving: 60 calories, 5 g carbohydrates, 1 g protein, 5 g fat

SWEET AND SOUR
CARROT-PARSNIP JULIENNE

Yield: 4 servings

This earthy mix of vegetables is given a lift with tangy citrus flavorings and a drizzle of maple syrup.

½ cup orange juice
1 teaspoon lemon juice
½ teaspoon salt
¼ teaspoon ground white pepper
¼ teaspoon ground ginger

⅛ teaspoon ground nutmeg
¾ cup julienned carrots
¾ cup julienned celery
¾ cup julienned parsnips
1 tablespoon maple syrup

Combine the juices, salt, pepper, ginger and nutmeg in a medium saucepan, Heat to boiling. Add the carrots, celery and parsnips; cover, reduce heat, and simmer until tender, about 20 minutes. Drain and spoon vegetables into a serving bowl. Drizzle with maple syrup.

Per serving: 58 calories, 14 g carbohydrates, 1 g protein, trace fat

QUICK CHILE-JUNIPER CABBAGE

Yield: 6 servings

The texture of the cooked vegetables should still be really crisp and the color, bright. The cabbage can be served either hot or cold, with any meat or fish main course.

3 tablespoons chicken broth
12 juniper berries, crushed
1 green chile, seeded and
  chopped
1 pound green cabbage,
  shredded
1 green bell pepper, seeded

and shredded
1 red bell pepper, seeded and
  shredded
2 tablespoons soy sauce
2 tablespoons white-wine
  vinegar
1 tablespoon sugar

Heat the broth, juniper berries and chile in a large nonstick skillet over medium-high heat, and when they are hot add the cabbage and peppers. Sauté 2 minutes, and then add the peppers, soy sauce, vinegar and sugar. Stir and cook until heated through, about 1 minute.

Per serving: 41 calories, 9 g carbohydrates, 2 g protein, trace fat

GINGER-CHILE OKRA STIR-FRY

Yield: 4 servings

This spicy vegetable dish is a fine side dish with grilled lamb.

$1/4$ cup sunflower oil
3 tablespoons cumin seeds
2 onions, diced
2-inch piece fresh gingerroot,
  peeled and grated
2 red chiles, finely chopped
8 ounces okra, sliced into
  $1/2$-inch pieces

3 tomatoes, chopped into
  8 chunks
2 tablespoons chopped fresh
  cilantro leaves
1 tablespoon chopped fresh
  mint leaves
salt to taste
freshly ground pepper

1. Heat the sunflower oil in a wok or nonstick skillet over medium heat. Add the cumin seeds and stir-fry until lightly browned. Add the onions and stir-fry until softened, 2 to 3 minutes. Stir in the ginger and chiles and stir-fry until fragrant, about 30 seconds

2. Add the okra to the pan and stir-fry until lightly coated with oil. Cook until the okra is softened, 5 to 6 minutes, stirring occasionally.

3. Add the tomatoes, cilantro, mint, salt and pepper. Stir well and cook 4 to 5 minutes longer.

Per serving: 197 calories, 16 g carbohydrates, 3 g protein, 15 g fat

ROASTED CARROT
AND CUMIN PUREE

Yield: 4 servings

8 large carrots, cut into
$^{1}/_{2}$-inch slices
2 tablespoons olive oil
1$^{1}/_{2}$ teaspoons ground cumin
$^{3}/_{8}$ teaspoon alt

$^{1}/_{4}$ teaspoon fresh-ground
black pepper
1 tablespoon butter
1 cup whole milk
$^{1}/_{2}$ teaspoon lemon juice

1. Heat the oven to 450 degrees. In a roasting pan, combine the carrots with the oil, cumin, $^{1}/_{4}$ teaspoon of the salt, and the pepper. Roast the carrots, stirring occasionally, until tender and browned, about 20 minutes.

2. In a food processor, puree the carrots with the butter, milk, lemon juice, and $^{1}/_{8}$ teaspoon salt. If necessary, reheat the puree in a small saucepan over low heat, stirring.

Per serving: 150 calories, 9 g carbohydrates, 3 g protein, 12 g fat

DUET OF STEAMED FRESH PEAS AND LETTUCE

Yield: 4 servings

This is the perfect example of classical French cooking. Here, unlikely partners are cooked in synchronicity and both emerge with their individual flavors intact. Try this with different types of lettuce, and you'll be amazed at how much you have taught your palate.

1 tablespoon butter
8 cups thinly sliced iceberg
   lettuce
2 cups fresh green peas

$1/2$ teaspoon sugar
$1/4$ teaspoon salt
$1/4$ teaspoon freshly ground
   pepper

1. Melt the butter in a large nonstick skillet over medium-high heat. Add the lettuce and cook until the lettuce wilts, about 3 minutes, stirring frequently.

2. Stir in the peas, sugar, salt and pepper and cook until the peas are bright green and crisp-tender, about 2 minutes.

Per serving: 99 calories, 13 g carbohydrates, 5 g protein, 3 g fat

HONEY-BAKED CABBAGE

Yield: 6 servings

You can use a mixture of cabbages to make the texture and flavor more interesting. Another way to make this a staple side dish that never gets boring is to use a different flavored vinegar every time you make it.

6 cups coarsely chopped Savoy
   or other cabbage (1 pound)
1 large garlic clove, thinly sliced
2 cups coarsely chopped onion
1 tablespoon olive oil

$1/8$ teaspoon salt
$1/8$ teaspoon freshly ground
   pepper
3 tablespoons cider vinegar
1 tablespoon honey

Preheat the oven to 400 degrees. Combine the cabbage, garlic, onion, oil, salt and pepper in a 2-quart baking dish and toss to mix. Cover and bake until tender, about 30 minutes, stirring after 20 minutes. Drizzle the vinegar and honey over cabbage mixture and toss to coat.

Per serving: 70 calories, 12 g carbohydrates, 8 g protein, 3 g fat

SHERRY-GLAZED SUGAR-SNAP PEAS AND CARROTS

Yield: 3 servings

You can use mirin, a Japanese sweet rice wine, or apple juice instead of the sherry.

2 medium carrots, peeled and cut diagonally into 1-inch pieces
8 ounces sugar-snap peas or peapods
2 tablespoons reduced-sodium soy sauce
1 tablespoon dry sherry
2 teaspoons sugar
2 teaspoons dark sesame oil
$1/8$ teaspoon salt

1. Arrange the carrot and sugar-snap peas in a vegetable steamer over boiling water. Cover, steam until crisp-tender, about 15 minutes, and drain.

2. Combine the soy sauce, sherry, sugar, oil and salt in a $1\frac{1}{2}$-quart saucepan and mix well. Heat over medium heat until hot. Add the vegetable mixture and cook, stirring, until the vegetables are heated through and glazed, about 2 minutes.

Per serving: 84 calories, 11 g carbohydrates, 2 g protein, 3 g fat

WARM PARSNIP SALAD

Yield: 3 servings

Cooked-vegetable salads are few and far between if you don't consider hot German potato salad. But carefully matched colors, flavors and textures highlight the pale but tasty parsnip.

6 leaves red-leaf lettuce
8 ounces parsnips, peeled and julienned
1 large celery stalk, julienned
1 medium red bell pepper, seeded and julienned
3 scallions, trimmed and julienned
1 large clove garlic, minced
1/4 cup white-wine vinegar
1 teaspoon Dijon mustard
1/8 teaspoon salt
1/8 teaspoon freshly ground pepper

1. Line 3 salad plates with 2 lettuce leaves each and set aside.

2. Grease a large nonstick skillet with cooking spray and heat the skillet over medium-high heat. Add the parsnips, celery, red bell pepper and scallions and sauté until the vegetables are crisp-tender, about 4 minutes.

3. Combine the garlic, vinegar, mustard, salt and pepper in a glass measure and whisk until blended. Add to the vegetables in the skillet and heat to boiling, stirring constantly.

4. Spoon the parsnip mixture onto the lettuce-lined salad plates and serve immediately.

Per serving: 85 calories, 20 g carbohydrates, 2 g protein, trace fat

MIRLITON MÉLANGE

Yield: 8 servings

Mirliton, also called chayote, was a staple of the Aztecs and Mayans. Its very mild flavor fits into any dish, with any seasoning. Use mirliton any way you would use summer squash, baked as you would winter squash or even used raw in salads. It is high in potassium.

2 cups cauliflower florets
2 cups cut green beans (1 inch pieces)
1 1/2 cups diagonally sliced peeled carrots
1 1/2 cups cubed peeled chayote
1 tablespoon vegetable oil
1 cup chopped onion
1 cup chopped green bell pepper
2 garlic cloves, finely chopped
3/4 teaspoon salt
1/2 teaspoon ground cumin
1/4 teaspoon freshly ground pepper
1/3 cup chopped fresh cilantro

1. Heat 3 cups water to boiling in a large dutch oven. Add the cauliflower and cook for 3 minutes. Add the green beans, carrots and chayote, cover and cook an additional 4 minutes. Drain and rinse under cold water, drain well, and set aside.

2. Heat the oil in large nonstick skillet over medium heat. Add the onion, bell pepper and garlic, cover and cook until tender, stirring occasionally, about 8 minutes. Add the cauliflower mixture, salt, cumin and pepper, cover and cook until heated through, about 5 minutes. Remove the pan from the heat, and stir in the cilantro.

Per serving: 58 calories, 10 g carbohydrates, 2 g protein, 2 g fat

QUICK-COOKING COLLARD GREENS

Yield: 7 servings

These take awhile to clean and shred but you'll save valuable nutrients with the short cooking time.

1 cup low-sodium chicken
  broth, divided
4 garlic cloves, finely chopped
4¹/₂ pounds fresh collard
  greens (yielding about 11
cups tightly packed,
  trimmed, shredded leaves)
¹/₄ teaspoon crushed red
  pepper flakes
¹/₈ teaspoon salt

1. Heat ¹/₂ cup chicken broth in a large dutch oven over medium heat until hot. Add the garlic, and cook 2 minutes, stirring frequently.

2. Add the collard greens and remaining ¹/₂ cup broth, stir well. Cover and cook 7 minutes, stirring occasionally. Remove from the heat and stir in the pepper flakes and salt.

Per serving: 97 calories, 18 g carbohydrates, 8 g protein, 1 g fat

HERB-STUFFED BAKED TOMATOES

Yield: 4 servings

This simple stuffing and method for baking any seasonal vegetable will serve you well. These tomatoes make a delightful first course or side dish for grilled meats or fish or creamy casseroles.

4 medium unpeeled, round red tomatoes
nonstick cooking spray
1 teaspoon olive oil
3/4 cup chopped onion
2 large garlic cloves, minced
2 tablespoons chopped fresh parsley

1 teaspoon chopped fresh thyme
1 teaspoon chopped fresh basil
1/4 teaspoon salt
1/8 teaspoon freshly ground pepper
1/2 cup dried breadcrumbs
3 tablespoons freshly grated Parmesan cheese

1. Preheat the oven to 375 degrees. Cut the stem ends off the tomatoes and discard. Carefully scoop the pulp into a bowl, leaving the shells intact. Coarsely chop the pulp and set aside.

2. Grease a medium nonstick skillet with the cooking spray and heat oil over medium-high heat. Add the onion and garlic, and sauté 1 1/2 minutes or until tender. Stir in the reserved tomato pulp, the parsley, thyme, basil, salt and pepper. Sauté 3 minutes or until moisture evaporates.

3. Remove the pan from the heat and stir in the breadcrumbs. Stuff the tomato shells with the breadcrumb mixture and sprinkle each with some of the Parmesan cheese.

4. Place the stuffed tomatoes in a small baking dish. Bake, uncovered, until the cheese melts, about 15 minutes.

Per serving: 120 calories, 19 g carbohydrates, 5 g protein, 3 g fat

CREAMY ROOT-VEGETABLE GRATIN

Yield: 6 servings

There is nothing uppity about this simply delicious vegetable combination. It makes a fine introduction to the sweet turnip-like flavor of rutabaga and we all know what happens when potatoes and cheese get together.

nonstick cooking spray

1 pound rutabaga, peeled and cut into 4-inch-by-¼-inch strips

8 ounces red potatoes, peeled and cut into 4-inch-by-¼-inch strips

2 tablespoons all-purpose flour

¾ teaspoon salt

¼ teaspoon freshly

ground pepper

1½ cups skim milk

1 (3-ounce) package Neufchâtel cream cheese, softened

1 tablespoon Worcestershire sauce

2 tablespoons dried breadcrumbs

2 tablespoons finely chopped fresh parsley

1. Preheat the oven to 350 degrees. Grease a 1½-quart baking dish with cooking spray and set aside.

2. Heat 3 quarts of water to boiling in a large dutch oven, add the rutabaga and boil until just tender, about 3 minutes. Add the potatoes and boil 1 minute. Drain the vegetables well, return to pan and set aside.

3. Combine the flour, salt and pepper in a medium saucepan. Gradually whisk in the milk until the mixture is blended and smooth. Heat to boiling over medium-high heat and cook until thickened, about 1 minute. Remove the pan from the heat, and add the cream cheese and Worcestershire sauce. Whisk constantly until the cream cheese melts. Pour the sauce over the vegetables and stir gently to coat. Spoon the mixture into the prepared baking dish. Cover with aluminum foil and bake until bubbly and the vegetables have cooked through, about 45 minutes.

4. Sprinkle the breadcrumbs and parsley over vegetables and bake, uncovered, 15 minutes longer.

Per serving: 134 calories, 20 g carbohydrates, 6 g protein, 4 g fat

PAN-ROASTED GARLICKY CAULIFLOWER AND BROCCOLI

Yield: 8 servings

You can buy many vegetables all ready washed and cut in the produce department of grocery stores these days. Garlic, too, comes sliced or chopped. So there's no excuse not to try this vitamin-rich tasty dish.

nonstick cooking spray
2 large garlic cloves, thinly sliced
1/4 teaspoon salt

2 tablespoons olive oil
4 cups cauliflower florets
4 cups broccoli florets

1. Preheat the oven to 400 degrees. Grease a 3½-quart casserole with cooking spray.

2. Crush the garlic with the salt until it is a paste and place in a large bowl. Add the oil and mix well. Add the cauliflower, broccoli and toss well to coat. Arrange the mixture in a single layer in the prepared baking dish and bake until tender and lightly browned, about 30 minutes, stirring every 5 minutes.

Per serving: 54 calories, 5 g carbohydrates, 2 g protein, 4 g fat

HOT MASALA MIXED-VEGETABLE PICKLES

Yield: 12 servings

Instead of grinding your spice mixture in a food processor, use a mortar and pestle or strong bowl and the end of a rolling pin.

1 cauliflower, cut into florets
4 ounces green beans, halved
1 carrot, peeled, cut crosswise into 1/4-inch slices

FOR THE MASALA AND PICKLING LIQUID
9 fresh red chiles, seeded if desired, and chopped
3 fresh green chiles, seeded if desired and chopped
2 teaspoons cumin seeds
1/2 teaspoon yellow mustard seeds

1/2 teaspoon fenugreek seeds, ground
2-inch piece of peeled fresh gingerroot, grated
1 1/4 cups distilled white vinegar or white-wine vinegar
5 ounces vegetable oil
8 bay leaves, crumbled
12 garlic cloves, roughly chopped
2 tablespoons sugar
1 tablespoon salt
6 black peppercorns

1. Combine the cauliflower, green beans and carrot in a large bowl, cover with cold water and set aside for 1 hour. Drain the vegetables in a colander and set aside.

2. For the masala: Grind the chiles, cumin, mustard and fenugreek seeds, ginger and a little of the vinegar in a food processor.

3. Heat the oil in a large skillet over medium heat and sauté the bay leaves and garlic until fragrant, 2 to 3 minutes, stirring frequently. Add the masala paste and sauté 5 minutes longer. Add the remaining vinegar and mix well. Add the sugar and salt and stir until dissolved. Add the vegetables and peppercorns, mix well and cook over a low heat until the vegetables soften. Remove the pan from the heat and leave to cool.

4. Store the pickles in the refrigerator and use within 2 weeks. Or, pack the pickles and their liquid into sterilized jars and seal according to the jar manufacturer's instructions. Store in a cool, dark place.

Per serving: 138 calories, 8 g carbohydrates, 2 g protein, 12 g fat

PICKLED STAR FRUIT

Yield: 16 servings

Bright yellow star fruit, or carambola, are a tropical vacation in a bite. Exotically aromatic, juicy and simultaneously sweet and tart, they are also geometric wonders when cut crosswise into perfect stars. If all that isn't enough, they do not require peeling or extensive seeding. Although the fresh fruit lasts for about a week in the fridge, you can pickle them for longer storage to serve as a fragrant accompaniment to cold meats and salads. Make several small jars and use them for gifts.

1 cup cider vinegar
3 tablespoons beet juice
  (optional, for added color)
1/2 cup sugar
1 inch fresh gingerroot, washed
  but not peeled

1 red chile
1 cinnamon stick
1 star anise
1 lime leaf (optional)
3 to 4 star fruit, thinly sliced
  crosswise

1. Place the vinegar, beet juice and sugar in a saucepan over medium heat and stir until the sugar has dissolved. Add the ginger, chile,

cinnamon stick, star anise and lime leaf and simmer for 1 minute.

2. Remove the pan from the heat. Arrange the star-fruit slices in a sterilized canning jar or jars and add the pickling liquid. Arrange the spices between the slices of star fruit. Seal the jar(s), allow to cool and refrigerate for up to 1 month.

Per serving: 34 calories, 9 g carbohydrates, trace protein, trace fat

QUICK CUCUMBER PICKLES

Yield: 4 servings

⅓ cup white-wine vinegar
3 tablespoons dry white wine
1 tablespoon chopped fresh
  cilantro

1 teaspoon sugar
salt to taste
freshly ground pepper to taste
½ English cucumber, peeled

Combine the vinegar, wine, cilantro, sugar, salt and pepper in a medium bowl and whisk until blended. Thinly slice the cucumber on a mandoline and add to the vinegar mixture. Toss to coat and set aside to marinate one hour.

Per serving: 18 calories, 3 g carbohydrate, trace protein, trace fat

PICKLED BABY CARROTS
WITH TARRAGON

Yield: 14 servings

These are quick to make and infused with a double-dose of tarragon.

1 (16-ounce) package peeled
  baby carrots
½ cup tarragon vinegar
1 tablespoon chopped fresh
  tarragon leaves or 1 teaspoon

dried leaves, crushed
1 tablespoon olive or vegetable
  oil
¼ teaspoon freshly ground
  pepper

1. Heat 2 quarts of water to boiling. Add the carrots and cook for 3 minutes.

2. Meanwhile, mix the vinegar, tarragon, oil and pepper in a large bowl.

3. Drain the carrots and stir into the mixture in the bowl. Cover and refrigerate for 24 hours, stirring once.

Per serving: 24 calories, 4 g carbohydrates, trace protein, trace fat

RUTABAGA PUDDING

Yield: 4 servings

This root member of the cabbage family is called rotabagge in Sweden, and/or a Swedish turnip or "Swede" in England. This recipe is an excellent way to get to know this tasty vegetable.

1 pound rutabagas
3 tablespoons fine dry
  breadcrumbs
3 tablespoons milk
2 teaspoons melted butter

1 teaspoon salt
1 teaspoon sugar
pinch of cinnamon or ginger
  (optional)
1 large egg, well beaten

1. Scrub, peel and cube the rutabagas. Place pieces in a medium saucepan and add enough water to cover. Heat to boiling and cook, covered, until tender.

2. Meanwhile, preheat the oven to 350 degrees. Butter a 2-quart casserole. When the rutabagas are cooked, drain, mash thoroughly, and add the remaining ingredients. Mix well and spread in the prepared casserole. Bake for 1 hour.

Per serving: 107 calories, 15 g carbohydrates, 4 g protein, 4 g fat

MIXED VEGETABLE PICKLES

Yield: 1 quart
(16 servings)

Preserve the pick of the garden by pickling a colorful, crunchy assortment of vegetables. Use them to dress up meals all year long.

2 cups thinly sliced zucchini	sliced
1½ cups, 2-inch pieces, green beans	salt to taste
	1 cup cider vinegar
½ cup thinly sliced onions	½ cup sugar
1 large red bell pepper, thinly	1 tablespoon pickling spice

1. Combine the zucchini, beans, onions and pepper in a large bowl, sprinkle lightly with salt, and let stand 15 minutes.

2. Meanwhile, bring a large pot of water to boiling. Rinse the vegetables well in a colander and cook, uncovered, in the boiling water 2 minutes. Drain in the colander and rinse with cold water.

3. Combine the vinegar, sugar and pickling spice in a small saucepan, and stir until the sugar dissolves. Heat to boiling and boil 1 minute. Reduce the heat to medium and simmer the vegetables for 15 minutes. Spoon the vegetables into sterilized ½-pint jars, top with the pickling liquid and seal according to the jar manufacturers' instructions. Refrigerate up to 2 weeks.

Per serving: 37 calories, 10 g carbohydrates, trace protein, trace fat

OVEN-ROASTED SHALLOTS WITH THYME

Yield: 8 servings

There's more to do with these wee members of the onion family than chopping them up and using them in a minor role in recipes. Once glazed with olive oil and seasoned with fragrant thyme, slow roasting caramelizes natural sugars and softens their garlicky flavor.

16 large shallots (about 1½ pounds)	thyme leaves
	thyme sprigs for garnish
1 tablespoon extra-virgin olive oil	kosher or coarse sea salt to taste
1½ tablespoons fresh thyme or 1 teaspoon dried	freshly ground pepper to taste

Preheat the oven to 400 degrees. Place the unpeeled shallots in a shallow baking dish and toss with olive oil, thyme and salt and pepper to taste. Roast uncovered until tender when pierced with knife, browned and some of papery skins have split, about 40 minutes. Sprinkle with more thyme and salt if desired. Garnish with thyme sprigs. Serve hot or at room temperature.

Per serving: 76 calories, 14 g carbohydrates, 2 g protein, 2 g fat

CHINESE VEGETABLES WITH TOFU

Yield: 6 servings

1 block firm tofu
1 pound daikon greens or bok choy
1 cup fresh or frozen shelled fresh soybeans (also
called edamame)
2 teaspoons dark sesame oil
1 teaspoon toasted sesame seeds
salt to taste

1. Wrap the tofu in a double-thickness of paper towels and place on a plate. Let sit 30 minutes.

2. Meanwhile, cut off the ends of the daikon stalks or trim off the ends of the bok choy. Cut large stalks and leaves lengthwise into ½-inch-long pieces. Cut leaf pieces crosswise into ½-inch-wide pieces. Steam greens over boiling water, until crisp-tender and bright green, 7 to 8 minutes. Steam the soybeans over boiling water about 2 minutes, until heated through. Toss together the steamed greens and soybeans.

3. Cut the tofu into 1-inch-square pieces. Steam the squares until heated through, about 5 minutes and toss with the steamed vegetables, sesame oil and sesame seeds. Season to taste.

Per serving: 167 calories, 9 g carbohydrates, 15 g protein, 10 g fat

SWISS CHEESE RÖSTI WITH TOMATOES

Yield: 6 servings

Hearty and healthful, this potato main course is (next to fondue) the national dish of Switzerland, where "rösti" means "crisp and golden." It's winter fare, perfect for après ski but a little too heavy for pre-surfing. Serve it as a fireside supper and meditate on the simple balance of perfectly matched ingredients.

1 pound potatoes, scrubbed,
   skins on
1 teaspoon paprika
salt and pepper to taste
4 tablespoons butter

2 large tomatoes, sliced
8 ounces grated Swiss or
   Gruyère cheese
chopped fresh parsley or
   shredded basil for garnish

1. Partially boil the potatoes until they are almost tender throughout, remove the skins, and coarsely shred the potatoes into a medium bowl. Toss with the paprika, salt and pepper.

2. Melt 1 tablespoon of the butter in a large nonstick skillet or cast-iron skillet over medium heat and lightly fry the tomato slices on both sides. Remove to a plate, sprinkle with salt and pepper, and keep warm.

3. Melt 2 tablespoons of the butter in the same skillet and spread out the potatoes to cover the bottom of the pan and form a cake. Press down lightly with a flat spatula. Cook quickly until the bottom is golden brown, loosen with a spatula and slide out onto a flat plate. Invert onto another plate. Melt the remaining 1 tablespoon butter in the pan and slide the cake back into the pan. Reserve 1/2 cup of the cheese and sprinkle the remainder over the cake. Cook until the cake is browned on the underside and the cheese has melted.

4. Slide out the cake onto a serving dish. Arrange the tomatoes over the cake and sprinkle with the remaining cheese and the parsley. Cut into 6 wedges asnd serve immediately.

Per serving: 283 calories, 18 g carbohydrates, 13 g protein, 18 g fat

ROASTED ASPARAGUS WITH HAZELNUT SAUCE

Yield: 6 servings

Roasted until golden and then drizzled with a chunky hazelnut and brown-butter sauce, asparagus spears make an awesome side dish. With a squeeze of lemon, the combination is magic. You may want to serve the roasted asparagus without the sauce sometimes—it's luxurious on its own.

$\frac{1}{3}$ cup shelled hazelnuts
2 pounds asparagus, trimmed
2 tablespoons olive oil
$\frac{1}{2}$ teaspoon salt

$\frac{1}{4}$ teaspoon freshly ground black pepper
8 tablespoons butter, cut into pieces
$\frac{1}{2}$ teaspoon lemon juice

1. Preheat the oven to 350 degrees. Place the hazelnuts on a baking sheet and toast in the oven until the skins crack and loosen and the nuts are golden brown, about 15 minutes. Wrap the hot hazelnuts in a kitchen towel and firmly rub them together to remove most of the skins. Discard the skins, cool the nuts and coarsely chop.

2. Increase the oven temperature to 450 degrees. Line a large baking sheet or pan with foil and add the asparagus. Drizzle with the oil, sprinkle with $\frac{1}{4}$ teaspoon of the salt and $\frac{1}{4}$ teaspoon pepper and toss to coat. Spread out the asparagus in a single layer and roast until just tender, 5 to 7 minutes for thin spears, 8 to 10 minutes for medium, or 10 to 12 minutes for thick spears.

3. Meanwhile, melt the butter in a small skillet over low heat. Add the toasted hazelnuts and the remaining $\frac{1}{4}$ teaspoon salt. Cook, stirring, until the butter is golden brown, about 5 minutes. Add the lemon juice and $\frac{1}{8}$ teaspoon pepper.

4. When the asparagus is cooked, drizzle with the hazelnut sauce and toss to coat. Place in a serving bowl and serve immediately.

NOTE: You can use pecans instead of hazelnuts. Since there are no skins on pecans, simply toast them in a medium frying pan over medium-low heat, stirring frequently, until golden brown, about 6 minutes or in a 350-degree oven for about 8 minutes.

Per serving: 262 calories, 8 g carbohydrates, 5 g protein, 25 g fat

ASPARAGUS WITH ORANGE-FLAVORED HOLLANDAISE SAUCE

Yield: 4 servings

The orange-flavored version of the classic egg-yolk and butter sauce is used to top many kinds of cooked vegetables but is especially nice with asparagus and green beans.

2 pounds asparagus
ORANGE-FLAVORED

HOLLANDAISE SAUCE (see page 331)

1. Snap off the tough ends from the asparagus and discard. Place the asparagus spears in 1 inch of boiling water in a large skillet, return to boiling, reduce heat, cover and simmer until tender, 5 to 8 minutes.

2. Drain the asparagus and serve topped with the sauce.

Per serving: 239 calories, 12 g carbohydrates, 8 g protein, 20 g fat

GARLIC-TOMATO RICE

Yield: 4 servings

1 teaspoon oil
2 garlic cloves
1 small onion, finely diced
1 cup long-grain rice, rinsed
  and drained

1¼ cups vegetable broth
1 teaspoon tomato paste
1 tomato, seeded and diced
fresh parsley or cilantro leaves
  for garnish

1. In a large nonstick skillet, heat the oil over medium heat. Add the garlic and onion and sauté until softened, about 7 minutes. Add the rice and stir until the grains are coated. Mix the broth with the tomato paste until blended. Stir the broth mixture into the rice and simmer until the rice has absorbed the liquid, 8 to 10 minutes.

2. Stir the diced tomato gently into the rice. Serve hot, garnished with parsley or cilantro leaves.

Per serving: 102 calories, 20 g carbohydrates, 2 g protein, 1 g fat

ASPARAGUS AND PEAS IN SOUR-CREAM AND PARSLEY SAUCE

Yield: 4 servings

Simple things can be surprisingly dramatic, as this side dish proves. The flavor of Italian flat-leaf parsley is more peppery than the curly leaf, but either is fine. If you are in a hurry, place the parsley sprigs in a measuring cup and use kitchen scissors to quickly snip them into bits.

1 teaspoon olive oil
2 garlic cloves, minced
2 tablespoons sour cream
2 tablespoons fresh lemon juice
2 teaspoons Dijon mustard

1 teaspoon white-wine vinegar
1/2 cup minced fresh parsley
1 pound asparagus
2 cups fresh or frozen green peas

1. Heat the oil in a small skillet over medium heat. Add the garlic, sauté 1 minute and place in a large bowl. Add the sour cream, lemon juice, mustard and vinegar and whisk until blended. Whisk in the parsley and set aside.

2. Snap off the tough ends from the asparagus spears and discard. Peel spears if desired and cut into 1-inch pieces. Place the asparagus in a vegetable steamer over boiling water, cover and steam until bright green and softened, 3 to 6 minutes, depending on the thickness of the spears. Add the peas and steam 2 minutes or until asparagus is crisp-tender. Add the vegetables to the parsley mixture and toss gently to coat.

Per serving: 116 calories, 18 g carbohydrates, 7 g protein, 3 g fat

WASABI-ASPARAGUS TEMPURA

Yield: 6 to 8 servings

Wasabi, the fiery pale green Japanese horseradish, is available in fresh, powdered and paste forms in specialty, gourmet, Japanese or "whole-foods" stores, but use the powdered, "straight" in this recipe. As a general-purpose dipping sauce, the fresh root is worth the search, but the powder and paste forms are the most readily available and conveniently stored at home. Just mix a spoonful or so of the peeled, grated fresh root or the powdered or the paste with cold water until it is the desired consistency for coating—first-timers may want a thinner, less intense sauce. The Japanese mix a little soy sauce into the wasabi sauce to add another flavor dimension.

16 asparagus spears
3/4 cup unbleached all-purpose
   flour
2 tablespoons cornstarch
1 teaspoon salt
1 teaspoon sugar
1 teaspoon baking powder

1 teaspoon ground
   ginger
1 to 2 teaspoons wasabi
   powder (to taste)
1/2 cup beer (any kind will do)
canola or corn oil for
   deep-frying

1. Snap off the tough ends from the asparagus spears and discard.

2. In a bowl, mix together the flour, cornstarch, salt, sugar, baking powder, ginger and wasabi. Add the beer and 1/4 cup water to the flour mixture and whisk slowly until the batter is smooth. Transfer the batter into a baking pan at least 8 inches wide.

3. In a deep 8-inch skillet or 8-inch wide saucepan, heat about 2 cups of the oil over medium-high heat. Test the oil temperature for cooking by dropping in 1/2 teaspoon of the wasabi batter. If it immediately bubbles and fizzes, the oil is ready.

4. Dip one asparagus spear into the batter, letting the excess drip off, then carefully drop it into the oil. Cook about 5 batter-dipped asparagus spears at a time, and let them fry for 2 to 3 minutes. Remove them to paper towels with a large slotted spoon to drain. Serve the tempura immediately.

Each of 8 servings: 81 calories, 13 g carbohydrates, 2 g protein, 2 g fat

SPICED SHREDDED CABBAGE

Yield: 4 servings

The warm, sweet flavor of nutmeg will entice everyone to eat more of this vitamin-C rich vegetable.

1 (1½-pound) head green
  cabbage
4 tablespoons butter
3 tablespoons bacon fat or
  water

½ teaspoon flour
¼ to ½ teaspoon grated
  nutmeg or ground mace
¼ teaspoon freshly ground
  pepper

1. Shred the cabbage. Melt half the butter in a heavy pot, then add the cabbage and toss until covered with the butter. Add bacon stock or water, cover and cook gently until the liquid is nearly absorbed and the cabbage is tender, about 20 minutes.

2. Stir in the flour, ¼ teaspoon of the nutmeg or mace and the pepper until blended. Add the remaining butter and toss until melted into the cabbage. Taste and add more nutmeg or mace if needed.

Per serving (with bacon fat): 232 calories, 10 g carbohydrates, 3 g protein,
22 g fat
Per serving (with water): 146 calories, 10 g carbohydrates, 3 g protein, 2 g fat

BARBECUED BAKED SOYBEANS

Yield: 18 servings

The members of the global bean family are an adaptable bunch of characters. Here, extra-healthful soybeans are given the Pilgrim treatment in a slowly bubbling bath of brown sugar and molasses. Smoky barbecue sauce and fragrant garlic are surprise melting-pot additions. This recipe makes enough to take to a family reunion.

9 cups cooked (3 cups dried) soybeans
1 medium onion, chopped
2 garlic cloves, minced
1/2 recipe CHILE AND ROSEMARY BARBECUE BASTING SAUCE (see page 322) or 1 1/2 cups other favorite bottled barbecue sauce
1/2 cup brown sugar
1/4 cup molasses
2 tablespoons Dijon-style mustard

1.   In a large pot, combine soybeans and 6 cups water. Bring to a boil over high heat, then reduce heat and simmer for 2 minutes. Remove from heat and let stand for 1 hour. Some skins will have come loose from the beans; skim these from the pot and discard.

2.   Drain beans, return to pot, and cover with 8 cups water. Heat to boiling over high heat, reduce heat, and simmer, covered, for about 3 hours, stirring occasionally, adding more water as necessary.

3.   In a 2-quart casserole, stir together the onion, garlic, barbecue sauce, brown sugar, molasses and mustard. Drain the beans, add to casserole, and mix well. The beans can be refrigerated at this point and baked later.

4.   Preheat the oven to 325 degrees. Cover the beans and bake for 5 to 6 hours, stirring occasionally, until the beans are tender, adding more liquid if beans become dry, and uncovering during the last 1/2 hour of baking if the beans are too soupy.

Per serving: 201 calories, 19 g carbohydrates, 14 g protein, 8 g fat

CARIBBEAN STEWED VEGETABLES

Yield: 12 servings

The colors and flavors of this hearty dish are as bright as the islands themselves. It tastes even better if cooked a day ahead of serving. Try it with jerked chicken and cooked rice or fresh crusty bread.

2 tablespoons vegetable oil
2 cups chopped onions
3 cups chopped cabbage
1/4 teaspoon cayenne pepper or 1 fresh chili, minced and seeded for a milder "hot"
1 tablespoon grated peeled fresh gingerroot
3 cups peeled sweet potatoes, chopped in 1/2-inch cubes

salt to taste
2 cups undrained chopped tomatoes, fresh or canned
2 cups sliced okra, fresh or frozen
3 tablespoons fresh lime juice
2 tablespoons chopped fresh cilantro plus (optional) sprigs for garnish
1 cup chopped peanuts

1. Heat the oil in a dutch oven over medium heat and add the onions. Sauté until softened, 4 or 5 minutes. Add the cabbage and the cayenne or chili and sauté, stirring often, until the onions are translucent, about 8 minutes.

2. Add the ginger and 2 cups water, cover and heat to boiling. Stir in the sweet potatoes, sprinkle with salt and simmer until the potatoes are barely tender, 5 or 6 minutes. Add the tomatoes, okra and lime juice. Simmer until the vegetables are tender, about 15 minutes. Stir in the chopped cilantro and salt to taste.

3. To serve: Sprinkle the stew with chopped peanuts. Top with a few sprigs of cilantro, if you like. Serve the stew on rice or with fresh crusty bread.

Per serving: 157 calories, 18 g carbohydrates, 5 g protein, 8 g fat

BRAISED GREEN BEANS

Yield: 6 servings

Cutting the beans in half lengthwise allows the simple seasoning to flavor them without taking away from their own delicate taste.

1 1/2 pounds green beans, trimmed, strings removed
1 tablespoon vegetable oil
1/2 cup low-salt chicken broth

1/4 teaspoon salt
1/8 teaspoon pepper
1 1/2 tablespoons fresh lemon juice

1. Cut beans in half lengthwise, slicing through the seam on each side of beans.

2. Heat oil in a large skillet over high heat. Add beans, and cook 5 minutes or until lightly browned, stirring frequently.

3. Reduce heat to medium and gradually add broth, salt and pepper. Cook 2 minutes. Remove from heat and stir in the lemon juice.

Per serving: 59 calories, 9 g carbohydrates, 3 g protein, 3 g fat

BEETS AND GREEN BEANS IN WALNUT-OIL DRESSING

Yield: 8 servings

The beets can be cooked and dressed a day in advance of serving. To heighten their sweetness and allow the walnut oil to melt and coat the quarters, warm the beets before finishing the salad.

2 pounds red, golden and/or striped beets

WALNUT OIL DRESSING
$^{1}/_{4}$ cup olive oil
2 tablespoons walnut oil
2 shallots, minced

2 tablespoons sherry vinegar
2 teaspoons salt
2 pounds green beans

FOR SERVING
$^{1}/_{2}$ cup walnut pieces

1. For the beets: Preheat the oven to 400 degrees. Scrub the beets, leaving the root tips and 1 inch of stems attached. Place the beets in a 13- by 9-inch glass baking dish with $^{1}/_{4}$ inch water, cover with aluminum foil, and bake until tender, about 40 minutes. Rinse beets under running water to remove the skins. Cut into quarters and keep warm.

2. For the beans: Combine the olive oil, walnut oil and shallots in small bowl and let stand at least 1 hour. Whisk together vinegar and salt in another small bowl and set aside. Snip off ends of green beans and discard. Blanch the beans in boiling salted water until crisp-tender, 3 to 5 minutes. Drain and immediately plunge beans into ice water to stop cooking process and preserve color, let chill 1 to 2 minutes. Drain well and wrap in towel until ready to serve.

3. Just before serving: Preheat the oven to 400 degrees. Place the walnuts on a baking sheet and bake until toasted and fragrant, about 5 minutes. Coarsely chop walnuts. Combine the shallot and vinegar mixtures and toss with the green beans. Mound the beets in center of a serving platter and surround with the green beans. Sprinkle with the walnuts.

Per serving: 216 calories, 20 g carbohydrates, 5 g protein, 15 g fat

SAUCES, SALSAS & MARINADES

CHILI-FLAVORED SALT

Yield: 16 servings

Sprinkle this mix over hot popcorn, a batch of freshly roasted nuts or a plate of steaming potato skins.

1 heaping tablespoon salt
1 small garlic clove
¼ teaspoon crushed
    red-pepper flakes

¼ teaspoon chili
    powder
1 teaspoon cracked black
    pepper

For the Chili-Flavored Salt: Place the salt in a small bowl, add the garlic and crush with the back of a spoon until the garlic disintegrates. Add the chiles, chili powder and pepper and mix well to combine.

Per serving: .3 calories, trace carbohydrates, 0 protein, 0 fat

---

ARABIAN SPICE MIX

Yield: 48 servings
(¹/₂ teaspoon)

Baharat means "spices" in Arabic. It is an all-purpose spice mix used in Lebanon, Syria, Jordan and Palestine and found in many prepared savory dishes.
¼ cup black

  peppercorns
¼ cup allspice berries
2 teaspoons cinnamon

1 teaspoon freshly grated
    nutmeg

Grind the peppercorns and allspice together and blend with cinnamon and nutmeg. Store the spice mix in tightly closed jar away from sunlight.

Per serving: 3 calories, 1 g carbohydrates, trace protein, trace fat

SPICY CHILE-PEPPER VINEGAR

Yield: 8 servings

Although there is really no way to tell how hot jalapeño peppers are, and often they are not hot at all, habañeros are no kidders. They are extremely hot. They are native to the Caribbean, Yucatan and the north coast of South America.

2 habañero or jalapeño
  peppers
1 cup white vinegar

4 thyme sprigs
2 garlic cloves,
  crushed

Pierce the peppers with a fork. Combine the peppers, vinegar, thyme, and garlic in a glass jar and let stand 2 to 3 days. Strain the seasoned vinegar before serving.

Per serving: 6 calories, 2 g carbohydrates, trace protein, 0 fat

BASIL OIL

Yield: ½ cup

¼ cup loosely packed fresh
  basil leaves
½ cup olive oil

salt to taste
freshly ground pepper to
  taste

Combine the basil and oil in a blender and season with salt and pepper. Puree until the oil is finely flecked with the basil.

Per serving: 120 calories, trace carbohydrates, 0 protein, 14 g fat

MAYONNAISE

Yield: about 2 cups

If the resulting mayo either looks too thin or has split and curdled, it is easy to rescue it by beating another yolk in a separate bowl and pouring the original mixture in gradually, beating well as before, but really taking plenty of time to whisk well together.

3 egg yolks
1 tablespoon white-wine vinegar
1 teaspoon good-quality Dijon
   smooth mustard
sea salt to taste

1 teaspoon lemon juice
freshly ground pepper to taste
5 ounces olive oil
1¼ cups sunflower oil

1. Whisk the yolks with vinegar, mustard and salt in a medium bowl until smooth. Gradually whisk in half the oils, drizzling the oil in a steady thin stream while whisking constantly. Whisk in the lemon juice and continue to drizzle in the oil while whisking.

2. Season with pepper and adjust the salt if necessary.

Per tablespoon: 120 calories, trace carbohydrates, trace protein, 13 g fat

SWEET AND HOT WHITE-WINE MUSTARD

Yield: 2 cups

Calling all cold cuts and sausages! This is a spread at the deli-in-your-dreams. It's also a great spread for grilled or roasted meats and it keeps several months in the refrigerator.

³/₄ cup sugar
³/₄ cup dry mustard
½ cup cider vinegar

½ cup dry white
   wine
3 large eggs

Combine the sugar, mustard, vinegar, wine and eggs in the top of a double boiler or heatproof bowl and whisk until well blended and smooth. Whisk over simmering water until thickened and smooth, about 8 minutes. Pour into small, sterilized jars and seal according to the jar manufacturer's instructions or cover and refrigerate.

Per tablespoon: 43 calories, 2 g protein, 5 g carbohydrates, 2 g fat, 24 mg cholesterol.t

BLACK-BEAN SALSA

Yield: about 3 cups
(12 servings)

The salsa can be made up without the cilantro and tomatoes and refrigerated up to one day in advance. Add the cilantro and tomatoes right before serving and mix well.

2 tablespoons olive or vegetable oil
1 bunch scallions, trimmed and thinly sliced (fresh green and white parts)
1½ teaspoons ground cumin
1½ tablespoons fresh lime juice
1 can (about 15 ounces) black beans, rinsed and drained
¼ teaspoon salt or to taste
freshly ground black pepper to taste
8 cherry tomatoes, cut into quarters
2 tablespoons chopped fresh cilantro

1. Heat the oil in a medium saucepan over medium heat. Add the scallions and cumin and cook for 2 minutes. Remove from the heat and stir in the lime juice. Add the beans, salt and pepper and toss to mix.

2. Just before serving, add tomatoes and cilantro.

Per serving: 37 calories, 7 g carbohydrates, 2 g protein, trace fat

AUTUMN SWEET-POTATO, APPLE AND-BEAN SALSA

Yield: 8 to 10 servings

Sweet potatoes and apples make this easy-to-prepare salsa a harvest-time ritual. Serve it as an appetizer with blue-corn chips, but it also makes a hearty pasta sauce! The flavors taste best if the salsa is made the night before or allowed to sit at least 6 hours before serving. If you can't find fresh sage, add a bit more fresh parsley (to taste). Feel free to adjust the amount of jalapeño and cayenne to suit your palate.

1 large sweet potato, baked and peeled
2 cups cooked or canned black beans, drained
1 red onion, diced
1 garlic clove, minced
1 yellow or orange bell pepper, seeded and diced
1 jalapeño pepper, seeded and diced
1 red apple, cored and diced
1/4 cup apple-cider vinegar
juice of 1 lime
1/4 cup chopped fresh parsley
1/4 cup chopped fresh sage
2 teaspoons ground coriander
1/8 teaspoon cayenne pepper
kosher salt to taste
grated sharp cheddar cheese for garnish (optional)
toasted pumpkin seeds for garnish (optional)

Divide the sweet potato in half. Place half in a mixing bowl and mash until smooth. Dice the remaining half and add to the bowl. Add the remaining ingredients and mix well. Cover and refrigerate the salsa a minimum of 6 hours. Top with a sprinkling of cheese and pumpkin seeds just before serving.

Per serving: (without cheese or pumpkin seeds) 86 calories, 18 g carbohydrates, 4 g protein, trace fat

EASY CORN SALSA

Yield: 12 servings

Use leftover corn cooked fresh from the cob or canned or frozen corn. Its sweetness and color complement the tart picante sauce.

2 cups bottled medium-hot picante sauce

1 cup cooked corn

Combine the picante sauce and corn in a medium bowl and mix well.

Per serving: 23 calories, 5 g carbohydrates, 1 g protein, trace fatt

ORANGE-TOMATO SALSA

Yield: 4 servings

You can make this salsa ahead of time except for adding the tomatoes. Stir those in just before serving.

juice of 1 orange
1 orange, peeled, sectioned and finely diced
4 plum tomatoes, finely diced
1 red onion, finely diced

1 hot red chile, seeded and sliced
1 hot green chile, seeded and sliced
½ cup coarsely chopped fresh cilantro leaves

Combine the salsa ingredients in a bowl and mix well. Serve at room temperature.

Per serving: 58 calories, 14 g carbohydrates, 2 g protein, trace fat

TOMATO-OLIVE SALSA

Yield: 8 servings

3 large plum tomatoes, seeded and finely chopped
⅛ teaspoon kosher salt
⅓ cup Calamata olives, pitted and finely chopped
1 tablespoon finely chopped fresh flat-leaf parsley
1 tablespoon finely chopped red onion

1 tablespoon balsamic vinegar
2 teaspoons fresh lime juice
1 teaspoon hot sauce
½ teaspoon minced garlic
¼ teaspoon dried oregano leaves (preferably Mediterranean)

In a strainer set in the sink, toss the tomatoes with the salt and let drain for 10 minutes. Transfer the tomatoes to a bowl and add the olives, parsley, onion, vinegar, lime juice, hot sauce, garlic and oregano. Mix well.

Per serving: 144 calories, 12 g carbohydrates, 2 g protein, 11 g fat

HOMEMADE FRESH PEACH AND MINT SALSA

Yield: 8 servings

Serve in a bowl with a sprig of fresh mint on top.

2 tablespoons extra-virgin olive oil
1 shallot, finely chopped
1 fat garlic clove, finely chopped
grated rind and juice of 2 limes
4 ripe peaches, blanched, peeled, pitted and chopped
1 red chile, seeded and finely chopped
1 teaspoon granulated sugar
1 large tomato, blanched, skinned, seeded and diced
1 tablespoon chopped fresh chives
1 handful chopped fresh mint
salt to taste
freshly ground pepper to taste

Heat the oil in a small nonstick skillet over medium heat. Add the shallot and garlic, cover and cook until softened but not browned, about 4 minutes. Place in a large bowl. Add the remaining ingredients and stir gently to mix. Taste for seasoning and adjust so that the mixture is generously seasoned. Chill well.

Per serving: 62 calories, 8 g carbohydrates, 1 g protein, 4 g fat

MANGO-TOMATILLO SALSA

Yield: 6 servings

Sweet mangos and tart tomatillos combine in this unique fruit salsa. Serve it with chips or grilled sausages, kabobs or ham. The veins are the hottest part of the chiles. You can cut them away if you want to tone down the heat.

8 ounces fresh tomatillos, finely chopped
1 mango, cut into ¼-inch chunks
1 jalapeño pepper, minced
¼ cup finely chopped red onion
¼ cup chopped fresh cilantro
⅓ cup fresh lime juice
salt to taste

Combine the tomatillos, mango, jalapeño, onion, cilantro and lime juice in a bowl and mix gently. Season with salt and mix again.

Per serving: 42 calories, 10 g carbohydrates, 1 g protein, 1 g fat

BEEFSTEAK-TOMATO
AND BASIL SALSA

Yield: 6 servings

Tearing the basil will make your fingers smell delicious and give the salsa a homey, fresh look.

2 large ripe beefsteak
  tomatoes, cored and diced
1 small bunch basil, rinsed, dried
  and torn into small pieces

2 shallots, peeled and finely
  diced
¼ cup extra-virgin olive oil
grated rind and juice of 1 lime

Combine the tomatoes, basil, shallots, oil, grated lime rind and the lime juice in a medium bowl. Mix gently but thoroughly.

Per serving: 100 calories, 5 g carbohydrates, 1 g protein, 9 g fat

TWO-TOMATO—AVOCADO SALSA

Yield: 2½ cups
(10 servings)

There may seem to be a lot of ingredients in this salsa recipe but each one serves a purpose. The surprising citrus complements of orange and lemon go well with tomatoes, and they also counter the rich avocado texture. Serve it with chips or as a tasty sauce for roasted or grilled pork or chicken. A garnish of basil sprigs makes the colors pop on the plate.

6 sun-dried tomatoes (not
  oil-packed)
1 garlic clove, crushed
1¼ cups diced plum tomatoes
1 large avocado, pitted, peeled
  and diced
¼ cup finely chopped red
  onion

2 tablespoons chopped fresh
  basil
2 tablespoons orange juice
1 tablespoon finely chopped,
  seeded, jalapeño pepper
2 teaspoons grated lemon rind
¼ teaspoon salt
¼ teaspoon pepper

Combine the sun-dried tomatoes and 1 cup boiling water in a medium bowl and let stand 30 minutes. Drain and chop the soaked tomatoes and return them to the bowl. Add the plum tomatoes, avocado, onion, chopped basil, orange juice, jalapeño, lemon rind, salt and pepper and mix well.

Per serving: 36 calories, 4 g carbohydrates, 1 g protein, 2 g fat

GRANNY SMITH-AVOCADO SALSA

Yield: 8 servings

This juicy and crunchy mix can be served as a dip with chips or as a relish for grilled sausages, steaks, pork chops or barbecued chicken.

1 large Granny Smith apple, peeled and diced
½ ripe avocado, pitted, peeled and chopped
1 small garlic clove, minced
¼ cup diced red bell pepper
¼ cup diced red onion
grated rind and the juice

of 1 lime
1 tablespoon chopped fresh cilantro
1½ teaspoons minced jalapeño pepper
salt to taste
freshly ground black pepper to taste

Combine the garlic, apple, avocado, garlic, bell pepper, onion, lime rind and juice, cilantro, jalapeño, salt and black pepper in a bowl and toss well to mix. Serve immediately.

Per serving: 35 calories, 6 g carbohydrates, 4 g protein, 2 g fat

PESTO SAUCE

Yield: about 12 tablespoons

2 garlic cloves, crushed
2 large bunches fresh basil leaves, torn
1 tablespoon pine nuts
a pinch of salt

3½ ounces olive oil
2 tablespoons freshly grated Parmesan cheese
2 tablespoons freshly grated pecorino cheese

1. Combine the garlic, basil leaves, pine nuts and a little salt in a food processor and puree. With the machine running, slowly pour in the olive oil. Scrape out the mixture into a bowl and stir in the cheeses.

2. To make the pesto the old-fashioned way, combine the garlic, basil leaves, pine nuts and a little salt in a mortar and pound with a pestle to a paste. Slowly pour in the olive oil as you keep pounding and add the cheeses.

Per tablespoon: 90 calories, 1g carbohydrates, 1 g protein, 9 g fat

BELL PEPPER COULIS

Yield: 1 cup, 4 servings

A coulis is a thick puree or sauce, and originally the French term meant the juices left from cooked meat. These days, restaurant menus expand the translation of this simple food with exciting interpretations ranging from a cooked relish to a fresh salsa. Use this thyme-tested, thick sauce with grilled meats or as a spread over a baked brie or pyramid of fresh goat cheese.

1 teaspoon butter
1 tablespoon chopped shallot
2 sprigs fresh thyme
1 garlic clove, crushed
3 cups low-sodium chicken broth
1 large green bell pepper, seeded and chopped
1 large red bell pepper, seeded and chopped
⅛ teaspoon salt
⅛ teaspoon freshly ground pepper
1 tablespoon vinegar

1. Melt the butter in a 2-quart saucepan over medium heat. Add the shallot, thyme and garlic and sauté 2 minutes. Add the broth, bell peppers, salt, and black pepper. Heat to boiling and cook 35 minutes.

2. Discard the thyme. Transfer the pepper mixture to a food processor and add the vinegar. Process until pureed. Taste and adjust seasoning if necessary.

Per serving: 44 calories, 7 g carbohydrates, 2 g protein, 2 g fat

CHILE AND ROSEMARY BARBECUE BASTING SAUCE AND MARINADE

Yield: 3 cups

The hot and herbal sauce can be used to marinate chicken, pork, ribs or meaty shrimp kebabs before and during grilling.

4 dried New Mexico red chiles
4 dried chipotle chiles
1 to 2 fresh habanero chiles or
   1 scotch bonnet chile
   stemmed and seeded
2 to 6 garlic cloves (to your
   taste), coarsely chopped
2 cups red-wine vinegar

⅓ cup loosely packed
   stemmed fresh rosemary
¼ cup coarsely chopped
   onion
¼ cup bourbon or
   3 tablespoons brown sugar
¼ cup fresh lemon juice
1 teaspoon coarse sea salt

1. Preheat the oven to 250 degrees. Stem and seed the dried chiles. Place in a skillet and roast for about 4 minutes, until they are fragrant, stirring the chiles after the first 2 minutes. Remove the pan from oven and add just enough hot water (just below the boiling point) to cover the chiles. Place a small plate on top to submerge the chilies. Let soak 20 to 30 minutes, until softened.

2. Drain the soaked chilies and coarsely chop. Place in a food processor or blender and add the fresh chiles, garlic, vinegar, rosemary, onion, bourbon or brown sugar, lemon juice and salt. Process until smooth, 3 to 4 minutes. Pour into a jar, cover and refrigerate to use as needed.

Data per 2 tablespoons: 22 calories, 3 g carbohydrates, trace protein, trace fat

GOLDEN SHALLOT-GARLIC SAUCE

Yield: about 2 ¼ cups
(10 servings)

2 tablespoons olive oil
5 shallots, sliced or 1 large
  onion, chopped
2 garlic cloves,
  crushed
2 teaspoons turmeric

1 ½ tablespoons all-purpose
  flour
2 ½ cups milk
2 bay leaves
salt to taste
freshly ground pepper to taste

Heat the oil in a saucepan and add the shallots or onion. Stir and cook for a couple of minutes. Add the garlic and turmeric and stir again. Cook over low heat until the shallots are tender without browning. Stir in the flour and then gradually stir in the milk. Heat to boiling and add the bay leaves and pepper. Simmer gently until the sauce is thick. Season to taste.

Per serving: 75 calories, 6 g carbohydrates, 3 g protein, 5 g fat

LEMON-CILANTRO SAUCE

Yield: 8 servings

1 cup MAYONAISSE (see pages
  313-314)
juice of 1 lemon
juice of ½ lime
chopped fresh cilantro to taste

salt to taste
freshly ground pepper to
  taste
olive oil to taste

Mix the Mayonnaise, lemon and lime juice, cilantro, salt and pepper in a small bowl until smooth. Whisk in a little olive oil until blended.

Per serving: 131 calories, 8 g carbohydrates, trace protein, 12 g fat

PARMESAN CHEESE SAUCE

Yield: 4 servings

1 garlic clove, halved
1 tablespoon butter
1 tablespoon flour

1 cup milk
¼ cup grated Parmesan
cheese

Rub a small skillet with cut edges of the garlic clove. Leave clove in pan. Add the butter and melt over low heat. Stir in the flour and cook 3 to 5 minutes over very low heat. Stir in the milk and heat to boiling. Remove from heat and add the cheese, stirring until melted.

Per serving: 99 calories, 5 g carbohydrates, 5 g protein, 7 g fat

CURRY-RAISIN SAUCE

Yield: 6 servings

Put this sauce in your repertoire and your life will change! You can use it to turn a bowl of leftover vegetables into a feast. Or use it to cloak a few sliced hard-cooked eggs. The only other things you need are hot white rice and homemade chutney. You can leave out the raisins or substitute dried cranberries or bits of chopped dried apricots.

3 ounces butter or margarine
3 tablespoons all-purpose flour
2 teaspoons curry powder
1 teaspoon salt

2 cups milk, heated, and more
if necessary to thin the
coating sauce
¼ cup raisins

Melt the butter in a small saucepan over medium heat. Whisk in the flour, curry powder and salt and cook until fragrant and bubbly, about 2 minutes. Whisk in the milk and raisins and whisk until the sauce boils and thickens.

Per serving: 186 calories, 12 g carbohydrates, 4 g protein, 14 g fat

EASY ASIAN PEANUT SAUCE

Yield: 8 servings

Add some cayenne if you like a hot finish. It's great for tossing over spaghetti for an appetizer or mix some into the mayonnaise you're using for a chicken or egg salad.

2 tablespoons creamy peanut butter
2 tablespoons low-sodium soy sauce
1 tablespoon dark sesame oil

Combine 1 cup hot water with the peanut butter, soy sauce and sesame oil in a small bowl and mix well.

Per serving: 41 calories, 1 g carbohydrates, 1 g protein, 3 g fat

---

CHINESE CHILI DIPPING SAUCE

Yield: 1 serving

1 tablespoon Chinese chili sauce
1 teaspoon unseasoned Japanese rice vinegar
$\frac{1}{2}$ teaspoon sugar

In a small bowl, combine 1 tablespoon hot water with the chili sauce, vinegar and sugar. Stir to dissolve the sugar. Let stand for at least 15 minutes and stir before serving.

Per serving: 10 calories, 3 g carbohydrates, trace protein, trace fat

RICE-VINEGAR AND GARLIC DIPPING SAUCE

Yield: 1 serving

2 tablespoons unseasoned Japanese rice vinegar
1 tablespoon plus 1 teaspoon minced garlic
1 tablespoon sugar

In a small bowl, combine the vinegar, garlic and sugar. Stir to dissolve the sugar. Let stand for at least 15 minutes and re-stir before serving.

Per serving: 19 calories, 5 g carbohydrates, trace protein, 0 fat

---

GINGER DIPPING SAUCE

Yield: 2 servings

1 tablespoon (packed) minced peeled fresh gingerroot
2 tablespoons peanut oil

¼ teaspoon kosher salt

Place the ginger in a small heatproof bowl. Heat the oil in a small saucepan until it sends up a wisp of smoke and pour it over the ginger and stir. Stir in the salt. Serve warm or at room temperature.

Per serving: 121 calories, 1 g carbohydrates, trace protein, 14 g fat

---

DEVILLED SAUCE

Yield: 4 servings

Demi-glace is a rich brown sauce made the classic French way from slow-simmering stock. You can buy it, usually frozen, in gourmet food stores.

1 cup white wine
1 tablespoon white-wine vinegar
1 shallot, chopped
1 sprig thyme
1 bay leaf

6½ ounces demi-glace
1 teaspoon chopped fresh parsley
¼ teaspoon cayenne pepper
2 ounces chilled butter

1. Combine the wine, vinegar, shallot, thyme and bay leaf in a small saucepan. Heat to boiling and boil until the liquid measures ⅓ cup. Add the demi-glace, parsley and cayenne pepper.

2. Return the sauce to boiling, remove the pan from the heat and add the butter. Whisk until the butter melts and the sauce thickens.

Per serving: 139 calories, 2 g carbohydrates, 2 g protein, 13 g fat

GINGER, THYME AND LIME SAUCE

Yield: 6 servings

Serve with roast chicken or pork, broiled fish or grilled vegetables such as scallions and radicchio. It's even a perfect match for baked or grilled fruits such as plums and pineapple that you can cook alongside meat and poultry.

1 medium carrot, peeled	1 sprig thyme
1 celery stalk	2 teaspoons butter
1 small onion	1/2 teaspoon finely chopped
1 garlic clove, crushed	gingerroot
1 tablespoon tomato paste	1 tablespoon freshly squeezed
1/2 cup beef broth	lime juice

1. Roughly chop the carrot, celery and onion. Heat the oil in a 2-quart saucepan over medium heat, add the chopped vegetables and sauté until they start to soften, about 7 minutes. Add the garlic and tomato paste and sauté 2 minutes longer. Stir in the beef broth and thyme and whisk to blend the tomato paste into the broth. Add 2 1/2 cups water and heat to boiling. Reduce the heat to low and simmer 30 minutes.

2. Strain the sauce into another pan and heat to boiling. Remove the pan from the heat, add the butter, and whisk until melted and blended. Stir in the ginger and lime and serve immediately.

Per serving: 27 calories, 3 g carbohydrates, 1 g protein, 1 g fat

WARM RHUBARB, SAGE AND GINGER SAUCE

Yield: 8 servings

The earthen flavor of sage gives this sweet and sour sauce a special character. It goes well with any kind of grilled meat or roasted poultry, especially turkey.

8 ounces rhubarb
⅓ cup sugar or to
  taste
⅓ cup orange juice
⅓ cup red wine
⅓ cup chicken broth

1 (3-inch) cinnamon stick
1 teaspoon finely chopped
  fresh sage
1 teaspoon finely chopped
  peeled fresh gingerroot
2 ounces butter

1. Peel and thinly slice the rhubarb and place into a 2-quart saucepan. Add the sugar, orange juice, wine, broth, cinnamon stick, sage and ginger and stir until the sugar is dissolved. Heat to boiling over medium heat, cover and simmer until the rhubarb is tender, about 10 minutes. Check the mixture occasionally to make sure the sauce isn't sticking to the pan. If it dries out too much, add a little water or a little extra of any of the liquids used.

2. When the sauce has reduced to the desired consistency, remove the pan from the heat. Remove the cinnamon stick. Add the butter and stir until melted. Keep the sauce warm until ready to use.

Per serving: 98 calories, 10 g carbohydrates, 1 g protein, 6 g fat

RED-CURRANT SAUCE

Yield: 8 servings

Drizzle a little of this over game, duck or pork dishes, on a meringue or into yogurt.

½ cup sugar   5 ounces red currants

1. Combine the sugar and ½ cup water in a small saucepan and stir until the sugar dissolves. Heat to boiling over medium heat.

2. Add the red currants, return to boiling and cook, uncovered, until the red currants burst, 4 to 5 minutes. Serve hot or cold.

Per serving: 58 calories, 15 g carbohydrates, trace protein, 0 fat

SHRIMP SAUCE

Yield: 6 servings

1 pound freshly cooked unshelled shrimp, with their heads on if possible
1¼ cups fish broth
1 tablespoon butter
3 tablespoons all-purpose flour
5 ounces half-and-half, or more if necessary
generous squeeze of lemon juice
1 tablespoon finely snipped fresh dill
salt to taste
freshly ground pepper to taste

1. Shell the shrimp and place their shells and heads in a food processor. Roughly chop the shelled shrimp and set aside.

2. Process the shell mixture using the pulse motion to a rough chop of debris. Combine the shell mixture with the fish broth in a small saucepan and heat to boiling over medium heat. Reduce the heat to low and simmer for 10 minutes. Strain the mixture through a cheese-cloth-lined sieve and reserve the broth.

3. Melt the butter and stir in the flour and stir over low heat for 1 minute. Remove the pan from the heat and gradually whisk in the broth, a little at a time, to form a smooth sauce. Whisk in the cream. Return to boiling and simmer for 5 minutes, stirring in a little more cream if the sauce is too thick. Stir in the chopped shrimp and simmer until heated through, about 1 minute. Add a generous squeeze of lemon juice and the dill and season with salt and pepper.

Per serving: 153 calories, 5 g carbohydrates, 18 g protein, 6 g fat

SAFFRON SAUCE

Yield: 6 servings

2 cups fish broth
½ cup chopped fresh fennel
1 tablespoon unsalted butter
¼ teaspoon saffron threads
1 star anise
½ cup dry white wine
1¼ cups heavy cream
salt to taste
freshly ground white pepper to taste

1. Heat the fish broth, fennel, saffron and star anise and reduce the liquid to 4 ounces. Add the white wine and reduce until the total liquid is 5 ounces. Add the heavy cream and heat to boiling.

2. Add the butter and whisk until melted. Season with salt and pepper.

Per serving: 91 calories, 2 g carbohydrates, 2 g protein, 8 g fat

SAFFRON HOLLANDAISE SAUCE

Yield: 6 servings

It's not exactly gilding the lily when you add more flavor to a buttery, egg-yolk rich sauce. In this case it is even more dramatic! Turning golden hollandaise into the color of the sun is as easy as infusing it with saffron. Serve the sauce with the usual suspects: asparagus, artichokes and eggs, but also with crab, oysters and mussels.

6 ounces butter	¼ teaspoon saffron threads
1 tablespoon white-wine vinegar	juice of ¼ lemon
1 tablespoon white wine	2 egg yolks
6 crushed white peppercorns	salt to taste

1. Melt the butter and skim off the foam. Carefully pour the clear portion into a glass measure, leaving the white milky portion behind.

2. Place the vinegar, wine, peppercorns and saffron into a small saucepan and boil to reduce the liquid to 3 tablespoons. Add 2 tablespoons water and strain into the top of a double boiler. Add the egg yolks to the liquid and whisk over a double boiler until light. Gradually whisk in the butter and finish with a squeeze of lemon and seasoning if required.

Per serving: 225 calories, trace carbohydrates, 1 g protein, 25 g fat

ORANGE-FLAVORED HOLLANDAISE SAUCE

Yield: 4 servings

The combination of orange and hollandaise sauce, the lemon-flavored egg-and-butter sauce, is classically known as Maltaise or Maltese sauce.

3 egg yolks	⅓ cup butter
2 tablespoons lemon juice	1 teaspoon grated orange peel
¼ teaspoon salt	3 tablespoons orange juice

Blend egg yolks, lemon juice and salt in saucepan or top of double boiler. Add half of butter and stir constantly over boiling water until butter melts. Add remaining butter and continue stirring until it melts and sauce thickens. Stir in orange peel and juice.

Per serving: 186 calories, 2 g carbohydrates, 2 g protein, 19 g fat

RED MOLE SAUCE

Yield: 16 servings

The ancient basic formula of Mexican mole sauce has withstood the test of time and variation. The result is a flavor complexity that is unlike anything in a European chef's repertoire. Here we use all classical ingredients except for a slice of egg bread instead of a traditional tortilla.

4 ancho chiles, stemmed and seeded	coarsely chopped
4 guajillo chiles, stemmed and seeded	1 cup chopped peeled plantain
3 tablespoons sesame seeds	½ bunch fresh thyme
1 (2-inch) stick cinnamon	½ teaspoon dried oregano
5 whole cloves, or ⅛ teaspoon ground cloves	¼ cup seedless dark raisins
5 whole black peppercorns	¾ cup blanched almonds
¼ cup vegetable oil	6 cups chicken broth
1 small yellow onion, peeled and coarsely chopped	1½ ounces Mexican chocolate, coarsely grated or finely chopped
6 garlic cloves, minced	1 thick slice day-old challah or brioche, crushed to fine crumbs
3 medium-size ripe tomatoes,	1 teaspoon salt

1. Rinse the chiles under cold running water and shake off the excess moisture, but do not dry them. Heat a griddle or cast-iron skillet over medium-high heat until a drop of water sizzles on contact. Place the chiles, a few at a time, on the griddle and let them heat, turning occasionally with tongs, just until the water evaporates and the chiles are fragrant. Allow between 30 to 45 seconds for the anchos, slightly less for the guajillos, which are very thin-skinned. The chiles should just become dry, hot and aromatic, do not allow them to start really roasting or they will have a terrible scorched flavor. Remove from the griddle as they are done. Place in a bowl and cover generously with boiling water. Let soak for at least 20 minutes. Drain.

2. In a small heavy skillet, cook the sesame seeds over medium heat, stirring constantly, just until you see them starting to turn golden. Scrape the seeds out into a small bowl and set aside.

3. Grind the cinnamon, cloves and peppercorns together in an electric coffee grinder or spice mill or in a mortar. In a medium skillet, heat 2 tablespoons of the vegetable oil over medium heat until rippling. Add the ground spices and cook, stirring, just until fragrant, 1 to 2 minutes. Add the onion, garlic, tomatoes, plantain, thyme, oregano, raisins, almonds and sesame seeds. Cook, stirring frequently, for 15 minutes. Let cool for 10 minutes.

4. In a large Dutch oven or deep skillet, heat the remaining lard over medium-high heat until rippling. Add the sauce, stirring well to prevent splattering. Stir in the remaining broth, a little at a time. Cover and cook, for 15 to 20 minutes, stirring frequently, until the chiles lose their raw edge. Stir in the breadcrumbs and cook, stirring frequently, until the sauce is lightly thickened, about 10 minutes. Add the chocolate and cook, stirring constantly, until it is well dissolved. Add the salt. Cover partially and cook, stirring occasionally, just until heated through, 7 to 10 minutes. Taste for seasoning and add another pinch or two of salt if desired.

5. Place half of the mixture in a blender with 1 cup of the chicken broth and half the drained chiles. Blend until smooth, about 3 minutes on high. Repeat with the remaining sauce mixture, another 1 cup of chicken broth, and the remaining chiles.

Per serving: 167 calories, 16 g carbohydrates, 6 g protein, 10 g fat

ANCHO-CASHEW MOLE SAUCE

Yield: 16 servings

7 dried ancho chiles
1 cup chopped peeled tomato
¼ cup sesame seeds
¼ cup cashews, chopped
1 (6-inch) corn tortilla
1 slice pumpernickel bread,
  toasted
1 tablespoon vegetable oil
½ cup sliced onion, separated
  into rings
1 garlic clove, minced

¼ cup raisins
1 tablespoon chopped pitted
  prunes
½ teaspoon ground cinnamon
¼ teaspoon ground coriander
¼ teaspoon aniseeds, crushed
⅛ teaspoon ground cloves
4 cups low-salt chicken broth,
  divided
1 teaspoon sugar
¼ teaspoon salt

1. Remove the stems and seeds from the chiles, reserving 2 tablespoons seeds, and discard the stems. Tear the chiles into large pieces, and place in a large skillet over medium heat. Cook for 5 minutes or until thoroughly heated, turning pieces occasionally (be careful not to burn the chiles). Combine the chiles and 4 cups boiling water in a large bowl, cover and let stand 1 hour.

2. Drain the chiles and place in a large bowl. Add the tomatoes and set aside.

3. Combine the sesame seeds and cashews in a skillet over medium heat. Cook for 3 minutes or until the sesame seeds are lightly browned, shaking the skillet frequently. Add the reserved chile seeds, cook an additional 2 minutes or until lightly browned. Add the sesame-seed mixture to the tomato mixture and set aside.

4. Place the tortilla in a skillet over medium heat. Cook 3 minutes or until thoroughly heated. Tear the tortilla and toasted pumpernickel bread into large pieces and add to tomato mixture.

5. Wipe the skillet clean with a paper towel. Heat the oil in skillet over medium heat. Add onion and garlic, sauté 4 minutes or until tender. Add the raisins and next 5 ingredients (raisins through cloves), cook 2 minutes or until raisins plump, stirring constantly. Combine the raisin mixture, tomato mixture, and 1 cup of the broth in a food processor and process until smooth. Press the mixture through a fine

sieve into a bowl and discard the solids. Combine the mixture and remaining broth in skillet, Heat to boiling. Reduce the heat and simmer, uncovered, 45 minutes or until thickened, stirring occasionally. Remove from the heat, stir in sugar and salt.

Per serving: 77 calories, 10 g carbohydrates, 3 g protein, 3 g fat

ASIAN LIME-MINT CHILI SAUCE

Yield: 4 servings

Each element that flavors this dipping sauce is more distinguished when the mixture is at room temperature. Serve it with chilled shrimp or with fingers of deep-fried okra, chicken or tofu.

1 garlic clove, minced
¼ cup tomato sauce
3 tablespoons fresh lime juice
2 tablespoons light-brown sugar
2 teaspoons fresh mint leaves, coarsely chopped

1 teaspoon grated lime rind
¼ teaspoon Chinese garlic chili sauce or Indonesian sambal oelek
1 tablespoon cornstarch

1. In a small saucepan, combine the garlic, tomato sauce, lime juice, brown sugar, mint, lime rind and chili sauce and mix well. Heat until simmering and cook for 2 minutes. Mix the cornstarch with 1 tablespoon water and stir into the sauce. Heat to boiling, stirring constantly, until it is clear and thickened.

2. Strain the sauce through a sieve placed over a small serving bowl and cool at least 10 minutes before serving.

Per serving: 34 calories, 9 g carbohydrates, trace protein, 0 fat

30-MINUTE TOMATO SAUCE

Yield: 6 servings

1 tablespoon extra-virgin olive oil
1 small onion, chopped
1 (28-ounce) can crushed tomatoes
½ cup chicken broth
1 tablespoon white-wine vinegar
1 sprig fresh rosemary
1 sprig fresh thyme
1 bay leaf
a pinch of sugar or to taste
salt to taste
freshly ground pepper to taste

1. Heat the oil in a 2-quart saucepan over medium heat. Add the onion, cover and cook until the onion is softened without browning, about 7 minutes. Add the tomatoes, chicken broth and the remaining ingredients. Mix well and heat to boiling. Simmer over low heat for 30 minutes. Adjust seasoning if necessary.

2. Remove the rosemary, thyme and bay leaf and blend the sauce with a hand blender until the sauce is smooth and fine. Set aside.

Per serving: 68 calories, 11 g carbohydrates, 2 g protein, 3 g fat

ALL-PURPOSE TOMATO SAUCE

Yield: 6 servings

This is the lip-smacking, quick and versatile sauce you've been looking for! It is right for pasta, pizza, spaghetti, chicken and anything else you need to flavor with an assertive tomato glaze.

1 tablespoon olive oil
1 cup chopped onion
4 garlic cloves, minced
1½ teaspoons sugar
¾ teaspoon dried basil leaves, crushed
½ teaspoon dried oregano leaves, crushed
½ teaspoon freshly ground pepper
⅛ teaspoon salt
1 (35-ounce) can tomatoes, undrained

Heat the oil in a large saucepan over medium heat until hot. Add the onion and garlic, sauté 3 minutes. Add the remaining ingredients and heat to boiling. Cover, reduce the heat to low and simmer until thickened to the desired consistency, about 15 minutes.

Per serving: 111 calories, 16 g carbohydrates, 3 g protein, 5 g fat

MARJORAM-TOMATO SAUCE

Yield: 6 servings

Marjoram is an herb prized by European cooks for its delicate flavor, which is more subtle than its cousin, oregano. It is easy to grow and, if you're going to use it by the handful, as in this recipe, you will want to grow it in abundance.

2 tablespoons extra-virgin olive oil
1 garlic clove
½ small red onion, chopped
10 ripe tomatoes, roughly chopped
1 (14-ounce) can crushed plum tomatoes
a handful of fresh golden marjoram leaves
½ teaspoon sugar
salt to taste
freshly ground pepper to taste

1. Heat the oil in a 2-quart saucepan over medium heat and add the onion and garlic. Cook, stirring, until softened, about 5 minutes.

2. Add the fresh and canned tomatoes, marjoram, sugar, salt and pepper. Heat to boiling and simmer over medium-low heat until the tomatoes are soft, about 15 minutes.

3. Puree the sauce in a blender until smooth and sieve or pass through a food mill into a clean saucepan. Add 1½ cups water and heat to boiling. Reduce heat to low and simmer until thickened, about 20 minutes. Check seasoning and adjust if necessary.

Per serving: 111 calories, 16 g carbohydrates, 3 g protein, 5 g fat

WALNUT-OIL AND FRESH-TOMATO SAUCE

Yield: 8 servings

1³/₄ pounds tomatoes, cooked and passed through a food mill
3 tablespoons extra-virgin olive oil
1½ tablespoons walnut oil
1½ tablespoons raspberry vinegar
salt to taste
freshly ground pepper to taste

Combine the ingredients in a medium bowl, whisk well and season with salt and pepper.

Per serving: 89 calories, 5 carbohydrates, 1 g protein, 8 g fat

TOMATO AND WALNUT SAUCE

Yield: 8 servings

This piquant tomato sauce is enriched with toasted walnuts and balsamic vinegar. Try it on steamed vegetables and with fish cakes.

½ cup olive oil
3 garlic cloves, chopped
2 green chiles
½ cup chopped walnuts
3 tomatoes, peeled, seeded and diced
2 tablespoons balsamic vinegar
salt to taste
freshly ground pepper to taste

Heat the oil in a small skillet over medium heat and sauté the garlic until fragrant, about 2 minutes. Add the chiles and walnuts and sauté until the walnuts are toasted, about 3 minutes. Add the tomatoes and cook until they are soft, about 5 minutes. Place into a food processor and process until smooth. Pour back into the skillet and stir in the balsamic vinegar. Season with salt and pepper, heat through and serve.

Per serving: 177 calories, 5 g carbohydrates, 2 g protein, 18 g fat

TOMATO AND OLIVE SAUCE

Yield: about 1¼ cups

Use this sauce to cloak stuffed vegetables such as cabbage leaves or zucchini boats.

6 tablespoons extra-virgin olive oil
1 shallot, finely chopped
1 large garlic clove, finely chopped
14 large ripe tomatoes, skinned, seeded and chopped
½ red bell pepper, skinned and diced
½ cup vegetable broth
½ teaspoon sugar or to taste
few drops Tabasco sauce or other hot sauce
salt to taste
freshly ground black pepper to taste
2 tablespoons chopped fresh marjoram
6 black olives, pitted and cut into 4 or 5 slivers

1. Heat the oil over medium heat in a 2-quart saucepan and add the shallot and garlic. Cook until soft but not colored, about 5 minutes.

2. Reserve ½ cup of the chopped tomatoes. Add the remaining tomatoes, bell pepper, broth, sugar, Tabasco, salt and pepper. Cook until soft, about 20 minutes. Puree in a blender until smooth. Return to the pan.

3. Stir in the reserved tomato, marjoram leaves and olives and heat through. Taste and adjust the seasoning if necessary.

Per tablespoon: 22 calories, 2 g carbohydrates, trace protein, 2 g fat

SPICY TOMATO SAUCE

Yield: 4 servings

1 cup peeled chopped tomatoes
1 medium hot red chile, seeded and chopped
a pinch of sugar
salt to taste
freshly ground pepper to taste

Combine the tomatoes, chile, sugar, salt and pepper in a small saucepan and simmer for 5 minutes. Keep warm or cool and serve at room temperature.

Per serving: 15 calories, 3 g carbohydrates, 1 g protein, trace fat

SOY-HONEY FRESH-HERB SAUCE

Yield: 6 servings

½ cup chopped fresh
   cilantro
¼ cup chopped fresh
   mint

½ cup vegetable broth
½ cup soy sauce
4 teaspoons cornstarch
4 teaspoons honey

Combine the cilantro, mint, vegetable broth, the soy sauce, cornstarch and honey in a small saucepan and mix until well blended. Heat just to boiling, stirring constantly, and cook until clear and thickened.

Per serving: 37 calories, 8 g carbohydrates, 1 g protein, trace fat

SHALLOT AND RED-WINE SAUCE

Yield: 8 servings

Keep this sauce on hand to serve with steaks and beef roasts. You can freeze it in 1-cup portions, which will be enough for four servings.

a bottle of good red wine
2 tablespoons olive oil
8 shallots
8 ounces beef trimming from
   beef steaks, tenderloins, etc.
12 black peppercorns
1 thyme sprig

1 bay leaf
1 tablespoon sherry vinegar
2¼ cups chicken broth
2¼ cups veal broth
salt to taste
freshly ground pepper to
   taste

1. Boil the wine in a wide saucepan until reduced to about 3 ounces and is syrupy.

2. Meanwhile, in a 2-quart saucepan, heat the oil and sauté the shallots, the reserved beef trimmings, the peppercorns, thyme and bay leaf, over medium heat until the shallots are caramelized. Deglaze the pan with the sherry vinegar, stirring until evaporated.

3. Pour in the reduced wine, all the chicken broth and one-third of the veal broth. Heat to boiling and simmer for about 20 minutes or until reduced by one third, skimming off any scum that accumulates

on the surface. Add the remaining veal broth and boil until the sauce has reduced to about 2 cups. Season to taste.

4. Pour the sauce through a sieve lined with wet muslin or a clean kitchen towel at least twice to remove all the particles.

Per serving: 61 calories, 2 g carbohydrates, 2 g protein, 4 g fat

CREAMED PARSLEY AND SPINACH SAUCE

Yield: 4 servings

Serve this beautiful, herbaceous sauce with grilled steaks, veal chops or fish fillets.

1 large bunch curly-leaf parsley
3 cups large spinach leaves
¼ cup half-and-half

sea salt to taste
ground white pepper to
 taste

1. Pick off the stalks from the parsley and spinach and wash the leaves thoroughly and drain. Add the parsley leaves to a saucepan of boiling water and the spinach leaves a minute later. Cook a total of 4 minutes. Drain well, but do not refresh under running cold water. To dry the leaves thoroughly, place them in a clean kitchen towel and wrap tightly, squeezing out all the water.

2. Place the cream in a small saucepan and boil until reduced by half. Meanwhile, put the parsley and spinach into a food processor and blend into a puree. Add the reduced cream and seasoning to taste.

Per serving: 36 calories, 3 g carbohydrates, 2 g protein, 2 g fat

SORREL SAUCE

Yield: 6 servings

The lemony tang of this leafy green is a palate-brightening experience either raw or heated through in this version of the classic sauce. It goes well with eggs, veal and chicken.

1¼ cups chicken broth or fish stock
3 ounces dry white wine
1½ ounces dry vermouth
2 shallots, finely chopped
1⅔ cups heavy cream

1 bunch sorrel leaves, washed, dried and shredded
salt to taste
freshly ground pepper to taste
fresh lemon juice to taste

1. Combine the chicken broth or fish stock, white wine, vermouth and shallots in a saucepan over a high heat and boil until the liquid has reduced by half. Add the cream and boil until the sauce coats the back of a spoon.

2. Just before serving throw in a handful of shredded sorrel and season with salt, pepper and a squeeze of lemon juice.

Per serving: 104 calories, 4 g carbohydrates, 3 g protein, 8 g fat

MORNAY SAUCE

Yield: 4 servings

You can add other cheeses in addition or instead of the Parmesan and Gruyère. A little mustard blended in with the egg yolk goes well with most cheeses.

1 ounce butter
2 tablespoons all-purpose flour
1 cup hot milk
1 small shallot, finely chopped
1 small bay leaf
1 egg yolk
2 tablespoons heavy cream

2 tablespoons freshly grated Parmesan cheese
2 tablespoons freshly grated Gruyère cheese
salt to taste
freshly ground white pepper to taste
cayenne pepper to taste

1. Melt the butter in a small saucepan over medium-low heat and whisk in the flour. Cook, whisking, until bubbly and fragrant, about 3 minutes. Gradually whisk in the hot milk, whisking until smooth. Add the shallot and bay leaf. Heat to boiling, whisking, and simmer for 15 minutes, until the sauce is thickened and smooth. Strain into another small saucepan.

2. Mix the egg yolk and cream in a small bowl and whisk in a little of the hot sauce. Whisk this mixture back into the sauce in the saucepan and heat through. Whisk in the cheeses and whisk until melted and smooth. Season to taste.

Per serving: 170 calories, 7 g carbohydrates, 5 g protein, 14 g fat

BECHAMEL SAUCE

Yield: about 1 cup
(about 4 servings)

Use this sauce as a base for flavoring. Add some white wine or pan juices from cooking vegetables and fish or chicken.

1 ounce butter
2 tablespoons all-purpose flour
1¼ cups hot milk

salt to taste
freshly ground white pepper to taste

Melt the butter in a small saucepan over medium-low heat and whisk in the flour. Cook, whisking, until bubbly and fragrant, about 3 minutes. Gradually whisk in the hot milk, whisking until smooth. Heat to boiling, whisking, and simmer for 15 minutes, until the sauce is the desired consistency.

Per serving: 114 calories, 6.5 g carbohydrates, 3 g protein, 9 g fat.

GRAND MARNIER SYRUP

Yield: 2 cups

1 cup sugar
½ cup plus 1 tablespoon

Grand Marnier liqueur

In a small saucepan, heat the sugar and 1 cup water, stirring until the sugar is dissolved. Stir in the Grand Marnier and let cool. Refrigerate in a covered jar for up to 1 week.

Per tablespoon: 41 calories, 9 g carbohydrates, 0 protein, 0 fat

BRANDIED SAUCE OF RED SUMMER FRUITS

Yield: 6 servings

1 pound fresh, rinsed, seeded, stemmed or hulled red summer fruit or a mixture of fruits, or frozen, thawed

2 to 3 tablespoons confectioners' sugar or to taste
1 tablespoon brandy or to taste

Combine the fruit in a 2-quart saucepan. Stir in the sugar and brandy. Heat gently until warmed through. Adjust the sweetness and brandy if necessary. Puree the fruit mixture in a food processor if desired, and pass through a sieve if desired.

Per serving: 53 calories, 11 g carbohydrates, 1 g protein, trace fat

GINGER SABAYON

Yield: about 2 cups
(8 servings)

This rich sauce is served hot or cold with a dessert such as grilled fruit, a mousse, cake or tart. The ginger will enliven just about any medium.

$^1/_2$ cup preserved stem ginger syrup
6 egg yolks

$^1/_3$ cup sugar
$^1/_2$ vanilla bean, cut open

Combine the syrup, egg yolks, sugar, seeds from the vanilla bean and $^1/_2$ cup water in the top of a double boiler set over simmering water. Cook, whisking constantly, until the sauce is creamy, pale, hot and thickened.

Per serving: 106 calories, 17 g carbohydrates, 2 g protein, 4 g fat

BALSAMIC-PORCINI DRESSING

Yield: 1 cup
(8 servings)

¼ ounce dried porcini
  mushrooms
1 cup chicken broth or water
¼ cup balsamic vinegar
½ cup virgin olive oil
salt to taste
freshly ground pepper to
  taste

Combine the porcini and the broth or water in a small saucepan. Let soak until soft, about 15 minutes. Heat to boiling and simmer until the liquid has been reduced to ¼ cup. Strain through a sieve lined with cheesecloth placed over a blender; reserve the porcini. Add the vinegar to the blender, and with the motor running, add the oil in a steady stream through the opening in the lid. Blend until the mixture is emulsified and season with salt and pepper.

Per serving: 140 calories, 4 g carbohydrates, 1 g protein, 14 g fat

PINK-GRAPEFRUIT
AND SAGE DRESSING

Yield: 8 servings

1/4 cup sunflower oil
3 tablespoons pink grapefruit
  juice
1 tablespoon finely chopped
  fresh sage
1 tablespoon white-wine
  vinegar
1 teaspoon grated pink
  grapefruit rind
½ teaspoon creamy prepared
  horseradish
½ teaspoon sugar
salt to taste
freshly ground pepper to taste

Combine the oil, grapefruit juice, sage, vinegar, grapefruit rind, horseradish, sugar, salt and pepper in a screw-top jar. Secure the lid and shake well until thoroughly combined.

Per serving: 63 calories, 1 g carbohydrates, trace protein, 7 g fat

MUSTARD-HONEY DRESSING

Yield: 8 servings

½ cup olive oil
1 teaspoon Dijon mustard or
  coarse-grain mustard
1 garlic clove, crushed
1 tablespoon cider or favorite

herb-flavored vinegar
2 teaspoons honey
salt to taste
freshly ground pepper to
  taste

Whisk together the oil, mustard and crushed garlic in a small bowl. Add the vinegar and honey. Season to taste and mix well.

Per serving: 126 calories, 2 g carbohydrates, trace protein, 14 g fat

CHAMPAGNE VINAIGRETTE

Yield: about 2 ¼ cups

A splash of sparkling wine makes this dressing special. It will give you an excuse to open a bottle to have with your first course.

1 ¼ cups mild olive oil
2 ½ ounces champagne vinegar
5 ounces Champagne

salt to taste
freshly ground pepper to taste
sugar if required

Whisk the vinaigrette ingredients together in a small bowl, adding sugar if necessary.

Per 2 tablespoons: 125 calories, trace carbohydrates, 0 protein, 14 g fat

GINGER DRESSING

Yield: about 1¹/₄ cups
(12 servings)

¹/₄ cup red-wine vinegar
2 tablespoons soy sauce
2 tablespoons dark sesame oil
1 teaspoon grated peeled fresh

gingerroot
6 tablespoons peanut oil
salt to taste
freshly ground pepper to taste

Combine the vinegar, soy sauce, sesame oil and gingerroot in a large bowl and whisk until blended. Add the peanut oil in thin a stream, whisking until the dressing is combined and emulsified. Season with salt and pepper.

Per serving: 70 calories, 1 g carbohydrates, trace protein, 8 g fat

WALNUT-OIL DRESSING

Yield: about ³/₄ cup
(12 servings)

2 tablespoons sherry vinegar
4 teaspoons balsamic vinegar
¹/₂ teaspoon salt and more to
  taste

freshly ground pepper to
  taste
¹/₂ cup olive oil
2 tablespoons walnut oil

Mix the sherry vinegar, balsamic vinegar, ¹/₂ teaspoon salt and the pepper in a large bowl. Add the walnut oil and olive oil and mix well. Taste and adjust seasonings.

Per serving: 101 calories, 1 g carbohydrates, 0 protein, 11 g fat

LIME-CILANTRO VINAIGRETTE

Yield: about ¾ cup
(12 servings)

¼ cup vinegar
¼ cup lime juice
3 tablespoons minced fresh
  cilantro

1 tablespoon Dijon mustard
salt to taste
freshly ground pepper to taste
¼ cup oil

Combine the vinegar, lime juice, cilantro, mustard and salt and pepper to taste in bowl. Slowly whisk in the oil and whisk until emulsified. Taste and add more salt and pepper if needed.

Per serving: 45 calories, 1 g carbohydrates, trace protein, 5 g fat

SESAME-GINGER DRESSING

Yield: 16 servings

3 garlic cloves, minced
⅓ cup finely chopped peeled
  fresh gingerroot
¼ cup rice vinegar
1 tablespoon tamari or soy
  sauce
½ teaspoon dried mustard
  powder

½ teaspoon salt, or to
  taste
freshly ground black pepper
  to taste
¾ cup peanut or vegetable
  oil
3 tablespoons dark
  sesame oil

In a blender, process the garlic, ginger, vinegar, tamari, mustard, salt, and pepper until smooth. With the blender running on low speed, slowly pour in the peanut or vegetable oil and the sesame oil through the opening in the blender lid and blend until smooth.

Per serving: 115 calories, 1 g carbohydrates, trace protein, 13 g fat

LIME-MINT DRESSING

Yield: 6 servings

juice of 1 lime
1/4 cup chopped fresh mint
6 tablespoons extra-virgin
  olive oil

1 teaspoon sugar
salt to taste
freshly ground pepper to
  taste

In a mixing bowl, mix the lime juice, mint, sugar and olive oil. Season with salt and pepper and whisk again. Set aside.

Per serving: 124 calories, 3 g carbohydrates, 1 g protein, 1 g fat

SPICED CRANBERRY CHUTNEY

Yield: 8 servings

rind and juice of 1 medium
  orange (remove the rind in
  strips)
1/2 cup red wine
8 ounces cranberries, fresh or
  frozen
1/2 medium onion, finely
  diced

2-inch piece peeled fresh
  gingerroot, julienned
3 tablespoons dark brown sugar
1/2 teaspoon cinnamon
  (optional)
salt to taste
freshly ground pepper
2 tablespoons Grand Marnier

1. Cut the orange rind into julienne strips. Heat the orange juice in a small saucepan with 1 ounce of the wine and cook until tender, about 10 minutes.

2. Combine the cranberries, onion, remaining wine, ginger, brown sugar, cinnamon, salt and pepper in a medium saucepan and cook until the relish thickens, 15 to 20 minutes, stirring occasionally.

3. Stir in the Grand Marnier and the reserved orange mixture. Cool and transfer to a serving bowl. Refrigerate until needed.

Per serving: 48 calories, 8 g carbohydrates, trace protein, trace fat

MANGO-DATE CHUTNEY

Yield: 16 servings

4 firm, slightly unripe
   mangoes, flesh cut into
   ½-inch cubes
½ cup sugar
⅓ cup white-wine vinegar or
   rice vinegar
a pinch of salt

⅓ cup chopped, pitted dates
⅛ teaspoon ground
   cinnamon
⅛ teaspoon ground nutmeg
⅛ teaspoon ground allspice
1 medium onion, finely
   chopped

Combine the ingredients in a nonstick skillet over medium heat and gently stir to combine. Heat to boiling and simmer until thick.

Per serving: 57 calories, 15 g carbohydrates, trace protein, trace fat

ZUCCHINI CHUTNEY

Yield: 6 servings

This combination of cooked and fresh ingredients makes a tasty table condiment. Serve it with grilled meats, fish or vegetables. It can easily become an appetizer using pappadams the wafer thin East Indian bread made from lentils, for dipping.

8 ounces zucchini, washed
   and roughly chopped
½ cup flaked coconut
1 teaspoon tamarind
   concentrate or
   1 tablespoon fresh lime
   juice
½ teaspoon salt

1 fresh green chile, seeded and
   chopped
1½ inch gingerroot, peeled
   and roughly chopped
1 small garlic clove,
   peeled
¾ cup fresh cilantro leaves,
   including the tender stalks

1. Combine the zucchini, coconut and 1¼ cups water in a wok or saucepan and place over a high heat. Heat to boiling and reduce the heat to low. Cover and simmer for 5 minutes. Add the tamarind and salt and stir until the tamarind is dissolved. Remove from heat and allow the ingredients to cool.

2. Puree the zucchini mixture with the remaining ingredients in a food processor until smooth.

Per serving: 39 calories, 5 g carbohydrates, 1 g protein, 2 g fat

PAPAYA-TOMATILLO CHUTNEY

Yield: 2 cups

Is this a chutney, salsa or relish? No matter what you call it, sweet papayas and tart tomatillos combine to make culinary magic in this unique fruit condiment. Serve it hot or cold, with just about anything—Indian curries, tacos, grilled sausages— you'll find endless partners.

1 pound fresh tomatillos, husks removed	¼ teaspoon ground cinnamon
1 small papaya cut into ¼-inch chunks	⅛ teaspoon cayenne pepper
1 tablespoon vegetable oil	⅓ cup cider vinegar
½ small onion, thinly sliced	¼ cup packed brown sugar
	¼ cup dried currants

1. Finely chop the tomatillos and place in a bowl. Cut the papaya in half and scoop out the seeds. Scoop out the flesh from the shells and cut into ¼-inch chunks. Add to the bowl with the tomatillos and set aside.

2. Heat the oil in a nonstick skillet over medium heat. Add the onion, cinnamon and cayenne. Cook, stirring often, until the onion is tender, about 7 minutes. Add the tomatillos and papaya, vinegar, brown sugar and currants. Heat to boiling over high heat, then simmer, stirring occasionally, until the liquid has evaporated. Pack into hot half-pint containers and seal according to the jar manufacturer's instructions or store, covered tightly in a container in the refrigerator for up to 3 weeks.

Per tablespoon: 48 calories, 7 g carbohydrates, 2 g protein, 2 g fat

PLANTAIN RELISH

Yield: 16 servings

4 plantains, unpeeled
3 plum tomatoes, chopped
4 tablespoons granulated sugar
juice of 1 lemon
2 tablespoons red-wine
  vinegar

1 red onion, peeled and finely
  chopped
1 tablespoon olive oil
1/2 teaspoon thyme leaves
salt to taste
freshly ground pepper to taste

1. Place the plantains in a deep skillet. Add enough water to cover and heat to boiling over medium heat. Cover and simmer until nearly tender throughout, about 20 minutes.

2. Drain and peel the plantains. Cut lengthways in half and 1/2 inch across. Return the plantains to the skillet and add the sugar, lemon juice and vinegar. Heat to boiling and cook over medium heat, stirring, for 5 minutes.

3. Add the onion, oil, thyme, salt and pepper. Mix well.

Per serving: 71 calories, 16 g carbohydrates, 1 g protein, 1 g fat

RED, RED WINE
CRANBERRY-ORANGE RELISH

Yield: 8 servings

This is too good a condiment to reserve just for the holidays. It's great with curries and you'll be surprised at how it tastes with macaroni and cheese.

1 medium orange
1/2 cup red wine
1 medium onion, chopped
2-inch piece fresh gingerroot,
  peeled and julienned
2 cups (8 ounces) fresh or
  frozen cranberries

3 tablespoons dark brown
  sugar
salt and freshly ground pepper
  to taste
ground cinnamon to taste
2 tablespoons Grand Marnier
  (optional)

1. Remove the orange peel by cutting down the "longitudes" of the orange. Cut the peel into julienne strips and place in a medium saucepan. Cut the orange in half and squeeze the juice over the peel strips. Add 2 tablespoons of the wine and cook over low heat until the orange strips are tender, about 10 minutes.

2. Add the remaining wine, onion, gingerroot, cranberries, brown sugar, salt, pepper and cinnamon and mix well. Heat to boiling and simmer over low heat until the relish thickens, 15 to 20 minutes, stirring occasionally.

3. Stir in the Grand Marnier, cool and transfer to a serving bowl.

Per serving (without the Grand Marnier): 53 calories, 11 g carbohydrates, 1 g protein, trace fat

SCALLION-TOMATO RELISH

Yield: about 1 1/4 cups

This sultry condiment will perk up just about anything. Try it with scrambled eggs or spread it on cucumber slices for a tasty, company-quality appetizer.

2 bunches scallions, trimmed and chopped
1 medium tomato, coarsely chopped
3 tablespoons chopped fresh basil
2 tablespoons finely chopped onion
2 tablespoons olive oil
1 tablespoon balsamic vinegar
1 tablespoon minced garlic
salt to taste
freshly ground pepper to taste

Combine the scallions, tomato, basil, onion, oil, vinegar and garlic in a medium bowl and mix well. Season with salt and pepper.

Per tablespoon: 22 calories, 2 g carbohydrates, trace protein, 2 g fat

MOCHA RUM SAUCE

Yield: 1 1/4 cups

1/2 cup packed dark-brown sugar
1/4 cup European-style
  unsweetened cocoa powder
2 teaspoons instant espresso-
  coffee powder
1/2 cup heavy cream

2 tablespoons unsalted butter,
  cut into bits
2 ounces chopped bittersweet
  chocolate
1 tablespoon dark rum
1/2 teaspoon vanilla extract

Combine the sugar, cocoa powder and coffee powder in a small saucepan and mix well. Gradually whisk in the heavy cream until blended and smooth. Add the butter and cook over medium-low heat, whisking constantly, until the butter is almost melted and the mixture is hot. Add the chocolate and whisk until the chocolate melts and the sauce is blended and smooth. Whisk in the rum and vanilla. Serve hot or warm.

Per tablespoon: 62 calories, 6 g carbohydrates, trace protein, 4 g fat

HOT CHOCOLATE SAUCE

Yield: about 1 cups

1 1/2 (1-ounce) squares
  unsweetened chocolate,
  grated

2 tablespoons sugar
small piece of vanilla bean or
  1/2 teaspoon vanilla extract

1. Combine the chocolate, sugar, 1 cup water and vanilla bean in a small heavy-bottomed saucepan. (If using vanilla extract, do not add it now.) Simmer 15 to 20 minutes, stirring occasionally.

2. Remove the pan from the heat and remove the vanilla bean. Keep the sauce warm until needed and stir in the vanilla extract, if using, right before serving.

Per tablespoon: 40 calories, 5 g carbohydrates, trace protein, 3 g fat

BREADS &
BAKED GOODS

PARATHA

Yield: 16 servings

This East Indian griddle bread is rolled out in a method that resembles making puff pastry in order to achieve its many flaky layers. There are many versions, including stuffings of various vegetables, spices, herbs and even fruits.

1⅓ cups sifted whole-wheat flour, plus extra for rolling

1¾ cups sifted all-purpose flour

½ teaspoon salt

5 ounces vegetable oil

1. Combine the two flours and the salt in a mixing bowl. Dribble 2 tablespoons of the oil over the top. Briefly rub the oil in with your fingertips until the mixture resembles coarse breadcrumbs. Slowly add 6 to 7 ounces warm water until you can gather the mixture together to form a softish ball of dough.

2. On a floured surface, knead the ball for about 10 minutes until you have a smooth, soft, but not sticky dough. Form into a ball, rub with a little of oil and slip it into a plastic food storage bag to rest for 30 minutes or longer.

3. Set a griddle or large heavy skillet to heat over medium-low heat to get hot.

4. Meanwhile, knead the dough again and divide it into 16 balls. Take out one to work with and keep the remainder sealed in the plastic bag.

5. On a floured surface, flatten the ball and dust it with flour. Roll it out into a 6-inch round, lightly brush with oil and fold it in half. Brush the new top surface with oil and fold in half again to form a triangle. Roll out this triangle into a bigger one with 7-inch sides.

6. Brush the skillet or griddle with oil and slap the paratha on to it. Let it cook for a minute or two, until the top has puffed up. Brush the top with 1 teaspoon of oil. Turn the paratha over and cook the second side for a minute or so. Both sides should now have reddish-brown spots. Move the paratha around as you cook so all corners are evenly exposed to the central heat of the pan.

7. Place the cooked parathas on a warm plate and cover either with an inverted plate or with foil. Make the remaining parathas in this same way.

8. If the parathas are not to be eaten right away, wrap them tightly in foil. The whole, wrapped bundle of parathas, including the plate, may be heated at 400 degrees for 15 to 20 minutes.

Per serving: 169 calories, 19 g carbohydrates, 3 g protein, 9 g fat

GARLIC BREAD TRIANGLES

Yield: 4 servings

These are nice crunchy potato alternatives for stews and steaks. Set the meat on top and the bread with absorb the flavorful juices.

2 thin slices white bread
oil for shallow frying

1 large garlic clove,
    crushed

Cut the bread diagonally each way to make 4 triangles from each slice. Heat the oil in a skillet over medium-high heat, add the crushed garlic and bread triangles and fry the bread on each side until crisp and golden. Drain on paper towels.

Per serving: 34 calories, 5 g carbohydrate, 1 g protein, 1 g fat

HONEY AND DRIED FRUIT TEA BREAD

Yield: 2 appetizer
or lunch servings

This is a delicious dairy-free quick bread. You can use cow's milk to make it if that's what you have on hand.

1 cup high-fiber bran cereal
2/3 cup sugar
2 tablespoons honey
2/3 cup chopped mixed

    dried fruit
1 cup soy milk
nonstick cooking spray
1 1/4 cups self-rising flour

1. Mix the cereal, sugar, honey and fruit in a bowl. Stir in the soy milk and leave to soak for 1 hour.

2. Preheat the oven to 350 degrees. Lightly grease a 9-inch loaf pan with cooking spray and line the bottom with parchment paper.

3. Sift the flour over the bran mixture and fold in. Spoon into the prepared pan and bake for 1 to $1\frac{1}{2}$ hours or until firm to the touch.

4. Remove from the oven and leave to cool 20 minutes in the pan. Turn out onto a cooling rack and leave to cool completely.

5. Brush the top with honey and decorate with more fruit.

Makes 20 servings (10 slices, each cut in half)

Per serving: 87 calories, 20 g carbohydrates, 2 g protein, trace fat

CARROT BREAD
FOR BREAD MACHINE

Yield: 12 regular servings
or 16 large servings

Use freshly grated carrots for best results. Spread the slices with pineapple cream cheese or peanut butter.

REGULAR LOAF
$\frac{1}{2}$ cup water
$1\frac{1}{3}$ cup white bread flour
$\frac{2}{3}$ cup whole-wheat bread
   flour
2 teaspoons powdered milk
1 teaspoon salt
$\frac{2}{3}$ grated carrots
1 tablespoon honey
2 tablespoons plain yogurt
1 tablespoon molasses
2 tablespoons chopped walnuts
1 teaspoon fast rising yeast or
   2 teaspoons active dry yeast

LARGE LOAF
$\frac{3}{4}$ cup water
$2\frac{1}{4}$ cups white bread flour
1 cup wheat bread flour
1 tablespoon powdered milk
$1\frac{1}{2}$ teaspoons salt
1 cup grated carrots
2 tablespoons honey
$\frac{1}{4}$ cup plain yogurt
2 tablespoons molasses
$\frac{1}{4}$ cup chopped walnuts
$1\frac{1}{2}$ teaspoons fast rising yeast
   or $2\frac{1}{2}$ teaspoons active dry
   yeast

Use the loading instructions per your owner's manual. This recipe can be used with the regular and rapid bake cycles.

Per serving: 90 calories, 17 g carbohydrates, 3 g protein, 1 g fat

YEAST-RAISED OAT PANCAKES

Yield: 20 servings

The pin-head size oats are essential to these hearty pancakes. They produce a texture that tickles the tongue rather than sticks to it.

2 cups fine oatmeal (not rolled oats)
1¹/₂ to 1³/₄ cups whole-wheat or all-purpose flour
1 teaspoon salt

¹/₂ ounce fresh yeast
3¹/₂ cups warm milk and water, mixed
1 teaspoon sugar
oil for greasing the griddle

1. Combine the oatmeal, flour and salt in a large bowl and mix well.

2. Dissolve yeast with a little of the warm liquid in a small bowl, and stir in the sugar. Set aside in a warm place until frothy, about 10 minutes. Add to the oatmeal mixture and stir in the remaining warm liquid to make a batter. Stir in a little more warm water if the batter is stiff or stir in a little more flour if the batter is runny. Cover the bowl with clean damp kitchen towel and leave in warm place for 1 hour to rise.

3. Heat a griddle (preferably cast iron) over medium-low heat until hot and grease with a little oil. Spoon enough batter onto griddle to produce an oatcake about 4 inches in diameter. The surface will be covered in holes as it cooks. Turn the oatcake after 2 to 3 minutes when the top appears dry and the bottom is golden brown, and cook for another 2 to 3 minutes. Eat as soon as possible. Oatcakes freeze well.

Per serving: 118 calories, 20 g carbohydrates, 5 g protein, 3 g fat

HOMEMADE-GRANOLA PANCAKES

Yield: 12 servings

Toppings for these little fruity pancakes can be as simple as the confectioners' sugar suggested or you can break out that pure maple syrup or imported honey you've been hoarding. Hot chunky applesauce or melted farmer's market preserves would be soothing in the wintertime for a fireside supper.

$2/3$ cup medium oat flakes
1 large egg, beaten
5 ounces milk
1 pinch salt
2 teaspoons baking powder
6 dried apricot halves, chopped

2 pieces dried pears, chopped
2 tablespoons raisins, chopped
1 tablespoon nuts, chopped (any kind)
1 apple, grated
butter for greasing the griddle
confectioners' sugar for dusting

1. Mix all the ingredients together in a medium bowl and let the mixture rest for about 30 to 60 minutes, until the oat flakes swell.

2. Heat a skillet or griddle and grease with a little butter. Drop the batter in by the scant tablespoonful to make about 3 pancakes at a time. Cook slowly until the edge starts to set, about 3 minutes, turn over and cook the other side until lightly browned. Keep warm. Repeat until the mixture is finished.

3. Serve immediately with a dusting of confectioners' sugar.

Per serving: 60 calories, 11 g carbohydrates, 3 g protein, 2 g fat

CHEDDAR-CHEESE SCONES

Yield: about 8 scones

1$\frac{1}{3}$ cups all-purpose flour
1 teaspoon baking powder
a pinch of salt
3 tablespoons butter
$\frac{1}{2}$ cup finely grated

cheddar cheese
$\frac{1}{3}$ cup milk or more if needed,
plus extra for glazing the
tops
1 egg yolk

1. Preheat the oven to 450 degrees. Combine the flour with the baking powder and salt in a medium bowl. Add the butter and cut it in using a pastry blender or two knives used scissors fashion until the mixture resembles coarse meal. Mix in the cheese. Mix $\frac{1}{3}$ cup milk with the egg yolk and stir into the flour mixture. Roll out to a thickness of $\frac{1}{2}$ inch and cut out with a 2-inch biscuit cutter.

2. Place on a baking sheet and bake until the scones are golden brown, 25 to 30 minutes.

Per serving: 166 calories, 16 g carbohydrates, 5 g protein, 10 g fat

PARSLIED BUTTERMILK BISCUITS

Yield: 12 servings

These tender, fragrant breads are quick to make and bake and always quick to be eaten. Serve them for brunch with eggs or try them on top of a pot pie.

2$\frac{1}{2}$ cups all-purpose flour,
divided
5 teaspoons baking powder
1$\frac{1}{2}$ teaspoons salt

$\frac{1}{4}$ cup shortening
$\frac{1}{4}$ cup chopped fresh parsley
$\frac{1}{4}$ cup buttermilk, or more if
necessary

1. Preheat the oven to 500 degrees. Lightly grease a large baking sheet. Combine 1 1/2 cups of the flour, the baking powder and the salt in a sifter and sift into a large bowl, setting remaining flour aside in a small bowl. Cut the shortening into the flour mixture with a pastry blender or a fork until the mixture resembles coarse meal and stir in the chopped parsley. Pour in the buttermilk all at once and stir with a fork until the mixture just holds together, adding a little more buttermilk if necessary to make a scoopable but not rollable dough. Do not overwork the dough—it should be wet and a little lumpy.

2. Flour your hands with the reserved flour and pull out a 1/4-cup piece of wet dough. Toss the dough lightly in the bowl of flour to coat and roll gently into a smooth ball between the palms of your hands—the inside of the biscuit will still be very wet. Place the biscuit carefully on the prepared baking sheet. Repeat the procedure with the remaining dough, flouring the hands as necessary and placing the formed biscuits on the baking sheet so they just touch each other. Pat each biscuit gently to flatten slightly. Bake until golden brown, 8 to 10 minutes.

Per serving: 135 calories, 20 g carbohydrates, 3 g protein, 5 g fat

LEMON-ANISE-POPPY MINI-MUFFINS

Yield: 36 muffins

These are not too sweet, so you can add them to the bread-basket and serve with lunch or dinner.

nonstick cooking spray
1 1/2 cups whole-wheat flour
1 cup all-purpose flour
1/4 cup sugar
2 tablespoons poppy seeds
2 teaspoons baking powder
1 teaspoon baking soda
1/2 teaspoon salt

grated rind of 1 lemon
1 egg, beaten, or powdered egg
   substitute for 1 egg,
   reconstituted
1 cup orange juice
1/2 cup plain yogurt
1 teaspoon lemon extract
1 teaspoon anise extract

1. Preheat the oven to 375 degrees. Grease 36 miniature muffin cups with cooking spray.

2. Combine the flours, sugar, poppy seeds, baking powder, baking soda, salt and grated rind in a large bowl. In separate bowl, whisk the egg, orange juice, yogurt and extracts until blended.

3. Make a well in the flour mixture and add the egg mixture. Whisk just until dry ingredients are moistened. Spoon the batter into the prepared muffin cups. Spread the batter tops flat with the back of the spoon or moistened fingers. Bake until the edges are golden and a wooden pick inserted in the center of a muffin comes out clean, 12 to 16 minutes. Cool in pan for 3 minutes, and serve warm.

Per muffin: 45 calories, 9 g carbohydrates, 2 g protein, trace fat

---

MELBA TOAST

Yield: 8 toasts

2 slices thin white or wheat bread

1. Preheat the broiler or toaster oven. Place the bread on a baking sheet and broil or toast under the grill and toast on both sides.

2. Remove the toast from under the heat, cut in half horizontally with a sharp knife and then diagonally across to make triangles. Toast the untoasted sides until crisp and slightly curled.

Per serving: 8 calories, 2 g carbohydrates, trace protein, trace g fat

---

NAAN BREAD WITH COCONUT, RAISINS AND PINENUTS

Yield: 10 servings

This bread comes from North India and is traditionally baked on the wall of a special very hot oven that cooks the dough in less than 60 seconds! The breads are slapped onto the wall, where they brown and take on a smoky flavor. Then they are speared with a skewer to remove them and served hot.

½ ounce quick-rising yeast
1 tablespoon sugar
a pinch of salt
1²/₃ cups bread flour

oil for coating
2 tablespoons flaked coconut
2 tablespoons raisins
2 tablespoons toasted pinenuts

1. Dissolve the yeast, sugar and salt in ³/₄ cup warm water and leave to sit for 10 minutes.

2. Oil a medium bowl. Sift the flour in a bowl and work the liquid into it, adding more tepid water if necessary to make a dough. Form into a ball, place it in the oiled bowl and turn the dough to coat it. Cover with plastic wrap and set aside in a warm place until doubled in bulk, about 1 hour.

3. Preheat the oven to 400 degrees. Lightly grease and flour 2 large baking sheets. Combine the coconut, raisins and pinenuts in a small bowl and mix well.

4. Punch down the dough and turn out onto a work surface. Divide the dough into 10 pieces. Lightly flour the work surface and gently roll each piece of dough into a 6-inch round. Sprinkle each with about 1 teaspoon of the coconut mixture and press it into the dough. Place the dough rounds on the prepared baking sheets and until golden and puffy, 10 to 12 minutes.

Per serving: 109 calories, 20 g carbohydrates, 4 g protein, 2 g fat

CORNBREAD MEXICALI

Yield: 10 servings

You may want to make this a meal in itself. With all the bright flavors and satisfying nutrients, this is one versatile dish. Try it baked in a corn-stick pan or make mini-muffins out of it for little appetizer-size portions.

nonstick cooking spray
1 small onion, chopped
1 to 2 jalapeño peppers, to taste, seeded and chopped
1 (4-oz) jar diced pimientos, drained

2 ounces butter, melted
1 cup self-rising cornmeal
1 cup shredded cheddar cheese
1 cup whole-kernel corn
1 cup skim milk
½ teaspoon garlic powder

1. Preheat the oven to 350 degrees. Grease a 10½-inch cast-iron skillet with cooking spray.

2. Combine the onion, jalapeño, pimientos, butter, cornmeal, cheese, corn, milk and garlic powder in a medium bowl, and mix well. Pour the batter into the prepared skillet and bake for 45 minutes or until golden. Cut into 10 wedges and serve warm.

Per serving: 164 calories, 16 g carbohydrates, 6 g protein, 9 g fat

BAKED APPLE-AND-HAM PANCAKE

Yield: 6 servings
(serving size: 1 wedge)

This egg-rich dish is inspired by Dutch and German versions of main-dish, baked-in-the-skillet pancakes.

nonstick cooking spray
2 teaspoons vegetable oil
¼ cup chopped onion
1 teaspoon sugar
1¼ cups chopped peeled
    Golden Delicious apples
1 cup diced reduced-sodium
ham
¼ teaspoon freshly ground
    pepper
3 large eggs
1 cup skim milk
¾ cup all-purpose flour
¼ teaspoon salt

1. Preheat the oven to 425 degrees. Wrap the handle of a large nonstick skillet with aluminum foil.

2. Grease the skillet with cooking spray, add the oil and heat over medium heat until hot. Add the onion and sugar and sauté until the onions starts to brown, about 10 minutes. Add the apples, ham and pepper and sauté until the apples are tender, about 6 minutes. Remove the pan from the heat.

3. Combine the eggs, milk, flour and salt in container of an electric blender. Cover, process until smooth and pour over the apple mixture.

4. Bake the pancake until slightly puffed and golden, about 18 minutes. Let stand 2 minutes before serving.

Per serving: 183 calories, 20 g carbohydrates, 10 g protein, 7 g fat

COUSCOUS CRÊPES

Yield: 12 crêpes

This is quite a clever use for that pasta-like "grain" that has easily moved from the Mediterranean into mainstream-American cuisine. The wheaty flavor goes well with ratatouille or grilled vegetables.

1 cup plus 1 tablespoon dry couscous
6 tablespoons all-purpose flour
1½ teaspoons ground coriander
¾ teaspoon baking powder
¼ teaspoon salt or more to taste

¼ teaspoon ground white pepper or to taste
3 large eggs, lightly beaten
1 cup milk
1½ tablespoons melted unsalted butter, plus extra for cooking the pancakes

1. Combine the couscous, flour, coriander, baking powder and ¼ teaspoon each salt and pepper in a bowl. Add the eggs and milk and mix well. Stir in 1½ tablespoons melted butter, mix just until combined, cover and set aside to rest for 20 minutes.

2. To cook the pancakes: Place an 8-inch skillet over medium heat and brush with a little melted butter. Stir the batter to recombine. Then spoon 2 to 3 tablespoons of batter per pancake into the skillet, making 3 pancakes at a time. Cook until bubbles rise to the surface of the pancakes and break, 1 to 2 minutes. Using a spatula, flip the pancakes and cook for 2 minutes. Remove pancakes from the skillet, cover and keep warm. Repeat with the remaining batter, using as little butter as possible without allowing the pancakes to stick to the bottom of the pan.

Per crêpe: 113 calories, 16 g carbohydrates, 5 g protein, 3 g fat

CLASSIC CRÊPES

Yield: 12 crêpes

1 cup unsifted all-purpose flour
2 large eggs
1¼ cups milk

1 teaspoon vegetable oil
a pinch of salt
oil for cooking the crepes

1. For the crêpe batter: Sift the flour with the salt into a bowl and make a well in the center. Break in the eggs and blend into the flour with a wooden spoon. Gradually add the milk and 5 ounces water, stirring until completely smooth. Stir in the oil and leave to stand in a cold place for 3 hours.

2. Cook the crêpes: Heat a 6- to 8-inch nonstick skillet over medium-high heat and brush with oil. Heat until hot but not smoking. Remove the pan from the heat and pour in 2 tablespoons batter (half-fill a $1/4$-cup measure). Immediately swirl the batter so it covers the bottom of the pan. Return the pan to the heat and cook until the underside is browned. Turn with a spatula and cook until brown spots appear on the underside. Turn out onto a plate and repeat with the remaining batter.

Per crêpe: 66 calories, 9 g carbohydrates, 3 g protein, 2 g fat

WHOLE-WHEAT CRÊPES

Yield: 12 crêpes

The hearty flavor of whole-wheat flour is an earthy addition to these paper-thin wraps.

$3/4$ cup all-purpose flour
$1/2$ cup whole-wheat flour
$1/4$ teaspoon salt
$1 1/2$ cups skim milk

2 tablespoons butter,
  melted
1 large egg
nonstick cooking spray

1. Combine both flours and the salt in a medium bowl and make a well in the center. Whisk the egg in a glass measure, add the milk and butter, and whisk to mix. Pour into the flour mixture and whisk until almost smooth. Cover the batter, and refrigerate for 1 hour.

2. Grease an 8-inch crêpe pan or nonstick skillet with vegetable cooking spray, and place over medium-high heat until hot. Remove pan from heat, and pour a scant $1/4$ cup batter into pan, quickly tilt pan in all directions so batter covers pan with a thin film. Cook about 1 minute.

3. Carefully lift the edge of the crêpe with a spatula to test for doneness. The crêpe is ready to turn when it can be shaken loose from pan and the underside is lightly browned. Turn over the crêpe

and cook 30 seconds on other side.

4. Place the crêpe on a towel and allow it to cool. Repeat procedure until all of the batter is used.

Per crêpe: 84 calories, 11 g carbohydrates, 3 g protein, 3 g fat

MUSHROOM AND CORN CRÊPE FILLING

Yield: enough to fill 12 crêpes

This vegetarian filling is very hearty and is tasty with couscous, classic or whole-wheat crêpes. Since crêpes freeze well, you can make a batch of each and keep them on hand to mix and match with various fillings. For even more convenience, fill the crêpes and refrigerate them in the baking dish until ready to heat through and serve.

3 tablespoons butter
12 ounces mushrooms, sliced
1 (11-ounce) can whole-kernel corn, drained
1¼ cups BECHAMEL SAUCE (see page xx)

½ cup chopped fresh parsley
salt to taste
freshly ground pepper to taste
COUSCOUS, WHOLE-WHEAT CRÊPES OR CLASSIC CRÊPES for filling (see page xx)

1. Melt the butter in a 2-quart saucepan over medium heat and add the mushrooms. Cook until they are cooked but not too softened Stir the corn into the mushrooms. Add the sauce and heat through, stirring until smooth. Stir in the parsley and season to taste. Set aside.

2. To finish: Preheat the oven to 350 degrees. Spread about ¼ cup filling on the side of a crêpe that was cooked second and fold or roll up. Place in the prepared baking pan. Repeat with the remaining crepes and filling. Bake until heated through, about 15 minutes. (Heat longer if the crêpes are cold.)

Per serving (filling only): 89 calories, 8 g carbohydrates, 3 g protein, 6 g fat

PIZZA DOUGH

Yield: 4 (12-inch) rounds
enough for 32 slices

1 cup warm water
1 teaspoon active dry yeast
3 cups all-purpose flour plus a

little extra for kneading
1½ teaspoons salt
olive oil

1. Place the water in a large bowl and sprinkle the yeast on top. Let stand until dissolved, about 5 minutes. Mix well. Stir the flour and salt into the water and mix until a stiff dough forms. Turn the dough out onto a floured surface and knead until smooth and elastic, about 10 minutes, sprinkling the dough with a little flour when it gets sticky.

2. Wash and dry the bowl and grease with olive oil. Place the dough in the bowl and turn to bring up the oiled side. Cover with plastic wrap and leave in a draft-free, warm place until doubled in bulk, about 1½ hours.

3. Punch down the dough and divide into portions. Place each on an oiled baking sheet and cover with plastic wrap. Let rise in the refrigerator until doubled in bulk, 12 to 24 hours. Punch down the dough and roll out. Continue as directed with the recipe.

Per slice: 43 calories, 9 g carbohydrates, 1 g protein, trace fat

SPICY SOUTHWESTERN PIZZA

Yield: 8 slices

Vegans will want to make this tasty pizza for any occasion. It's ideal for entertaining guests of any age or topping persuasion. Serve with a crisp green salad.

1 (5-ounce) package soy
  ground-meat substitute
1 tablespoon olive oil
1 (1.25-ounce) envelope
  taco-seasoning mix
2 tablespoons sun-dried
  tomato paste
1 (12-inch) round PIZZA
  DOUGH (see recipe above)
½ green bell pepper, seeded

and thinly sliced
½ red bell pepper, seeded
  and thinly sliced
½ yellow bell pepper, seeded and thinly sliced
1 red onion, sliced into rings
8 black olives, pitted and
  sliced
shredded fresh basil leaves
  for garnish

1. Place a pizza stone on the lowest rack of the oven (optional). Preheat the oven to 400 degrees.

2. Reconstitute the soy mix according to package directions Heat the oil in a skillet, add the soy mixture and taco seasoning and mix well. Sauté for 5 minutes, stirring frequently.

3. Spread the sun-dried tomato paste evenly over the pizza dough and spoon the soy mixture evenly on top. Arrange the peppers, onion, olives and basil on top.

4. Bake the pizza on the middle oven shelf for 20-25 minutes.

Per slice: 148 calories, 20 g carbohydrates, 13 g protein, 2 g fat

NEW ORLEANS-STYLE PIZZA

Yield: 2 medium pizzas
8 slices each

Andouille is a spicy smoked Louisiana sausage. If you can't find it, substitute any garlicky sausage.

4 ounces Monterey jack
  cheese, grated
½ cup sour cream
4 ounces cooked Andouille sausage,

thinly sliced at an angle to make large elliptical pieces
2 (12-inch) rounds PIZZA DOUGH (see page 369)

1. Place a large pizza stone on the lowest rack of the oven (optional). Preheat the oven to 400 degrees.

2. Combine the cheese and sour cream in a bowl. Spread half the sour cream mixture to within ¼ inch of the edges of the pizza dough rounds and arrange 6 slices of the sausage on top of each. Slide the pizzas onto the pizza stone or place on metal baking pans. Bake until the crust is golden brown, about 15 minutes.

Per slice: 92 calories, 9 g carbohydrates, 4 g protein, 4 g fat

DESSERTS

SWEET SPIKED OATS AND CREAM (CRANACHAN)

Yield: 4 servings

This Scottish dessert, also called "Crowdie Cream," is made of all local ingredients, specifically and traditionally heather honey and single-malt Scotch whisky.

1¼ cups heavy cream
2 tablespoons whisky
1 to 2 tablespoons honey, depending on the
desired sweetness
8 ounces raspberries, cut into halves
2 ounces cracked oats, lightly toasted and cooled

1. Lightly whip the cream, whisky and honey together until soft peaks form.

2. Fold in the raspberries and cracked oats (reserving some of each for garnishing). Transfer to individual serving dishes, garnish and chill thoroughly before serving.

Per serving: 360 calories, 20 g carbohydrates, 4 g protein, 29 g fat

---

CALVADOS PEAR TARTLETS

Yield: 10 servings

An open-face fruit tart is a European tradition. Because you can see the fruit inside, great care is used to arrange the fruit artistically or the top is decorated temptingly. As if you needed to be coaxed to eat a buttery pastry-cased, honey-sweet pear!

LOWFAT PASTRY
1 egg, separated
1 rounded tablespoon fine cornmeal
10 small halves canned pears in
water and ¼ cup Calvados or other apple brandy
2 tablespoons sugar
1 (8-ounce) container crème fraîche for serving

1. Preheat the oven to 400 degrees. Line a baking sheet with parchment paper.

2. Roll out the pastry to a thickness ¼ inch. Cut out 10 rounds of pastry using a 4-inch plain cutter.

3. Combine the canned-pear juice with the brandy in a saucepan. Set the pears on paper towels.

4. Brush each pastry round in the center where the pear base will sit with egg yolk, sprinkle with the cornmeal. Set a whole pear on top. Fold up the pastry edge around the pear, pleating the pastry casually. Do not worry how rough and raggedy it looks! Brush with the egg white and sprinkle with the sugar, repeating the process until all the pears have been used.

5. Transfer the tartlets to the prepared baking sheet, and bake for 15 to 20 minutes, or until golden brown and the sugar has started to caramelize. Meanwhile, boil the pear liquid to reduce it by half in a saucepan over medium heat.

6. Serve immediately with a spoonful of crème fraîche and a drizzling of the reduced syrup.

Per serving: 191 calories, 19 g carbohydrates, 3 g protein, 10 g fat

FROZEN MOCHA-MASCARPONE MOUSSE

Yield: 6 servings

8 ounces mascarpone
  cheese
2 tablespoons brandy
2 tablespoons fine ground
  espresso coffee

¼ cup confectioners' sugar
3 ounces deluxe chocolate,
  grated
5 tablespoons half-and-half
1¼ cups heavy cream

1. Beat the mascarpone cheese in a bowl with the brandy, espresso coffee and confectioners' sugar. Reserving 1 tablespoon of grated chocolate, stir in the remainder, with the half-and-half.

2. Whip the heavy cream until just peaking and fold into the mascarpone mixture. Turn the mixture into a freezable container and freeze for 2 to 3 hours.

3. Serve scooped into cups. Drizzle with brandy if liked and decorate with lightly whipped cream and sprinkle with chocolate.

Per serving: 366 calories, 18 g carbohydrates, 3 g protein, 32 g fat

CHOCOLATE-HAZELNUT MOUSSE

Yield: 4 servings

3 ounces bittersweet
   chocolate
1 tablespoon hazelnut liqueur
2 large egg whites

⅓ cup heavy cream
¼ cup chopped toasted
   hazelnuts
½ pint raspberries

1. Combine the chocolate and 2 tablespoons water in a small saucepan and heat, stirring, over low heat until the chocolate melts. Remove the pan from the heat and stir in the liqueur. Pour into a medium bowl and cool.

2. Beat the egg whites until stiff and gently fold into the chocolate mixture using a rubber spatula until no white streaks remain. In the same bowl used for the egg whites, beat the cream until stiff and gently fold into the chocolate mixture.

3. Spoon the mousse into 4 stemmed glasses and sprinkle with the hazelnuts and raspberries. Serve immediately or refrigerate until serving.

Per serving: 249 calories, 20 g carbohydrates, 4 g protein, 18 g fat

CREAM PUFFS

Yield: 12 to 16 large puffs

For cocktail puffs, pipe 1-inch high mounds of the dough, bake for about 30 minutes in all and fill with egg salad or other savory mixture. A batch of dough should make about 90 baby puffs.

DOUGH
nonstick cooking spray or
  parchment paper
2 ounces unsalted butter, cut
  into bits
2 teaspoons sugar
1/4 teaspoon salt
1 cup unsifted all-purpose
  flour

4 large eggs
1 egg yolk

FILLING AND TOPPING
1 cup whipping cream
2 tablespoons sugar
1/2 teaspoon vanilla extract
confectioners' sugar for
  dusting

1. Preheat the oven to 400 degrees. Grease a large baking sheet with cooking spray or line with parchment.

2. For the dough: Combine the butter, sugar, salt and 1 cup water in a heavy 2-quart saucepan and heat to boiling over medium heat. When the butter melts, immediately remove the pan from the heat and add the flour all at once. Beat vigorously with a wooden spoon until blended and smooth. Cook the dough over medium heat, stirring constantly, until the dough comes away from the sides of the pan and is a smooth mass, about 30 seconds. Remove the pan from the heat and let cool 3 minutes.

3. Scrape the dough into a food processor or, using a wooden spoon or portable mixer, blend or beat in the eggs, one at a time, blending or beating until the dough is smooth before adding the next egg.

4. Place the dough in a pastry bag fitted with a large plain or star tip and pipe out into 12 or 16 high mounds 2 inches apart on the prepared baking sheet. (You can simply spoon it onto the baking sheet rather than pipe it.) Mix the egg yolk with 1 teaspoon water in a small cup and brush the mixture onto the pastry, being careful not to drip on the baking sheet.

5. Bake the dough until doubled in size and golden brown, about 25 minutes. Remove the cream puffs from the oven and with the tip of a small knife, make a slit into the side of each to let the steam escape. Return the puffs to the oven and reduce the heat to 325 degrees. Bake until browned and very crisp, about 15 to 20 minutes. Remove from the baking sheet and let cool on a wire rack. Split the cream puffs horizontally or along a ridge in the puff and pull out any raw-looking dough.

6. For the filling and topping: Beat the cream with the sugar and vanilla until stiff and spoon into the bottom half of the pastry puffs. Replace the tops and sprinkle with confectioners' sugar.

Each of 16 servings: 142 calories, 9 g carbohydrates, 3 g protein, 11 g fat

PROFITEROLES

Yield: 18 profiteroles

nonstick cooking spray or
   parchment paper
CREAM PUFF PASTRY DOUGH
   (see page 375)

1 pint vanilla ice cream
MOCHA RUM SAUCE or HOT
   CHOCOLATE SAUCE (see
   page 353)

1. Preheat the oven to 400 degrees. Grease a large baking sheet with cooking spray or line with parchment. Drop or pipe the Cream Puff pastry dough onto the prepared baking sheet in 18 high mounds 2 inches apart. Bake the dough as directed for Cream Puffs, about 40 minutes in all. Cool, split and fill with ice cream. To serve, drizzle with hot sauce.

Per profiterole: 105 calories, 9 g carbohydrates, 3 g protein, 7 g fat

MINI CHOCOLATE ÉCLAIRS WITH LEMON CURD FILLING

Yield: 40 éclairs

nonstick cooking spray or
  parchment paper
CREAM PUFF PASTRY DOUGH
  (see page 375)

2 recipes LEMON CURD
CHOCOLATE SATIN GLAZE
  (see page 378)

1. Preheat the oven to 425 degrees. Grease 2 large baking sheets with cooking spray or line with parchment.

2. Place the pastry dough in a pastry bag fitted with a $\frac{1}{3}$-inch plain or round tip and pipe the éclairs onto the prepared baking sheets in finger-size strips about 3 inches long. Bake for 15 minutes, reduce the oven temperature to 350 degrees and bake until the pastry is golden and dry, about 20 minutes longer.

3. Cut the éclairs in half lengthwise and separate. Using a small palate knife, spread the Chocolate Satin Glaze on the tops. Fill the bottoms with Lemon Curd (piping it in is the easiest and neatest way) and replace the tops. Serve immediately.

Per éclair: 165 calories, 17 g carbohydrates, 2 g protein, 11 g fat

LEMON CURD

Yield: 1 cup

4 large egg yolks
$\frac{1}{2}$ cup plus 2 tablespoons
  sugar
3 ounces fresh lemon
  juice

2 ounces unsalted butter,
  softened, in pieces
pinch of salt
2 teaspoons finely grated
  lemon rind

1. Combine the egg yolks and sugar in a heavy bottomed nonreactive saucepan and whisk until blended. Add the lemon juice, butter and salt and whisk until the mixture is a thick but pourable consistency. (Do not allow the curd to boil or it will curdle.) Pour through a sieve into a bowl. Stir in the lemon rind and set aside to cool. Store in the refrigerator.

Per tablespoon: 73 calories, 9 g carbohydrates, 7 g protein, 4 g fat

CHOCOLATE SATIN GLAZE

Yield: 2 cups

12 (1-ounce) squares
  bittersweet or semisweet
  chocolate, chopped
6 ounces unsalted butter,
  softened

1 tablespoon light corn
  syrup
1 tablespoon vanilla extract

1. Melt the chocolate in the top of a double boiler set over hot, not boiling water or in a microwave on HIGH power, stirring every 10 seconds. When the chocolate is fully melted and smooth, whisk in the butter, 1 tablespoon at a time. Add ½ cup hot water all at once and whisk until blended. Whisk in the corn syrup and vanilla.

Per tablespoon: 92 calories, 8 g carbohydrates, trace protein, 8 g fat

PASTRY CREAM

Yield: 2 cups

1½ cups half-and-half
¼ vanilla bean
⅓ cup sugar
2 tablespoons flour
2 tablespoons cornstarch

a pinch of salt
4 large egg yolks
2 tablespoons unsalted butter,
  cut up, softened
¼ cup heavy cream

1. Combine the half-and-half and vanilla bean in a medium saucepan and heat to simmering. While the mixture heats, mix the sugar, flour, cornstarch and salt in a medium bowl. Whisk in the egg yolks until blended and smooth. Whisk in the hot half-and-half and the vanilla bean, adding the liquid in a thin, steady stream. Pour the mixture back into the same saucepan. Cook over low heat, whisking constantly, until boiling, 3 to 5 minutes. (The mixture will start to form clumps when very hot so whisk vigorously to keep it smooth.)

2. Remove the mixture from the heat and whisk in the butter. Sieve into a clean bowl and immediately place plastic wrap directly on the surface to keep a skin from forming. Refrigerate until cold.

3. To serve, whip the heavy cream until soft peaks form and gently fold it into the pastry cream using a rubber spatula.

Per tablespoon: 93 calories, 7 g carbohydrates, 2 g protein, 7 g fat.

MOCHA POTS DE CRÈME

Yield: 8 servings

You will have to go by the baking time and not the look of the mixture to take it out the oven. The custard will be jiggly and a knife inserted in the center of the dishes will not come out clean, as is the test for most custards. Don't worry, though, because the mixture will firm up upon cooling and chilling.

1 cup semisweet chocolate
  morsels
⅓ cup sugar
2½ teaspoons espresso-
  coffee powder
3 cups half-and-half
6 large egg yolks

1 teaspoon vanilla
  extract
FOR GARNISH
whipped cream (optional)
  chocolate-covered coffee
  beans or plain coffee beans
  for garnish (optional)

1. Day before serving: Preheat the oven to 325 degrees. Combine the chocolate, sugar, coffee powder and 1 cup half-and-half in a medium saucepan and heat over low heat, whisking constantly, until the chocolate melts and the mixture is smooth.

2. Mix the egg yolks and vanilla in a medium bowl and gradually whisk in the chocolate mixture. Add the remaining half-and-half and whisk until smooth.

3. Pour the mixture into eight 6-ounce pot de crème dishes or ramekins placed in a shallow roasting pan. Place the pan on the center oven rack. Pour enough hot water into the pan to come halfway up the sides of the dishes. Bake until the mixture is set, 40 to 45 minutes.

4. Remove the pots de crème from the roasting pan and cool on a wire rack. Cover loosely with plastic wrap and refrigerate overnight. Garnish each with whipped cream and coffee beans, if desired.

Per serving: 273 calories, 20 g carbohydrates, 6 g protein, 21 g fat

FLOURLESS CHOCOLATE CAKE

Yield: 16 servings

nonstick cooking spray
1 cup milk
16 (1-ounce) squares semisweet chocolate, chopped
8 ounces butter, softened, in pieces
2 tablespoons brandy

1 tablespoon vanilla extract
8 large egg yolks
½ cup heavy cream, whipped, for garnish
½ cup fresh raspberries for garnish
fresh mint leaves for garnish

1. Preheat the oven to 350 degrees. Grease a 9-inch springform pan with cooking spray.

2. Heat the milk in a large heavy-bottomed saucepan over low heat until little bubbles form around the edge of the pan. Add the chocolate and whisk until the mixture is smooth and all the chocolate has melted. Whisk in the butter, brandy and vanilla. Whisk until the butter melts, and remove the pan from the heat.

3. Place the egg yolks in a small bowl and whisk until smooth. Whisk in about ½ cup of the hot chocolate mixture until blended and gradually whisk the egg-yolk mixture into the chocolate mixture in the pan. Pour the mixture into the prepared pan and bake 20 minutes or until the center is set. Remove the cake to a wire rack and allow the cake to cool completely in the pan. Cover with plastic wrap and refrigerate until cold.

4. To serve, run a knife around the edge of the cake and remove the sides of the pan. Place on a serving dish and garnish with the whipped cream, raspberries and mint. To cut, use a thin-bladed knife and dip the blade in hot water and wipe it off between cuts to keep the edges of the slices clean and neat.

Per serving: 309 calories, 20 g carbohydrates, 3 g protein, 26 g fat

CRÈPES WITH VANILLA PASTRY CREAM AND CHOCOLATE SAUCE

Yield: 12 servings

12 Classic Crepes
VANILLA PASTRY CREAM
  (see pages 378-379)
½ recipe HOT CHOCOLATE SAUCE (see pages 353-354)

1. For each crêpe: Place one crêpe on a plate with the nice brown side down. Spread with pastry cream and roll up. Place on a serving dish and drizzle with Hot Chocolate Sauce. Repeat with the remaining crêpes, pastry cream and sauce.

Per serving: 211 calories, 20 g carbohydrates, 5 g protein, 12 g fat

LEMON-POLENTA CAKE

Yield: 16 servings

1 cup self-rising flour, sifted
¾ cup fine polenta semolina
¼ teaspoon baking powder
⅔ cup sugar
pinch of salt

3 eggs
3 tablespoons extra-virgin olive
  oil
juice and grated rind of 1
  lemon

1. Preheat the oven 400 degrees. Grease an 8-inch square cake pan.

2. Place the flour, polenta and baking powder in a bowl with the sugar and salt. Stir well to combine.

3. Whisk together the eggs, oil until thick. Whisk in the lemon juice and rind. Pour the mixture into the flour mixture and fold together using a gentle stirring action, until thoroughly combined. Spoon into the prepared pan. Bake in the preheated oven for 10 minutes and lower the heat to 350 degrees. Cook for a further 15 minutes. Transfer to a wire rack to cool before cutting into squares.

Per serving: 110 calories, 20 g carbohydrates, 3 g protein, 2 g fat

RASPBERRY TIRAMISÚ

Yield: 6 to 8 servings

Everyone knows by now that the translation of tiramisú means "lift you up" or at least something like that. This fruity version has plenty of spirit and will certainly lift up the spirits of those who eat it. If you can't find raspberries, you can use sliced strawberries or blueberries.

1 cup heavy cream
1 (8-ounce) container mascarpone cheese
2 tablespoons Tia Maria liqueur

1¼ cups strong black coffee
8 ounces purchased crisp ladyfingers (French or Italian)
⅓ cup fresh raspberries

1. Place the cream in a bowl and add the mascarpone and 1 tablespoon liqueur. Whisk well until the cream is thick.

2. Mix the coffee and remaining liqueur in a shallow bowl.

3. To assemble the tiramisú, spoon one-third of the cream mixture into the bottom of a deep 2-quart glass serving bowl. Taking one crisp ladyfinger at a time, dip half of the ladyfingers into the coffee mixture and arrange a single layer on the cream. Spoon another one-third of the cream mixture on top and cover with the remaining ladyfingers moistened with the remaining coffee mixture.

4. Spread the remaining cream mixture on the top and sprinkle with the raspberries. Cover the tiramisú with plastic wrap and refrigerate for at least 6 hours. Serve chilled.

Each of 8 servings: 266 calories, 20 g carbohydrates, 5 g protein, 19 g fat

DATES STUFFED WITH GOAT CHEESE

Yield: 6 servings

This unusual combination of savory and sweet ingredients makes an unforgettable dessert.

4 ounces fresh goat cheese
½ garlic clove, crushed
grated rind of ½ lemon
1 small red chile, seeded and
    chopped

12 medjool dates
5 ounces ruby port
5 ounces chicken broth
5 ounces balsamic vinegar
1 teaspoon cracked peppercorns

1. Preheat the broiler. Combine the cheese, garlic, lemon rind and chile in a small bowl. Mix well and set aside.

2. Combine the port, broth, vinegar and cracked pepper in a saucepan and heat to boiling. Boil until it has reduced to a light syrup and keep warm.

3. Split each date lengthways and fill with a generous amount of the cheese mixture. Place on a baking sheet and broil for 6 to 7 minutes or until lightly glazed.

4. Place 2 dates on each plate and drizzle with the syrup. Serve immediately.

Per serving: 167 calories, 15 g carbohydrates, 6 g protein, 7 g fat

CHOCOLATE BAKED BANANAS

Yield: 4 servings

Say goodbye to s'mores! Here are the next hottest things off the campfire.

4 small ripe finger bananas
1/4 cup white-chocolate chips

1/4 cup semisweet-chocolate chips

1. Use the last of the coals from barbecuing or preheat the oven to 400 degrees.

2. Cut through the peel along one side of each of the bananas. Slide in a mixture of the chips. Wrap tightly in tin foil and bake for 15 minutes.

3. Serve in the foil wrapping with a small spoon.

Per serving: 128 calories, 2 g carbohydrates, 1 g protein, 6 g fat

NO-BAKE GINGER-ORANGE CHEESECAKES

Yield: 4 servings

nonstick cooking spray
1/2 cup crushed gingersnaps
1 ounce butter, melted
3 tablespoons dark cocoa
   powder
grated rind and juice of 1
   orange

1/4 cup heavy cream
2 tablespoons confectioners'
   sugar
10 ounces mascarpone cheese
4 fresh strawberries, hulled and
   halved lengthwise
fresh mint for garnish

1. Grease the inside of two 2- or 3-inch metal rings and place one on each of 4 dessert plates.

2. Combine the gingersnap crumbs in a bowl with the melted butter and stir with a fork until mixed. Spoon one-fourth of the mixture into each ring and pack lightly.

3. Place the cocoa powder in a bowl and mix with the orange rind and juice to form a paste. Add the cream, confectioners' sugar and the mascarpone cheese and slowly mix. Spoon the mixture into the rings and spread flat on the top. Drizzle the remaining juice around the plate and garnish with the strawberries and fresh mint. With a twist, remove the rings from the cheesecakes.

Per serving: 328 calories, 19 g carbohydrates, 4 g protein, 28 g fat

CARROT CAKE

Yield: 24 servings

No one can refuse carrot cake. This one is especially good because it has many non-traditional ingredients such as olive oil and whole-wheat flour. Be sure to grate your carrots just before using so they will be juicy.

1 (8-ounce) can crushed, unsweetened pineapple, well drained, juice reserved
1/2 cup dark raisins
1 cup liquid egg substitute at room temperature
2 teaspoons vanilla extract
1/4 cup light olive oil
2 cups grated carrot
2 tablespoons fresh lemon juice
1 1/2 cups cake flour
1/2 cup whole-wheat pastry or regular flour

3/4 cup packed brown sugar
1 teaspoon ground allspice
2 teaspoons ground cinnamon
1 teaspoon baking powder
1 teaspoon baking soda
1/2 teaspoon freshly ground sea salt
1 cup plain yogurt
2 tablespoons packed brown sugar
1/4 cup chopped walnuts
1 tablespoon confectioners' sugar

1. Pour the reserved pineapple juice into a small saucepan and heat to boiling. Remove from the heat, stir in the raisins, and let them sit until plumped, about 15 minutes. Drain, discarding the pineapple juice.

2. Preheat the oven to 350 degrees. Grease and flour an 11-inch-by-17-inch baking pan.

3. In a large bowl, sift together all the dry ingredients. In a separate bowl, combine all the wet ingredients until mixed well. Slowly add the wet ingredients to the dry, stirring gently. Pour the cake batter into the prepared pan and bake for 40 minutes or until a toothpick inserted in the center comes out clean. Remove from the oven and let sit for 15 minutes. Turn the cake out of the pan and onto a wire rack.

4. For the filling, while the cake is cooling, mix the yogurt with the brown sugar and vanilla in a bowl until blended.

5. To assemble, place the cake on a serving platter and slice it horizontally into two even layers. Slide a rim-less cookie sheet between the layers and remove the top layer. Spread the bottom layer with the filling and sprinkle with the walnuts. Cover with the top layer and garnish with a sprinkle of confectioners' sugar.

Per serving: 122 calories, 19 g carbohydrates, 3 g protein, 7 g fat

POACHED RHUBARB WITH MANGO AND STAR ANISE

Yield: 4 servings

The magenta-red rhubarb and the hot-afternoon-sun orange color of the mango make this a dessert that makes you want to get up and tango.

1 pound thin rhubarb stalks, cut into 2-inch pieces
1/2-inch piece peeled fresh gingerroot, thinly sliced
2 or 3 whole star anise
1 tablespoon fresh

lime juice
1 tablespoon sugar
1 large or 2 small ripe mangos, pitted, peeled and cut into large dice
mint leaves for garnish

1. Preheat the oven to 325 degrees. Combine the rhubarb, ginger and star anise in a baking dish and set aside.

2. Combine 5 ounces water, the lime juice and sugar into a saucepan and heat to boiling, stirring until the sugar has dissolved. Boil for 2 minutes, and then pour over the rhubarb mixture. Cover and bake on the middle oven rack until the rhubarb is very soft, about 1½ hours.

3. Remove the rhubarb from the oven, cool slightly and spoon into a wide glass serving bowl or individual bowls. Mix the mango with the rhubarb without breaking it up too much and refrigerate until serving.

4. To serve: With a fork, pull up the star anise to the top of the fruit mixture in each bowl so they are visible. Decorate each serving with mint leaves.

Per serving: 83 calories, 20 g carbohydrates, 1 g protein, trace fat

SPICED POACHED PEARS WITH GINGER SABAYON

Yield: 8 servings

The buttery sweetness of pears makes them one fruit that always makes you smack your lips. When they are cooked in a spicy syrup, their honey fragrance and glorious nectar are even more pronounced.

2 teaspoons granulated
  unrefined sugar
1 star anise
1 (2-inch) cinnamon stick
1 bay leaf

rind of ¼ lemon
4 small crisp pears, peeled,
  halved lengthwise and cored
GINGER SABAYON (see
  page 343)

1. Combine 1½ cups water, the sugar, star anise, cinnamon, bay leaf and lemon rind in a large skillet and stir until the sugar is dissolved. Heat to boiling over medium heat and simmer gently 15 minutes.

2. Place the pears in the syrup and add more water if necessary to cover the pears. Boil gently, covered, until the pears are tender when pierced with a thin skewer, about 30 minutes, turning the pears frequently with a wooden spoon to avoid damaging the pears. Serve warm or cold with the Ginger Sabayon.

Per serving: 98 calories, 20 g carbohydrates, 2 g protein, 4 g fat

BENNE SEED WAFERS

Yield: 24 servings

These cookies, pronounced BEHN-nee, trace their origins to the early settlers of the Deep South. African slaves introduced sesame seeds, which they called benné, to American cuisine. These delicately flavored, fragile cookies make much-appreciated gifts if you can part with them.

½ cup firmly packed brown
  sugar
5 tablespoons butter, melted
⅔ cup all-purpose flour

2 tablespoons sesame seeds,
  toasted
⅛ teaspoon salt
1 egg white, lightly beaten

1. Preheat the oven to 300 degrees. Cover a baking sheet with parchment paper and secure to baking sheet with masking tape.

2. Combine the brown sugar and butter in a medium bowl and beat until smooth. Add 2 tablespoons water and the remaining ingredients and stir until well blended.

3. Spoon the batter by teaspoonfuls 3 inches apart onto the prepared baking sheet. Using the back of a spoon, spread the batter into 2-inch rounds.

4. Bake until edges are lightly browned, about 6 minutes. Let cool 1 minute. Remove wafers from the paper and let cool completely on wire racks.

Per serving: 50 calories, 6 g carbohydrates, 1 g protein, 3 g fat

BAKED CHEESES WITH HONEY AND OATCAKES

Yield: 8 servings

Oatcakes are chewy, crisp thin wafers beloved by Scots and anyone else who has tread on land settled or visited by the British. You can find various brands of oatcakes (and they vary in flavor) in specialty food stores.

1 whole Camembert cheese (in wooden box)
1 garlic clove
2 fresh thyme sprigs
1 (2-ounce) wedge Gorgonzola cheese
8 oatcakes

2 teaspoons honey
8 small slices crusty bread
1 small ripe pear, cored and sliced (peeled if desired)
1 small cluster of grapes
1 small apple, cored and sliced

1. Preheat the oven to 400 degrees. Remove the Camembert from its wrappers and place on a baking sheet. Cut the garlic into slivers and push them and bits of the thyme sprigs into the cheese with the thyme sprigs. Bake until the cheese begins to soften and melt, about 20 minutes.

2. Cut 8 slices of Gorgonzola and place one on top of each oatcake and drizzle with the honey.

3. Remove the Camembert from the oven and serve with crusty bread, ripe pears, grapes, and apple slices for dipping and spreading.

Per serving: 233 calories, 20 g carbohydrates, 11 g protein, 12 g fat

CHOCOLATE-CAPPUCCINO DREAM CREAMS

Yield: 4 servings

A sweet finish to a meal makes everyone leave the table in a good mood. Most of the preparation can be done ahead of time so you'll just have to leave the table to put it together.

$3/4$ cup heavy cream
1 tablespoon sugar
1 (8-ounce) container crème fraîche
1 tablespoon strong

expresso coffee
6 amaretti cookies, roughly crushed
2 ounces bittersweet chocolate, grated

1. Pour the cream into a large bowl and add the sugar. Whip until it just begins to hold its shape and then fold in the crème fraîche and coffee.

2. Add a layer of amaretti crumbs to 4 small stemmed elegant glasses. Sprinkle with one-third of the chocolate. Cover with half of the cream mixture and repeat the layers, finishing with a grated chocolate. Set on a serving plate and serve at once.

Per serving: 407 calories, 20 g carbohydrates, 5 g protein, 37 g fat

LOW-FAT PASTRY

Yield: enough for 2 crusts,
16 servings

To make the most of this indulgence, use it to make vegetable-rich meat pies and quiches or double-fruit pies and tarts.

$1^3/4$ cups all-purpose flour
$1/4$ teaspoon baking powder

6 tablespoons cold vegetable shortening

Mix the flour and baking powder in a medium bowl and add the shortening. Using your fingers or a pastry blender or two knives used scissors fashion, cut the shortening into the flour mixture until it resembles coarse meal. Drizzle ⅓ cup ice water over the dough and toss with a fork and then your hands until the dough holds together. Divide into 2 portions and wrap separately in plastic wrap. Flatten each into a disk. Refrigerate 30 minutes before rolling out into a thin crust.

Per serving: 92 calories, 10 g carbohydrates, 1 g protein, 5 g fat

JAM BARS

Yield: 24 bars

These cookies are fruity and not too sweet.

12 tablespoons cold unsalted butter plus extra for greasing the pan
1½ cups all-purpose flour
1 cup quick-cooking rolled oats
⅔ cup brown sugar
½ teaspoon salt
¼ teaspoon baking soda
2/3 cup favorite-flavor jam

1. Preheat the oven to 350 degrees. Line a 9-inch square pan with foil, letting the foil extend over the edges. Butter the foil and set aside.

2. Combine the flour, oats, brown sugar, salt and baking soda. Cut the 12 tablespoons butter into pieces and add to the mixture, cutting them in using a pastry blender or two knives used scissors fashion until the mixture is crumbly.

3. Set aside 1½ cups of these crumbs and press the remainder over the bottom of the pan. Spread jam to within ¼ inch of the edge of the pan. Sprinkle the remaining crumb mixture on top of jam. Bake until golden brown, 45 to 55 minutes. Cool completely before cutting into 24 bars.

Per bar: 119 calories, 16 g carbohydrates, 1 g protein, 6 g fat

BISCOCHITOS

Yield: 6 dozen cookies

These Mexican cookies were traditionally cut into fleur-de-lis shapes but they will disappear regardless of how they look. You can substitute sherry or even apple juice for the brandy.

6 cups all-purpose flour
1 tablespoon baking powder
¼ teaspoon salt
2 cups lard or shortening
1¾ cups sugar

2 teaspoons anise seeds
2 eggs
¼ cup brandy
1 tablespoon
  cinnamon

1. Sift together the flour, baking powder and salt and set aside. Beat together the lard and 1½ cups sugar in a large bowl with a mixer at medium-high speed until light and fluffy. Add the anise seeds and beat in the eggs, 1 at a time. Beat in the brandy. Add the flour mixture and beat with a mixer and then a wooden spoon until the dough pulls cleanly away from sides of work bowl, about 1 minute. Chill the dough 1 hour.

2. Remove the dough from refrigerator at least 30 minutes before rolling out. Preheat oven to 350 degrees. Combine the remaining ¼ cup sugar and the cinnamon and set aside.

3. Roll out the dough ¼ to ½ inch thick on a lightly floured board and cut into desired shapes (fleurs-de-lis are traditional). Transfer to an ungreased baking sheet, dust with cinnamon-sugar and bake until lightly browned, about 10 minutes.

Per cookie: 115 calories, 13 g carbohydrates, 1 g protein, 6 g fat

ANISETTE-ALMOND BISCOTTI

Yield: about 3 dozen

2½ cups all-purpose flour plus more for shaping
1½ teaspoons baking powder
½ teaspoon salt
3 tablespoons unsalted butter, softened
1¼ cups sugar
2 tablespoons anisette
1 cup chopped toasted blanched almonds

1. Preheat the oven to 350 degrees. Line a large baking sheet with parchment paper.

2. Combine the flour, baking powder and salt in a large bowl. In another large bowl, beat the butter until creamy. Gradually beat in the sugar and anisette. Add the flour mixture and the almonds and stir with a wooden spoon until smooth.

3. Divide the dough in half and shape each into a 3-inch wide log, sprinkling the dough with flour if it is sticky. Place the logs at least 2 inches apart on the prepared baking sheet and at least 2 inches from the edges of the baking sheet. Bake until golden and the tops spring back when lightly pressed, about 30 minutes.

4. With a serrated knife, cut the logs diagonally into ½-inch thick slices. Arrange the slices cut side down on the baking sheet (you may need another baking sheet) and bake until crisp, about 10 minutes, turning the slices over after 5 minutes. Cool the biscotti on wire racks and store in an airtight container.

Per biscotto: 104 calories, 16 g carbohydrates, 2 g protein, 3 g fat

DRIED CRANBERRY AND HAZELNUT BISCOTTI

Yield: about 3 dozen

1 cup dried cranberries
2 large eggs
3/4 cup sugar
1/2 cup vegetable oil
2 tablespoons finely grated
  orange rind
1 teaspoon cinnamon

1 1/4 teaspoons baking powder
1 teaspoon vanilla extract
1/4 teaspoon salt
2 cups all-purpose flour plus
  more for shaping
1 cup chopped skinned,
  toasted hazelnuts

1. Preheat the oven to 350 degrees. Soak the cranberries in hot water in a small bowl for 10 minutes.

2. Meanwhile, whisk the eggs, sugar, oil, orange rind, cinnamon, baking powder, vanilla and salt in a large bowl until blended. Add 2 cups flour and the hazelnuts. Drain the cranberries and stir with a wooden spoon until combined.

3. Turn out the dough onto a floured work surface and knead 20 turns, sprinkling the dough and your hands with flour as necessary to keep the dough from sticking. Divide the dough in half and shape each half into a 2-inch thick log. Place the logs well apart on a baking sheet and bake until golden brown and firm, about 30 minutes.

4. Leave the oven on and let the logs cool 10 minutes. With a serrated knife, cut the logs diagonally into 1/2-inch thick slices. Arrange the slices cut side down on the baking sheet (you may need another baking sheet) and bake until crisp, about 20 minutes, turning the slices over after 10 minutes. Cool the biscotti on wire racks and store in an airtight container.

Per biscotto: 107 calories, 13 g carbohydrates, 2 g protein, 6 g fat

HAMANTASHEN

Yield: 4 dozen cookies

These cookies are traditionally made for the Jewish holiday of Purim. The word hamantashen is Yiddish for "Haman's pockets" and recalls the story of Haman, a wicked Persian prince whose plot to destroy the Jews was foiled by Mordecai and Esther.

FILLING
3/4 cup pitted prunes
1/3 cup raisins
1/3 cup coarsely chopped
   apple
1/4 cup walnut pieces
2 tablespoons sugar
2 tablespoons fresh lemon
   juice
1 teaspoon grated lemon rind

COOKIE DOUGH
1/2 cup sugar
1/4 cup canola oil
2 tablespoons butter or margarine at room temperature
1 large egg
1 teaspoon pure vanilla extract
2 cups all-purpose flour
1 teaspoon baking powder
a pinch of salt

1. For the filling: Combine the prunes, raisins and 1/2 cup water in a small saucepan. Heat to boiling and simmer over low heat until the prunes are tender but still firm and liquid has been absorbed, about 10 minutes. Transfer the mixture to a food processor and add the apples, walnuts, sugar, lemon juice and lemon rind. Process until smooth, transfer to a small bowl and set aside. The filling can be made up to 2 days ahead and kept covered in the refrigerator.

2. For the cookie dough: Combine the sugar, oil and butter in a medium bowl and beat on medium speed until smooth. Add the egg and beat until smooth. Beat in the vanilla until blended. Combine the flour, baking powder and salt in a sifter and sift into the butter mixture. Using a wooden spoon, stir just until combined. Gather the dough together into a ball, cover with plastic wrap and flatten slightly. Refrigerate for 2 to 3 hours or overnight.

3. To make the cookies: Line 2 baking sheets with parchment paper or coat with nonstick cooking spray. Set aside. Preheat oven to 350 degrees. Divide the dough in half. Cover and refrigerate one half and roll out the other half onto a lightly floured surface to a $^{1}/_{2}$-inch thickness. Using a $2^{1}/_{2}$-inch round cookie cutter, cut out the dough. Place $^{1}/_{2}$ tablespoon of the filling in the center of each round of dough. Bring the edges together to cover the filling, forming a 3-cornered cookie, and pinch the corners together to seal. Place about $1^{1}/_{2}$ inch apart on the prepared baking sheets.

4. Bake the cookies until the tops are golden, 10 to 15 minutes, and transfer to wire racks to cool. Store cookies in an airtight container for up to 3 days or freeze for longer storage.

Per cookie: 59 calories, 9 g carbohydrates, 1 g protein, 2 g fat

DRINKS

BORANI

Yield: 4 servings

This Pakistani drink is surprisingly refreshing in the summer. Make sure you season it well with pepper.

1 cup plain yogurt
1 teaspoon finely grated lemon rind
1/2 teaspoon chopped fresh mint

1/8 teaspoon chili powder
salt and pepper to taste
freshly ground pepper to taste

Combine the ingredients in a bowl and whisk in 2 cups ice water. Refrigerate until serving.

Per serving: 37 calories, 3 g carbohydrates, 2 g protein, 2 g fat

---

ORANGE CAFE AU LAIT MIX

Yield: about 1 cup mix
(24 servings)

Put on the kettle and prepare to chill out. Keep a batch of this special flavorful coffee on hand so you have it ready and waiting for you and friends to enjoy. It makes a nice gift, too.

1/2 cup powdered nondairy creamer
1/2 cup sugar

1/4 cup instant coffee powder
1 teaspoon dried orange peel
1/4 teaspoon ground cinnamon

1. Place the creamer, sugar, coffee powder, orange peel and cinnamon in a blender or food processor. Cover and blend on high speed 30 seconds, stopping blender after 15 seconds to stir, or process 5 to 10 seconds, until well mixed. Store in a tightly covered container at room temperature for up to 6 months.

2. For each serving, place 2 teaspoons mix in a mug or cup. Fill with 2/3 cup boiling water and stir to dissolve.

Per serving: 29 calories, 5 g carbohydrates, 17 g protein, trace fat

LIMONCELLO COSMOPOLITAN

Yield: 2 serving

2 ounces lemon-flavored
  vodka
2 teaspoons Cointreau

2 teaspoons fresh orange juice
4 teapoons limoncello
lemon twist

Combine the vodka, Cointreau, orange juice and limoncello in a shaker with ice and shake to combine. Strain into a martini glass and garnish with the lemon twist.

Per serving: 166 calories, 5 g carbohydrates, trace protein, trace fat

TROPICAL TEA PUNCH

Yield: 12 servings

2 cups freshly brewed tea
$1/2$ cup sugar
1 cup Cognac
1 cup pineapple juice

2 ounces light rum
1 (750-ml) bottle sparkling
  wine
ice or an ice ring

Make the tea in a large glass measure and while the tea is hot, add the sugar and stir until dissolved. Add the Cognac, pineapple juice and rum and stir. Chill until cold. Just before serving, pour into a punch bowl and add ice and the sparkling wine.

Per serving: 152 calories, 12 g carbohydrates, trace protein, 0 fat

COCONUT-RUM COOLERS

Yield: 6 servings

3 cups unsweetened coconut
  milk
$1^{1}/_{4}$ cups fresh orange
  juice

$3/_{4}$ cup aged Jamaican rum
$1/_{3}$ cup pure maple syrup
$3/_{4}$ teaspoon pure vanilla
  extract

Combine all of the ingredients in a blender and blend until smooth, in batches, if necessary. Pour into a tall pitcher, fill with ice and stir well. Pour the mixture into white-wine glasses and serve.

Per serving: 367 calories, 20 g carbohydrates, 3 g protein, 26 g fat

CAFÉ BRÛLOT

Yield: 8 servings

This flaming brew is a New Orleans specialty. It gets its name from the French word for "burnt brandy."

1½ (3-inch) sticks cinnamon, broken
julienned rind of 1 orange
julienned rind of ½ lemon
½ teaspoon whole allspice

8 sugar cubes
½ cup Cognac or bourbon
2½ cups freshly brewed strong coffee

Combine the cinnamon sticks, julienned rinds and allspice in a chafing dish or flameproof bowl and add the sugar. Add all but 1 tablespoon of the Cognac or bourbon and heat until warmed. Heat the remaining Cognac or bourbon in a metal ladle and ignite. Add it to the mixture in the chafing dish and when it ignites, ladle it over the sugar cubes until they melt. Add the coffee and stir well. When the coffee is hot, ladle it into demitasse cups, using a tea strainer.

Per serving: 51 calories, 4 g carbohydrates, 0 protein, 0 fat

VICTORIAN COCKTAIL

Yield: 1 serving

Angostura bitters to taste
small ice cubes or cracked ice
2½ ounces bourbon, (at least

8 years old)
sugar syrup to taste
1 (2-inch) strip orange rind

1. In a whisky glass add a few splashes of bitters. Add one ice cube and a splash of the sugar. Stir, using the muddler end of the bar spoon. Add two more ice cubes. Stir. Add some more ice. Stir. Add half the bourbon and some more ice. Stir.

2. Add some more ice and the rest of the bourbon. Stir again. Over the top of the glass, squeeze the oil out of the orange rind. Place the orange rind in the glass.

Per serving: 209 calories, 13 g carbohydrates, 0 protein, 0 fat

ALMOND-FLAVORED TEQUILA LIQUEUR

Yield: 3½ cups
(16 servings)

The piloncillo syrup is made from unrefined sugar and can be found in Mexican grocery stores. You can replace it in a recipe with the same amount of brown sugar.

8 ounces unblanched almonds
½ vanilla bean, split
1 (3-inch) stick cinnamon
1 bottle gold tequila

2 tablespoons spicy piloncillo syrup
¼ teaspoon pure almond extract

1. Preheat the oven to 325 degrees. Place the nuts on a baking sheet and toast until dark brown, turning occasionally to keep from burning. When done, remove from the pan to prevent overcooking.

2. Coarsely chop the nuts. Place in jar along with the vanilla bean and cinnamon stick. Cover with tequila and steep for 2 weeks in a cool, dark place, occasionally shaking the jar gently. (A murky sediment is natural). Strain several times through paper coffee filters placed in a sieve placed over large glass measures for easy pouring back and forth.

3. When the liqueur is clear, add the piloncillo syrup and almond extract in small increments, tasting after each addition, until you are satisfied with the flavor. Pour into a sterilized dark-colored jar or bottle and allow it to set for 2 weeks, tasting it occasionally and adding more syrup if needed.

4. Pour into pretty decorative jars for gifts. Serve either poured into hot coffee or served over ice in brandy snifters with a twist of lemon.

Per serving: 140 calories, 1 g carbohydrates, 0 protein, 0 fat

ORANGE-YOGURT SHAKE

Yield: 5 servings

In one cold blast of flavor you can boost your body full of calcium and vitamin C.

1 (6-ounce) can frozen orange
  juice concentrate

1 cup skim milk
3/4 cup plain nonfat yogurt

Combine the frozen concentrate, milk and yogurt in a blender or food processor, cover and process until smooth. Pour into individual glasses, and serve immediately.

Per serving: 92 calories, 18 g carbohydrates, 5 g protein, trace fat

BEEFY BLOODY MARY

Yield: 1 serving

This recipe works just as well with clam-tomato juice cocktail instead of the beef-flavored variety.

1 (5.5-ounce) can Beefamato
  juice
1 1/2 ounces vodka
1 tablespoon fresh lime juice
dash of Seasoned Salt

freshly ground pepper to
  taste
Tabasco sauce to taste
Worcestershire sauce to taste
ice

Combine the ingredients except ice in a tall glass and stir until blended. Add ice and stir until cold.

Per serving: 195 calories, 16 g carbohydrates, 1 g protein, trace fat

SWEET MANHATTAN

Yield: 1 serving

For a dry Manhattan, use dry vermouth instead of the sweet and a lemon or lime twist instead of an orange twist.
cracked ice
4½ ounces bourbon or rye whisky
1½ ounces sweet vermouth
dash of juice from maraschino cherries
dash of Angostura bitters (optional)
maraschino cherry with a stem
twist of orange rind

1. Combine the ice, whisky, vermouth, cherry juice and bitters in a cocktail shaker. Cover and shake to mix. Pour through a cocktail strainer into a tall glass. Garnish with a cherry and the orange twist.

Per serving: 525 calories, 18 g carbohydrates, trace protein, 0 fat

OLD-FASHIONED COCKTAIL

Yield: 1 serving

Legend has it that this American drink was first made from "Old 1776" brand Kentucky bourbon whisky in the late 1800s. Its popularity is proved by the fact that the squat tumbler it is traditionally served in is called an "old-fashioned" glass.

1 lump sugar or 1 teaspoon sugar
2 dashes Angostura bitters
2 ounces bourbon or rye
   whisky

cracked ice or ice cubes
1 strip orange peel
1 strip lemon peel
1 maraschino cherry with a stem

Place the sugar in a tumbler and add a small spoonful of warm water. Stir to dissolve, using the muddler end of the bar spoon. Stir in a few splashes of bitters. Add ice and the whisky and stir. Garnish with the orange and lemon peels and the cherry.

Per serving: 167 calories, 5 g carbohydrates, 0 protein, 0 fat

---

FRESH-PEACH BELLINIS

Yield: 8 servings

2 ripe peaches
juice of 1 orange
juice of 1 lemon
1 cup crushed ice

1 (750-ml) bottle Champagne
or prosecco, chilled

Blanch the peaches in boiling water and place in a bowl of ice water to chill. Remove the skins, cut in half and remove the pits. Place the peaches in a blender with the orange juice, lemon juice and ice and puree. Strain into a pitcher. Add the Champagne, mix gently and pour into fluted glasses.

Per serving: 77 calories, 4 g carbohydrates, trace protein, 0 fat

---

GINGER COLADA PUNCH

Yield: 24 servings

1 (5-ounce) jar stem ginger in syrup

$2^1/_2$ ounces coconut rum, chilled
$2^1/_2$ quarts pineapple juice, chilled

ice for serving

1. Combine the ginger and its syrup and 2½ cups ice water in a blender and blend until smooth. Strain into a pitcher and refrigerate until serving.

2. To serve, pour the ginger mixture into a punch bowl. Stir in the rum, pineapple juice and ice.

Per serving: 60 calories, 16 g carbohydrates, 0 protein, 0 fat

MOCK CHAMPAGNE

Yield: 8 servings

1 quart fresh chilled apple cider or juice

¼ cup fresh lemon juice

1 (1 liter) bottle club soda

8 strips lemon rind

Combine the cider and lemon juice in a pitcher and pour equal amounts into 8 champagne flutes. Fill each with club soda and add a strip of lemon rind to each glass.

Per serving: 60 calories, 16 g carbohydrates, 0 protein, 0 fat

WHITE-WINE AND MINT PUNCH

Yield: 18 servings

Ice

2 bottles white wine, chilled

1 cup creme de menthe, chilled

½ pint fresh strawberries, washed and hulled

fresh mint sprigs for garnish

1. Fill the punch bowl with ice to chill well. Just before serving, remove the ice.

2. Fill the punch bowl with the wine and creme de menthe and mix well. Add the strawberries and mint sprigs and serve.

Per serving: 126 calories, 16 g carbohydrates, trace protein, trace fat

PINK SPICED-TEA PUNCH

Yield: 40 servings

You won't need to roll out the barrel. Just take down that punch bowl from the attic and have a barrel of fun! Add some hooch if you're inclined.

12 bags green tea, black currant tea, rosehip tea or other favorite tea

2 (3-inch) cinnamon sticks

1 (12-ounce) can lemonade concentrate, thawed

1 (12-ounce) can orange-juice concentrate, thawed

1 cup grenadine syrup

1 (1 liter) ginger ale, chilled

1 (1-liter) club soda, chilled

1. Combine the tea bags and cinnamon in a large glass measure and add 3 cups boiling water. Stir and let steep 4 minutes.

2. Meanwhile, in an empty milk or orange-juice container, combine the juice concentrates and 3 cups water. Shake until blended and pour into a punch bowl.

3. Strain the tea mixture into the punch bowl. Add the grenadine syrup and mix well. Add the ginger ale and club soda and serve.

Per serving: 63 calories, 16 g carbohydrates, trace protein, trace fat

MULLED WINE

Yield: 6 servings

1/3 cup sugar
3 cloves
1 star anise
1 (3-inch) cinnamon stick

1 lemon, thinly sliced
1 bottle red wine
orange slices to
  decorate

Combine the sugar, spices and 1 1/4 cups water in a small saucepan and stir until the sugar dissolves. Heat to boiling and boil 3 minutes. Let stand 10 minutes. Add the wine and heat until hot but not boiling. Strain the mixture into a heat-safe pitcher. Add the orange slices and serve.

Per serving: 154 calories, 19 g carbohydrates, trace protein, 0 fat

OLD-FASHIONED HOT COCOA

Yield: 6 servings

1/4 cup unsweetened cocoa
  powder
3 tablespoons sugar
1/2 teaspoon cinnamon

pinch of salt
pinch of nutmeg
3 cups scalded milk
1/4 cup miniature marshmallow

Combine the cocoa powder, sugar, cinnamon, salt and nutmeg in the top of a double boiler. Add 1 cup boiling water and whisk until smooth. Add the milk and cook, whisking, over hot, not boiling water over low heat, for 10 minutes. Pour into mugs and add a few marshmallows to each serving.

Per serving: 122 calories, 18 g carbohydrates, 5 g protein, 5 g fat

CARIBBEAN TODDY

Yield: 2 servings

You get to call how you serve this soother according to the weather. Hot or cold, it will take you to the islands inside your head. Swill at will on a wind-swept veranda or inside a lively city apartment.

juice of 1 large
  lemon
2 tablespoons honey
1 to 2 teaspoons Caribbean

rum, brandy or whisky
  (optional)
$1/2$ teaspoon mild or hot
  pepper sauce

Combine $1^1/_4$ cups boiling water with the lemon juice, honey, rum and pepper sauce in a large heatproof glass measure and mix well. Cover and leave to stand for 5 minutes. Strain, and drink hot or cold.

Per serving: 2 calories, 75 g carbohydrates, 19 g protein, 0 fat

INDEX